THROUGH A
NOIR LENS

THROUGH A
NOIR LENS

Adapting Film Noir Visual Style

SHERI CHINEN BIESEN

Columbia University Press
New York

Columbia University Press
Publishers Since 1893
New York   Chichester, West Sussex
cup.columbia.edu

Copyright © 2024 Columbia University Press
All rights reserved

Library of Congress Cataloging-in-Publication Data
Names: Biesen, Sheri Chinen, 1962– author.
Title: Through a noir lens : adapting film noir visual style / Sheri Chinen Biesen.
Description: New York : Columbia University Press, 2024. |
    Includes bibliographical references and index.
Identifiers: LCCN 2023054703 | ISBN 9780231215633 (hardback) |
    ISBN 9780231215640 (trade paperback) | ISBN 9780231560894 (ebook)
Subjects: LCSH: Film noir—History and criticism.
Classification: LCC PN1995.9.F54 B537 2024 |
    DDC 791.4309/04—dc23/eng/20240216
LC record available at https://lccn.loc.gov/2023054703

Cover design: Elliott S. Cairns
Cover image: TCD/Prod.DB/Alamy Stock Photo

For lovers of film noir and its enduring shadows.

CONTENTS

Acknowledgments   ix

Introduction   1

1. Film Noir Visual Style from Wartime to the Postwar 1940s Nitrate Era   9
2. Fade to Gray and Color Noir   51
3. Neo-Noir: The Legacy of Noir Visual Style   111
4. From Noir to Netflix: Streaming Darkness in the Digital Era   149

Epilogue. The Persistence of Noir in the COVID-19 Era: 2020 and Beyond   183

Notes   197
Index   243

ACKNOWLEDGMENTS

This journey exploring the dark world of film noir began over twenty years ago and is greatly indebted to many people. I would especially like to thank my editor, Ryan Groendyk, Jennifer Crewe, Michael Haskell, Ben Kolstad, Zachary Friedman, Elliott Cairns, John Belton, Marianne L'Abbate, Deshraj Chaudhary, and the editors and staff at Columbia University Press for their kind efforts, which enabled this project to come to fruition. Special thanks go to Ned Comstock and the archival staff at the University of Southern California (USC) Cinematic Arts Library Special Collections; Academy of Motion Picture Arts and Sciences Margaret Herrick Library Center for Motion Picture Study; USC Warner Bros. Archive; Digital Media History Library; Motion Picture Producers and Distributors of America, Inc. (MPPDA) Digital Archive at Flinders University; University of California, Los Angeles (UCLA) Young Research Arts Library Special Collections; Harry Ransom Humanities Research Center at the University of Texas; New York Public Library for the Performing Arts Special Collections; George Eastman Museum and Technicolor Online Research Archive; Library of Congress; American Film Institute; British Film Institute; Indiana University Lilly Library; National Archives; and Museum of Modern Art for their research assistance, as well as for the research sabbatical grant support and funding received from my institution at Rowan University, which made this project possible. I would also like to thank Thomas Schatz, Brian Neve, Noah Isenberg, Emily Carman, Richard B. Jewell, Thomas Doherty, Charles Maland, Eric Hoyt, Anthony L'Abbate, Robert Boddingham, Scott Curtis, Fred Metchick, Walter Metz, Rebecca Martin, Shelley Stamp, Mahinder Kingra, my colleagues and students over the years for their inspiration and enthusiasm about film noir, Nate Chinen, John Gizis, and my family and grandparents, who lived through the era.

THROUGH A
NOIR LENS

INTRODUCTION

"That's cute. Say it again." The crackling hard-boiled dialogue is laced with ice. "For once I believe you. Because it's just rotten enough." "Goodbye, baby." The room is pitch-black in shadow as deadly lovers Walter Neff and Phyllis Dietrichson jealously spar and gun each other down, in the dark after closing the windows and drawing the shades—and their weapons—at the end of the classic 1944 film noir *Double Indemnity*. Film noir, the well-known period style that emerged during World War II, was famous for its silhouettes; venetian blinds; unlit spaces; and bleak depictions of crime, corruption, and crooked protagonists. The hard-boiled "red meat" crime cycle was recognized in the United States in 1944–1945, and the French critics Nino Frank and Jean Pierre Chartier coined the term "film noir" in 1946 to describe these dark crime films exported from Hollywood after the war.[1] Noir's brooding milieu exuded a distinctive atmosphere of deep shadows, dark alleys, swirling smoke, and rain-slicked city streets—iconic elements of the film noir visual style. "One is lost in the dark of the night," the film noir stylist John Alton observed, calling cinematography "painting with light." "In the dark there is mystery . . . ghosts do exist, but only in the absolute darkness of night."[2]

Film noir style influenced and transformed many different genres. Noir was not a single genre, nor was it static. The dark noir aesthetic trend evolved and was forged and developed in relation to industrial and institutional historical pressures, thematic and narrative concerns, censorial constraints (or lack thereof), technological advances, and material production considerations.

In particular, the noir visual style was catalyzed during and just after World War II, and the legacy and influence of noir continued vis-à-vis color film production in the postwar period and into the later postclassical and digital-streaming eras.

In fact, the influential 1940s cinematic legacy of the "noir impulse" continues to persist even today. In a digital era, eighty years after noir's emergence in the 1940s, we have seen a resurgence of film noir style in new media. For instance, Netflix has thrived offering low-lit noir-styled programming. Cinematic Netflix dramas such as *The Chilling Adventures of Sabrina* (2018–2020) are visually steeped in blackness and comment on the absence of light: projecting darkness permeates its murky milieu as murderous underworld gangs destroy lights and black out a city and tormented characters experience nightmares flashing back to the 1940s then meet their demise in an existential abyss.

The look, imagery, and style of film noir were especially impressive on nitrate film. For instance, the George Eastman Museum's Nitrate Picture Show recently unveiled a gorgeous, restored nitrate film print of the 1947 film noir *Dead Reckoning*, starring Humphrey Bogart, to showcase its blackened high-contrast chiaroscuro cinematography. Nitrate was highly volatile and explosive, however, and thus was rationed during the war and used to make bombs. In 2015, *The Verge* observed, in an article called "Film from the Ashes: A Beautiful but Deadly Art Is Reborn at the Nitrate Picture Show," that "this version of *Casablanca* [1942]," a 1947 print made from a base of nitrocellulose, a cousin to gunpowder, "had the potential to kill us all."[3]

Indeed, we typically view these films through the lens of evolving technology: most of us in a contemporary digital new media era now watch noir films either via digital streaming or on DVD or Blu-ray discs that have been digitally transferred from acetate "safety" film release prints of the original nitrate films, which also affects noir style. In many cases, these digital incarnations of noir films are much lighter than the original films, and their cinematic aesthetic looks increasingly digitized. Such a technological shift reveals how rare it is for viewers today to see films noir on the original 1940s nitrate film stock used when they were originally shot, produced, and theatrically screened.

Nevertheless, the Nitrate Picture Show demonstrated that screening noir in the original nitrate film format is a vast improvement over digital projection on the big screen at a few other film festivals. In 2020, Netflix acquired Hollywood's historic Grauman's Egyptian Theatre, capable of screening nitrate and 70mm film, to enable a sweeping restoration and technological upgrade of its streaming capabilities.[4] The Egyptian, partnering with American Cinematheque, programs classic cinema and films noir and hosts premieres of such noir-inspired Netflix films as Afonso Curón's *Roma* (2018) and Martin Scorsese's *The Irishman* (2019). When theatrical viewing and noir festivals were abruptly interrupted by the COVID-19 pandemic, streaming gained importance and was essential for virtual events like Spike Lee's neo-noir *Da 5 Bloods* (2020) and the Film Noir Foundation's Noir City.[5] The move from nitrate to digital streaming signaled a remarkable synergy of old and new technologies for optimal viewing of film noir visual style.

This volume is a technological and industrial history of the evolution of film noir visual style and how it was adapted throughout the decades. It is a follow-up to my earlier monographs, *Blackout: World War II and the Origins of Film Noir* (2005); *Music in the Shadows: Noir Musical Films* (2014); and *Film Censorship: Regulating America's Screen* (2018), and it traces film noir from the origins of the dark cinematic style to the present day. This book gives a historical perspective on film noir visual style; aesthetic technique; narrative/thematic and censorship considerations; and the technological, industrial, and material production conditions that contributed to its multifaceted evolution. It explores film noir from its 1940s emergence in wartime to its changing nature in the postwar era and the persistence of the "noir impulse" in American film and new media legacy in the streaming era. The chiaroscuro imagery of classic noir visual style continues to be cinematically reimagined in later neo-noir films and digital iterations of noir darkness. This volume considers the evolution of film noir and in particular film noir style from the forties to the present, paying particular attention to variations in the product in its classical period (1940s and 1950s) and the reuse and reimagining of elements of it (particularly its look or looks) as material conditions of film production change and new technologies emerge.

The visual style of film noir, with its iconic blackened imagery shot in deep focus on nitrate film stock, permeated many classic Hollywood genres and evolved from the 1940s into the 1950s and beyond. Primary archival evidence and contemporaneous industry trade discourse suggest that, as film noir emerged and proliferated during the 1940s, the style responded to new technologies. Since then, changes in motion picture technology, film stock, cameras, lenses, cinematography, lighting, color, projection and digital shooting/compression, ultra-high-definition television, and the streaming revolution have affected the development and evolution of noir visual style and its aesthetic technique.

As motion picture technology, the film industry, visual style, and cinema-viewing markets shifted with World War II and its aftermath, film noir was transformed. Postwar noir was different from the wartime noir films *Double Indemnity* (1944), *Murder, My Sweet* (1944), *Jane Eyre* (1944), *Phantom Lady* (1944), *Laura* (1944), and *The Big Sleep* (1945–1946), which were shot amid war-related constraints; blackouts; and rationing of film stock, electricity, and set materials. All these factors contributed to its development. After the war, noir visual style, aesthetic techniques, and technology adapted because noir films were shot on location on nitrate film in broad daylight, which juxtaposed deep shadows with a lighter sunlit visual style in the virile yarns *Dead Reckoning* (1947), *Out of the Past* (1947), *Dark Passage* (1947), *The Lady from Shanghai* (1948), and *Act of Violence* (1949), which saw protagonists framed in murderous labyrinths of deceit. A semidocumentary technique also influenced the aesthetic style of visually brighter film *The Naked City* (1948), and topical social realist noir message pictures like *The Lost Weekend* (1945), with darker imagery in *Crossfire* (1947), and *Body and Soul* (1947).

Postwar developments altered the iconic look and visual style of film noir. The film stock on which shadowy noir was shot shifted after 1950 from the stark black chiaroscuro high contrast of nitrate stock to grayer acetate safety stock and the vibrant hues of color film. *Sunset Boulevard* (1950), one of the last major features shot on nitrate, was a key transitional film. As Hollywood shifted from nitrate to acetate safety stock from 1950 onward, a less shadowy semidocumentary style was seen in films shot on location, such as *The Enforcer* (1951). The visual style and film technology of noir films shot on acetate featured a lighter aesthetic as classic noir ebbed by the end of the 1950s. For instance, *Ace in the Hole* (1951), *The Big Heat* (1953), *The Big Combo* (1955), *Kiss Me Deadly* (1955), and *Touch of Evil* (1958) included a grayer, sunlit, high-key "gris" visual style and cinematography distinctive from *Sunset Boulevard* and very different from the nitrate noir look of the classic 1940s films noir.

Hollywood rechanneled low-budget B film production, including noir B films, into noir-inspired telefilms and television crime dramas that were also shot in low-contrast imagery with a brighter, grayer visual style. Color became a new technological and aesthetic vehicle for channeling film noir visual style. As part of Hollywood's response to television, a distinctive color noir aesthetic arose, emulating shadowy noir style with color film, using muted tones to simulate the look of black-and-white film (while often also adding the color red). The noir aesthetic also adapted to new technology in the postwar industry move to color widescreen spectacles with stereophonic sound.

As gritty black-and-white crime films became grayer and more masculine and shifted away from hard-boiled femme fatales, brooding color noir melodramas like *The Red Shoes* (1948) resonated with postwar women, visually and thematically employing a darker noir style. Classic film noir visual style continued to decline after 1953 as new technological developments by Technicolor and Kodak Eastmancolor enabled single-strip color film processes, which contributed to studios producing more color films. Hollywood sought to differentiate its cinema product from small-screen television by using color films—along with widescreen technologies and stereophonic sound—to meet the industry's "desperate need to lure people away from their black-and-white television sets."[6]

Hollywood responded to competition from television with spectacular color noir films such as *Niagara* (1953), *Rear Window* (1954), and *North by Northwest* (1959) and the noir musicals *A Star Is Born* (1954) and *West Side*

Story (1961). Standard screen (Academy 1.37:1 aspect ratio) pictures morphed into widescreen noir films such as *The Big Combo, Kiss Me Deadly*, and *Touch of Evil*. Alfred Hitchcock pushed the color noir impulse by re-envisioning black-and-white noir in a new color light in *Rear Window* and *North by Northwest*. Fox required that films shot in CinemaScope be filmed in color, compelling competitors like Warner Bros., which had begun filming the juvenile delinquent crime film *Rebel Without a Cause* (1955) in black and white, to start over using color.

The legacy of film noir style continued to resonate in later incarnations of neo-noir color films such as *The Godfather* (1972), *'Round Midnight* (1986), *Dark City* (1998), and *Bridge of Spies* (2015). Following the refinement of film lab processing techniques—and the conversion of network television to color—in 1966, Hollywood studios abandoned black-and-white film and shot entirely in color by 1967.[7] But the black-and-white film noir imagery and the color noir visual style of 1940s and 1950s films influenced a new aesthetic in neo-noir films after 1967 and through the present day. The harsh violence, blackouts, and filmmaking constraints of World War II created unique production and reception conditions that catalyzed the development of film noir in the 1940s, but the brutal carnage of the Vietnam War—coupled with the end of Hollywood's Production Code censorship—contributed to a gritty cultural climate receptive to neo-noir. From the late 1960s through the 1970s, Hollywood renaissance films explored the darker themes and visual style of classical film noir in neo-noir films of a new postclassical era.

Arthur Penn's *Bonnie and Clyde* (1967) reimagined 1930s gangster film outlaws in the spirit of the 1949 noir *Gun Crazy*. Francis Ford Coppola harkened back to the 1940s in his cinematic incarnation of New York mobsters in *The Godfather* and *The Godfather Part II* (1974). As New Hollywood innovations progressed, advances in color film technology refined color noir visual style. Martin Scorsese's gritty neo-noir rendering of New York City in *Mean Streets* (1973), *Taxi Driver* (1976), and *Raging Bull* (1980) re-envisioned film noir. *Mean Streets, Taxi Driver*, and *The Godfather* films were also developed in Technicolor, which enhanced their color noir style.

The surge in neo-noir continued into the 1980s and 1990s with *'Round Midnight, Barton Fink* (1991), *L.A. Confidential* (1997), and *Dark City*. Kodak Eastman made improvements in color film stocks in the 1980s, 1990s, and 2000s with faster, more light-sensitive film requiring shorter exposure times. These new stocks and advancing technology aided the ability to achieve high contrast in low-light conditions for darker noir imagery in the visual style of later neo-noir films. Bertrand Tavernier's neo-noir *'Round Midnight*, for example, was beautifully shot using an improved version of Eastmancolor in Panavision 35mm, with moody art direction from production designer Alexandre Trauner inspired by film noir and color noir.

As technological advancements refined neo-noir style in the new millennium, filmmakers paid homage to classic noir. Steven Spielberg's Cold War film *Bridge of Spies* reimagines film noir in the divided cities of East and West Berlin to replicate cinematically the stark imagery of Cold War noir style in a color neo-noir. Spielberg's cinematographer, Janusz Kaminski (originally from Poland), and production designer, Adam Stockhausen, re-created the harsh, chilling climate of the Cold War and captured the brooding, paranoid zeitgeist and shadowy visual aesthetic of 1940s–1950s film noir. Kaminski, who also shot *Schindler's List* (1993) and *Saving Private Ryan* (1998), shot *Bridge of Spies* on 35mm Kodak color film stocks with anamorphic lenses using two different crews—and different gaffers—for shooting in the United States and Germany, saying, "The lighting style is very much film noir, I was going for shadows."[8] Recent neo-noir films such as *The Irishman* (2019), *Rebecca* (2020), and *Nightmare Alley* (2021) reveal the influence of the ongoing dark noir-styled trend.

Netflix has emerged as a trailblazer in new digital media technologies that fundamentally transform distribution and exhibition, changing the way consumers engage with media. Netflix even created a short neo-noir film, *Meridian* (2016), for developers, engineers, and filmmakers to pay homage to the noir visual style while testing the digital-streaming technical capabilities in handling smoke and chiaroscuro shadows onscreen. Netflix has also appropriated noir as an important part of its business model, strategically infusing noir visual style into original programs such as *Daredevil* (2015–2018), *Jessica Jones* (2015–2019), *Luke Cage* (2016–2018), *Babylon Berlin* (2017–), *Shadow* (2019), *House of Cards* (2013–2018), *Collateral* (2018), *Ozark* (2017–2022), and *The Night Agent* (2023–), and noir style featured prominently in the AMC series *Mad Men* (2007–2015) and *Breaking Bad* (2008–2013). All have strong noir elements: flawed or corrupt protagonists, elaborate overlapping plot lines that concern criminal underworlds and immoral debauchery, and a distinct noir visual style. Even sun-scorched New Mexico in *Breaking Bad* evokes the parched desert in Billy Wilder's noir *Ace in the Hole*. In the wake of COVID-19, Netflix provided an ideal home-viewing environment for binge watching noir and invited viewers into the dark, disturbing nocturnal world of noir cinema. As fewer theaters screen actual celluloid, with 35mm (or 70mm) films no longer shown in most movie theaters, there is also less incentive for cinema viewers to leave their homes just to see digital projection in theaters.

Neo-noir visual style is darker than ever as advances in digital technology allow much greater image contrast in long-form streaming dramas that emulate extended noir movies rather than conventional broadcast television. Netflix's adaptation of *House of Cards* is much more shrouded and expressionistic in its noir visual design than the original 1990 British TV series. The Netflix adaptation actually incorporated an homage to the noir classic *Double Indemnity*. Like *House of Cards*, Netflix's *Jessica Jones*, *Daredevil*, and *Luke Cage* are soaked in shadowy noir cinematography, exploring a dangerous after-hours underworld metropolis (New York City), and *Babylon Berlin* reimagines a noir-styled retro-urban Berlin. Netflix's noir serial dramas *Ozark, Jessica Jones, Daredevil,* and *The Chilling Adventures of Sabrina*—like HBO's *Perry Mason* (2020–2023) and *Game of Thrones* (2011–2019) and Disney's *The Mandalorian* (2019–)—are so steeped in blackened noir imagery that they were criticized for being "too dark" and "filmed in unrelenting noir shadows."[9]

✳ ✳ ✳

This book investigates how the noir impulse persists. It considers the legacy of film noir in an evolving technological, industrial production, distribution, and reception context. After the 1940s, film noir was never quite the same. The influential shadowy visual style responded to technological and industrial changes, even adopting a brighter sunlit look in 1950s pictures, and transformed many different film genres and digital streaming media productions, in black and white and in color, into the new millennium.

Chapter 1 examines film noir visual style from wartime to the postwar 1940s nitrate era. It explores the wartime chiaroscuro style of noir shot on nitrate film stock and its unique production context amid war-related constraints—blackouts; the rationing of film, electricity, and set materials; censorship regulations; and restrictions on location shooting—which aided film noir style. Following the war, location shooting resumed its prominence, and noir was filmed outdoors in broad daylight using a semidocumentary social-realist style for films noir and noir message pictures as seen in *Notorious, Dead Reckoning, Out of the Past, The Lady from Shanghai,* and *Act of Violence.*

Chapter 2 considers how noir visual style came apart in the 1950s as it faded to gray and shifted to color in response to an evolving postwar climate influenced by emergent technology, production, and reception contexts. *Sunset Boulevard* was a key transitional film. Film noir also became so self-aware that the director Robert Aldrich posed with the first book on film noir, *Panorama du film noir américain*, by the French critics Raymonde Borde and Etienne Chaumeton,[10] on the set of *Kiss Me Deadly* in 1955, and films like *The Big Combo*, shot by John Alton, intentionally harken back to a darker 1940s nitrate noir aesthetic. Chapter 2 also looks at color noir visual style from the late 1940s to the early 1960s as postwar Hollywood adapted to new technologies and the industry shifted from black-and-white to color film. The industry also moved from three-strip Technicolor to single-strip monopack Eastmancolor film, which affected the evolution of noir style in color. The influence of film noir style is seen in the emergence of color noir and technical innovation in *The Red Shoes, Niagara, A Star Is Born, The Barefoot Contessa,* Rear Window, North by Northwest, and *West Side Story.*

Chapter 3 explores the legacy of noir visual style in the explosion of neo-noir productions in postclassical Hollywood from the 1960s onward. Early neo-noir visual style is seen in *Bonnie and Clyde, Bullitt* (1968), and *The Godfather*. New technology such as advances in color film refined color noir visual style in neo-noir films. For example, Eastmancolor film stock improved to allow low-lit shadowy exposure of film after the mid-1970s, which, along with portable mobile equipment and new lab techniques, eventually resulted in enhanced color noir style in later neo-noir during the 1980s, 1990s and 2000s. Color neo-noir pastiche, experimentation, and homage to classic film noir is seen in films like *'Round Midnight, Bird* (1988), *The Fabulous Baker Boys* (1989), *Dead Again* (1991), *Barton Fink, The Big Lebowski* (1998), *L.A. Confidential*, and *Dark City*.

Chapter 4 traces the shift to digital darkness in the new millennium—streaming noir visual style in the digital era. Netflix has spawned a noir revival in the contemporary digital era, streaming transnational noir in an evolving media production, technology, and global reception context. Neo-noir cinematic productions—from postclassical, New Hollywood noir-inspired films such as *Bridge of Spies, The Irishman, Rebecca*, and *Nightmare Alley* to an array of long-form dramas nostalgically invoking noir—are streamed domestically and beamed digitally overseas. Noir visual style is reimagined in these neo-noir dramas, paying homage to classic noir.

From the 1940s to an emergent digital era, whether producing or streaming worldwide classic film noir, color noir, neo-noir, or long-form original neo-noir dramas, classic noir visual style and aesthetic technique has been reimagined into the new millennium. This volume relies on extensive primary archival and trade research, as well as formal and stylistic analysis, to place in historical context these stylistic, technological, aesthetic, industrial, and material production issues regarding film noir visual style vis-à-vis cinema history, technology, and global convergent culture.

CHAPTER 1

FILM NOIR VISUAL STYLE FROM WARTIME TO THE POSTWAR 1940s NITRATE ERA

"Film History Made by *Double Indemnity*," the *Los Angeles Times* heralded in 1944. The murder mystery film spurred a trend, recognized by contemporaneous critics at the time (1944–1945), as a "decisive" motion picture with its definitive noir style. Renowned master of suspense Alfred Hitchcock wired the director: "Since *Double Indemnity* the two most important words in motion pictures are Billy Wilder." Wilder admitted he deliberately set out to "out-Hitch Hitch," and declared: "I like to set Hollywood back on its heels."[1] World War II revealed the deadly side of human nature on screen as Hollywood films noir proliferated in wartime. Film noir was distinctive for its shadowy iconography, and motion pictures such as *Double Indemnity* spawned a new 'red meat' 'crime and romance' cycle, saving film by delivering darkness, developing a brooding style of 'black' chiaroscuro cinematography.[2]

"SAVE FILM! HELP WIN THE WAR!" is typed on the cover of Billy Wilder and Raymond Chandler's September 25, 1943 script for *Double Indemnity*, which opens with a 1938 coupe screeching through the murky streets of downtown Los Angeles in the dead of night. The script included four pages describing the atmosphere of the setting. Amid war-related blackouts, rationing of electricity, limited set materials, and restrictions on location shooting, which constrained Hollywood filmmaking for the duration of the war, dim lighting, shadows, fog machines, dry ice, mirrors, and artificial rain cloaked recycled sets in noir productions like *Double Indemnity*.[3] Ill-fated antihero Walter Neff and deceptive seductress Phyllis Dietrichson are shrouded in silhouette and visually splintered by venetian blinds as they verbally spar and plot murder in a haze of cynical hard-boiled dialogue: "Look, baby, you can't get away with it. You want to knock him off, don't you?" "I think you're rotten." "I think you're swell. So long as I'm not your husband." Later, as rain streaks the windows and they kiss in the dark, he offers her a drink, admitting: "All I have is bourbon," as they plan to kill her husband, run off together, and scam Walter's insurance company. Her eyes glisten in the shadows of the pitch-black frame as Phyllis insists the murder would be worth it to her.

The signature motifs of films noir like *Double Indemnity*, *Murder, My Sweet* (1944), *Phantom Lady* (1944), and *The Big Sleep* (1946)—which were used initially in response to wartime blackouts and filmmaking constraints—have long endured: rain-soaked city streets, brooding shadows, smoke, fog, dark alleys, late-night milieus, pools of water and reflective surfaces, oblique crisscrossing bars of entrapment from window shades, and expressionistic high-contrast deep-focus photography. Film noir was originally shot on 35mm nitrate film stock, which contributed to its distinctive shadowy visual style. Its light-sensitive silver emulsion produced blackened images and accentuated the stark high contrast of film noir visual style with its murky shadows, chiaroscuro cinematography, and "composition-in-depth" mise-en-scène on theater screens.

1.1 Phyllis's (Barbara Stanwyck) eyes glisten in nitrate shadows in Billy Wilder's *Double Indemnity*. Paramount, 1944

1.2 Stark noir shadows and shady bars of entrapment contrast with shafts of light in *Phantom Lady*. Universal, 1944

Nitrate film's jet-black imagery looked stunning in creating an ominous noir milieu. Actor Robert Mitchum joked about film noir: "the big stars got all the lights. We lit our sets with cigarette butts."[4] However, the reality was more complex. Filmmaker Mark Robson noted that, when shooting low-budget film noir with necessary war-related cost cutting and rationed material shortages (of building supplies, set materials, and wardrobe fabrics), "the less light we put on" recycled sets at a soundstage with back-lot streets, "the better they looked."[5] Studio executive Jack Warner insisted: "There is a war on, and we are trying to save film"—and film wasn't the only limited commodity.[6] War-related material constraints; government-mandated rationing; $5,000 set construction limits; and restrictions on lighting, electricity, location shooting, rubber, tires, cars, and gas hit the film industry as wartime blackouts, dimouts, and air raid drills affected Hollywood and the West Coast.

The noir style cut across genres and achieved critical and box office success, including Academy Awards and nominations, for *Double Indemnity, Jane Eyre* (1944), *Laura* (1944), *Gaslight* (1944), *The Lost Weekend* (1945), *Spellbound* (1945), and *Notorious* (1946). After Humphrey Bogart became an iconic noir crime-and-romance antihero on the heels of *To Have and Have Not* (1944) and

Casablanca, which won the Academy Award for Best Picture in March 1944, other studios sought the Warner Bros. star for noir films *Gilda* (Columbia, 1946) and *Out of the Past* (RKO, 1947). The new crime film trend was recognized in 1944–1945 by newspapers such as the *New York Times* and the *Los Angeles Times* and industry trade papers like *Variety* and the *Hollywood Reporter*, and its distinctive noir visual style of shadowy photography was praised in *American Cinematographer*. Studios joined the trend and tried to replicate the success of *Double Indemnity*—trying, for instance, to produce other films of censorable and previously banned Raymond Chandler and James M. Cain hard-boiled fiction adaptations. Film noir pushed the envelope of Production Code Administration (PCA) censorship, forcing filmmakers to find creative ways around the Code and encouraged cinematic artistry. Wilder's film was called an "emancipation for Hollywood writing."[7]

"Crime certainly pays on the screen," industry analyst Lloyd Shearer of the *New York Times* observed, noting the "growing crop of homicidal films" and the studio bandwagon mentality fueling the growth of the hard-boiled noir crime film trend. He explained the "main reason behind the current crop of hard-boiled, action-packed cinema murders is the time-honored Hollywood

1.3 Iconic femme fatale Gilda (Rita Hayworth) in noir silhouette in the film *Gilda*. Columbia, 1946

production formula of follow-the-leader. Let one studio turn out a successful detective-story picture and every other studio in the screen capital follows suit . . . Result: a surfeit of motion pictures of one type." *Double Indemnity* is generally accorded the honor of being the "first of the new rough, tough murder yarns . . . [and starting] the cinema's cycle of crime."[8] The prevalence of the noir trend from 1944 to 1946 is shown in the box "Definitive Films Noir Cycle Recognized in the United States (1944–1945) and France (1946)."

"Forever watchful of audience reaction, the rest of the industry almost immediately began searching its story files for properties like *Double Indemnity*,"

Definitive Films Noir Cycle Recognized in the United States (1944–1945) and France (1946)

Double Indemnity, 1944
Murder, My Sweet, 1944
Laura, 1944
Phantom Lady, 1944
The Woman in the Window, 1944
To Have and Have Not, 1944
Jane Eyre, 1944
Detour, 1945
Mildred Pierce, 1945
The Lost Weekend, 1945
Scarlet Street, 1945
Spellbound, 1945
Ministry of Fear, 1945
The Big Sleep, 1946
The Postman Always Rings Twice, 1946
Gilda, 1946
The Blue Dahlia, 1946
The Stranger, 1946
Notorious, 1946
The Lady in the Lake, 1946
The Killers, 1946*

---

* Early noir antecedents included: *Stranger on the Third Floor* (1940), *Citizen Kane* (1941), *Suspicion* (1941), *The Maltese Falcon* (1941), *This Gun for Hire* (1942), *Street of Chance* (1942), *Moontide* (1942), *Casablanca* (1942), *Shadow of a Doubt* (1943), and *Gaslight* (1940, 1944).

Shearer explained, describing it as a "fast-moving story" that studios could "buy cheap," thus encouraging the production of other "tough, realistic homicide yarns." He added: "RKO suddenly discovered it had bought Chandler's novel, *Farewell, My Lovely*, on June 3, 1941. If *Double Indemnity* was so successful, why not make *Farewell, My Lovely*? [retitled *Murder, My Sweet*] . . . 20th Century-Fox followed with *Laura*. Warners began working on Chandler's *The Big Sleep* for Humphrey Bogart and Lauren Bacall. MGM excavated from its vaults an all-but-forgotten copy of James Cain's *The Postman Always Rings Twice* [1946]. The trickle swelled into a torrent and a trend was born."[9]

The carnage of war and brutality of combat affected screen images, undermined censorship with violence, and added misogynistic gender distress to noir films. For instance, publicity for *Phantom Lady, Jane Eyre, Scarlet Street* (1945), and *Gilda* promoted misogynistic brutality, sexual violence, and men beating the women. Raymonde Borde and Étienne Chaumeton recognized the "eroticization" of violence, especially sexual violence, and provocative gender polemics in films noir. Filmmakers' reliance on a documentary newsreel style of cinematography, which grew out of the war years, would also affect the look and imagery of film noir and female gothic noir films.[10]

Noir Variants: Newsreel Style and Female Gothics

The visual style of film noir flourished in a number of different classic Hollywood genres in the 1940s. Even before the term "film noir" was coined, this brooding strain of dark cinema emerged during and just after World War II and permeated a range of atomic age crime films of the Cold War. When *Double Indemnity* previewed in late spring 1944, Fred Stanley of the *New York Times* observed the popularity of a women-centered variation on noir films "bulging with screams in the night, supercharged criminal phenomena and esthetic murder" and noted, "Every studio has at least one such picture in production and others coming to a witching boil."[11] Female gothic noir narratives like *Jane Eyre, Notorious*, and the supernatural love story *The Ghost and Mrs. Muir* (1947) redeployed the shadowy visual style of films noir.

Hollywood's female gothic noir films developed a darker visual style with disturbing stories set against dangerous landscapes involving toxic relationships. Gothic noir films *Rebecca* (1940), *Suspicion* (1941), *Shadow of a Doubt* (1943), *Jane Eyre, Gaslight* (1940, United Kingdom; 1944, United States), *Spellbound* (1945), and *Notorious* centered on murder and tormented unstable psyches, hysteria, and crimes of passion—hallmarks of female gothic *roman noir* narratives—and revolved around "gender difference, sexual identity, and the 'gender distress' that accompanied the social and cultural disruption of the war and postwar eras." Thomas Schatz observes that, like hard-boiled detective narratives, the gothic centered on an "essentially good though flawed and vulnerable protagonist at odds with a mysterious and menacing sexual other."[12] In the female gothic's harsh, remote settings of steep cliffs, violent surf, and haunted mansions, a young, innocent female meets, becomes romantically involved with, and marries a suave enigmatic stranger. The gothic noir heroine's mysterious, charming older lover or husband (such as Laurence Olivier's brooding Heathcliff in *Wuthering Heights* [1939] and Maxim in *Rebecca*, and Orson Welles's moody Rochester in *Jane Eyre*), with a dubious past and secrets to conceal, becomes an alluring but potentially predatory sexual presence. Gothic film noir coincided with a wartime labor market of aging men and younger women in Hollywood, as younger men went off to war.

These female gothic noir thrillers involved toxic dark love romances, lethal attraction, and brooding psychological trauma. In perilous noir gothic settings, "seeds of romantic estrangement" pervade the homme fatale's "moodiness and unpredictability [which] sometimes signal potential danger to the heroine even before she marries," as in George Cukor's *Gaslight* (1944), where criminal spouse Charles Boyer preys on a young, unsuspecting Ingrid Bergman. Helen Hanson observes the "rapid move from the romance stage of the narrative to one of suspicion and investigation shows the transition in the heroine's perception of her husband."[13] Women-centered noir mysteries *Phantom Lady, Laura, Woman in the Window* (1944), *Spellbound*, and *Gilda* infused elements of *roman noir* gothic romance and were called "psychological" "horror" films. Screen censors fretted over the growing "crime-horror" trend by the 1940s, after previously discouraging salacious brutality, criminality, and instead encouraging a cinematic shift from "rawness to romance" in the 1930s.[14] By 1944–1946, female gothic thrillers coalesced with a darker shadowy noir style in *Jane Eyre, Spellbound*, and *Notorious*.

Film noir has long been recognized for its disturbing psychological "nightmare" underworld on-screen. Gothic novels also featured nightmarish psychology, for example, Emily Brontë's *Wuthering Heights*, Charlotte Brontë's *Jane Eyre*, and Daphne du Maurier's *Jamaica Inn* and *Rebecca*. Alfred Hitchcock and Orson Welles thrived on portraying subjective prisms of psychological anguish in noir thrillers. Given war-related restrictions on location shooting in Los Angeles for the duration, most gothic noir films were shot on Hollywood studio soundstages and back lots, but Alfred Hitchcock and cinematographer Joseph Valentine avoided set construction limits by leaving Los Angeles and shooting *Shadow of a Doubt* on location outdoors in Santa Rosa, California.[15]

Jane Eyre

Gothic noir *Jane Eyre*, produced, designed, and partially shot by Orson Welles—and credited to director Robert Stevenson (after Hitchcock passed on the project)—featured an impressive, fog-shrouded, blackened landscape

1.4 Shadowy, noir-styled night imagery on an enclosed soundstage set in *Jane Eyre*. Twentieth Century-Fox, 1944

of noir imagery. The bleak gothic Thornhill mansion was shot entirely on enclosed Twentieth Century-Fox studio soundstages with huge sets cloaked in deep shadows and abundant dry ice. Although he did not receive screen credit, production correspondence reveals that "Welles did a great deal more [than] producing" *Jane Eyre* and "worked on the sets, changes in the script, in casting, among other things, and [was in] charge of the editing."[16] Cinematographer George Barnes, who also shot Hitchcock's gothic noir films *Rebecca* and *Spellbound*, created a brooding noir tableau in *Jane Eyre*.

Newsreel Style

Film noir visual style benefited from World War II documentary trends and what 1940s cinematographers James Wong Howe and John Seitz and director Billy Wilder called newsreel style. In *American Cinematographer*, Howe insisted that this technique enhanced the visual look of sets built in an era of rationing (i.e., of building materials, rubber, lighting, electricity) to achieve production economy in the lean filmmaking environment of wartime Hollywood.[17] Newsreel realism and stark real-life violence defined noir cinematography, which simulated the gritty filming limitations of frontline news coverage: existing "natural" lighting produced darker high-contrast images, which were exposed using "faster" light-sensitive film stock and shot with portable lightweight cameras designed to capture military action. Howe observed darker shadows in war-related combat documentaries filmed with little available light with silhouettes of soldiers in battle cast against dim cellar windows: "Magazines like *Life* and *Look* acquainted us with the documentary 'still' [photograph]," he explained, and newsreels presented an "intimate" portrait of death: "Film taught us what war looked like."[18]

Director George Stevens recalled the "tremendous experience" of watching the film noir *I Wake Up Screaming* on the front with twenty thousand troops during the war, which he felt had even greater impact overseas while he was "cut off" from the "simple life" back home. Films noir like *The Big Sleep* and gothic thrillers such as *Gaslight* were promoted as being shown on the front lines in combat zones. Soldiers living through the war were attracted to the gritty verisimilitude of films that emulated newsreel style. Stevens experienced the brutality of the conflict first hand, filming concentration camps "beyond description" at Dachau, where "the only way you can talk about it is in photographs."[19]

In filming *Double Indemnity*, director Billy Wilder (whose family perished at Auschwitz) and cinematographer John Seitz noted the film's documentary technique. "We attempted to keep it extremely realistic," Seitz explained. "The effect of waning sunlight" was created by using "some silver dust mixed with smoke" to accentuate the shimmering contrast of low-key lighting.[20] Wilder recalled using newsreel style and described filming at art director Hans Dreier's home: "Whenever I opened the door and the sun was coming in, there was always dust in the air." Wilder noted, "Once the set was ready for shooting on *Double Indemnity* . . . I would go around and overturn a few ashtrays in order to give the house in which Phyllis lived an appropriately grubby look because she was not much of a housekeeper. I worked with the cameraman to get dust into the air to give the house a sort of musty look. We blew illuminant particles into the air and when they floated down into a shaft of light it looked just like dust." He remarked, "I wanted to get away from what we described in those days as the white satin decor associated with MGM's chief set designer, Cedric Gibbons."[21]

Hitchcock worked on the 1945 British government World War II documentary *German Concentration Camps Factual Survey* about the genocide of the Holocaust. On his return to Hollywood, he considered using a clinical, scientific nonfiction newsreel style for the 1945 gothic noir thriller *Spellbound*, which was produced by David O. Selznick and scripted by Ben Hecht. But *Spellbound* also included elaborate dream sequences—drawn from painter Salvador Dali's surrealist design—that enhanced the brooding noir visual style with nightmarish imagery. Hitchcock created dark personas and psychological turmoil in *Spellbound* (with Ingrid Bergman and Gregory Peck) and in *Suspicion* (with Joan Fontaine and Cary Grant), recasting romantic antiheroes as potential murderers.

Notorious

Hitchcock produced and directed the gothic noir espionage thriller *Notorious* just after the war. The film involved a uranium plot among fugitive Nazis in Brazil as the atomic bomb was being tested—the film was shot after the atomic bomb was used in Hiroshima and Nagasaki. Gregg Toland directed second unit photography and Robert Capa shot stills (both uncredited) for *Notorious*. The film was promoted as: *"Love! burning in danger's deepening shadow!"* with outdoor location footage of Rio de Janeiro included in the trailer. Hitchcock cloaked stars Cary Grant and Ingrid Bergman in ominous shadows in *Notorious*, invoking noir style to project disturbing gender polemics and tapping into cultural tensions in the immediate postwar espionage climate. Bergman plays Alicia, daughter of an imprisoned Nazi, who is recruited by the U.S. government to be a spy. She becomes entangled in a romantic love triangle: a smoldering affair with American agent Devlin (Cary Grant) while posing as the wife of suspected Nazi Alex (Claude Rains), from whom she tries to get information—until Alex (and his mother) plot to murder her.

As working women were channeled into the home, postwar noir gothic heroines were constrained: entrapped into sublimating their intelligence (or career) and forced to adopt feminine, submissive qualities. Noir gothics reveal gender distress as women moved from professional careers (in *Spellbound*) to a dangerous domestic space (in *Notorious*) as sexuality is transmuted into violent eroticism and misogyny. Alfred Hitchcock created dark sinister noir visual spaces and defied Production Code censorship with torrid kisses between Cary Grant and Ingrid Bergman to visually express the intensity of their clandestine sexual relationship—inviting the camera and viewer to share in the heated intimacy and cinematic experience of their embrace. Hitchcock also creates tension and suspense in *Notorious* by filming an overhead crane shot of Bergman's Alicia socializing at a cocktail party in her husband Alex's (Claude Rains) mansion. The camera slowly pulls in to an extreme close-up shot of Alicia secretly holding Alex's key to the wine cellar, which she has stolen to give to Devlin (Cary Grant). Hitchcock then crosscuts between Alicia and Devlin looking for clues to her Nazi husband's activities. Devlin finds (and accidently shatters) a wine bottle in the cellar that contains uranium ore. Alicia and Devlin passionately kiss in the shadows as they are discovered, Alex and his mother slowly poison Alicia, then she wastes away and nearly dies. Hitchcock worked with

1.5 Cary Grant and Ingrid Bergman driving dangerously on a dark night in *Notorious*. RKO, 1946

writer Ben Hecht on a treatment in scripting the film. Censor Joseph Breen originally rejected early drafts of the screenplay, complaining that Bergman's Alicia was a "grossly immoral woman" who was "portrayed as a dying glorious heroine." Breen objected to and censored her having an affair dressed in her negligee at the opening of the film, then, due to the uranium plot, suggested submitting the script to J. Edgar Hoover and the FBI, the Navy, and the Brazilian government for approval. It is notable that, by the end of the war, industry censorial discourse grew increasingly hostile toward noir pictures; Hoover even wrote articles in local newspapers like the *Hollywood Citizen-News* denouncing these "low" "sordid" crime films that did not uphold law and order.[22]

Shot at RKO studio from October 1945 through early 1946, *Notorious* premiered in New York and Los Angeles in August. *American Cinematographer* called Hitchcock the "cameraman's director," renowned for his "suspense-mystery" style.[23] Hitchcock and cinematographer Ted Tetzlaff employed noir style to convey a subjective point of view in *Notorious*, simulating Alicia's disoriented perspective with an upside-down shot (created using mirrors) of her view of Devlin, which rotates as she lays disheveled and hungover in bed. In another scene, stylized iris shots show a horse race through her binoculars. Hitchcock used rear projection as an aspect of noir style in a distinctive way when Alicia's hair blowing in the wind obscures the camera as she drives recklessly, speeding while intoxicated on a dark dangerous night. *Notorious* (and 1946–1947 noirs *Dead Reckoning*, *Out of the Past*, and *The Big Sleep*) featured what appeared to be exterior scenes—for example, of noir couples driving in automobiles—with rear-projected process-shot images of second-unit footage in the background. Rear projection (popular in studio system films during the sound era in the 1930s and 1940s) sought to resemble and emulate filming on actual locations, thus eliminating the need for additional shooting. When used in films noir, this practice of filming in-studio with rear projection accentuated noir visual style combined with shadowy low-key lighting and artificial rain and fog to create an atmospheric milieu. These simulated locations saved time, avoided expensive delays, and avoided bad weather while creating a more contained, controlled studio production environment on soundstages that further emphasized noir visual style.[24] To enhance noir style in *Notorious*, Hitchcock ensured control over shooting conditions by filming almost entirely on RKO soundstages (and studio back lots), with an outdoor horse-riding scene shot in nearby Arcadia

1.6 Murky noir shadows and dim backlighting shroud Cary Grant and Ingrid Bergman in *Notorious*. RKO, 1946

(at the Los Angeles Arboretum Botanical Garden), and Toland's second-unit crew filmed additional footage of Miami, Rio de Janeiro, and Santa Anita racetracks for use in process shots with rear projection. As a result, *Notorious* is shrouded in chiaroscuro shadow and claustrophobic unlit spaces. It features impressively dark mise-en-scène and the most expressionistic noir-style visual design of Hitchcock's films.

When *Notorious* was released in 1946, Hitchcock recognized that he had garnered a substantial female audience.[25] *Notorious* made $7,150,000 in 1946, including $4,850,000 in North America and $2,300,000 overseas, signaling the vast popularity of film noir and woman-centered gothic noir romance. Hitchcock's gothic noir espionage thriller was the most successful RKO film that year. And many other noir films were also huge box office hits, as shown in the box "Film Noir Box Office Earnings of $5 Million."[26]

Film noir was so popular after the war that technology companies used noir films and aesthetics to promote filmmaking equipment and film stock. In *American Cinematographer*, an August 1946 Mitchell camera ad featured *The Big Sleep*, and an April 1947 Kodak ad used noir imagery to sell film with the tagline: "Artist . . . with light and shadow."[27] In late 1945, the *New York Times* noted that the film industry anticipated the end of war-related filmmaking constraints and production restrictions (e.g., limits on location shooting) and welcomed a revival of lavish Hollywood sets, expensive costumes, and crowd scenes with the easing of wartime shortages.[28] Studios were planning spectacular

---

Film Noir Box Office Earnings of $5 Million

Along with *Notorious*, other films noir enjoyed strong box office earnings, with many noir pictures making approximately $5 million by 1946:

Double Indemnity, 1944
Spellbound, 1945
The Lost Weekend, 1945
Mildred Pierce, 1945
Scarlet Street, 1945
The Big Sleep, 1946
The Postman Always Rings Twice, 1946
Gilda, 1946
The Blue Dahlia, 1946
The Stranger, 1946

color pictures for 1946. As a result, instead of the shrouded, enclosed nocturnal tableau of *Jane Eyre* or the dark urban jungle of *Double Indemnity*, Welles shot the gothic espionage noir *The Stranger* (1946) outdoors on a bright sunlit back lot at Goldwyn and Universal studios with huge sets to create a small town. Welles even included graphic documentary newsreel footage of the Nazi Holocaust in *The Stranger*, fusing nonfiction style and cinematic techniques, blackened stylized mise-en-scène, baroque noir design, and Cold War espionage in his brooding narrative.[29] The suspense film culminates in Welles's Franz Kindler—a Nazi war criminal who masterminded the genocide at concentration camps—meeting his demise in the shadows as he is shot by his wife Mary (Loretta Young) and speared on a clock tower in an elaborate finale.

While female gothic noir films like *Jane Eyre*, *Notorious*, and *The Stranger* targeted women, who dominated domestic (and Allied) home-front viewing markets during and immediately after the war, films noir grew more male-centered as the war ended and men returned home. For instance, industry discourse recognized the connection between the war's violence and the popularity of film noir as the conflict ended. "Because of the war the average moviegoer has become calloused to death, hardened to homicide and more capable of understanding a murderer's motives . . . getting rid of our wives or husbands and making off with the insurance money," industry analyst Lloyd Shearer of *New York Times* wrote on August 8, 1945. He called the noir crime film trend a "violent escape in tune with the violence of the times" and explained that the war has "made us psychologically and emotionally ripe" for these kinds of films. "After watching a newsreel showing the horrors of a German concentration camp," cinematic violence elicits "no shock, no remorse, no moral repugnance." Many filmmakers and viewers at the time had witnessed the carnage, saw graphic newsreels, experienced combat, or enlisted in military service overseas. Shearer opined, "These are times of death and bloodshed and legalized murder; these are times when, if an audience can stomach newsreels of atrocities, it can take anything."[30] Growing out of this climate, Hollywood produced a spate of virile hard-boiled film noir that were shot more and more often on sunlit exteriors.

Postwar Hard-Boiled Noir: *Out of the Past*

After the war, location shooting gained prominence as film noir moved outside into broad daylight, with sunlit techniques emulating nonfiction filming utilizing semidocumentary style as in *The Postman Always Rings Twice*, *The Stranger*, *Out of the Past*, *Dead Reckoning*, *The Lady from Shanghai*, and *Dark Passage* (1947). As film technology, censorial constraints, and markets shifted following the war, film noir evolved. Noir visual style, aesthetic techniques, and

1.7 *The Postman Always Rings Twice* featured outdoor filming on location in bright sunlight. MGM, 1946

technology adapted as postwar films noir shot on nitrate film in daytime sun on actual locations juxtaposed deep shadows with a more brightly lit semidocumentary visual style (paler than earlier wartime newsreel-style techniques shot amid war-related limitations on lighting). Noir protagonists were trapped in murderous labyrinths of deceit in masculine hard-boiled noir pictures. Examples include Robert Mitchum's cynical detective in *Out of the Past*, Bogart's tormented noir antiheroes in *Dead Reckoning* and *Dark Passage*, and Welles's patsy in *The Lady from Shanghai*.

In September 1945, RKO considered *Out of the Past* as "worthy" of the "rough, tough school of Chandler, Cain and [W. R.] Burnett." Directed by Jacques Tourneur, *Out of the Past* featured Robert Mitchum as Jeff Bailey, a deadpan private eye hiding from gangster Whit Sterling (Kirk Douglas) after running off with his gorgeous, doe-eyed femme fatale mistress Kathie Moffat (Jane Greer)—who stole $40,000, fled to Acapulco, then gunned down his partner Jack Fisher (Steve Brodie), who tracked them down. Based on Daniel Mainwaring's (aka Geoffrey Homes) novel *Build My Gallows High*, the film adaptation of *Out of the Past* was scripted by Mainwaring (Homes), Frank Fenton, and James M. Cain (uncredited). While the noir picture opened in bright

1.8 Hard-boiled detective Robert Mitchum is cloaked in deep shadows as he holds a cigarette in *Out of the Past*. RKO, 1947

sunshine on location, the film's pithy narration reflexively commented on its brooding visual style descending into shadow. Mitchum's moody voice-over explained, "She walked in out of the moonlight . . . We seemed to live by night. What was left of the day went away like a pack of cigarettes you smoked."

Mitchum comments wryly on the film's noir mise-en-scène and duplicitous narrative: "I'm in a frame . . . All I can see is the frame. I'm going in there now to look at the picture." Indeed, the picture exuded darkness. Mitchum hides in shadows in an unlit room. The screen is pitch-black as Kathie double-crosses him, arranging his set up and expressing dismay that he's eluded her assassination. When Kathie's deadly duplicity is revealed, the screen is black as Jeff enters her bedroom through the window, as the curtains blow in the dark. The stinging barbs of the characters in silhouette are iconic of hard-boiled noir—as she cries, "I don't wanna die," he replies: "Neither do I baby, but if I have to, I'm gonna die last." He adds: "You're like a leaf that blows from one gutter to another." The film's Cain-style hard-boiled dialogue included punchy repartee such as Mitchum's lines: "Baby, I don't care," "That's a mean river," "You don't go fishing with a .45 in your hand," and "Look, get out . . . I have to sleep in this room." Kathie betrays Jeff and returns to Whit, who frames Jeff for murder.

When Jeff foils her attempt to frame and kill him, Kathie's futile efforts to murder Jeff result in Whit's tough-guy assassin Joe (Paul Valentine) getting killed. Jeff tries to make a deal with Whit for $50,000 "to spend my waning years in Mazatlán." He adds, "Not Acapulco, because I'd keep thinking about you, Kathie, up there in the women's prison in Tehachapi." Setting up the femme fatale who killed his partner Jack: "It won't be too bad. Hills all around you. Plenty of sun." When Whit tries to punch him, Jeff dryly says, "I wouldn't try it, Whit, you're out of shape. Besides, it's not a frame. She shot him . . . You see, Whit, self-defense. A cinch to beat. She might not even have to do time." Whit yells, "Get out!" then violently slaps Kathie. "You dirty little phony," he growls, threatening to kill her and telling her she's taking the rap in a vicious exchange. "What a sucker you must think I am. I took you back when you came whimpering and crawling. I should have kicked your teeth in." Then Kathie knocks Whit off. She and Jeff die in a fiery car crash at a roadblock when Kathie guns Jeff down behind the wheel.[31]

Hollywood's growing penchant for location shooting influenced the postwar noir visual style. *Out of the Past* is notable for its stunning noir cinematography shot by Nicholas Musuraca. It combined shadowy interiors with sunlit outdoor locations. *American Cinematographer* commented on how RKO tried to cast Bogart in *Out of the Past*, had Cain rewrite the script, and applauded Musuraca's chiaroscuro noir photography with its sparse minimal lighting.[32] It was shot at RKO and at Pathe in Culver City, with extensive location filming in Lake Tahoe and second-unit shooting in Acapulco, New York, and San Francisco. RKO's pressbook publicity exploited the look of the film's expressionistic

1.9 Noir shadows loom as "lightning kisses thunder": Robert Mitchum, "a guy without a future," grabs femme fatale Jane Greer, "a girl with too much past," in *Out of the Past*. RKO, 1947

visual style and promoted the noir picture with murky black storm clouds splintered by crackling lightning; hard-boiled star Robert Mitchum, with a fedora and cigarette dangling from his mouth; femme fatale Jane Greer; and the tagline: "It's like *LIGHTNING* kissing *THUNDER* when Mitchum makes love to a girl with a gun!" *Out of the Past* was pitched as a "high-powered romance that begins with a double-cross and ends in double-trouble . . . for a guy without a future and a girl with too much past!" Italian *Catene della colpa* (*Chains of Guilt*) posters featured color noir images of Mitchum and Greer, who holds a gun and wears a bright scarlet dress, and lightning piercing the stormy night sky.[33]

The brooding noir style and provocative narratives in these films alarmed Hollywood's industry censors. *Out of the Past* met resistance from the PCA. In April 1946, censor Joseph Breen addressed executives and producers at RKO. Breen condemned films noir, criticized producer Val Lewton, and denounced "low tone" pictures with "unpleasant people, set down in squalid or sordid surroundings and engaged not only in criminal but in brutal activity."[34] Breen tried to prevent the production of *Out of the Past* in June 1946, deploring its "objectionably sordid flavor" and "gross illicit sex, blackmail and murder," then

1.10 Robert Mitchum and femme Jane Greer drive by night in shadowy noir darkness as they flee the scene of the crime before crashing and meeting their demise in *Out of the Past*. RKO, 1947

suggested RKO shelve the film project and "dismiss any further consideration of making motion pictures of this type" as "I am sure that a picture of this kind will do a definite disservice to this industry."[35] Breen again bewailed the "unsatisfactorily low tone" of *Out of the Past* in late August.[36]

Despite Breen's objections, the beautifully shot, atmospheric film noir was a success and would become one of the all-time classic noirs. *Variety* praised the "hardboiled melodrama," noting director Tourneur's moody realism, location settings, and the "topnotch lensing" by Musuraca. *Out of the Past*, said *Variety*, was a "flashy addition to the tough-guy film archives . . . plenty of blood-and-thunder for action and mystery fans," adding: "Jacques Tourneur's direction demonstrates plenty of know-how in the knock-down-drag-out genre."[37] *Hollywood Reporter* observed, "Nicholas Musuraca keeps his camerawork at a low key throughout, thus implementing the suspense values" and admired the "intriguing geographic canvas" from Reno, San Francisco, Los Angeles, and Mexico in the melodrama that "is the kind of satisfying show which for years has been the industry's bread and butter."[38] Bosley Crowther of the *New York Times* compared *Out of the Past* and deadpan star Robert Mitchum to Bogart's "tough detective films."[39]

Yet the huge box office popularity of the cycle was already beginning to ebb as the postwar era progressed into the late 1940s. While *Out of the Past* earned $1,865,000, netting a modest $90,000 profit for RKO in 1947, it was nowhere near the $5 million profits of many earlier successful films noir at the height of the noir cycle in 1944 to 1946, or the $7 million box office of Hitchcock's *Notorious* only the year before.[40] Despite their success and critical acclaim, not everyone was happy with these noir films. Like the dustup between Breen and RKO over censorable content in *Out of the Past*, Hollywood censors considered noir pictures "sordid," "brutal," "low tone," "unpleasant," and "unacceptable."[41] Industry censors had earlier banned the sex and violence in hard-boiled noir source material, such as James M. Cain novels in the 1930s, and warned against crime-horror films arising by the war years. PCA censors criticized films noir, discouraged producing more of them, and attempted to sanitize the contents of the films they could not block completely. In early January 1947, *Variety* reported that some industry executives cautioned that the "psychological murder drama [noir] cycle" had run its course and the novelty had worn thin; they wanted to promote Hollywood's "movement toward realism" yet projected a waning hard-boiled crime trend and ebbing box office returns in the future.[42] By 1947, industry discourse was already becoming more critical and even hostile toward violent hard-boiled noir crime films. As with *Out of the Past*, Breen expressed concern to studios over other noir films, which he referred to as the "types and kinds of pictures which are stirring up a storm of protest." Breen also complained about another 1947 noir picture, Columbia's *Dead Reckoning*.

Dead Reckoning

Directed by John Cromwell, *Dead Reckoning* (produced in 1946 and released in 1947) showcased postwar noir visual style, fusing gorgeous shadowy chiaroscuro studio interiors with outdoor sunlit locations. As *Dead Reckoning* opens, it is visually difficult to recognize Bogart, who is on the run and cloaked in blackness. His character Rip Murdoch is shot from afar in a downpour. He clings to the shadows as he flees gangsters and the cops on wet city streets and disappears into the murky night. He ducks out of the storm, seeking refuge in a church and hiding in pitch-black darkness. It is so dark that Bogart is in complete silhouette and his face cannot be seen as he recounts his story to a priest and the noir film launches into a flashback of past events.

Columbia producer Virginia Van Upp cast Bogart in *Dead Reckoning* as paratrooper-turned-detective Rip Murdoch pursuing mobsters in a shady nightspot to solve the murder of his war buddy. Originally set to star Rita Hayworth opposite Bogart, *Dead Reckoning* instead featured Lizabeth Scott as deadly femme fatale Coral (aka Dusty or Mike) Chandler, a lethal married blonde bombshell—recalling Barbara Stanwyck in *Double Indemnity*, Lana Turner in

1.11 Humphrey Bogart hides in a church cloaked in deep shadows in *Dead Reckoning*. Columbia, 1947

The Postman Always Rings Twice, and Rita Hayworth in *The Lady from Shanghai*. Lizbeth Scott was borrowed from Hal Wallis's company, and Humphrey Bogart was borrowed from Warner Bros. to star in the Columbia film noir.

As mobsters turn out the club's lights, husky-voiced Dusty (nicknamed Mike) performs, singing the blues and dancing with Rip (Bogart). In early drafts of Columbia's screenplay for *Dead Reckoning*, Breen rejected the "brutality," "gruesomeness," "sex-suggestive flavor" and also decried the "loose morals," "drinking," and "attitude towards women" of the film's tough-guy antihero Rip in seducing girls at the bar and committing crime.[43] Rip suffers from post-traumatic stress symptoms: when he is beaten by gangsters and blacks out, the combat paratrooper has vivid nightmare hallucinations of skydiving and freefall imagery that are shown in elaborate montages. Dusty romances then betrays Rip, attempting to kill him in quintessential noir style, nearly gunning him down on a black rainy night. She tries again to shoot Rip as they drive off. Then the car veers off the road, and she dies after a violent fiery crash. Director John Cromwell filmed stars Bogart and Scott driving in a car on an automobile set to try to obtain the look of shooting on location in *Dead Reckoning*.

Pointed barbs punctuated the tough noir film. Bogart asks, "Is this the city of brotherly love?" when the train stops in Philadelphia. The local Philly photographer responds: "That's what New Yorkers call it. They don't live here." The grisly hard-boiled dialogue in *Dead Reckoning* seemed to fly in the face of Breen's censorial concerns. In the wake of the war's horrific genocide of the Holocaust and the devastation of the atomic bomb (which challenged screen censorship with actual [nonfiction] images of atrocities), Rip finds his combat buddy's body in the morgue burned "crisp as bacon." In tune with the violence of the war, and suggesting torture, a sadistic thug (with the moniker Krause, evocative of the Nazi menace) brutally roughs up Rip while taunting: "Make with the music, friend." A cynical safecracker gives Rip stolen weapons of war, destructive munitions taken from dead soldiers overseas. Rip uses them to terrorize the hoodlums who brutally beat him, whom he suspects of killing his buddy. Nazi "creeping jelly" grenades blaze with spiderlike tendrils to terrorize hoodlums. Gangsters recognize in horror the deadly German bomb devices as Rip seeks to burn them alive. He caustically inquires: "How would you like to be broiled? Medium rare?" As the room bursts into flames, crooks smash through a window, and are gunned down by the femme fatale. Cromwell and cinematographer Leo Tover used three cameras and fire explosives experts to film the "creeping jelly" grenade special effects, which were achieved using hidden pipes, gasoline vapors blown through holes in the carpet with air pumps, black powder, and electric wires. (After filming the fiery scene, the set was consumed in flames within two minutes.)[44]

Publicity for *Dead Reckoning* featured tough guy Bogart embracing femme fatale Scott, who wore a black gown and held a gun, and the tagline: "That's how guys get hurt . . . Trusting a beautiful woman!"[45] As postwar location shooting resumed free of war-related restrictions, Columbia pressbooks promoted the film noir's location shooting and in-studio effects combined with soundstage shots, which heightened its visual style. It publicized how the *Dead Reckoning* crew avoided crowds while filming at Penn Station in New York City.[46] According to *Hollywood Reporter*, actual locations and second-unit and background footage for *Dead Reckoning* were shot in Philadelphia, Pennsylvania; LaGuardia airport in New York; St. Petersburg, Florida; and Biloxi, Mississippi.[47] In January 1947, the *New York Times* called *Dead Reckoning* a "slug 'em-love 'em and leave 'em picture" for "those with a taste for rough stuff . . . almost certain to satisfy" and warned "all others . . . to proceed at their own risk."[48] *Variety* praised the film's suspense, smart direction, and photography, and Bogart's tense performance.[49]

The Lady from Shanghai

While many postwar noirs such as *Kiss of Death* (1947) boasted a lighter visual style,[50] another film—Orson Welles's *The Lady from Shanghai*—artfully combined outdoor locales with a brooding noir aesthetic with deep shadows. Welles adapted, produced, and directed *The Lady from Shanghai*, filmed in late 1946 to early 1947, but its release was delayed until May 1948. It remains one of Welles's great films noir. Welles and cinematographer Charles Lawton's stylized, deep-focus, composition-in-depth imagery created a provocative cinematic aesthetic. Welles and Lawton shot on location and on elaborate studio sets to accentuate the film's remarkable visual style.

The Lady from Shanghai featured brooding noir photography that emphasized realism. It was filmed deftly on location in Mexico, San Francisco (at Union Square, the Mandarin Theatre in Chinatown, the Steinhart Aquarium in Golden Gate Park, and a deserted amusement park boardwalk), and Sausalito. *American Cinematographer* observed how Welles and Lawton infused the entire production with an "ominous mood" by combining darker "low-key interior lighting" with "natural light sources." Welles and Lawton created harsh noir images in deep focus and sharp contrast by using few reflectors (which typically soften the facial features of actors and eliminate shadows with flattering diffused light) for outdoor scenes. Instead, they filmed in glaring full sunlight with extreme camera angles and "heavily filtered skies" to "dominate the exteriors." Welles and Lawton shot with filters to achieve menacing shadows with "dramatic" "highlight" using wide-angle lenses to film close-up shots from "weirdly grotesque angles" of duplicitous characters and deadly landscapes—visually simulating the chaotic subjective point of view of the tormented noir antihero.[51]

1.12 Orson Welles and Rita Hayworth, in noir silhouette, are backlit against sharks and eels at the Steinhart Aquarium in Golden Gate Park in San Francisco in *The Lady from Shanghai*. Columbia, 1948

In addition to the extensive location filming, Welles went to incredible lengths to accentuate noir visual style in *The Lady from Shanghai* with its pitch-black shadows. For instance, on Hollywood soundstages, Welles pushed the noir visual style further, filming the chiaroscuro, fog-shrouded opening sequence using an extended dolly shot with huge arc lights, a sound boom, and camera mounted on a crane rolling along a horse-drawn Victoria carriage. It was promoted as the longest dolly shot at the time.[52] In another famous example, actors are shot in blackened silhouette at San Francisco's Steinhart Aquarium in Golden Gate Park and Chinatown's Mandarin Theatre. *American Cinematographer* praised the "striking" aquarium sequence—a "masterpiece of mood" illuminated only by "simulating the light from the display tanks" to cast Welles and Hayworth in deep shadow backlit against huge sharks, eels, and an octopus.[53]

Antihero Michael O'Hara (Welles) is framed for murder and literally becomes the fall guy. He and femme fatale Elsa Bannister (Hayworth) sit in the darkness of the Mandarin Theatre in Chinatown, beautifully shot in a blackened variation of documentary-style realism as they watch actors perform a Chinese opera. Then Michael discovers Elsa is the killer and draws a gun from her purse. After Michael is drugged and blacks out, he is taken to an amusement park where his drug-induced hallucination becomes a real nightmare as he falls down a curving slide and through a dragon's mouth to enter a surreal, expressionistic world evocative of *The Cabinet of Dr. Caligari* (1919).

Welles took a week to design the disorienting funhouse sets for the famous noir-style mirror sequence finale in *The Lady from Shanghai*. He combined Columbia soundstages 8 and 9 for the massive set, which was specially designed to enable filming as camera operators moved down the slide to enhance its atmospheric noir visual style. Welles's impressive set included a giant slide rising to the roof with an eighty-foot-long/forty-foot-wide/twenty-foot-deep pit at the far end, a thirty-foot dragon's head with moving jaws, and thirty-five-foot geared turntables. Lawson and camera operator Irving Klein used overhead crane shots but also had to lie flat to "slide on their stomachs down the 125-foot zigzag chute"—with the camera mounted on a specially constructed mat to fit the contours of the chute—to film Welles's tumbling descent down the topsy-turvy slide.[54]

The film's unique noir visual style is especially evident in Welles's remarkable shattering hall-of-mirrors climax, which remains one of the extraordinary

1.13 Femme fatale Rita Hayworth and Everett Sloan in Welles's stunning noir mirror montage sequence in *The Lady from Shanghai*. Columbia, 1948

moments in cinema history. Welles accentuates the eerie imagery and creates elaborate geometric patterns of mirrors that slice and splinter the screen to reflect the deception of Elsa and her crooked attorney spouse Arthur Bannister (Everett Sloan). They confront each other in a labyrinth of mirrors, shooting and smashing reflections in a montage of explosive shattering shards of cracked glass— even splintering the camera lens. To achieve this visual effect, Welles mounted a 2,912-foot maze of reflected glass distortion mirrors on the set with transparent two-way mirrors to allow camera operators to shoot through them. Much of the sequence (including a decaying skull) was cut, but what remains is nonetheless superb. Preservationists continue to discover footage cut from the film.

Welles did encounter challenges filming *The Lady from Shanghai* on location in Acapulco, Mexico. He enhanced realism and noir visual style shooting on actual locales. Columbia chartered Errol Flynn's yacht *Zaca* to film at sea. Welles shot cramped interior compositions to emphasize noir claustrophobia. It was technically very difficult to shoot scenes on the water. Sunlight reflections off the ocean's surface spoiled light meter readings and caused overexposure of scenes, making them too bright and thus necessitating reshooting. Along with the outdoor locations of Acapulco Bay and Morro Rocks, Welles filmed chiaroscuro night-for-night shots at Ciro's nightclub atop the Casablanca Hotel, a shadowy, low-angle chase through Acapulco, and a moonlit stretch of sandy beach at Pied de la Cuesta for a darker style of noir realism with authentic atmosphere.[55]

Columbia promoted *The Lady from Shanghai* with menacing noir-style images of Welles and femme fatale Hayworth and a racy tagline, a warning that resembled a noir voice-over: "Men remembered her in the dark of night" and "I told you . . . you know nothing about wickedness," referring to Hayworth as a "blonde bombshell," the "Notorious" "Woman of the World." Posters for *The Lady from Shanghai* in the United States and overseas featured muted tones to simulate black and white with the dominant color scarlet red, which were repeated in U.S. publicity and racy Italian *La Signora di Shanghai* ads.[56] *American Cinematographer*'s Herb Lightman applauded Welles and cinematographer Lawton for achieving "extraordinary" and "unusual" effects with an "uninhibited camera" in *The Lady from Shanghai*, "but the real importance of the picture is its originality, as departure from stereotyped techniques—a healthy sign for an industry that continues to grow."[57]

Dark Passage

As seen in noir films such as *The Lady from Shanghai, Dead Reckoning,* and *Out of the Past,* postwar filmmakers combined shadowy in-studio photography shot on 35mm nitrate film with location shooting techniques that enhanced the moody noir imagery and realism of these pictures. As Hollywood's trend toward filming on location accelerated, a brighter visual style emerged in films such as *Dark Passage* (1947). Delmer Daves's *Dark Passage* features extensive location shooting filmed with a semidocumentary technique on the streets of San Francisco, California—often in broad daylight—to showcase the sweeping vistas of the city from the very opening credit sequence. This approach visually reinforces the fact that the film's locations are the star of the show. The opening sequences of *Dark Passage* are a nod to Robert Montgomery's experimental 1946 noir *Lady in the Lake*, in which the entire film is shot from the detective's viewpoint.

In *Dark Passage*, framed fugitive antihero on the run Vincent Parry (Humphrey Bogart) is initially only an unseen entity with Bogart's recognizable voice, which becomes the structuring absence of the film. The stunning location filming of the Bay Area in *Dark Passage* is combined with cinematic direct address for the first sixty-two minutes of the 106-minute film noir. Thus, Bogart is not visible for an hour (over half of the movie). The opening sequences are shot from his first-person point of view. The film's initial images approximate Bogart's viewpoint as he escapes San Quentin: the subjective camera spins inside a

1.14 Humphrey Bogart against the spectacular sunlit backdrop of one of the San Francisco locations in *Dark Passage*. Warner Bros., 1947

barrel rolling down the hills near Sausalito to show his perspective tumbling, running through brush, being picked up, hitching a ride with a huckster in a convertible, and punching the driver out cold, thus breaking the rules of classical Hollywood film style and anticipating Jean-Luc Godard's famous jump cutting sequence in the 1959 French New Wave noir *Breathless*. Impressive filmed locations in *Dark Passage*—the hills of Marin County, the Golden Gate Bridge, and San Francisco—are juxtaposed with exquisite close-up shots of Lauren Bacall (as beautiful redeemer heroine Irene Jansen), who helps the mysterious unseen fugitive escape by hiding him under a tarp on the floor of her wood-paneled station wagon—all shown from his first-person subjective view.

Shot by Sid Hickox, *Dark Passage* was for the most part lighter, brighter, and more high key in its sunlit daytime rendering of Union Square, the Presidio, the Filbert Steps, San Quentin prison, and Irene's Malloch Apartment Building. However, *Dark Passage* also includes some filming at Warner Bros. studio and shadowy afterhours nocturnal sequences of Harry's Wagon all-night diner (evocative of Edward Hopper's 1942 color noir painting *Nighthawks*) and fugitive Parry riding in a taxicab, which are so dark that the actors' faces are in blackened silhouette (briefly making Parry's first-person point of view direct address unnecessary). The noir style itself thus hides Parry's visible features in high-contrast chiaroscuro before he has plastic surgery and finally appears as Bogart.

In the last forty-four minutes of the noir film, *Dark Passage* presents Bogart against the spectacular backdrop of San Francisco locations, including his rooftop view of the city, then descending a fire escape (combining closer shots of Bogart with long-shot images of his stunt double) and running across steep hills and streets. The film captures his point of view as the Warner crime star rides a cable car and beats up a blackmailing thug at the foot of the Golden Gate Bridge. *Dark Passage* also reimagines the iconic noir femme fatale Madge (Agnes Moorehead) not as an enticing seductress but rather as a "pest," a nosy, vain busybody manipulating and murdering others for power and framing Parry for her crimes. Lethal femme fatale Madge turns out to be a vicious spurned lover who throws herself out a window—shown with a high-angle semidocumentary shot of the street below—in a final effort to frame Parry. In the end, Bogart and Bacall blissfully reunite at a beachside café in Peru (shot in-studio in shadowy noir style).

Dark Passage was promoted and compared to Bogart and Bacall's earlier noirs *To Have and Have Not* and *The Big Sleep* in its trailer. Warner Bros. studio pressbook publicity for *Dark Passage* also promoted Bogart and Bacall in noir-style imagery with evocative noir taglines: "YOU CAN GET THINGS DONE IN THE DARK!" As for Bogart's character: "He was the hunted turned hunter. The guilty half of his story all 'Frisco knew. The other half was a love story—with a threat in it he had to do something about!" *Dark Passage* cost $1,678,000, and grossed $3,430,000 ($2,318,000 in North America and $1,112,000 abroad), a huge box office success for Warner Bros. in 1947, revealing the ongoing popularity of Bogart and Bacall and the enduring appeal of film noir.[58]

As postwar Hollywood gravitated toward an increasing use of location filming and heightened realism, the semidocumentary cycle continued. As seen in *Dark Passage*, heavy reliance on location shooting with sunlit outdoor filming that employed semidocumentary cinematography techniques contributed to a brighter photographic style. Thus, *Dark Passage* was visually lighter in its overall aesthetic look than many noir films, including other hard-boiled noirs like *Dead Reckoning*, *Out of the Past*, and *The Lady from Shanghai*.

From Documentary Technique to Cultural Critique: *The Lost Weekend*

Extensive filming on location and a brighter high-key semidocumentary aesthetic technique lightened and undermined the shadowy conventions of noir visual style in films such as Billy Wilder's social-realist *The Lost Weekend* (1945); Henry Hathaway's *Kiss of Death*; Jules Dassin's *The Naked City* (1948), which showcased spectacular images of actual New York City locales; and Joseph Lewis's *The Undercover Man* (1949). As seen in postwar Italian neorealist films overseas, the trend toward location shooting influenced visual style in social-realist noir pictures that emphasized hard-hitting themes, as in *Crossfire* (1947), *Body and Soul* (1947), and influential antecedent *The Lost Weekend*.

Rather than centering on sex or murderous crime, Wilder's acclaimed *The Lost Weekend* was a social-realist drama infusing newsreel style with extensive location shooting on the streets of New York. The film anticipated later social problem noir and neorealist pictures.[59] Based on Charles Jackson's novel about the perils of alcoholism, censors deemed it sordid and objectionable in its unvarnished portrayal of excessive drinking, illicit sex and prostitution, and suicide. *The Lost Weekend* was a brooding narrative of obsession that was adapted by Wilder and Charles Brackett. *The Lost Weekend* portrayed the bleak vision of its unglamorous self-destructive writer Don Birnam (Ray Milland). It featured stunning noir cinematography shot on location by John Seitz, who also filmed *Double Indemnity*. *The Lost Weekend* focused on the downward spiral and addiction to drink of its antihero. Don plummets down a flight of stairs on an alcoholic binge, and the film culminates in his late-night imprisonment in a shrouded, horrifying, *Caligari*-like psychiatric ward with a caustic male nurse. Oppressive shadows and crisscrossing bars undulate to splinter Milland visually as doors swing shut. Suffering delirium tremens, called a "disease of the night," inhabitants are trapped and visually consumed by darkness. Miklós Rózsa's creepy score uses the theremin and amplifies Don's horror-inspired hallucination of a bat eating a rat in a hole in the wall. Rózsa also scored *Double Indemnity* and *Spellbound*, using the theremin in Hitchcock's eerie Dali dream sequences in the latter film. (Although Wilder denied it, Milland's tormented, hard-drinking writer in *The Lost Weekend* seemed to resemble *Double Indemnity* collaborator Chandler.)

Milland's antihero in *The Lost Weekend*, described as "that nice young man who drinks," is driven not by sex or money or violent sadistic thrill but by thirst for booze. He hides his liquor in a chandelier. He steals a woman's purse in a swanky bar to pay for his booze. Wilder shows his hand clasping her purse under the table, but he is humiliated when he is caught and thrown out. Don pawns his typewriter and his girlfriend's leopard coat, and gets a gun and attempts suicide. He calls the autobiographical novel he is writing "morbid stuff . . . a horror story, confessions of a booze addict," which he simply titles *The Bottle*. His drinking is an obsessive "merry-go-round[,] you got to ride it all the way" (an homage to the lethal trolley ride described in *Double Indemnity* that the criminals ride "straight down the line" together to their doom.)

While *Double Indemnity* dealt with an unscrupulous insurance salesman out to score some cash and sex in murderous fatal attraction, Wilder's *The Lost Weekend*—and later *Sunset Boulevard* (1950) and *Ace in the Hole* (1951)— centered on flawed, washed-up writers filled with cynical loathing hitting rock-bottom. *The Lost Weekend* projected a noir urban jungle shot on location: revealing New York City pawnshops, the Bellevue Hospital psychiatric ward, 55th Street and Third Avenue, and the Metropolitan Opera. Wilder's dark sense of humor torments Don with *La traviata*'s "Drinking Song." Yet in terms of gender, the antihero's girlfriend Helen (Jane Wyman) in *The Lost Weekend* is a warm-hearted, maternal redeemer, unlike *Double Indemnity*'s dangerous femme fatale Phyllis, who tries for over three years to curb his addiction. Even the prostitute Gloria (Doris Dowling) is portrayed as humane, humorous, and sympathetic as Don exploits her for money to buy another bottle to feed his obsession. Censors urged Wilder to clean up his depiction of unsavory prostitution, drinking, and suicide—all of which remained in the film.

The Lost Weekend ends where it begins: with a bottle of booze stealthily hanging outside Don's apartment window as he still tries to hide his drinking from his girlfriend and brother. The film has a vaguely optimistic closing, however, as he is heard narrating his story: "I stood in there packing my suitcase, only my mind wasn't on the suitcase, and it wasn't on the weekend, nor was it on the shirts I was putting in the suitcase either," Don explains in the voice-over narration, flashing back to his story of obsession and addiction. "My mind was hanging outside the window. It was suspended, just about eighteen inches below. And out there in that great big concrete jungle, I wonder how many others there are like poor bedeviled guys on fire with thirst, such colorful figures to the rest of the world as they stagger blindly towards another binge, another bender, another spree." Thus, the finale reveals that he eventually survives and overcomes his destructive habit to write his story and that alcoholism has not destroyed him. In this way, Wilder ultimately channels the sex and murderous crime of hard-boiled film noir into redemption from obsession, addiction, and self-destruction. After Wilder's *Double Indemnity* was nominated for seven Academy Awards the year before, *The Lost Weekend* won the Academy Awards for Best Picture, Best Director for Wilder, Best Actor for Milland, and Best Screenplay for Brackett (who produced) and Wilder. The fact that the film earned $5 million further validated the appeal of the noir style melded with social-realist cultural critique.

Body and Soul

The trend toward realism and cultural commentary continued in other social-realist noir films of the postwar era.[60] The documentary impulse of shooting on location informed the visual aesthetic of topical noir films ever shadier in their imagery. For example, social-realist noir pictures *Crossfire, Act of Violence* (1949), and *Body and Soul* were shot with a darker aesthetic. While *Crossfire* featured more in-studio shooting on the RKO back lot, *Body and Soul* achieved social-realist noir visual style filmed on location.

Body and Soul was an independent Enterprise Productions picture directed by Robert Rossen, scripted by Abraham Polonsky, and released through United Artists. Initially titled *The Burning Journey*, star John Garfield purchased the original story for *Body and Soul* in 1945 and was involved in all aspects of production. *Body and Soul* was shot by cinematographer James Wong Howe, who had championed filming with newsreel-style photography to enhance cinematic production values with darker, natural-source lighting during the war-related shooting constraints of World War II. Shot primarily on location in New York City, *Body and Soul* also had three second units film boxing arenas in twenty-six cities around the United States to provide background fight footage.

Garfield plays boxer Charlie Davis, who rises to fame and then loses everything, including his entire fortune, by standing up to the mob and winning his match rather than taking a dive and throwing a fight. The film opens in shadows as Charlie wakes from a traumatic nightmare, screaming in the dark for his friend Ben. Garfield, who performed his own fight sequences for his role, trained with sparring coach Mushy Callahan. Real-life 1930s middleweight boxing champ Canada Lee movingly plays Charlie's friend Ben, a black boxer who perishes after his health deteriorates from many years of being pummeled in the ring, set up to lose by gangsters. *Body and Soul* faced censorship delays due to its depictions of violence, suicide (which was removed), and PCA censor Joseph Breen's insistence that interracial fight scenes between white and black

1.15 John Garfield is covered in shadow as he meets the mobster trying to pay him off to fix a fight in *Body and Soul*. Enterprise/United Artists, 1947

boxers be removed. Garfield was reportedly injured and knocked out while filming a fight scene. For first-unit filming on *Body and Soul*, cinematographer James Wong Howe used eight cameras to shoot the fight sequences, placing three cameras on cranes for overhead bird's-eye-view shots of the boxing ring, with three cameras mounted on dollies and two handheld cameras to create a newsreel effect. Howe also shot handheld footage of boxing sequences while wearing roller skates.

Despite the innovative cinematography, topicality, and powerful cultural critique of the social-realist 1947 noir message picture, publicity for *Body and Soul* promoted the film's romantic sex appeal, with star boxer John Garfield and an array of beautiful women in alluring poses with taglines: "The story of a guy women go for! *Body and Soul*!" *Daily Variety* applauded the boxing scenes in *Body and Soul*, writing, "Seldom has the camera caught such exciting ring sequences."[61] The *New Yorker* called the fight scenes "marvelously realistic."[62] *Body and Soul* was nominated for Best Actor (Garfield) and for Best Original Screenplay (Polonsky), and won an Academy Award for Best Editing (Francis Lyon and Robert Parrish). Considered the quintessential boxing film, it also heavily influenced director Martin Scorsese's 1980 neo-noir *Raging*

Bull. Garfield's next hard-hitting noir picture, *Force of Evil* (1948), directed by Abraham Polonsky, featured lighter high-key cinematography shot on actual New York locales. Ads for the independent Enterprise Studios film (released by MGM) promoted its location shooting: "story of New York, many of its thrilling scenes filmed in this city!" It included sexy dames and lawyer-turned-racketeer Garfield firing a gun in "MGM's Inside Story of Gambling on Numbers! John Garfield puts his Body and Soul into *Force of Evil*!" As in *The Lost Weekend* and *Body and Soul*, other noir films engaged in cultural critique, as seen, for example, in the provocative topical commentary of noir pictures like *Crossfire*.

Crossfire

Critically acclaimed social problem films such as *Crossfire* (1947) raised serious issues, such as anti-Semitism, growing out of the war years in the wake of the horror and genocide of the Holocaust. *Crossfire* also dealt with the pervasive exposure to brutality as a result of military combat and the global conflict's potential to foster hate and xenophobia. The powerful film tackled hate crimes, racial-ethnic prejudice, anti-Semitic violence, and intolerance. It faced censorship for its original theme of homosexuality and its topic of a gay hate crime and the murder of a civilian committed by a service veteran.

Crossfire was considered controversial. PCA censor Joseph Breen objected to the project for two years, insisting it violated Hollywood's Production Code. Based on Richard Brooks's hard-hitting 1945 novel, *The Brick Foxhole*, *Crossfire* centered on a veteran (Robert Ryan as Sergeant Montgomery) who kills a Jew (a homosexual in the book). Robert Mitchum plays a veteran, Keeley, who helps police captain Finlay (Robert Young) as a detective solving the crime. Filmed at RKO studios *Crossfire* was cloaked in deep shadows. Shot in thirty-four days on a lean $589,000 budget, it was a huge critical and box office success, a "sleeper" hit grossing $1,270,000 that became the biggest release for RKO in 1947.[63]

Publicity for *Crossfire* showed gun-toting tough guys in fedoras (with Gloria Grahame's cigarette-smoking dance hall dame) to connote hard-boiled noir. Ads heralded: "Sensational? . . . No, It's Dynamite!" RKO gave hate crime violence a social-realist spin with the tagline: "Hate is like a loaded gun."[64] *Crossfire* was nominated for several Academy Awards, including Best Picture (losing to Twentieth Century-Fox's topical *Gentleman's Agreement*), Best Director, Best Screenplay (Adaptation), Best Supporting Actor (Robert Ryan), and Best Supporting Actress (Gloria Grahame), and it won Best Social Film at the Cannes Film Festival in September 1947. *Crossfire* was also applauded and criticized for depicting anti-Semitism in the United States. In March 1947, the *New York Times* called it one of Hollywood's first 1940s films to "face questions of racial and religious prejudice with more forthright courage than audiences have been accustomed to expect."[65] In 1947, the African American magazine, *Ebony*, recognized *Crossfire* with an award for its tackling of social issues as a film "improving interracial understanding."[66]

Noir reached its pinnacle at the end of the war, evolved into the 1940s and 1950s, and steadily declined amid new challenges in the postwar era. In fact, just months after the release of *Crossfire, Dead Reckoning*, and *Kiss of Death*, the postwar Red Scare produced a chilling effect, with House Un-American Activities Committee (HUAC) hearings investigating Hollywood in October 1947. Controversial, provocative screen material was discouraged, and industry executives denigrated downbeat noir crime pictures as sordid and disreputable. *Crossfire* was the last RKO film for director Edward Dmytryk and producer Adrian Scott after the HUAC labeled them "unfriendly" witnesses. Members of the so-called Hollywood Ten, they were blacklisted by the industry (Dmytryk also served time in prison). Orson Welles was shut out of the industry and prevented from making Hollywood films for a decade following *The Lady from Shanghai* and *Macbeth*. Welles then moved to make films in Europe, working with British director Carol Reed on *The Third Man*. Welles shot films in exile overseas as the Cold War escalated, until his return for film noir *Touch of Evil*. Other blacklisted noir filmmakers such as Jules Dassin, Edward Dmytryk, Robert Siodmak, Joseph Losey, and John Berry made films abroad. Abraham Polonsky, Robert Rossen, John Garfield, Carl Foreman, Dashiell Hammett, and Arthur Miller were also blacklisted.[67]

Deep Focus, Natural Lighting and Social Realism in *Act of Violence*

While noir message pictures like *Crossfire* relied on studio filming (using indoor soundstages on Hollywood back lots), other social-realist films noir such as Fred Zinnemann's *Act of Violence* filmed more extensively on location, which enhanced the message film's topical, hard-hitting social realism. *Act of Violence* allegorically commented on the growing Red Scare climate in postwar Hollywood. Zinnemann's *Act of Violence* created a shadowy chiaroscuro visual style even on location by using semidocumentary cinematic techniques and night-for-night shooting rather than relying solely on in-studio photography.

As in *Crossfire, The Lost Weekend*, and *Body and Soul*, the topical noir film *Act of Violence* deployed postwar documentary technique, deep focus, natural lighting, and social realism to reimagine Hollywood cinema's social issues and cultural critique of 1940s America. Directed by Zinnemann and shot by Robert Surtees, *Act of Violence* is an underrecognized noir gem that continues to resonate in its socially conscious themes, taut narrative, and innovative formal-aesthetic style. Zinnemann is better known for his 1950s films, such as *The Men*

(1950), *High Noon* (1952), and *From Here to Eternity* (1953). Yet the talented Jewish European émigré, born in Vienna, Austria, was a consummate stylist and was involved much earlier in noir films. In 1929, Zinnemann collaborated with other (future) Hollywood filmmakers (and Jewish European émigrés) Robert Siodmak, Edgar Ulmer, and Billy Wilder in Germany on *Menschen am Sonntag* (1930, *People on Sunday*). Zinnemann had previously worked with Surtees when they were fellow camera operators at European Film Alliance (EFA) in Berlin. He also worked with documentary filmmaker Robert Flaherty, which inspired his naturalistic, visual aesthetic technique and social-realist directorial style. Zinnemann's work with Paul Strand on *Redes* (1936, *The Wave*), shot in Mexico in 1934, earned him an MGM contract. Zinnemann came to Hollywood in December 1934 and worked his way up at MGM. In 1942, he directed low-budget MGM B mysteries *Kid Glove Killer* (1942) and *Eyes in the Night* (1942), before directing *The Seventh Cross* (1944), with Spencer Tracy as an escaped fugitive aided by the anti-Nazi Resistance. Zinnemann also contributed uncredited directing to *The Clock* (1945).

As a European émigré, Zinnemann's formal aesthetic and social commentary was informed by his wartime experiences and personal trauma, and was influenced by documentary and neorealist technique. Zinnemann had explored similar issues in his Academy Award–winning message film *The Search* (1948), about displaced postwar refugees, which was shot on location among the ruins in Germany (with studio filming in Switzerland). Starring Montgomery Clift and Czechoslovak child actor Ivan Jandl, *The Search* was acclaimed for its verisimilitude, nonfiction aesthetic style, and topical critique. In *The Search*, Zinnemann movingly portrayed the plight of families torn apart by war amid the rubble in postwar Europe. After the war, Zinnemann learned his own family had been killed in Nazi concentration camps, like Billy Wilder's and so many others.

After exploring the destruction and trauma of war in *The Search*, Zinnemann's semidocumentary technique, cinematic naturalism, and social-realist concerns in film noir crystallized in *Act of Violence*. Produced in 1948 and released in 1949, *Act of Violence* presents an extraordinary cultural critique. Zinnemann recalled that upon completing *The Search* in Europe and returning to the United States to film *Act of Violence*, "I felt that I already knew what I was doing, rather than going by instinct." He admitted that after *Act of Violence* (and *The Men*), "I felt that I had arrived."[68] Yet it was remarkable that the film noir *Act of Violence* was even made. It encountered many challenges, was shelved more than once, and was Zinnemann's final picture for MGM.

Act of Violence explored postwar tensions such as the Hollywood Blacklist; informing and "naming names;" and issues of masculinity, honor, loyalty, and betrayal. Filmed on location in Los Angeles, Big Bear Lake, and San Bernardino Forest, *Act of Violence* shifted the noir setting from shadowy urban jungle to a sunny, brightly lit rural terrain. Zinnemann drew outstanding performances from Van Heflin and Robert Ryan portraying volatile self-destructive noir antiheroes. Troubled veteran Frank Enley (Heflin) is celebrated as a war hero, but his dark past is revealed as he is pursued by vengeful former war buddy, Joe (Ryan). Women in *Act of Violence* are nurturers and helpmates—wives, girlfriends, even compassionate washed-up streetwise working girls—redeemers of tormented combat veterans. As Frank flees from Joe and hides in the shadows of his dark home, he tells his young wife, Edith (Janet Leigh), "A lot of things happened in the war that you wouldn't understand. Why should you? I don't understand them myself." Throughout the course of the film, as Frank unravels and tries to hide his past misdeeds to save his own skin, Zinnemann creates a disturbing atmosphere in *Act of Violence*.

Scripted by Robert Richards and based on a story by Collier Young, *Act of Violence* was originally called *The Traitor* and set up at Warner Bros. The project bore obvious similarities to *Crossfire* in dealing with murderous crimes committed by returning combat veterans. Warner Bros. director Don Siegel and producer Jerry Wald praised *Act of Violence* as a film noir project akin to *Crossfire*, and at one point Raoul Walsh was assigned to direct. Robert Mitchum, Humphrey Bogart, and Dana Andrews were all considered for the lead role. Like earlier postwar films noir, it faced scrutiny from industry censors, and in October 1947—as Washington's HUAC hearings ramped up—Warner executives' interest in the project began to cool. Somewhat surprisingly, the studio suddenly wanted to eliminate night exterior scenes in the film. Doing so would, of course, have undercut the dark, atmospheric noir style in *Act of Violence*. Sounding like Joseph Breen attacking noir pictures, Eric Johnston, the chief at the Hollywood film industry trade association, the Motion Picture Association of America (MPAA), insisted at the time: "We'll have no more films that show the seamy side of American life."[69] These developments indicate the various types of ongoing industry and Cold War cultural pressures facing films noir, social-realist message pictures, and shadowy noir visual style during this postwar period. In December 1947, Warner sold *Act of Violence* to independent producer Mark Hellinger (*Naked City*), who suddenly died a few weeks later, leaving the project dormant.

In 1948, socially minded executive Dore Schary, who had backed *Crossfire* at RKO before moving to MGM, acquired *Act of Violence* and supervised production. He assigned the picture to Zinnemann, who saw an opportunity as he had in *The Search* to utilize the "raw material of history" to "make a dramatic document."[70] *Act of Violence*, like *The Search*, was a product of its time after the war years—another ideal project for Zinnemann. Contrary to Warner Bros.' original conception of *The Traitor*, Zinnemann and cinematographer Robert Surtees deliberately decided to emphasize documentary technique, deep focus, natural lighting, high-contrast photography, and realism. Key here were stark

1.16 Robert Ryan against a shadowy noir Manhattan night skyline in *Act of Violence*. MGM, 1949

location shots of Los Angeles at night to emphasize visually the film's topical social themes and ominous milieu. *Act of Violence* captures the urban jungle's oppressive entrapment vis-à-vis the tormented antihero's subjective point of view to reflect his psychological peril.

The film opens in New York City at night. Zinnemann and Surtees immediately establish a shrouded, chiaroscuro style and menacing mood against the dark silhouette of a Manhattan skyline. Bronislav Kaper's riveting, atonal minor-key music score (conducted by André Previn) builds tension as obsessed veteran Joe drags himself across the rain-soaked street and grabs his gun from the shadows of his room. The music blares as the title *Act of Violence* blazes across the screen, but there are no opening credits. Joe boards a bus and rides clear across the country.

The noir setting rapidly shifts from its urban terrain to a quiet California town, where World War II veterans march in a Memorial Day parade and family man and war hero Frank smiles with his wife and baby in the sunshine as he receives an award from the community. All seems blissful in this peaceful rural setting until Joe arrives, bent on vengeance. Zinnemann builds suspense in broad daylight and outdoor wilderness as Frank goes fishing on the lake in the mountains—and Joe pursues him.[71] Joe rows out on a boat across the lake and crouches, hidden behind a boulder, waiting, then aims his gun to shoot Frank

1.17 Robert Ryan shot in bright sunlight outdoors and on location in *Act of Violence*. MGM, 1949

as his boat goes by, but Joe misses the opportunity when Frank turns the motor on and goes to shore blissfully unaware. Once ashore, Frank realizes he is being stalked because Joe appears rowing in the distance behind him. He abruptly leaves, cutting his trip short to return home.

The noir imagery that Zinnemann and Surtees create in *Act of Violence* projects the guilt-ridden antihero's dark prism of physical and psychological entrapment. Frank's entire demeanor changes as he returns home that night. He locks the doors, turns out the lights, stands cloaked in shadows, cowers in the blackened corner, apprehensively draws down the blackout shades, and silences his wife in the dark. He clings to the shadows and avoids the light—as if he fears it will expose him. The kitchen faucet runs as Joe tries to force his way into the house, then waits in his car outside. Frank's home becomes not a domestic sanctuary but rather a trap imprisoning him as he hides in fear, concealing the terrible, guilty lie on which he has built his life. Frank is hiding a dark, disturbing secret: He betrayed his men to the Nazi enemy, which led to their brutal murder. Surtees's brooding, low-key, deep-focus cinematography shows the expressionistic darkness of Frank's house and blackness of the night. Joe lights his cigarette from the shadows inside his unlit automobile across the

1.18 Van Heflin and Janet Leigh shrouded in noir shadow as he hides in the dark trying not to reveal his secret in *Act of Violence*. MGM, 1949

street. Sound is used brilliantly to heighten suspense in the noir thriller—even the sound of Frank's baby's cry becomes a startling shriek of terror.

Tormented, afraid, and unable to forgive himself, Frank flees in the night to a convention in Los Angeles. Zinnemann accentuates darkness and a claustrophobic noir mise-en-scène as Frank's wife Edith (Janet Leigh) tracks him down in LA. Frank pulls her into a dim cramped stairwell so they won't be seen. "Do I have to spell it out for you? Do I have to draw you a picture? I was an informer." The visual piercing of compositional space in the frame and oblique obstructions between camera and subject in the brooding noir cinematography suggest Frank's entrapment as he reveals his horrible betrayal to his wife. Splintering diagonal patterns of crisscrossing bars and ominous shadows cover him.[72]

In filming *Act of Violence*, Zinnemann stressed the importance of fusing documentary realist technique with a darker, moody noir style, as did Surtees, who said that "reflected lighting, no makeup, natural locations and use of a 28mm lens are some of the new production trends explored in the making of this picture" to achieve deep-focus images with no diffusion.[73] Zinnemann recalled that his "most vivid memory" of making *Act of Violence* was "the many sleepless nights we spent shooting exteriors in the eerie slums of downtown Los Angeles," which were among the film's unforgettable highlights.[74] Zinnemann and Surtees employed noir style to expose the seamy side of Los Angeles, as Frank runs for his life through skid row at night in the howling wind, trying to flee Joe and escape his secret betrayal. The most powerful sequences are the nocturnal sights and disturbing sounds in Los Angeles. In this noir universe, life on the street and in shady nightspots is presented as undesirable and dangerous. Zinnemann effectively conveys a treacherous waking nightmare. The strong gusts wail and blow debris through the air, littering the slick wet asphalt of a harsh urban jungle. Surtees's breathtaking night-for-night location shooting creates gripping suspense with menacing shadows of the city, which come vividly to life and capture the antihero's tormented mentality.

Zinnemann depicts the traumatized veteran as a diminutive figure dwarfed by huge, imposing, soaring structures that are shot from extreme angles to create visual depth and emphasize the deep-focus composition and the blackened mise-en-scène. Frank is pressed up against the sides of buildings and descends to shabby tenements, neon signs, and dive bars. The deteriorating

1.19 Frank (Van Heflin) runs through the dark streets of late-night Los Angeles, at one point moving under the Angel's Flight funicular railway in *Act of Violence*. MGM, 1949

noir environment visually reflects Frank's psychological tumult in the low-lit spaces of Los Angeles with towering edifices in the bleak, disturbing, nocturnal city. He wanders dark alleys, dodgy joints, and cheap hotels, and ends up in the slums on skid row, descending steep stairs and the slopes of Bunker Hill. The Angels Flight funicular railway passes above him and slices diagonally across the frame. Frank runs screaming through a long, claustrophobic Third Street tunnel, where he is haunted by the memories of his past.[75] In crisis, Frank emerges disoriented, then, in a psychotic state, breaks down and tries to commit suicide by standing in front of an oncoming train.[76]

Adding to the unvarnished realism of their performances, actresses Janet Leigh and Mary Astor were deglamorized with harsh deep-focus photography, high-contrast lighting (without softly flattering diffusion), and very little makeup.[77] Zinnemann recalled, "It was a special delight to be working with Mary Astor, playing an aging streetwalker who picks up the exhausted, desperate Van Heflin running for his life through the creepy, crumbling night time streets."[78] Surtees explained that he shot *Act of Violence* in deep focus in natural locations using a 28mm lens to achieve its noir visual style, using no reflected lighting to beautify the features of Leigh and Astor, who looked good on camera nonetheless.[79] Astor's dress was not from the MGM wardrobe but rather off the rack at a cheap department store.[80]

1.20 In brooding noir shadows, Frank hears voices and runs screaming through the long, dark, claustrophobic Third Street tunnel in *Act of Violence*. MGM, 1949

MGM publicity ads for *Act of Violence* promoted Zinnemann's topical social message noir like a gothic suspense thriller, clamoring: "The Killer with the Limp Arrives Today!! Night and day he stalks his prey. Slowly, surely his shadow of doom darkens the life of his terrified victim." Tapping into the Cold War paranoia of its postwar cultural climate, Heflin was described as: "The Hunted! What suddenly made him a fugitive?" Ryan was "Menacing . . . The Hunter! He came from nowhere to avenge" in "the manhunt no woman could stop!" Ads for *Act of Violence* targeted war veterans and their wives in the suburbs, as depicted in the film, with mysterious taglines: "One morning Frank kissed me goodbye . . . and everything was as it always had been. That evening, he came home with horror in his eyes . . . and told me things that changed my life forever." Previews also featured Heflin standing on the tracks before a blaring oncoming train. The film's trailer announced: "'ACT OF VIOLENCE' VAN HEFLIN *CLASHES WITH* ROBERT RYAN" as Heflin punches Ryan, "and *Three Women Cross Their Evil Path!*"[81]

Reviews praised *Act of Violence* for Zinnemann's direction and the actors' performances. *Variety* applauded the "realism," "suspense," and "dramatic intensity" in Zinnemann's noir production as a "masterpiece," calling it "stark" "strong meat" and an "excellent" "grim melodrama." Critic William Brogdon observed that the film noir exuded "tight excitement" filled with "topflight," "punchy performances" by Heflin and Ryan that "give substance to the menacing terror." He concluded, "It's grim business, unrelieved by lightness, and the players belt over their assignments under Zinnemann's knowing direction," and praised Astor as a "brassy, blowzy femme . . . woman of the streets who gives Heflin shelter during his wild flight from fate."[82] Bosley Crowther of the *New York Times* insisted that Zinnemann's "smart direction" was the "best thing" about the film noir.[83] Despite the fact that Zinnemann's taut, beautifully shot, social-realist film noir was critically praised, *Act of Violence*, which cost $1,290,000, earned only $1,129,000 ($703,000 in North America and $426,000 overseas) and ultimately lost $637,000.[84]

It was nowhere near the huge $5 to $7 million box office successes of many films noir at the height of the booming trend in 1944–1946, just a few years earlier. Indeed, industry trade analysts and studio executives even complained of the declining popularity of noir films and social-realist pictures at the end of the decade, a trend that would persist into the 1950s. However, other films such as *The Naked City, The Undercover Man*, and *Dark Passage* were more successful than *Act of Violence*. These films relied more heavily on brighter, high-key, sunlit location shooting and visually lighter, semidocumentary technique, which offset shadowy iconic noir visual style.

Act of Violence is important and significant as an underrecognized postwar noir film depicting a chilling Cold War climate and mounting industry pressures—as Hollywood faced declining viewership from 1947 onward after peaking in 1946. Surtees's masterful cinematography in *Act of Violence* powerfully illustrates the use of documentary technique, deep focus, and natural lighting to articulate cultural tensions in films noir toward the end of the decade.

The postwar noir trend would continue to move away from chiaroscuro imagery and the brooding expressionistic shadows of the earlier war years and increasingly employ bright sunlit documentary-style photography. The evolution of film technology and pervasive outdoor location shooting would affect the noir visual style as the actual nitrate film stock shifted to lighter acetate safety film. The initial 1940s dark cinema trend entered its closing stages as the classic cycle started to ebb, and its box office success eventually receded over the course of the next decade. Films noir were reimagined in the 1950s in relation to brighter, low-contrast televisual conventions as the noir visual aesthetic faded to gray and color imagery—and it began to come apart and adapt to new technologies.

CHAPTER 2

FADE TO GRAY AND COLOR NOIR

Black-and-white film noir was changing by the 1950s, adopting a new look and style in response to postwar industrial and cultural challenges and shifting gender roles and themes, and adapting to changing filmmaking conditions and new technologies. As the technological, industrial, and material production conditions contributing to the development of film noir transformed its filmmaking and transnational reception context, the distinctive style of film noir was eventually reconceived, reworked, and adapted in new monochrome, color, and widescreen formats. Film noir—and the Hollywood studio system that produced these dark crime films—transformed throughout the 1940s and rapidly declined in popularity over the 1950s, yet the resilient noir impulse spurred an ongoing cinematic legacy. As primary archival evidence, studio records, and contemporaneous industry trade discourse suggest, film noir emerged and proliferated in the 1940s and evolved in the 1950s as the stylish cycle of films responded to new technologies.

Postwar developments altered the iconic look and visual style of film noir. As we have seen, technological innovations and new shooting techniques transformed noir imagery and mise-en-scène during this period. Typical of the grayer, lighter semidocumentary visual style so prevalent in postwar films noir from the late 1940s into the 1950s, *The Naked City* (1948), produced by Mark Hellinger and directed by Jules Dassin, displayed what Dana Polan called "the flip side of film noir." Acclaimed for its realistic, documentary-style images shot on location in New York City, *The Naked City* was promoted by Universal not as a story about lust, murder, or red-meat criminals. *The Naked City* was publicized instead—in a comparatively tame manner—as a "truthful" and "exciting" story that depicts a safe, reassuring postwar world. In *The Naked City*, the cops are the heroes (telling the story from their "law-abiding" point of view), and the authorities ultimately restore order by apprehending criminals—a pleasing resolution for censors.[1]

Film noir, in its quintessential, inky, jet-black visual style, started splintering, dispersing, and coming apart as early as 1950 and 1951 because of many factors. Not only was its chiaroscuro aesthetic style fading to gray, but even the hard-boiled innuendo and witty repartee—so distinctive in 1940s films noir like *Double Indemnity* (1944)—began to wane as viewers and critics grew weary of the cycle. The grayer, visually lighter films in the 1950s were ultimately very different than classic shadowy 1940s noir and were not even really noir anymore in aesthetic style, look, or temperament. For instance, in 1950, an incongruous array of films—*Sunset Boulevard, The Asphalt Jungle, Whirlpool, In a Lonely Place, Gun Crazy, Panic in the Streets, Where the Sidewalk Ends*—are typically considered noir.[2]

Filmmaker and critic Paul Schrader noted in his influential essay "Notes on Film Noir" that noir declined after 1953, with the exception of some late stragglers in the cycle. "By the mid-fifties *film noir* had ground to a halt. There were a few notable stragglers, *Kiss Me Deadly* [1955], the Lewis/Alton *The Big Combo* [1955], and film noir's epitaph, *Touch of Evil* [1958], but for the most part a new style of crime film had become popular." Schrader observed: "As the rise of McCarthy and Eisenhower demonstrated, Americans were eager to see a more bourgeois view of themselves. Crime had to move to the suburbs. The criminal put on a gray flannel suit and the footsore cop was replaced by the 'mobile unit' careening down the expressway. Any attempt at social criticism had to be cloaked in ludicrous affirmations of the American way of life." He added, "Technically, television, with its demand for full lighting and close-ups, gradually undercut the German 'Expressionist' influence, and color cinematography was, of course, the final blow to the '*noir*' look. New directors like [Don] Siegel, [Richard] Fleischer, [Phil] Karlson and [Samuel] Fuller and TV shows like *Dragnet, M-Squad, Lineup* and *Highway Patrol* stepped in to create the new crime drama."[3] All these developments undermined the noir aesthetic.

The noir cinematic aesthetic became an evolving postwar visual style as it responded to new emergent technology and to a shifting production and reception context in a changing industry. Classic film noir had been recognized for its stark expressionistic visual style shot in high-contrast deep focus on 35mm black-and-white nitrate film. Yet television would surge in popularity during the 1950s, influencing the look, visual style, and technology of noir feature films. As the noir visual style evolved, the iconic "black" look and feel of postwar films began to ebb as acetate safety film eventually began to replace the motion picture industry standard nitrate film stock by the end of the 1940s, and studios converted in 1950. As the *New York Times* reported, "the motion picture industry continued to use nitrate film until 1950, when the nonflammable cellulose triacetate base was universally adopted."[4] Not only would the film stock shift from the stark black chiaroscuro of nitrate to the grayer acetate safety stock after 1950, but the vibrant hues of color film (discussed later in this chapter in the Color Noir Visual Style and The Emergence of Color Noir sections) would also be added to the noir repertoire. The industry shift from nitrate to acetate film stock was just one of many changes transforming film noir visual style in the postwar era.

As seen even during the late 1940s, extensive location filming infused a paler nonfiction style and subjective point of view in films noir. Shooting on location and semidocumentary techniques, which became prevalent by the late 1940s, continued with a vengeance during the 1950s and certainly lightened noir style. For example, Twentieth Century-Fox cinematographer Norbert Brodine shot films noir entirely on location to emulate a lighter semidocumentary style. He admitted that he resisted the temptation to go "overboard" in striving for realism or moody shadows in his photography and used restraint to avoid a "too dark" style or "extreme" style. "Those of us in the industry, along with theatregoers in the large key cities, recognize and appreciate the artistry of low-key, cross-lighting, and the more extreme mood effects," Brodine insisted. "However, in making pictures, we must think of the people in the smaller towns who make up the majority of our audiences. The butcher, the baker and the candle-stick-maker who pay their 35 cents to go to the movies on Saturday night, are anxious to watch certain stars and be able to *see* their faces." He added, "I personally believe in avoiding effects that are too dark and extreme, and might prevent the audience from seeing the face of their favorites."[5] *American Cinematographer* recognized the noir trend had "become standard fare on the menu of the American moviegoer"—praising its experimental lighting, subjective camera, montage, excellent screen drama, and perfection of camera techniques—but noted that public taste began to shift away from the cycle.[6]

This cinematic trend in the age of television undermined a darker film noir aesthetic style. A brighter, high-key, low-contrast televisual-style aesthetic would become increasingly prevalent in films noir during the 1950s and would employ techniques that would preclude chiaroscuro noir visual style. For example, in January 1952, *American Cinematographer* recognized "a revolution imminent in the production methods of motion picture making in Hollywood" as "major film producers ... take a lesson" from Desilu Productions "turning out 22 minutes of TV program film in 60 minutes of actual shooting time" for the "best-filmed," top-rated *I Love Lucy* television show. With veteran cinematographer Karl Freund—who shot *Metropolis, Dracula, Frankenstein, Key Largo*, and *Dr. Jekyll and Mr. Hyde*—"directing the photography ... the photographic methods employed by Freund and his camera crews are creating widespread interest among producers of motion pictures—both major and television. Production executives from nearly every Hollywood studio have 'scouted' the show during filming and have lauded Freund for his achievements." To create a bright, high-key, low-contrast visual aesthetic that would become increasingly prevalent during the 1950s, "[a]ll lighting is from overhead, with units so mounted they can be changed with a minimum of time and effort... photographed with three Mitchell 35mm BNC cameras [Blimped Newsreel Cameras], all shooting simultaneously." Such high-key, low-contrast, three-camera televisual shooting techniques mitigated against shadowy chiaroscuro noir visual style.[7]

As early as 1955, French critics Raymonde Borde and Étienne Chaumeton noted in their pioneering study *Panorama du Film Noir Americain (1941–1953)*, the first book on film noir, that a different style of film noir emerged in the late 1940s and early 1950s, straying from its earlier shady, defiant mid-1940s tendency to challenge the strictures of screen censorship with a perspective of criminality presented from the criminal's point of view. They contrasted the iconic subjective perspective in film noir—distinguished by a "different angle of vision" concerning corruption "from within, from the criminals'" point of view centering on a "whole host of angelic killers, neurotic gangsters, megalomaniac gang bosses," and "disturbing or depraved stooges"—with later, more documentary-oriented crime films such as the police procedural, which "considers the murder from without, from the official police viewpoint."[8]

As noir morphed into Cold War crime films and police procedurals, films unveiled a crime-fighting network of government agencies and laboratories to crack down on wrongdoers. In semidocumentary style, they showed the office buildings and federal headquarters in Washington or vast metropolises like New York City, as in *The Naked City, The Enforcer* (1951), *The Thief* (1952), or Los Angeles, as in the TV series *Dragnet* (1951–1959), adapted as a film in 1954. The "cop on the beat" is shown to be part of a vast crime-fighting, scientific organization. The 1951 shift from nitrate to acetate safety film also changed the noir aesthetic.

Sunset Boulevard and the Decline of the Noir Aesthetic

As film noir's cinematic imagery and aesthetic visual style changed, the industry sentiment toward films noir and their box office prospects also shifted. The *New York Times* noted an "Uneasy Hollywood" in 1950, and Warner Bros. producer Jerry Wald reported that no top-grossing 1949 films included gangsters or crime or had "violence as its theme or basic subject," suggesting the waning popularity of noir.[9] Nevertheless, just across town, Billy Wilder and John Seitz began filming *Sunset Boulevard* at Paramount in the summer of 1949.

Sunset Boulevard (1950), one of the last major features shot on nitrate, was a key transitional film. As film noir visual style transformed and grew lighter after 1950, its iconic shadowy imagery ebbed—as did the classic noir cycle by the end of the 1950s—as Hollywood responded to emergent technologies. In the mid- to late 1950s, the industry's adoption of new technologies led to widescreen noir films, which included *The Big Combo, Kiss Me Deadly, Sweet Smell of Success* (1957), *A Face in the Crowd* (1957), *Touch of Evil*, and *Odds Against Tomorrow* (1959). As the industry moved from standard-screen black-and-white films, noir creative talent brought darker, realistic dramatic tendencies to color, widescreen, and stereophonic sound films. In response to these myriad technological changes, the multifaceted evolution of noir and how its distinctive visual imagery is adapted to new innovations reinforces the fact that it is a period style (rather than a single genre) that splintered and influenced many different film genres, from noir musicals to noir sci-fi and noir westerns in the postwar period. Film noir itself grew intrinsically self-conscious and more aware of the noir cycle. The bright high-key lighting of noir during this period was seen on sunlit sets: director Robert Aldrich was even photographed as he filmed *Kiss Me Deadly* on location in broad daylight holding and reading Borde and Chaumeton's *Panorama du Film Noir Americain* book.

Wilder's *Sunset Boulevard*, a swan song to nitrate stock, featured iconic examples of noir visual style and an unlikely romantic pairing of washed-up misfits: delusional, eccentric, past-her-prime, silent screen star Norma Desmond (Gloria Swanson) and her younger kept man Joe Gillis (William Holden), a frayed, unemployed B-movie screenwriter hiding from a collection agency. *Sunset Boulevard* is an example of noir as a style rather than a genre: there are not many films about Hollywood writers moving in with old silent movie stars. *Sunset Boulevard* includes a noir love triangle with the classic noir gender paradigm, contrasting "good girl" Betty, a fresh-faced young script reader (Nancy Olson), versus aging star Desmond, who embodies unstable noir psychosis.

While *Double Indemnity* conveys its story via a murder confession given by a dying man, Wilder tops himself in *Sunset Boulevard* with a voice-over narrated by a dead man floating face down in a pool! Wilder shot the sequence with a mirror to show the corpse's face through the water from below. The studio crew built a swimming pool on the site and placed a mirror at the bottom of the pool to film the striking reflection of the extraordinary floating body's visage downward in the water during the opening scene. The crew then filled the pool in after shooting was completed. Wilder's noir love triangle is doomed from the start: his narrator is already murdered. Joe ends up shot, but *Sunset Boulevard* is not really about crime in the usual sense of a detective mystery story; like *Double Indemnity*, everything is revealed up front. (The film originally opened in the morgue, with Joe's corpse talking to cadavers, but Wilder reshot the opening after preview audiences laughed.)

In the spring of 1949, when Wilder submitted the script for *Sunset Boulevard* to the industry's Production Code censors for approval, chief censor Joseph Breen exclaimed, "[W]e are most anxious." He objected to the sex affair and to star Desmond being married three times, insisting that "mandatory intimate parts of the body—specifically breasts of women—be fully covered at all times." Breen also complained: "There is no indication of a voice for morality by which the sex affair would be condemned nor does there appear to be" any punitive "compensating moral values for the sin," adding, "[w]e are quite aware that the story is told in flashback and the leading man is shown to be dead when the story opens."[10] Narrated by a dead antihero murdered by his aging, psychotic divorced lover, *Sunset Boulevard* certainly did push the envelope of Code censorship.

Wilder's film also faced resistance to its scathing cinematic critique of the motion picture industry. Taking shots at Hollywood, *Sunset Boulevard* exemplifies Wilder's assertion that "psychopathy sells" in pictures—a self-reflexive commentary on film noir, exploring the difference between his noir films *Double Indemnity*, *The Lost Weekend* (1945; a message picture), and *Sunset Boulevard*.

2.1 "I am big. It's the pictures that got small." Washed-up silent star Norma Desmond (Gloria Swanson) in noir shadow and backlit by a projector in Billy Wilder's *Sunset Boulevard*, one of the last major films shot on nitrate. Paramount, 1950

Script girl Betty says: "I just think that pictures should say a little something . . . I think you should throw out all that psychological stuff—exploring a killer's sick mind." Joe replies, "Psychopaths sell like hotcakes." Betty insists people's "threadbare lives, their struggles . . . worry about getting enough money to resole their shoes . . . can be as exciting as any chase, any gunplay." In *Sunset Boulevard*, Joe's viewpoint obviously prevails.

Wilder and cinematographer John Seitz capture a dying era of old Hollywood in *Sunset Boulevard*, casting famous silent stars such as Swanson; filmmakers Erich von Stroheim (as Norma's butler and ex-husband Max), Buster Keaton, and Cecil B. DeMille; and gossip columnist Hedda Hopper. Shot in shadowy noir style, the film provides scathing critique and insider commentary on the motion picture industry with an ugly backstage glimpse of Tinseltown. Wilder and Seitz invoke gothic conventions: Norma's rundown mansion resembles a haunted house of surreal insanity that becomes a prison entrapping Joe. He is entombed in a shrine to a flamboyant long-faded star. Images of Swanson as a young ingénue are everywhere. She sinks her claws into Joe as they watch Swanson's real-life silent films (*Queen Kelly*, directed by Stroheim) backlit by the projector in the dark. Norma pantomimes Charlie Chaplin's Tramp. Norma's obsessive web closes in, controlling and manipulating Joe's every move.

Sunset Boulevard features iconic noir elements: a doomed antihero, entrapment, claustrophobia, a femme fatale, and a naïve redeemer. Wilder reveals a corrupt Hollywood with crooked agents, washed-up stars, and writers trying to get a gig—where life is a daunting struggle. Joe never lands a job on a picture; he instead becomes Norma's gigolo, selling sex and services for some hard cash while moonlighting with another woman, writing for free. *Sunset Boulevard* opens with Franz Waxman's exhilarating score, police cars blaring across asphalt at dawn with screaming sirens, and newsreel cameras. Joe narrates,

> Yes, this is Sunset Boulevard . . . the Homicide Squad—complete with detectives and newspaper men. A murder has been reported from one of those great big houses . . . You'll read all about it in the late editions . . . You'll get it over your radio, and see it on television because an old-time star is involved, one of the biggest. But before you hear it all distorted and blown out of proportion, before those Hollywood columnists get their hands on it, maybe you'd like to hear the facts, the whole truth . . . If so, you've come to the right party.

Wilder and Seitz create a creepy atmosphere of eccentric ruin from a lost age, indulgent yet hypnotically alluring and seductive. The grandiose excess of Norma's ostentatious, empty mansion personifies her overwhelming silent-era presence deglamorized and dissected as tragic and oppressive, a suffocating, bizarre relic of faded grotesque splendor. Joe admits, "The whole place seemed to have been stricken with a kind of creeping paralysis, out of beat with the rest of the world, crumbling apart in slow motion . . . I knew there was something wrong . . . It sure was a cozy set-up." As in *Double Indemnity*, Wilder and Seitz sprinkled dust on the sets to enhance a musty shrouded look. They employ an ornate baroque visual style of worn opulence and decadent decay with a cluttered, claustrophobic mise-en-scène. *Sunset Boulevard* reveals a clash of styles and eras: Norma's melodramatic intensity, hyperbolic exaggerated gestures, makeup, and silent-era performance style versus Joe's caustic barbed wit and the mocking deadpan humor of a cynical, hard-boiled sound-era screenwriter. "You're Norma Desmond. You used to be in silent pictures. You used to be big." She famously replies, "I am big. It's the pictures that got small." In silent star Norma's critique of sound pictures, Wilder's dialogue seems to also metaphorically suggest Hollywood's rival: small-screen television siphoning viewers from the big screen. Wilder visually articulates Joe being drawn into Norma's web with snarled dead branches as he climbs dark stairs to his room above the garage. Joe misleadingly thinks he has a "cozy setup" and does not recognize the dangerous mess he's getting into.

When Joe ultimately tries to leave, Norma attempts suicide; then in manic delusion she breathes, "No one ever leaves a star. That's what makes one a star," and shoots him dead. Wilder ends his noir where it began, with Joe's sardonic narration: "They got a couple of pruning hooks from the garden and fished me out . . . ever so gently. Funny, how gentle people get with you once you're dead. They beached me, like a harpooned baby whale, and started to check the damage . . . By this time the whole joint was jumping—cops, reporters, neighbors, passersby." Wilder skillfully handles Production Code censorship: Norma is arrested after gunning down Joe, but her famous departure becomes a memorable moment. As TV crews, cameras, and newsreels roll, von Stroheim directs the finale. "Life, which can be strangely merciful, had taken pity" on Norma, deluded by fame as the "dream she had clung to so desperately had enfolded her." Swanson delivers a mesmerizing performance. Self-absorbed, she exclaims to imaginary fans, "I'll never desert you again . . . this is my life! . . . I'm ready for my close-up."[11]

Sunset Boulevard was shot from April through July 1949, with additional filming in January 1950. Norma's mansion had been owned by oil tycoon J. Paul Getty; its interiors were filmed on soundstages. Art director Hans Dreier (who also worked with Wilder and Seitz on *Double Indemnity* and *The Lost Weekend*) and John Meehan designed Paramount soundstage sets replicating the interiors of Norma's Gothic mansion and Schwab's drugstore. Seitz, a veteran cinematographer from the silent era, used a small "dance dolly" platform on wheels attached to the front of the camera to film a moving 360-degree turn around the room to shoot the doomed antihero and aging femme fatale dancing a tango.[12] The powerful shimmering backlight makes faded star Norma Desmond come alive in the deep chiaroscuro shadows with stark high contrast captured in the beam of a movie projector as "strong sidelight edges her hair in a white blaze."[13] For *Sunset Boulevard*, the quest for realism prompted night-for-night shooting and exterior filming at actual locations—a deserted twenty-five-room mansion, the Bel-Air golf course, the Alto-Nido apartment buildings, and Paramount's back lot filmed at night for the first time. For the final murder shooting scene, a compressed-air gun fired by an electric solenoid valve with half-inch, steel, ball-bearing bullets and striking force of 180 pounds pressure per square inch was used to break a heavy plate glass door—and miss the actor.[14]

American Cinematographer applauded *Sunset Boulevard* as "masterful" and "cinematic." It praised Seitz's brilliant realistic photography "suffused with an aura of otherworldliness," using "subjective" camerawork to film the lavish, decadent ghostly mansion shot in deep focus with "no varnishing of the truth for manufactured glamour, no mushy diffusion" to soften the image. The trade journal recognized how the film emphasized its [noir] visual style and "photographic mood" for "dramatic effect," with intense sequences in "low-key," "restrained" lighting and wide-angle shots using extreme depth of field "forcefully" to focus sharply on deep shadows and allow shooting with limited natural light. Herb Lightman insisted Seitz was at the "top of his profession," an "expert experimentalist" willing to "stick his neck out" for an "unusual," "original" "exciting" shot (Wilder described him as "gutsy") in filming *Sunset Boulevard*, *Double Indemnity*, and *The Lost Weekend*, which "prove the force of his photography" with "no clichés in his style—as modern as tomorrow, rugged, forceful" and "alive." Lightman noted that, to achieve the film's visual style, innovative photographic techniques, and extreme depth of field, it was necessary to use a "greatly intensified light level and to latensify the film in order to stop down the lens aperture sufficiently."

As Hollis Moyse reported in *American Cinematographer* in December 1949, the "latensification" process involves treating shot film footage with extra light or chemicals (in addition to the normal film developing process) to increase the "emulsion speed" of the film negative, thereby making it "faster" and more "light sensitive" to enable greater visual details and depth of field for deep focus in the shadows and to allow shooting with limited natural light. "The latensification process," Lightman explained, "added about two stops to the speed of the film—allowing a scene lighted for f3.5 to be shot at f7. This method was used for shooting about 15 percent of the total footage of the picture," allowing Seitz to use a "practical lamp in the composition" on the set as the "key light illumination" as "ultimate" "source lighting" with a "minimum of fill-light being used to soften the shadows" in scenes. Latensification also made it possible to film realistic night exteriors and street scenes shot at night instead of in daylight with red lens, day-for-night filters, thus enabling night-for-night shooting.[15] This technique contributed to Seitz's cinematography on *Sunset Boulevard* being lighter than *Double Indemnity*.

Sunset Boulevard's final cost was $1,572,000. It was released in August 1950 and earned $2,350,000 in the United States by the end of the year, a critical and popular hit.[16] Sunset Boulevard was critically acclaimed as one of Hollywood's finest films. Nominated for eleven Academy Awards, including best picture, director, cinematography, performances, and editing, it won Academy Awards for writing for Wilder and Charles Brackett (who produced) and for art direction and music. It also won Golden Globes for best picture, Wilder's direction, and Swanson's performance.

While the film industry had earlier praised *Double Indemnity*'s success, a film that had spurred the noir trend, just six years later, in a sign of the declining popularity of the noir cycle, studio executives criticized Wilder and *Sunset Boulevard* for its unvarnished portrayal of Hollywood. It was a metaphoric wake-up call signaling the end of a creative, economic, and political era in a changing Hollywood. At an industry premiere of *Sunset Boulevard* for studio executives, MGM's Louis B. Mayer castigated the film's critique of Hollywood and called émigré director Billy Wilder a "foreigner" who was disparaging the industry, thus revealing the period's Cold War xenophobia. Mayer was heard to say: "Billy Wilder should be run out of town"—to which Wilder responded by telling the head of MGM studio where to go.[17] Hollywood executives' hostile response to *Sunset Boulevard* indicated the growing resistance to provocative, hard-hitting noir films by 1950. Even Twentieth Century-Fox executive Darryl Zanuck advised studio producers to avoid making censorable "downbeat," violent, "sordid," films noir featuring "psychopathic" brutality, unsympathetic "underworld" or "low" criminality, deeming these dark pictures as risky to produce in terms of box office appeal and insisting that the public was no longer interested in these kinds of films. Zanuck panned *Sunset Boulevard* as a "masterpiece until it was released throughout the country and failed to do business. It is not so big a masterpiece today . . . Pictures in this category are certainly a very high risk."[18]

Ace in the Hole

Sunset Boulevard's success enabled Wilder to produce, write, and direct a visually lighter if thematically even darker film: *Ace in the Hole* (1951). Indicative of the fading noir style as Hollywood shifted to acetate, it was shot by Charles Lang and filmed outdoors in bright, remote, New Mexico desert locations rather than a dark shadowy urban setting on a Hollywood back lot. Wilder and Lang used an array of huge solar reflectors bouncing scorching sunlight onto the set.

Ace in the Hole was Wilder's last and most cynical noir (it was based on the true story of the tragic death of Floyd Collins), in which ruthless reporter

Charles (Chuck) Tatum (Kirk Douglas) exploits a mining cave accident and has a toxic affair with the cave-in victim's unfaithful wife Lorraine (Jan Sterling) while her war veteran husband Leo slowly dies. Chuck delays Leo's rescue a week to milk his sensational tabloid story while thousands cash in on the tragedy with a media circus that makes the hoopla in *Sunset Boulevard* look tame. *Ace in the Hole* amplified Wilder's scathing cultural critique of media sensationalism.[19] Its sunlit noir look offset a bleak worldview.

In *Ace in the Hole*, everyone is corrupt: Leo's "friend" Chuck, his wife, the crooked sheriff, the contractor hired to rescue him (and paid off to delay), the news media who should be helping Leo but instead exploit him, and the public feeding on the carnival frenzy. No one is innocent; even Leo was stealing from Native American burial sites. When Chuck realizes Leo will die, he tries to save him, but it's too little, too late.[20] In the end, Chuck literally "takes the fall" and dies in an incredible shot, crashing face down toward the camera on the floor, shifting from ironic extreme power angle to extreme close-up of his dead face.

Most of the film was bathed in the scorching desert sunlight of a new acetate film era. Despite its high-key visual style, *Ace in the Hole* was certainly caustic and unvarnished thematically. It encountered a hostile critical reception from the press as well as the film-going public and was not successful at

2.2 Kirk Douglas in the final shot of Billy Wilder's *Ace in the Hole*, which was more shadowy than most of the film. *Ace in the Hole* was shot on location, with an array of huge solar reflectors bouncing scorching sunlight onto the set in the New Mexico desert. Paramount, 1951

the box office.²¹ Paramount bungled the film's release and retitled it *The Big Carnival* after it opened poorly as *Ace in the Hole*. It was a huge disappointment for Wilder and was his last noir. But while the scathing response and box office failure of *Ace in the Hole* were clearly contributing factors, particularly in a chilly Cold War era increasingly resistant to film noir and social message pictures, Wilder insisted there were no specific reasons why he never made another noir. He had a shrewd commercial sensibility, however, and, like the industry itself, turned to lighter fare. Wilder was a remarkable noir stylist, and an inspired trendsetter. His cynical vision, biting wit, and perceptive human insight, so influential to noir, was a tremendous loss to the noir cycle itself.²²

Joseph Lewis's 1950s Noirs: From *Gun Crazy* to *The Big Combo*

Like Wilder's films noir, director Joseph H. Lewis's noir films provide a microcosm of the changing aesthetic visual style and vision of postwar American culture in Hollywood's classic noir crime cycle. Lewis's films reveal changes in noir stylistics, the film industry, and evolving gender roles, evincing noir's rapid transition from its shadowy emergence in World War II to its postwar emphasis on psychotic antiheroes, Cold War gangsters, and tormented cops. Lewis elevated low-budget noir filmmaking and worked at many different studios as independent production flourished in postwar Hollywood. After directing wartime combat films, Lewis helmed B noirs such as the gothic crime thriller *My Name Is Julia Ross* (1945), the inexpensive sunlit noir *So Dark the Night* (1946), Cold War G-men and gangsters in *The Undercover Man* (1949), the outlaw cult classic *Gun Crazy* (1950), and the stylish noir gangster yarn *The Big Combo* (1955).²³

Lewis's 1950 noir classic *Gun Crazy*, the quintessential outlaw lovers movie, has gained a huge cult following since its original release. *Gun Crazy* was based on MacKinlay Kantor's 1940 short story in the *Saturday Evening Post* and was adapted by blacklisted writer Dalton Trumbo. It was produced by the King Brothers, Maurice and Frank, with cinematography by Russell Harlan. *Gun Crazy* was shot extensively on location using Kodak Plus-X Cine Panchromatic 5231 nitrate film with inventive mobile equipment techniques accentuating natural available lighting from May to June 1949 for about $450,000. It was much leaner than *The Undercover Man*, which was shot at Columbia for $1 million.

Gun Crazy featured Peggy Cummins and John Dall as a wild, gun-obsessed, sex-crazed outlaw couple who get their kicks committing violent crimes until they meet their brutal demise in a fog-shrouded swamp. The film opens with a rain-drenched noir flashback sequence of a juvenile delinquent (Russ Tamblyn as Dall's younger self), then jumps ahead to a much brighter sunlit-noir look. In March 1949, *Hollywood Reporter* noted alluring blonde siren Veronica

Lake was considered for the film's femme role. Like *The Undercover Man, Gun Crazy* was a postwar noir gangster film—but from the criminals' point of view. It included an androgynous femme fatale who is a cold-hearted, violent gunslinger who seems stronger and more masculine than her male counterpart. Suggesting provocative postwar gender relations, Lewis's noir film title was changed to *Deadly Is the Female* in October 1949, then released through United Artists in January 1950. Reviewed by many publications as *Deadly Is the Female*, the film's title was later changed back to *Gun Crazy* by the time it opened in New York in August 1950.[24]

Filmed in bright sunlight in Montrose, Reseda, and Angeles Crest Highway just outside Los Angeles, *Gun Crazy* was innovative for its adroit technical skill, location shooting, and semidocumentary visual style—as well as its violent sexual innuendo, which played havoc with Hollywood screen censorship. Censor Joseph Breen rejected the grisly violence and sex in the first draft of the screenplay.[25]

Gun Crazy displayed remarkable technical style. Lewis acknowledged that, although the film was not successful during its original release, studios clamored to know how he shot it. "Every studio wanted to run that film, because they wanted to know how we used four and five rear-projection machines at the same time." Lewis and Harlan actually shot the film live on location with portable equipment—most notably in a long take depicting the criminals' robbery and getaway, which was shot from the backseat through the car windshield. Lewis created a makeshift dolly to fit in a car, explaining, "I wanted to make dolly shots and you can't put a dolly in a sedan. I got my crew together and said . . . I *know* it can be done." They filmed a bank holdup by the fugitive couple and their getaway in a car for over two miles with one shot. After extensive preproduction planning with test shots of two extras on 16mm film, the crew filmed on location in Montrose, California. Lewis completed the getaway sequence (originally scheduled for four days) in three hours by renting a stretch limousine with a crew of eight technicians (including himself) behind the front seats. His camera operator sat on a jockey's saddle on a greased plank pushed back and forth to simulate a dolly shot. "Improvised dialogue outside the limo was captured by tiny microphones hidden under the sunshades and outside sounds by two mikes on poles held by technicians strapped to the car's roof."[26] This extraordinary shot revealed how postwar changes in technology dovetailed with the desire to shoot more often on location to produce a change in noir aesthetics.

Lewis gave *Gun Crazy* a western flavor by dressing his sharpshooter fugitives in matching cowboy-cowgirl outfits, thus eroticizing violence and crime as a sexual thrill and provoking censors. Selling rough sex and weapons, lobby cards for *Gun Crazy* proclaimed the film's antiheroine: "She Believes in Two Things . . . *love and violence!*" and depicted her in a strapless slit-skirt gown, in contrast to her more androgynous garb in the film. Ads blazed: "Thrill Crazy! Kill Crazy! Gun Crazy!" Peggy Cummins's blonde, skin-tight, sweater-clad femme fatale was more masculine, in one ad wearing a black beret with a cigarette dangling from her mouth and both hands holding loaded pistols cocked and ready to fire.[27]

Despite its technical innovation, *Gun Crazy* was panned as low-budget, pulp fiction fare. "Even with some adroit camouflaging," Howard Thompson of the *New York Times* wrote in August 1950, the "new picture . . . is pretty cheap stuff. *Gun Crazy* just about covers it." Hard-boiled fiction praised during World War II was dismissed five years later: "this spurious concoction is basically on a par with the most humdrum pulp fiction. This time we have a hard-boiled young carnival markswoman teaming up with a confused veteran for a career in banditry on the West Coast. Guns blazing away like twin forest fires, the pair bolt from one robbery to the next until finally trapped on a mountain top. So much for the plot, as episodic as it is familiar."[28] *Gun Crazy* was viewed more positively in the industry. It earned acclaim, which opened a few doors for Lewis, who scored a gig at prestigious MGM, known for its lavish resources and high production values. Lewis said MGM hired him after being impressed with his documentary style on *Gun Crazy*, but he later complained of the studio's unnecessary opulence.[29]

In 1953, Lewis suffered a heart attack at the age of forty-six, after years working at a breakneck pace. He took more than a year off, eventually leaving MGM to direct his noir classic, *The Big Combo* (1955). In July 1954, in the midst of Hollywood's rising postwar trend toward independent production, the *New York Times* reported Allied Artists would coproduce *The Big Combo* (aka *The Hoodlum*) with star Cornel Wilde and wife and costar Jean Wallace's independent company Theodora Productions and Security Pictures, headed by writer Philip Yordan and producer Sidney Harmon.[30] *The Big Combo* was released by Allied Artists.[31] In the taut shadowy noir dubbed a "gangster melodrama," Wilde plays dogged cop Lieutenant Leonard Diamond, a police detective pursuing sadistic, psychotic, corporate crime boss Mr. Brown (Richard Conte, in a role originally intended for Jack Palance), out to nail him. Diamond reaches out to Brown's mistress Susan Lowell (Wallace), a classical pianist whom he desires and pressures to break free of the abusive kingpin.

The Big Combo surpasses some of Lewis's earlier low-budget ventures. It afforded Lewis, Wilde, and its independent filmmakers greater creative leeway and control. As low-budget film production at many Hollywood studios across the industry retooled for television in the 1950s, low-budget B films were increasingly reformulated into TV series and telefilms. In March 1953, for example, NBC broadcast an adaptation of *My Name Is Julia Ross* as television increasingly targeted women and families at home while noir films targeted men.

Film noir visual style also evolved as regulatory strictures changed and Production Code censorship eased. Breen retired from the Production Code Administration (PCA) in 1954. In a sense, it was the end of an era. As Hollywood's classical studio system unraveled by 1954, even the Academy Awards, Thomas Doherty observed,

> plays more like a grim wake than a joyous celebration. The controlling gaze of television, the extinction of the short film, the risky gamble on CinemaScope, and the retirement of the long-serving chief of the censorious Production Code Administration—all seemed to punctuate the end of a Golden Age, a shimmering epoch when Hollywood held a monopoly over the moving image, when throwaway shorts garnished a beautiful motion picture menu, when the square-shaped motion picture screen was plenty big enough, and when the moral universe projected by the medium was patrolled by a watchful sentinel.[32]

Indeed, filmmakers pushed the cinematic envelope after Breen left the PCA. Independent films like *The Big Combo*, produced as Breen was leaving, allowed more latitude in evading censorship of salacious screen content. Despite Breen's retirement, however, a chilly Cold War climate in the wake of the postwar Red Scare increasingly challenged and disparaged films noir, as seen in the case of *Crossfire* and the industry criticism of *Sunset Boulevard* and hostile reception toward *Ace in the Hole*. In this evolving 1950s production climate, noir filmmakers Wilder, John Huston, and Fred Zinnemann turned to lighter fare such as comedy, musicals, and widescreen color spectacle pictures.

Just a decade after praising the gritty realism, graphic violence, and hard-boiled narratives of earlier mid-1940s film noir, critics called for Hollywood to curb cinematic violence, graphic realist noir style, tough gangsters, and juvenile delinquency in 1950s films. Thus, filmmakers pushing the envelope with censorable content in independent films noir also risked facing a critical backlash. For instance, many reviewers noted the violence and brutality in *The Big Combo* when a mobster tortures the police detective protagonist. *Daily Variety* called it "particularly brutal" and the *Hollywood Reporter* referred to it "as nerve-wracking as anything seen on the recent screen."[33]

The Big Combo was inspired by legendary real-life gangster Al Capone, crime fighter Elliot Ness, and Lewis's earlier film *The Undercover Man*. *The Big Combo* was originally planned to be photographed in Kodak Eastmancolor but instead was beautifully shot in stunning noir black and white in widescreen on acetate film by famed cinematographer John Alton at Kling Studios.[34] One wonders whether Lewis's classic noir would have had any noir style if it had been shot in bright high-key visual style in Eastmancolor; I can only imagine that Alton's gorgeous black-and-white homage to classic 1940s film noir style was more shadowy, high-contrast, and impressive than a color version would have been. Alton's moody photography had previously cast noir shadows on low-budget independent films that fused expressionistic aesthetic with semi-documentary location filming, as in *T-Men* (1947), *Raw Deal* (1948), *He Walked by Night* (1948), *Border Incident* (1949), *The Crooked Way* (1949), *Mystery Street* (1950), and *Witness to Murder* (1954), before shooting *The Big Combo*. Production ran from August 26 to September 18, 1954, with additional scenes filmed in late November 1954.

Tantalizing the imagination, *The Big Combo* included many salacious elements that Breen would have found censorable. Lewis craftily suggested racy innuendo and provocative violence in the film to challenge the Code, then remarked, "There's nothing I can put on screen that's half as interesting as what you have in your head."[35] It included grisly homicide crimes, sadism, and scandalous sexual affairs on-screen, which were sensationalized in its publicity. It was a bleak noir vision. *The Big Combo* opens with David Raksin's moody jazz soundtrack over Alton's stunning chiaroscuro imagery of a noir-style cityscape, with long shadows cloaking the dark dead-end corridors of shady urban jungle nightlife, which permeates the film. Susan (Wallace) flees her gangster lover's thugs in a shrouded boxing arena.[36] Lewis used sound, music, and silence effectively in *The Big Combo*, including a murder sequence with no sound at

2.3 For *The Big Combo*, John Alton shot murky noir figures in stark, shadowy silhouette, backlit against thick dense mists of fog created on soundstages. Theodora/Security/Allied Artists, 1955

all from the point of view of a deaf victim (Brian Donlevy), who did not have his hearing aid. Richard Conte's cold-blooded kingpin and other hoodlums torture and torment Wilde with a radio blasting. Then Conte pours a bottle of hair tonic down the victim's throat. In a powerful, gut-wrenching scene, Conte removes the hearing aid of his henchman (Donlevy), and his thugs (Earl Holliman and Lee Van Cleef) shoot him with a machine-gun, with only horrifying silence on the soundtrack. According to Lewis, "One of the grips came to me with that and I accepted it."[37] Lewis even cleverly got homosexuality by the Code. Gangsters (Holliman and Van Cleef) are portrayed as gay lovers before they too meet their demise.

The Big Combo is one of Lewis's finest films, notable for its bold noir style shot on widescreen acetate—an homage to the classic noirs of World War II. With its striking noir cinematography, Alton filmed on soundstages with a fog machine (swirling around black velvet sets) using very little light to create the stunning silhouette images in its fog-shrouded finale. *The Big Combo* remains one of the most beautifully shot of all Lewis's pictures. Its ending, with stark shadows, deep-focus photography, and murky figures backlit against thick dense mists of fog, is an iconic breathtaking noir image. Lewis gave credit to the film's talented cinematographer for the remarkable noir style and its gorgeous finale: "I must pay tribute to the cameraman, John Alton, a brilliant cameraman. They wanted us to go out to the airport and fog it in for the final scene. He said: 'Look, let's put black velvet around there, and one light up there, and that's it.' He did it all on the stage."[38] There was no fade to gray here.

Publicity still photographs and lobby cards promoting *The Big Combo* featured black-and-white chiaroscuro lighting and shadow that resembled Alton's cinematography in the film's blackened finale and was combined with scarlet red. Taglines read, "The most startling story the screen has ever dared reveal!" and included a macho warning, "Once you get trapped, there's no escape from them. Girls like Susan never learn!" with spicy intimation: "He knew what she was, but he couldn't forget the sight of her . . . the scent of her . . . the touch of her!" alongside images of the gangster grabbing and leaning down to kiss the neck of a beautiful blonde in a strapless dress throwing her head back.[39]

When the film was released in February 1955, *Variety* praised Lewis's "bare-knuckle direction," Alton's "low-key photography," and Raksin's "noisy, jazzy score," which were in keeping with the film's "tough mood . . . cut out to order" for the crime fan who "likes his action rough and raw." In contrast to 1940s noir (with its intricate mystery stories in a flurry of witty, hard-boiled repartee), mid-1950s critics panned the censorable content and narrative complexity of *The Big Combo*. It was the stuff noir was made of and hard-boiled noir viewers could immensely enjoy, but *Variety* cautioned, "[In] this stress on the seamier side of gangland and its denizens," it "gets too realistic. One torture scene in particular will shock the sensibilities and cause near-nausea . . .

The moronic fringe of sadists will enjoy this." Unlike the penchant for crime and violence praised earlier at the end of World War II, critics instead suggested the film should make more effort to sanitize its noir violence and show that justice will prevail.[40]

New York Times reviewer Howard Thompson—who panned Lewis's classic *Gun Crazy*—dismissed *The Big Combo* in March 1955, complaining it "isn't very big or good," and calling it a "shrill, clumsy and rather old-fashioned crime melodrama . . . for all the frenzied attempts at realism." He complained that Lewis's noir picture was "carefully and expansively rigged with brutality and violence (six corpses, for the record). Most of the tactics employed went out with Prohibition." The *New York Times* knocked its punchy, hard-boiled noir repartee and downbeat performances: "Philip Yordan, the scenarist, may know his shady lingo, but it would have been wonderful to have heard someone simply ask for the time and get a straight answer. Both he and director Joseph Lewis share responsibility for the open-throttle monotonous serving of mayhem." Critics were unimpressed with *The Big Combo*, concluding it "remains a sputtering, misguided antique."[41]

Yet *The Big Combo*, Lewis's last noir, endures as a fitting culmination of his innovative cinematic career, marking a film noir master at work. While cult classic *Gun Crazy* is his most famous noir, *The Big Combo* is underrecognized and worthy of much greater critical and scholarly attention. It displays some of Lewis's most impressive noir work, and it deserves far more credit than it receives. Years later, when honoring his career, the *New York Times* referenced *Cry of the Hunted* and praised *Gun Crazy* but neglected to mention *The Big Combo*. Even Lewis preferred *Gun Crazy* to *The Big Combo*. In recent decades, however, the *Los Angeles Times* film critic Kenneth Turan recognized Lewis as a "cult favorite" and his final noir masterwork *The Big Combo* as "a genuine noir classic . . . stunningly shot by John Alton, the absolute master of noir cinematography . . . a thrilling experience on all levels."[42]

The ambivalent critical reception to Lewis's brilliant collaboration with Alton may have indicated that his stylized crime homage to earlier classic noir conventions had become outmoded in an era of color; widescreen; and lighter, high-key visual style. Revealing how prevalent Hollywood's realistic semidocumentary visual style was in crime films by 1949 into the 1950s, critics complained that its frequent overuse was a "dreary" recurrence that was visually uninteresting.[43] Despite Lewis's subsequent critical following for his economical, low-budget B noir techniques, he was rarely promoted in studio publicity, and his films were more critically reviewed upon their initial release. Lewis forged a sophisticated standard of B noir in the artistry of *Gun Crazy* and *The Big Combo* during a growing Cold War climate. His move away from films noir after *The Big Combo* (he shifted to lighter visual-style westerns *Terror of a Texas Town* and TV series such as *The Rifleman*, *The Detectives*, and *The*

Investigators) coincided with the decline of film noir in the 1950s and contributed to an evolving noir aesthetic style in a changing Hollywood system a decade after World War II.

Televisual Style and the Twilight of Noir

As television took off, the motion picture industry and its directors of photography retooled for a burgeoning postwar television market. To the detriment of film noir visual style, Hollywood studios strongly encouraged cinematographers to avoid shadows; low-key chiaroscuro photography; expressionistic shots; blackened, high-contrast imagery; and night scenes. Filmmakers, cinematographers, and camera operators observed how the small, low-resolution monochrome television screen (a mere three to twelve inches) favored medium shots and close-ups over wider long shots, and pondered whether the television industry would shift from predominantly live New York–based production to shooting on film. By 1951, with the popular success of *I Love Lucy*, the television industry began its decade-long conversion to filming television shows in Hollywood.[44] In fact, 16mm color film was used to shoot low-contrast, black-and-white images for monochrome television.

As Hollywood slowly but steadily shifted to shooting on film for television, the inherent technological limitations of the new medium certainly mitigated against film noir visual style and affected the cinematography of feature films. "Motion pictures for TV demand exacting photography, special lighting and careful processing by the laboratory," NBC television engineer Robert Frasier wrote. To produce satisfactory films for television, it was essential to understand the technical limitations of the medium: "scenes lit in low-key or scenes having predominantly black areas will not televise with fidelity" because the iconoscope tube flares with dark or black areas, and compression washes out the image when televised. He insisted that "arty" lighting, shadows, and high contrast—that is, the distinctive style of film noir—should be restrained or avoided altogether in lieu of low-contrast imagery in keeping with televisual limitations. The Society of Motion Picture Engineers stated that the "limited range of picture tube brightness" in television requires visual contrast to be controlled and maintained when filming: "even lighting is essential," and illumination should be kept constant so the television signal does not change. "For this reason, night scenes should be avoided."[45] As Hollywood adopted televisual style shooting conventions, filming for a smaller black-and-white screen, industry directors of photography expressed concern that the technical limitations of television did not guarantee sharp focus and severely degraded image quality and visual style, losing much of the half-tone shading and contrast of the image.

"Lighting is the basic problem," *American Cinematographer* complained, insisting bright, flat uniform "high-key illumination is the best for photography of TV films for present conditions. Unfortunately, many of the best effects used in the theatre film are lost on the television tube. These include atmospheric low-key scenes, night scenes, and firelight or candlelight scenes." Also, complex montages (so crucial to noir visual style) were to be avoided because of the inherent lack of sharpness, and special effects should also be used sparingly. "Until the video mechanism is improved," it was deemed best to simplify design, refrain from dramatic shadowy lighting, and instead stick to high-key lighting.[46]

As Hollywood shifted from nitrate to acetate film and adopted a brighter, high-key, low-contrast televisual style, early 1950s films noir like *Ace in the Hole*, *The Enforcer*, *The Thief*, and *The Big Heat* (1953), featured a virile masculine underworld in film gris ("gray film") imagery rather than the blackened shadowy imagery of earlier 1940s films noir. By the 1950s, as seen in the sunlit 1951 noir *The Enforcer*, which was shot in semidocumentary visual style in outdoor exterior locations, Bogart—no longer a 1930s gangster or hard-boiled 1940s noir loner—was a crime-fighting law man trying to get a hoodlum to testify and inform on "Murder Inc." In Bogart's last Warner Bros. film noir, the aging crime star was promoted as an everyman beating the bad guys.[47] Although *The Enforcer* opened in moody nocturnal shadow, most of the remaining picture was shot in the brighter, high-key visual style that permeated 1950s crime pictures that were now flooded with light on sunny outdoor locations. The *New York Times* complained about the gruesome and graphic killings in *The Enforcer*, insisting: "murder on such a gaudy scale tends to become monotonous—and a little ridiculous . . . No matter how naturalistic and grisly the boys have made the deeds . . . the sheer accumulation of ugly violence and brutality eventually becomes dull."[48] Not only had noir style evolved away from its iconic black look, but in terms of gender, femme fatales had morphed into more submissive redeemers relegated to the periphery of virile masculine crime melodramas.

In Hollywood's persistent shift to lighter cinematography and televisual style, the 1952 espionage noir *The Thief*, independently produced by Harry M. Popkin and released by United Artists, was shot on acetate with a bright, high-key visual style and extensive outdoor locations. It was remarkable because it included no dialogue throughout the entire film but rather stunning semidocumentary photography. In fact, the realistic nonfiction-like photography was the star of the film. *American Cinematographer* noted that it was shot using Dupont acetate film stock. The noir film was also informed by the intensifying Cold War, Red Scare, and industry blacklist. Starring Ray Milland as a government nuclear scientist who steals secrets for the Communists, *The Thief* featured striking sunlit location filming in Washington, DC, and New York City, including stealthily capturing documentary style candid shots of New Yorkers filmed with a hidden camera. In its spectacular climax, *The Thief* culminates atop the Empire State Building, where Milland (who refused to use a stunt double) flees FBI agents in roaring fifty-five-mile-an-hour winds while climbing steep, winding stairwells from the eighty-sixth to the 102nd floors and towering observation deck. *The Thief* combined deep shadowed interiors and nocturnal streets on location in New York's Times Square with a lighter semidocumentary style, privileging its stunning visuals. *American Cinematographer* editor Herb Lightman called *The Thief* outstanding, forceful, and refreshing, praising Sam Leavitt's cinematography as a "style of realistic photography that perfectly complements the brooding atmosphere."[49]

Fritz Lang's 1953 noirs *The Big Heat* and *The Blue Gardenia* were also filmed on acetate in a lighter semidocumentary, low-contrast, televisual aesthetic style—versus Lang's darker classic 1940s nitrate noir *Scarlet Street*. *The Big Heat* featured cops, gangsters, and misogynistic violence toward their molls: one of the hoodlums (Lee Marvin) scalds and scars his mistress's (Gloria Grahame) face with boiling coffee and explosively blows up the detective's (Glenn Ford) wife in a failed attempt to assassinate the police officer. Columbia studio publicity for *The Big Heat* featured cop Ford roughly grabbing moll Grahame: "Somebody's Going To Pay . . . because he forgot to kill me . . ." and "Vice . . . Dice . . . and Corruption!"[50] Yet publicity for *The Big Heat* was tame compared to the violence in the 1953 noir film. Even *American Cinematographer* noted the sadistic violence, social and political corruption, and pessimism infusing Lang's film.[51]

As the industry eventually adapted to new technologies, widescreen and color became more prevalent. Noir films like *Ace in the Hole*, *The Enforcer*, *The Thief*, *The Big Heat*, and *The Blue Gardenia* were shot in a lighter, semidocumentary televisual style in standard Academy aspect ratio, but other noir pictures shot on acetate saw a new dimension in 1953 with the introduction of widescreen. Produced and directed by Robert Aldrich for independent Parklane Productions (owned by Victor Saville) and released by United Artists, the 1955 low-budget B noir *Kiss Me Deadly*, shot by Ernest Laszlo for $410,000, was one of the later noir films as the cycle declined in the 1950s. Aldrich was assistant director on *Body and Soul* before directing *Kiss Me Deadly*. Released the year after censor Breen retired and the PCA relaxed its regulation, provocative and suggestive publicity for *Kiss Me Deadly* raucously declared, "I Don't Care What You Do To Me, Mike—Just Do It Fast!" and "Blood-Red Kisses! White-Hot Thrills! Mickey Spillane's Latest H-Bomb!"[52] Ads featured star Ralph Meeker grabbing and kissing a partially bare, alluringly clad woman wearing skin-tight leopard pants holding a gun. In was a cinematic cocktail of sex and violence in the atomic era.

The opening sequence of *Kiss Me Deadly* is wonderfully experimental, highlighting the burgeoning technology of widescreen in a brooding noir visual style more shadowy than the rest of the film.[53] In a cold open before the credits, a woman, Christina Bailey (Cloris Leachman, in her film debut), desperately trying to hitch a ride, runs fearfully from an unseen pursuer on a long dark road in a way that emphasizes the expansive width of the screen. Detective Mike Hammer (Meeker) zooms through the pitch-black night in his convertible sports car. He screeches to a stop, veering off the long highway when Christina jumps out blocking the road in front of him. Credits begin to scroll in reverse from the bottom of the screen toward a distant z-axis point at the top. The opening title card reads: "Victor Saville presents Mickey Spillane's *Kiss Me Deadly*."[54] Director of photography Ernest Laszlo used wide-angle lenses to accentuate the breadth of the images.

Aldrich's widescreen noir *Kiss Me Deadly* is, for the most part, lighter visually; it features extensive outdoor location filming with a grayer televisual aesthetic and mischievously plays with the new widescreen technological visual style, as seen in the wonderfully experimental opening credits emphasizing the expansive elongated width of the frame. Considered a straggler in the declining cycle of noir over the course of the 1950s, *Kiss Me Deadly* is another key transition point in the ebbing trend as new postwar technologies emerge. The film is a notable point on the spectrum of noir style in relation to widescreen filmic considerations and grayer film gris televisual-style imagery. Filmed from late November through December 1954, *Kiss Me Deadly*'s pressbook publicity noted that 75 percent of the film was shot on exterior locations around Los Angeles. Its sunny Southern California locales included a Malibu beach house, a service station in Calabasas, a swanky estate in Beverly Hills, a Hollywood athletic club (where an atomic Pandora's box was kept in a locker), a Black club in South Los Angeles (at the 4800 block of South Figueroa), a fading Victorian mansion, and boardinghouses in the Bunker Hill neighborhood of downtown Los Angeles. The interiors of Hammer's modern apartment were shot at Sutherland Studio on Occidental Boulevard in Los Angeles.[55] Night scenes included the innovative experimental opening on a dark road and the fiery cataclysmic final sequences shot in widescreen with deep-focus, night-for-night photography filmed on location as the detective and his girlfriend escape from the blast by running across a vast expanse of the beach, looking back at the explosion.[56]

Kiss Me Deadly faced numerous censorship problems. Mickey Spillane's 1952 novel concerned narcotics, which was changed to radioactive atomic material for the film. Private eye Mike Hammer originally battled the Mafia and organized crime. The enemy was changed to a mysterious band of Communists, heightening its Cold War, Red Scare production context. Censors objected to "illegal drug traffic," narcotics, violence, "sex-suggestiveness," and depicting Mike Hammer as a "cold-blooded murderer" whose vigilante "killings are completely justified," and cautioned against excessive sex and brutality. Aldrich eventually thanked PCA censor Geoffrey Shurlock for approving the film in

February 1955, expressing how difficult it was to adapt Spillane's novels: "In the Spillane pictures we have a unique and difficult problem. The properties are of great commercial value, and yet there is no morality, or integrity, or respect for American tradition, or the due process of law." In April, however, Aldrich noted "a most rude and expensive surprise" that, although the motion picture industry's PCA censors had finally endorsed the film, the National Catholic Legion of Decency "has taken violent exception" to *Kiss Me Deadly* and has "requested that over thirty changes, cuts and deletions be made." The Legion later gave the film a B "partly objectionable" rating instead of a C "condemned" rating, declaring: "This film tends to glorify taking the law into one's own hand. Moreover, it contains excessive brutality and suggestiveness in costume, dialogue and situations."[57]

Visual style and narrative content also faced constraints from television. The film encountered still more censorship interference when Los Angeles CBS-TV station censor Ed Nathan criticized *Kiss Me Deadly* and refused to air preview trailers, complaining that it had "no purpose except to incite sadism and bestiality in human beings." But Aldrich protested that other U.S. CBS stations had agreed to broadcast the previews. United Artists even negotiated with major television networks in 1955 and planned to "set up a half hour coast-to-coast telecast featuring live enactments of scenes from the picture" to promote *Kiss Me Deadly*. "It is expected that the exploitation program, first of its kind, will reach a video audience of twenty-five million." It remains unclear whether their planned telecast was ever produced.[58] It is worth noting that many of these postwar films noir were, of course, later shown on television. These 1950s pictures, shot with lighter televisual conventions and visual constraints in mind but filmed in widescreen, were eventually cropped when aired on television.

In terms of its aesthetic imagery, the blackened nocturnal opening and explosive atomic finale of *Kiss Me Deadly* are the darkest, most visually noir-style moments in the film and the most narratively disturbing in illustrating its Cold War cultural production and reception context. For years (since the early 1970s), *Kiss Me Deadly* was shown with a butchered "truncated" ending that concluded with an apocalyptic atomic explosion, which changes the meaning of the film to suggest that Mike and Velda both die, perishing among the flames. The original restored ending shows Mike and Velda getting away, running along the wide stretch of beach at night, a scene that was emphasized by its deep-focus, widescreen, night-for-night cinematography, as the house explodes and burns in a fiery atomic blast. Scholars have speculated that perhaps censors may have sought a more punitive ending and cut the film.

Kiss Me Deadly earned a mere $726,000 in North America. The *Los Angeles Times* noted that the film was a "failure when originally released." The film was denounced by the influential Kefauver Commission on organized crime for its violence.[59] Nevertheless, it remains a vanguard noir classic. *Kiss Me Deadly* is highly visceral and modern in its provocative nature, challenging the audience and censorship. Like *The Big Combo*'s homage to earlier noir imagery, the visually lighter, grayer, widescreen noir films *Kiss Me Deadly*, *Sweet Smell of Success*, *A Face in the Crowd*, *Touch of Evil*, and *Odds Against Tomorrow* were also indicative of the twilight of black-and-white noir visual style and Hollywood's increasing reliance on emergent technologies and innovations such as widescreen spectacles (discussed later in this chapter in the Color Noir Visual Style and The Emergence of Color Noir sections) to compete with the exploding postwar popularity of television in the 1950s. Indeed, as black-and-white noir was influenced by television to become grayer, less shadowy, and less high-contrast, Hollywood—and the fading noir cycle—nevertheless tried to differentiate itself from small-screen monochrome television by adopting widescreen and color as well as focusing on bolder, provocative narrative screen content and themes that would be censored on television.

As the classic noir cycle ebbed by the late 1950s, the fade to gray continued in a visually lighter but thematically darker jazz noir, *Sweet Smell of Success* (1957). Shot on location in widescreen on black-and-white acetate film, it also employed a high-key televisual aesthetic. Independently produced by Burt Lancaster, Tony Curtis, James Hill, and Howard Hecht and released by United Artists, *Sweet Smell of Success* was British director Alexander Mackendrick's first U.S. film.[60] It projected a bleak noir vision of deceit, duplicity, graft, and exploitation and revealed gritty corruption in a brooding black-and-white semidocumentary style. The film provided a harsh glimpse of malicious betrayal and informing in the Cold War McCarthy era in America's urban jungle. Cinematographer James Wong Howe shot stunning widescreen images of New York City nightlife. Lancaster and Curtis played caustic opportunistic antiheroes, vicious power-hungry hucksters trading barbs and verbally sparring as they plot to destroy people over cocktails, in sequences filmed at Manhattan's famed 21 Club.[61]

The basis for the film was Ernest Lehman's novella, *Tell Me about It Tomorrow!*, which was published in *Cosmopolitan* in 1950. Lehman adapted his story with Clifford Odets and Mackendrick. Inspired by New York gossip columnist Walter Winchell, *Sweet Smell of Success* portrayed an icily brutal Broadway columnist, J. J. Hunsecker (Lancaster) and sleazy press agent Sidney Falco (Curtis) in their manipulative lust for power and money, hustling movie stars and senators schmoozing and mingling at 21. Howe put petroleum jelly on Lancaster's glasses to heighten and emphasize his piercing glare. The film featured an atmospheric music score by Elmer Bernstein and jam session jazz performances by the Chico Hamilton Quintet.[62]

In May 1949, Breen rejected Lehman's story, considering it unacceptable because of incest and marijuana. The story originally concluded with Hunsecker murdering Falco after Hunsecker's younger sister Susie accuses Falco of rape, which censors objected to. Breen's PCA successor Geoffrey Shurlock eventually approved *Sweet Smell of Success* in 1957.[63] The fact that it was an independent production—and Breen had retired in 1954—allowed more censorial latitude for the hard-hitting film. Lehman was originally set to direct when his story was purchased in 1955. He even scouted locations in 1956 but was fired when producers and United Artists were reluctant to allow a first-time director to helm the project. After considering Frank Sinatra and Orson Welles, Lancaster and Curtis cast themselves as the lead antiheroes. The role of Steve Dallas was originally intended for Robert Vaughn, who was drafted into the military. *Sweet Smell of Success* was shot on location in New York City from November 1956 through March 1957 (additional filming continued through May). Like the film itself, it was a contentious shoot, and tensions were rife on set. After a dispute, Lancaster even threatened to hit Lehman, who responded: "Go ahead, I need the money."[64] Shooting locations included Times Square, the Brill Building in Tin Pan Alley, and the Broadway theater district in New York, as well as the 21 Club, with additional shooting on soundstage 6 at Goldwyn studios in Culver City. Lehman eventually left the project, moving on to write scripts for *North by Northwest* and *West Side Story*. Clifford Odets rewrote the screenplay for *Sweet Smell of Success*, and there were many revisions and production delays. There were also creative disputes and disagreements between producer-star Lancaster and director Mackendrick over the ending. Susan Harrison admitted the tension and conflicts were overwhelming. Nevertheless, Howe's widescreen, deep-focus cinematography was breathtaking and emphasized the sweeping expanse of the film's spectacular New York City locations.

Publicity for *Sweet Smell of Success* promoted the film with sensational taglines describing Hunsecker: "They know the venom that flickers in those eyes behind the glasses—and they fawn—like Sidney Falco, the kid who wanted 'in' so much, he'd sell out his own girl!" With menacing shots of Lancaster and Curtis, *Sweet Smell of Success* ads warned: "Beware these Gentlemen of the Press!"[65] When it was released in June 1957, the film received a hostile reception from critics and viewers who balked at the unflattering roles for Lancaster and Curtis. Yet *Time* and *New York Herald-Tribune* praised it as one of the year's best films, but noted it would not recover its $1.3 million production cost. By 1959, it was even blocked by the U.S. Information Agency in twelve countries for "painting a false picture abroad of the United States."[66]

Sweet Smell of Success is a thematically biting, albeit visually lighter, televisual-style, blistering social realist cultural critique woven into an intense male melodrama rather than a shadowy 1940s-style film noir. Howe's high-key cinematography was much brighter than his brooding blackened photography for *Body and Soul* a decade earlier.

As Schrader notes, Welles's *Touch of Evil* marks the epitaph of film noir, ending the classic cycle in all its baroque excess and at a point of utter exhaustion.

76 Fade to Gray and Color Noir

2.4 Charlton Heston and Janet Leigh walk by a convertible car, stopping at a U.S.-Mexico border crossing beside a ticking bomb in the trunk of the car in the opening shot of Orson Welles's *Touch of Evil*, filmed on location. Universal, 1958

Touch of Evil was written and directed by Welles and filmed by Russell Metty in widescreen acetate to emphasize its extraordinary expansive composition-in-depth mise-en-scène. It was shot on location at night in Venice, California, from February to April 1957.[67] Filmed for $900,000 in thirty-nine days, the moody, noir, night-for-night, widescreen photography was stunning. Welles's remarkable opening shot, an elaborate, extended, three-minute take, shot with a fluidly moving camera on a crane as a time bomb ticks away, moves from a close-up, pulling back to a high-angle wide shot rising aerially over buildings, sweeping down expansively across stretches of roads that was emphasized by the wide breadth of the screen. Then the amazing expanded long take continues as the camera swings around street corners to meander alongside newlywed couple Mike (Charlton Heston) and Susan (Janet Leigh) Vargas conversing as they stroll leisurely through a Mexican-American border town, visually lingering and passing shops, crossing gates, following automobiles and pedestrians stepping over the border and chatting with the guard as a convertible rolls past, stopping and starting and ticking through the elongated frame in a mesmerizing expanded duration of time. The incredible three-minute take culminates in a deafening bang as a car explodes. Welles then shifts to shaky handheld camera shots as people flee in the chaos and destruction, and seedy, menacing corrupt detective Hank Quinlan (Welles, with 60 pounds of rotund padding) appears, shot from an extremely low camera angle. Welles's *Touch of Evil* remains a spectacular homage to the innovative cinematography of film noir. It was also the last studio film Welles directed in the United States. It was a fitting end to film noir.[68]

In many ways, however, film noir visual style actually died with *Ace in the Hole*, when Hollywood abandoned the original nitrate noir aesthetic, moving instead to acetate film shot at luminous locales where sunlight permeated a realistic semidocumentary cinematic fade to gray; employed a low-contrast televisual style mirroring the image constraints of early television; and retooled for color and widescreen spectacles. Like Wilder's doomed antihero crashing dead into the camera, the entire style of cinematography had changed since the blackouts and filming constraints produced the inky black, nitrate noir aesthetic fashioned by James Wong Howe, John Seitz, and Wilder during the war years. Eventually, that noir style declined and came apart, fading over the course of the 1950s in response to new technologies and myriad postwar pressures. As Hollywood adapted to emergent techniques, however, the shadowy noir aesthetic was repurposed and channeled into films with a 'color noir' visual style.

Color Noir Visual Style

The influence of film noir visual style on an array of different films, including improbable generic strains not typically associated with noir style such as darker color musicals, illustrates how noir is not a single genre nor a static style. Rather, noir is a complex visual style that responds to industrial and generic/thematic considerations, censorial pressures, and technological changes and advances, influencing even unlikely genres as the style evolves. This trend is evident in 'color noir' films, which emulate shadowy noir visual style in adapting to new color technology using muted tones to simulate the look of black-and-white film noir. Established noir scholars such as Alain Silver, Elizabeth Ward, and James Ursini, as well as Paul Schrader, have argued and recognized noir as a *style* and the inclusion of thematic and narrative elements such as suicide, obsession, self-destruction, and other downbeat themes intertwined with noir style.

The evolution of film noir visual style continued and evolved in response to developments such as the Hollywood film industry's embrace of and conversion to new color film technologies in the postwar era—and later in the postclassical New Hollywood and digital streaming eras—which contributed to a color noir visual style. Such developments reveal that noir is a complex, nuanced, multifaceted visual style that influences the aesthetic look of color films during the postwar period. As the original classic black-and-white noir films faded in response to myriad factors over the course of the 1950s, the noir look adapted to new technologies. This is certainly evident in the influence of black-and-white noir visual style on the emergence of a color noir aesthetic in the industry's adapting to and adopting color film technology. The noir visual style—and the legacy and influence of noir—continued with color film production in the postwar period and into the later postclassical and digital streaming eras.

In this section, I will highlight how noir adapts to color technology. In particular, I will discuss the evolution of color noir style in important films such as *The Red Shoes* (1948), *Niagara* (1953), *The Barefoot Contessa* (1954), *A Star Is Born* (1954), Hitchcock's color noir films *Rear Window* (1954) and *North by Northwest* (1959), and *West Side Story* (1961) and how the evolution of noir style in relation to Hollywood adapting to color film technology also powerfully illustrates the multifaceted influence of noir across different generic strains of the evolving style. It is important to distinguish that there is a difference between conceiving of a picture as a film noir versus considering the evolution of the noir style as an influence of earlier noir film techniques, as we see in color noir films and later neo-noir and digital streaming noir productions.

The chiaroscuro aesthetic of classic 1940s noir was never the same after the shift to bright sunlit films shot outside on location with lighter acetate film stock and adopting televisual techniques, as we have seen with *Ace in the Hole* in 1951. The deep shadows of black-and-white film noir style declined after 1953.[69] World War II studio filmmaking production constraints and technological and industrial considerations contributed to how and why many 1940s films noir were, for the most part, so much darker overall than earlier 1930s films preceding the classic noir cycle and the later postwar 1950s productions produced in the absence of those war-related filmmaking constraints on entirely different acetate film stock with more light on brighter sets.[70] The industry shift to color also intensified this stylistic shift.

Film noir and its brooding atmospheric visual style thrived during the classical studio system in the 1940s, but as the studio system unraveled during the 1950s, noir visual style also diminished.[71] Hollywood retooled for color, and thus black-and-white film noir began to wane. Its distinctive style was eventually reconceived, however, in color noir films. As the noir aesthetic evolved, it adapted to new technology in the postwar move to color spectacles. The film industry developed and employed a variety of technological advances, such as single-strip monopack color film, a variety of large-frame widescreen formats, and stereophonic sound to enhance large screen spectacles (and provide an alternative to grainy, small-screen, black-and-white monochrome television), all of which eventually contributed to a color noir cinematic style. As the black-and-white noir aesthetic faded to shades of gray, a darker, more shadowy noir visual style permeated postwar color cinematography invoking elements of the noir aesthetic.

"ALL PIX IN COLOR WITHIN 5 YRS": this bold headline splashed across the top of *Variety*'s front page on Wednesday, January 7, 1948, with the subhead: "New Tint Cuts Cost Way Down." The industry trade journal projected an explosion of color films that would revolutionize the cinematic output of the Hollywood studio system by 1953, significantly curtailing black-and-white films—a development that would further constrain the monochrome aesthetic of noir visual style. It was a stunning forecast. "As with two world wars within the same generation," *Variety*'s Abel Green predicted, "so will the motion picture industry see the two most revolutionary milestones in its history. The first was sound, some 20 years ago, and within the next three to five years motion pictures in black-and-white will be obsolete." *Variety* observed, "A new [color] process with which Eastman Kodak scientists have been experimenting the last few years, in close cooperation with some of the major studios—most notably 20th Century-Fox—is expected to bring down the cost of color to make it available for every producer."[72]

Technological advances would dramatically transform the look and visual style of postwar Hollywood motion pictures, including noir films, in the late 1940s and 1950s. As has already been shown, the industry prediction that all films would be made in color by 1953 was mistaken. Although film noir (in its black-and-white mode) stylistically faded to lighter shades of gray and eventually ebbed, it scarcely disappeared.[73] Rather, it was repurposed and reconceived in other forms. Black-and-white and color films coexisted for longer than anticipated. The iconic chiaroscuro aesthetic of monochromatic films noir was channeled into color noir imagery. By the end of the year, Philip Scheuer reported in the *Los Angeles Times*, "Movie Realism at Peak in 1948, But Signs Begin to Hint That Postwar Hardness is Cracking." Scheuer noted the film industry's surging boom in tough realism, suspenseful thrills, "crime and the 'psycho' mind" psychological "mood dramas," "neorealism," and "semidocumentary" techniques—so influential to noir films such as *The Naked City, Call Northside 777* (1948), *Street with No Name* (1948), *The Search* (1948), and *The Snake Pit* (1948). "Man against society, the villain pursued and punished—the 'gangster,'" he added, "remains basic, A No. 1 cinema stuff." However, he recognized waning "signs that the hard crust was cracking," with a reaction to this hard-boiled trend, noting the Technicolor "triumph" of *The Red Shoes* cinematic ballet and musical spectacles.[74]

After 1953, technological developments by Technicolor and Kodak Eastmancolor utilizing single-strip color film processes enabled studios to produce more color films and thus to differentiate their cinema products from small-screen television and meet the industry's "desperate need to lure people away from their black-and-white television sets."[75] Hollywood responded to competition from television by producing fewer but bigger films, with more stars in glorious color and widescreen formats (briefly in 3D from 1952 to 1953) with multitrack stereophonic sound, which contributed to the postwar industry rechanneling small-screen (or standard Academy 1.37:1 aspect ratio) black-and-white noir films into color noir dramas and musicals. These technological innovations included a spate of widescreen formats that were rolled out in the early to mid-1950s, notably Cinerama, an extravagant three-camera/projector system, as well as Twentieth Century-Fox's CinemaScope anamorphic widescreen system, MGM's Panavision, and Paramount's VistaVision.

The Emergence of Color Noir

A few moody color films—across an array of different and even unlikely genres—made savvy use of new advances and cinematic techniques in adopting and adapting to innovations in color film technology to reimagine the brooding, iconic, visually darker look of classic black-and-white film noir style in color, for example, in the color noir imagery in films such as *The Red Shoes, Niagara, Rear Window*, and the dark musical-melodramas *A Star Is Born* and *The Barefoot Contessa* that effectively employed a more shadowy, chiaroscuro, noir-style visual aesthetic, which influenced later films such as *North by Northwest* and *West Side Story*.[76] As the industry moved away from standard-screen, black-and-white films, noir creative talent moved to other genres, including musicals, where they brought their darker, realistic dramatic tendencies to color and stereophonic sound films. These darker color films presented a distinctive color noir aesthetic, emulating shadowy noir style with color film and using muted tones to simulate the look of black-and-white film (while also emphasizing the color red). Studios also employed this color noir aesthetic in ads and promotions, even in artwork for black-and-white noir pictures, as in *The Lady from Shanghai* (1947), *Out of the Past* (1947), and *The Big Combo*.

In the industry's postwar shift to color, even color films across an array of different genres employed cinematography that invoked elements of the noir style aesthetic visually and thematically, as in the variations of color noir imagery seen in *The Red Shoes, The Barefoot Contessa*, and *A Star Is Born*, which explored a brooding melodramatic color musical world in dark hues.[77] Talented European émigrés, women, and jazz musicians had influenced the black-and-white film noir style during Hollywood's wartime labor shortage. By the 1940s, a color noir style began to coalesce in films such as the Chopin biopic *A Song to Remember* (1945), and the extraordinary shadowy imagery of Michael Powell and Emeric Pressburger's *The Red Shoes*. Blackouts and rationing of film stock and lighting contributed to the development of a shadowy black-and-white film noir aesthetic in wartime, but the industry's postwar location shooting and competition with television helped move motion pictures away from expressionistic mise-en-scène to bright lighting and colorful spectacle. Visually brighter color films such as *Leave Her to Heaven* (1945), *Desert Fury* (1947), *Inferno* (1953), *Dragnet* (1954), and *Black Widow* (1954) included noir *thematic* elements but were much brighter, comparatively high-key in visual style, and mainly void of shadowy noir imagery. This was especially the case because many postwar films were shot on location outdoors in sunlight, as was the melodrama *Leave Her to Heaven*.

By the 1950s, many industry executives discouraged production of hard-hitting noir pictures tackling social problems—preferring popular escapist

2.5 Gene Tierney sits in bright outdoor sunlight in a rowboat on a lake, an uncharacteristically sun-soaked, visually light scene for a murder in *Leave Her to Heaven*, shot on location. Twentieth Century-Fox, 1945

color musicals, comedies, melodramas, historical period epics, science fiction, Westerns, fantasy, and presold Broadway adaptations, which also contributed to the rechanneling of black-and-white film noir visual style into postwar color noir films. In some cases, filmmakers shifted from making black-and-white noir films to color musicals and comedies that seemed antithetical to noir style. For example, after filming definitive shadowy noir-style features *Double Indemnity* and *Sunset Boulevard*, Billy Wilder moved to brighter sunlit location shooting for *Ace in the Hole*, which was shot in the desert of New Mexico, then made high-key color comedies like *The Seven Year Itch* (1955). After filmmaker Fred Zinnemann made the powerful noir *Act of Violence* (1949) and won the Academy Awards for Best Picture and Director in 1953 for *From Here to Eternity* (1953), he directed the sunny color 1955 musical *Oklahoma!* Even the noir veteran director of *The Maltese Falcon* (1941) and *The Asphalt Jungle* (1950), John Huston, took on color films like the musical-melodrama *Moulin Rouge* (1952) and the widescreen adventure *Moby Dick* (1956), and noir stylist Henry Hathaway made Technicolor films with a moody color noir aesthetic as in *Niagara*. As gritty black-and-white crime films became grayer and more masculine and shifted away from hard-boiled femme fatales, darker color noir musical melodramas targeted postwar women with brooding chromatic spectacle, as in *The Red Shoes*.

The Red Shoes featured quintessential three-strip Technicolor noir-style imagery that was very influential for Hollywood's postwar color noir aesthetic.

After it opened in Britain in mid-1948, it was a magnificent success when it was released in the United States and opened in October 1948 in New York, in Los Angeles in December, then roadshowed in art houses across the United States. Philip Scheuer of the *Los Angeles Times* called *The Red Shoes* "[t]he most ambitious—and probably the most dazzlingly successful—use of traditional-type ballet in any motion picture," referring to Powell and Pressburger as "conscientious movie makers in England who paint with color as Josef von Sternberg once painted in black and white."[78] The film cost over £500,000. It grossed $5 million, running for two years in New York, and received five Academy Award nominations, becoming the most successful British film ever released in the United States by 1952.[79]

The Red Shoes adapted and reenvisioned the Hollywood star-is-born, backstage musical drama with deep, shadowy, noir-style mise-en-scène to project a destructive, intoxicating whirlwind of dark romance, fame, and performance in the realm of ballet. The film featured a deadly ill-fated love triangle: the conflict between Boris Lermontov (Anton Walbrook), a possessive, arrogant impresario who mentors aspiring up-and-coming prima ballerina Victoria Page (Moira Shearer) but clashes with young classical music composer Julian

2.6 Vicky (Moira Shearer) dances in brooding Technicolor noir shadows with menacing red backlighting in *The Red Shoes*. Eagle-Lion, 1948

Craster (Marius Goring). Lermontov hires Craster to score *The Red Shoes* ballet, a Hans Andersen tale of a girl driven to dance who perishes in red shoes, which makes Page a star. Upon making her a star, Lermontov, who represses his desire for Page, jealously resents it when Page abandons her dance career, wasting her talent to marry Craster. She eventually becomes a muse for Craster, who in turn begrudges her passion for dance. Tensions fly in a turbulent deadly climax as they confront each other. The stormy obsessive tensions are reflected in Page's dressing room mirror as tears streak and distort her makeup. "Nobody can have two lives, and your life is dancing!" Lermontov furiously demands. "Go with him. Be a faithful housewife with a crowd of screaming children and finish with dancing forever!"[80] When Craster walks out, the red shoes draw Page down spiral stairways to leap off a balcony toward an oncoming train as black smoke fills the screen.

The Red Shoes infused its moody melodrama with three-strip Technicolor noir style. Lermontov is often hidden in darkness, his face cloaked in a blackened abyss. The demanding impresario is in complete silhouette and backlit through a window covered in shadow, inhaling a smoldering cigarette as tendrils of smoke surround him. Page and Craster are shrouded in blackness as

2.7 Boris Lermontov (Anton Walbrook) is cloaked in murky noir darkness and backlit through a window as smoke swirls in *The Red Shoes*. Eagle-Lion, 1948

they embrace, riding along the glistening, late-night Mediterranean seaside, a visual foreshadowing of their doomed affair. Craster sits in the dark at a Villefranche café listening to melancholy jazz, depicting his unemployed blues after Lermontov fires him to try to break them up. The unlit room is pitch black as Lermontov chain-smokes, bursts into a vicious rage, and smashes a mirror after Page leaves the company with Craster. Lermontov confronts Page in the cramped confines of a claustrophobic train cabin. Chiaroscuro color mise-en-scène permeates director of photography Jack Cardiff's cinematography. The film was cloaked in deep Technicolor shadows shot on Pinewood studio soundstage sets, as well as at atmospheric locations in London, Paris, Monaco and the Côte d'Azur.[81]

American Cinematographer's Herb Lightman applauded the impressive technological innovations that enabled the brilliant, brooding, three-strip Technicolor visual style in *The Red Shoes*. Trailblazing transatlantic cinematographer Cardiff flew between Britain and Hollywood to develop new lighting equipment and cinematic techniques with technical experts at the Mole-Richardson stage lighting company. Cardiff used huge new 225-amp "Brute" and three-hundred-amp water-cooled "monster lamp" spotlights to create stark menacing shadows and elaborate expressionistic imagery. The set was pierced by harsh, high-contrast beams of light for *The Red Shoes* ballet sequence drawn from Hein Heckroth's gothic sketch-storyboard designs.[82] Powell and Pressburger created the elaborate, seventeen-minute, expressionistic, color noir ballet-within-a-film, with spectacular surrealist nightmare images evoking *The Cabinet of Dr. Caligari* (1919) to reflect Page's conflicted psyche. Powell and Pressburger (known collectively as the Archers) wanted to cast actual dancers in the roles and created their own ballet company of fifty-three dancers for the film. Powell pursued the rising twenty-year-old star of Sadler's Wells Theatre ballet, dancer Moira Shearer, for a year before she agreed to do the film, her screen debut. Other dancers included Robert Helpmann (who also choreographed the film), Leonide Massine, and Ludmilla Tcherina. Walbrook, a gay Jewish Austrian émigré actor (Adolf Wohlbrück) who trained in Germany at UFA, infused misogyny into his powerful performance as Lermontov.[83] Shearer recalled a grueling shoot. Walbrook wore dark sunglasses and remained aloof like impresario Lermontov on set.[84] Shearer reprised her tragic role in *The Red Shoes* with James Mason in MGM's Technicolor *The Story of Three Loves* (1953).

The shadowy, low-key color noir aesthetic seen in *The Red Shoes* continued with *Moulin Rouge, Niagara*, and *The Story of Three Loves*, and crystallized in 1954 with *The Barefoot Contessa*, the noir musical *A Star Is Born*, Hitchcock's *Rear Window*, and the moody melodrama *Young at Heart* (1954). Hollywood's increasing use of color was enabled by the wider availability of Technicolor technology. In 1950, Technicolor agreed to share its patents after an antitrust decree terminated contracts requiring film producers to use only Technicolor camera equipment, services, and processing for color pictures. In March 1953, Technicolor announced it would develop single-strip color film (such as the cheaper Kodak Eastmancolor monopack stock) to create three color separated strips (in a dye-transfer imbibition [I-B] process emulating three-strip Technicolor) derived from a single strip of film shot with any regular black-and-white camera. This technological innovation was a huge cost saver, thus opening the door for color filming and contributing to the post-1953 decline in black-and-white noir production.[85] As Technicolor became more available for use by Kodak and filmmakers across the industry, it also advanced color noir style. For more on color film technology, see the box "Color Film Technology."

Color Film Technology

By 1953, Kodak Eastman color single-strip monopack stock (and the ability to create three color separated strips in a dye-transfer imbibition [I-B] process) was a less expensive alternative to Hollywood's three-strip Technicolor film process. This advancement contributed to a color noir aesthetic visual style. "The money differential on the new process is said to be startling," Abel Green of *Variety* reported. "The secret lies in the new film, with its three master colors (red, blue and green) which can be used in the same camera as black-and-white film. The additive colors are invisible on the negative, the pigmentation being derived from a disk placed in the front of the lens. The process is said to permit one-third more light." He further explained that "[i]t will cost around 2½ [cents] per foot, and less, as against the 6¼ [cents] of today's Technicolor." *Variety* added that "the industry looks to this new low-cost color process to revitalize the industry . . . at a time when the industry perhaps may need a radically new lift," acknowledging that the "idea of color" for "all product" has been a "dream" in the industry but was limited by cost, noting that "color (usually of the Technicolor quality), adds 25 percent to the gross of the film."* Eastman's new, quick, economical process allowed the use of standard cameras for shooting (and printing facilities), similar to those used for black-and-white film, with the ability to develop enhanced color using the dye-transfer imbibition (I-B) process by sending film to Technicolor for processing to create three color separated strips in a less expensive alternative to Hollywood's three-strip Technicolor process.

* Abel Green, "All Pix in Color Within 5 Yrs," *Variety* 169, no 5 (January 7, 1948): 3, 158; "Technicolor Alters Practice On Output," *New York Times*, March 13, 1953, 23.

In 1954, for the first time, Hollywood produced more color films than black-and-white motion pictures—58.4 percent were color, 41.6 percent were black and white—as Kodak Eastmancolor film stock improved and the industry shifted away from three-strip Technicolor. In 1954, Eastman Kodak's less costly, single-strip monopack color systems replaced Technicolor's more expensive original three-strip process. The new single-strip color films were easier to shoot (especially with widescreen and CinemaScope films, which required more light), used regular black-and-white cameras, and were more economical, although they offered inferior color compared to the superior hues of the original three-strip Technicolor process, which can be seen in *A Star Is Born* (1937), *The Adventures of Robin Hood* (1938), *Gone with the Wind* (1939), *The Wizard of Oz* (1939), *Blood and Sand* (1941), *The Red Shoes*, and *Niagara*. Color noir visual style was so pervasive that it permeated postwar three-strip Technicolor spectacles and even a darker strain of musicals. By 1954, color noir visual aesthetic style was affected by improvements in Kodak's Eastmancolor stock. The introduction of new "faster" light-sensitive, higher-speed color negative and print films (in 1952 and 1953) soon became an industry standard—leading to cinematic enhancements that allowed more rapid, light-sensitive exposure times and that in turn contributed to Hollywood studios shifting to color films over the course of the 1950s and into the 1960s. Thus, films shot with the same amount of light looked brighter and needed less illumination, reducing shadowy imagery. Needing fewer lights for cinematic images to be exposed was especially important because color and widescreen formats such as CinemaScope required more light. These developments eventually mitigated against color noir visual style in the late 1950s to 1960s, especially when coupled with outdoor location shooting and televisual conventions.

A color noir visual aesthetic proliferated by 1954, however, as Hollywood adapted to new technology. After earlier Technicolor noirs *The Red Shoes* and *Moulin Rouge*, among the last three-strip Technicolor Hollywood films were the 1953 color noir *Niagara* and the 1954 color noir musical-melodramas *The Barefoot Contessa* and biopic *The Glenn Miller Story* (1954). Color noir musical melodramas *A Star Is Born* and *Young at Heart* and Hitchcock's *Rear Window*, *Vertigo* (1958), and *North by Northwest* (1959) were shot on Eastman single-strip monopack safety stock and developed using the Technicolor dye-transfer process (which replaced three-strip). By 1955, the Warner Bros. color film *Rebel Without a Cause* (1955) and MGM's noir musical *Love Me or Leave Me* (1955) were shot in widescreen CinemaScope with Eastmancolor rather than three-strip Technicolor. Hitchcock's *Rear Window* was filmed in widescreen, and *Vertigo* and *North by Northwest* were shot in widescreen VistaVision.[86]

Fox studio executive Darryl Zanuck championed color, widescreen, CinemaScope, and stereophonic sound films, insisting that these new technologies added "new dimension" to musicals, amplifying spectacle with darker edgier

2.8 A shadowy, overhead color noir shot with ominous bars of entrapment (with bells hanging from the roof) becomes a murder scene with silhouettes of the femme fatale and her estranged husband in *Niagara*. Twentieth Century-Fox, 1953

style. Noir musicals fused film noir visual style with color, and Zanuck believed that three-strip Technicolor noir musical *Moulin Rouge* was successful not only because of its beautiful color and spectacular imagery of Henri Toulouse Lautrec's paintings but also because it deals with darker themes in a moody atmospheric setting (not unlike film noir) permeated by sex, illicit affairs and prostitution, where color and showmanship were enhanced by "a heavy, downbeat, depressing story [that] can be lifted if it contains a really strong, violent sex situation."[87]

Niagara was one of the last films shot in three-strip Technicolor at Twentieth Century-Fox before the studio shifted to CinemaScope with monopack Eastmancolor in 1953.[88] Fox veteran Henry Hathaway, who directed black-and-white noir films *Kiss of Death* (1947) and *Call Northside 777*, and cinematographer Joseph MacDonald shot *Niagara* on location at Niagara Falls in summer 1952. *Niagara* featured blackened shadows; bars of entrapment; and a sultry femme fatale, Rose (Marilyn Monroe, in her first color picture), who gets knocked off by obsessed, unstable Korean War veteran husband George (Joseph Cotten) after trying to have her lover dispose of him. Screenwriter Walter Reisch recalled that cowriter/producer Charles Brackett—who cowrote and produced Billy Wilder's noir films *Sunset Boulevard* and *The Lost Weekend*—wanted to shoot a picture at Niagara Falls. Reisch suggested making a murder mystery set against the sweeping backdrop of the falls. As he explained, "Anybody hearing the name Niagara thinks of honeymoon couples and of some sentimental story of a girl walking out on her husband on their wedding night and their getting together again. It would be foolish to start up with Sonja Henie tricks here or Esther Williams-type swimming extravaganzas. I would like to make it a mystery story, with a real murder in it."[89]

In *Niagara*, shadowy noir interiors, atmospheric venetian-blind lighting, and shrouded sites of murder contrasted with the stunning outdoor location of the falls. Fox publicity showed a curvaceous noir temptress being manhandled, as taglines clamored: "Marilyn Monroe and 'Niagara': a raging torrent of emotion that even nature can't control!" *Hollywood Reporter* praised *Niagara* as "one of a very few murder yarns to be filmed in Technicolor;" Hathaway's "wonderful use of the falls to heighten the suspense;" and MacDonald's "fine photography . . . around the scenic splendor of Niagara Falls, Charles Brackett

2.9 Deep shadows and bars of entrapment cover the dead body of femme fatale Marilyn Monroe ("a raging torrent of emotion that even nature can't control") in a color noir shot from *Niagara*. Twentieth Century-Fox, 1953

has produced and co-scripted a gripping murder melodrama that is loaded with sex and suspense." The industry trade magazine also applauded Monroe's "finest acting performance" as a "sexy tart with a provocative abandon that has a powerful impact" and Cotten's "unfortunate" "psychopath."[90] The *New York Times* called Marilyn Monroe "seductive," observing that "cameras . . . have caught every possible curve both in the intimacy of the boudoir and in equally revealing tight dresses," and her unstable antihero spouse Cotten "brooding."[91] *Variety* complained, however, about the color noir film's lethal sex and intrigue, calling *Niagara* a "morbid, clichéd expedition into lust and murder. The atmosphere throughout is strained and taxes the nerves with a feeling of impending disaster . . . The camera lingers on Monroe's sensuous lips, roves over her slip-clad figure and accurately etches the outlines of her derriere as she weaves down a street to a rendezvous with her lover." But *Variety* did allow that the "natural phenomena" of Niagara Falls were "magnificently photographed on location."[92] Shot for about $1.5 million, *Niagara* was a major hit for Fox, earning $2.35 million in 1953 and eventually grossing $6 million.[93]

The Barefoot Contessa was another three-strip Technicolor noir shot by *The Red Shoes* cinematographer Jack Cardiff, with exquisite Mediterranean imagery filmed on location in Italy at San Remo, Portofino, Rome, and the famed Cinecitta studios. It starred Ava Gardner, Humphrey Bogart, Edmund O'Brien, Rossano Brazzi, and Marius Goring (another *Red Shoes* alum). Written, produced, and directed by Joseph Mankiewicz for his independent company Figaro and financed by United Artists, it was his first color film. Mankiewicz directed the shadowy chiaroscuro romance *The Ghost and Mrs. Muir* (1948), higher-key noirs *House of Strangers* (1949) and *No Way Out* (1950), and the backstage drama *All About Eve* (1950) before filming *The Barefoot Contessa*.[94] *The Barefoot Contessa* opens in stark color noir style with dreary shades of gray at the heroine's funeral in the pouring rain, simulating the look of black-and-white film noir. Gorgeous dancer–turned–movie star Maria Vargas (Gardner) has been killed—gunned down by her jealous, impotent, war-scarred spouse Count Vincenzo Torlato-Favrini (Brazzi) for philandering. Her mentor-director-friend Harry Dawes (Bogart) mourns her loss. Bogart mentions Hans Andersen in *The Barefoot Contessa*, saying, "[L]ife is not a fairy tale," and removes Gardner's shoes when she dies (recalling Page's death as Craster removes her red shoes.) *The Barefoot Contessa* included a noir-style voice-over narration with a flashback structure told from multiple points of view. It was filmed overseas in three-strip Technicolor from early January to late March 1954. Meanwhile, *A Star Is Born* was being shot at Warner Bros. It premiered in Los Angeles on September 29, 1954, the same day *The Barefoot Contessa* opened in New York.

The emergence of a color noir visual style in the postwar era demonstrates how film noir style influenced and transformed many different genres and how it developed and evolved in responding to technological advances. Brooding noir musicals such as *A Star Is Born* illustrate how noir is a style and not a single genre. Director George Cukor's 1954 version of *A Star Is Born* is specifically significant in terms of its important original contribution to color noir visual style. In fact, in *A Star Is Born*, filmmakers adapted to and adopted new technologies when the color noir picture was being filmed. The Hollywood film industry was changing during the 1950s, and these changes affected noir visual style in color and in black-and-white films (as discussed earlier in this chapter). *A Star Is Born* reveals the influence of noir visual style on color noir and noir musicals. For example, color noir films such as *A Star Is Born* adopt techniques of noir style in their visual aesthetic to convey the kinds of downbeat themes that Silver, Ward, and Schrader identified with noir style. *A Star Is Born* is also a very important film in terms of shifting to new CinemaScope widescreen color technology and the dye transfer process as well as a significant example of color noir style. It is important to understand the distinction and difference between conceiving of a picture as a film noir versus considering the evolution of noir as a style influencing color films, often drawn from adapting and reimagining earlier film noir techniques in new and different ways, as we see in color noir films (and later neo-noir and digital streaming noir productions).

A Star Is Born actually began filming in three-strip Technicolor but switched to single-strip monopack Eastmancolor with CinemaScope to attain an equally stunning, anamorphic, widescreen color noir look.[95] A brooding musical drama, *A Star Is Born* gave Judy Garland a comeback role as jazz singer Esther Blodgett, who gains fame as Hollywood star Vicki Lester. She is swept into a doomed romance with self-destructive, alcoholic, aging star-mentor, Norman Maine (James Mason), who discovers her, watches her rise to fame, and eventually commits suicide after losing his career. *A Star Is Born* was an adaptation of two nonmusical dramas, Cukor's *What Price Hollywood?* (1932) and William Wellman's color remake *A Star Is Born* (1937), both produced by David O. Selznick. Cukor's 1954 version of *A Star Is Born* presented a dark, disturbing vision for a musical—portraying Hollywood fame as rife with addiction, self-loathing, egomania, and suicide.[96]

A Star Is Born captures the obsession, alienation, toxic corruption, misleading appearances, and duplicity of film noir. Its unvarnished, deglamorized portrayal of stardom in a harsh backstage world of empty dreams was evocative of *Sunset Boulevard*. *A Star Is Born* emulates film noir visual style in color while embracing its brooding thematic tone. Chiaroscuro high contrast, splintering lines, and deep shadows are used throughout the film, infusing geometric patterns of light and bars of darkness to symbolize entrapment. When Maine is in a sanitarium, sharp diagonal shards of light cut through and splinter his image on a black shadowed staircase, piercing compositional space like the chain mesh glass on the windows imprisoning him. Jail bars loom in the background as the couple are married, suggesting their doomed fate. Reflective surfaces, mirrors, and water expose the duality and false façade of the noir milieu they inhabit. Extreme camera angles and a magnifying mirror distort Esther's image as cosmeticians make her over and destroy her natural beauty; Cukor uses a wide lens and extremely low angles as they tower over her to show her vulnerable subjective point of view. Warped reflections cubistically slice Esther's image, taking it apart, dissecting it like an insect—a visual comment on how the studio destroys people in remaking them into stars. Backstage, Maine punches caustic press agent Libby (Jack Carson), shoving him into a mirror that shatters, thus revealing their loathing and duplicitous rapport cloaked under a thin veneer.

A Star Is Born is stylistically and thematically evocative of film noir with its destructive violence, suicide, fighting, gambling, obsession, addiction, and psychological instability in bleak shadowy settings: jail rooms, sanitariums, funerals, the Downbeat bar after hours, and dark claustrophobic interiors. Alain Silver notes the noir antihero's "loss of self-control," "undercurrent of social alienation," and inability to "distinguish between benign and malign" moving through a "complex noir underworld."[97] Paul Schrader describes 1950s films noir typified by the noir protagonist's "psychotic action and suicidal impulse" and psychological battle with "forces of disintegration." Maine expresses these themes as well: his isolation, alienation, obsession with drinking, psychological deterioration, and instability land him in a sanitarium, a fate reminiscent of Milland in *The Lost Weekend*.[98]

Cukor's design and color composition throughout *A Star Is Born* emphasizes high-contrast expressionist hues, emulating black-and-white noir—usually with black, deep indigo, white, and gray. Typical of color noir style, however, the color red stands out juxtaposed against shadows and muted tones, as it does in *The Red Shoes*. Red walls are the backdrop of the dark bar as Esther sings "The

2.10 Color noir shot from *A Star Is Born* as Esther Blodgett (Judy Garland) sings "The Man That Got Away," in a dark bar with red walls. Her indigo wardrobe disappears in blackened chiaroscuro shadows in the foreground. Warner Bros., 1954

Man That Got Away," contrasting with her dark indigo wardrobe, which disappears into the blackened chiaroscuro shadows in the foreground. Red highlights the Downbeat club's midnight "Bleu" neon sign, lighting, stage curtains, as well as Esther's scarlet dresses, her lipstick, and the satin robe she wears as she sings "It's a New World" in a dark cramped hotel room (resembling a lonely Edward Hopper painting) after she marries Norman Maine. Red carnations adorn black-and-white tuxedos as Esther sings "Gotta Have Me Go with You." Bright red lights illuminate the walls backstage as Cukor's Degas-like ballet dancers shriek and scream when Maine violently attacks them. Spectators wear black, white, and red and hold crimson programs. Red becomes a color variation on noir to connote danger (as in a cautionary stop sign), passion, violence, and bloodshed. However, red also suggests vitality. Images without red are desolate and void of joy, vibrancy, or passion. Maine is cloaked in darkness in his murky unlit bedroom as he contemplates suicide. After his death, Vicki looks pallid in a shadowy sitting room, her wardrobe a decaying shade of brown, her eye makeup smeared from crying (like Vicky Page in *The Red Shoes*), and her lips pale (rather than red). Even the carpet is a queasy burnt orange.

A Star Is Born explored the dark side of Hollywood, and its production revealed the uncertainty surrounding the adoption of new technologies as the industry tried different formats in its quest to outshine television with big-budget color musical spectacles. Jack Warner initially wanted to film *A Star Is Born* in 3D and also considered filming using the new WarnerScope anamorphic widescreen process with WarnerColor film. Not satisfied with the subpar results of the new technologies, the studio decided *A Star Is Born* was "too intimate for WarnerScope" and instead began shooting in three-strip Technicolor. But after eight days of filming, Warner Bros.—impressed with the huge success of Twentieth Century-Fox's new anamorphic CinemaScope widescreen process

2.11 Norman Maine's (James Mason) face is covered in silhouette shadow as he looks at the ocean in twilight and then commits suicide in *A Star Is Born*. Warner Bros., 1954

used in *The Robe*—shot test footage and chose to switch to CinemaScope with multitrack stereophonic sound. Thus, they threw out the $300,000 worth of three-strip Technicolor footage already shot. *A Star Is Born* was the first CinemaScope picture for Warner Bros. and only the third film shot in Hollywood using the new anamorphic process. It was shot in single-strip WarnerColor—Warner's version of Kodak Eastmancolor monopack—and developed using the new Technicolor dye-transfer process, then promoted as being filmed in "Technicolor."[99] In October 1953, Fox expert Milton Krasner made test shots of Garland's "The Man That Got Away" jazz club musical number in CinemaScope and helped the transition from three-strip Technicolor. Photographer Sam Leavitt, who shot the documentary-style noirs *The Thief* and *Tension* (1949) as well as Vincent Minnelli's Technicolor musical *The Pirate* (1948), and who was familiar with the new Eastman monopack color process, replaced three-strip Technicolor camera operator Winton Hoch.[100]

Al Harrell of *American Cinematographer* later recognized *A Star Is Born*'s "controlled, darkly picturesque style, 'the musical noir' style," and its "dark color scheme" that "gives the movie a weight and resonance that is very atypical of movie musicals."[101] Cukor was so insistent on creating a shadowy visual style for the film that he had a Technicolor cinematographer fired for not lighting the set dark enough. Cukor wanted "low light levels, the impressionistic feeling of the musical instruments, Garland moving in and out of pools of light with the camera following," as in shadowy black-and-white film noir. As Ronald Haver observes, "Instead of using lots and lots of color, which was the thing you were supposed to do in those days, they kept subtracting color. So the primary color scheme is very natural, subdued pastels . . . no blatant anything. It's all very, very dark, even the daylight scenes."[102] In fact, the limitations of Eastman Kodak's less expensive monopack single-strip color process actually aided the film's color noir visual style. As Haver explains, "The wide range and delicacy of color available with the sophisticated Technicolor three-strip method" was "replaced by the more primitive and garish effects of single-strip WarnerColor, with its much more restricted palette."[103]

In creating a color noir aesthetic, filmmakers had to respond creatively to the drawbacks of using the new single-strip Eastmancolor monopack film technology. Cukor and the film's designers developed new cinematic techniques in response to Eastmancolor's limitations, which influenced the visual appearance of *A Star Is Born* and, as a result, evoked the look of a black-and-white film in color. Art director Gene Allen described the challenges in adapting to the new Kodak Eastmancolor film technology, for instance, "You didn't have the separation of colors we were used to. We didn't have the grays and the interesting rich blacks and darks" with Eastmancolor that Technicolor had. "We really had to control what we did and be very careful," Allen explained. "It was a moody picture at times, and director George Cukor wanted to play it for mood" to emphasize the story's blue tones and dark themes. So Cukor, Allen, and designer George Hoyningen-Huene (who worked on Huston's Technicolor noir musical melodrama *Moulin Rouge*) started "eliminating color; *we damned near did a black-and-white picture*," Allen recalled, "except for little accents of color . . . all controlled and related and in good taste."[104]

Cukor, Allen, Huene, and Leavitt establish a bleak noir milieu as beams of stark white light crisscross a black nighttime Hollywood skyline, searchlights explode, and drunken Maine shatters mirrors and violently assaults screaming performers backstage. Haver, who was instrumental in painstakingly restoring *A Star Is Born*, recalled, "Cukor was a great student of art. He got his ideas for composition, especially for lighting, from his study of paintings. Gene Allen and George Hoyningen-Huene backed him up on it."[105] Cukor experimented with color, light, shadow, CinemaScope widescreen, and the new technology. Rather than fill the entire widescreen CinemaScope space of the frame with action in each shot, when deciding how to compose images for the film, Cukor and Allen sought to "leave parts of the screen in darkness or to only use a section of the screen. The technique of isolating sections of the screen is used throughout the picture"—as in Garland's powerful blues number "The Man That Got Away" performed in the darkness of an after-hours nightspot. He effectively musicalizes film noir in color by surrounding Esther's performance of "The Man That Got Away" with deep shadows, silhouettes, and red walls behind the bar. It was shot in one fluidly moving long take to visually capture Garland's powerful vocal rendition of Harold Arlen and Ira Gershwin's bluesy jazz number. Allen recalled, "Cukor believed in trying to shoot musical numbers as if they were one shot. We had great camera movements."[106] The scene is filmed to emulate Maine's subjective point of view, visually evoking film noir as he surreptitiously watches her behind empty tables in the back of the darkened jazz club.

A Star Is Born was filmed from October 1953 through February 1954, with additional retakes and shooting continuing through late July 1954. It was produced by Garland's husband Sid Luft's independent company Transcona Enterprises in a partnership with Warner Bros. "The Man That Got Away" was reshot in February 1954 with different colors (black and navy blue instead of brown), a new costume for Garland—designed by Jean Louis, who did Rita Hayworth's gowns in the film noir *Gilda* (1946)—making her wardrobe more flattering for the anamorphic widescreen CinemaScope format and WarnerColor process. Garland had silk flesh-colored stockings, the same ones Shearer wore in *The Red Shoes*, flown in from Paris. The film's cost rose to $5,020,000—one of Hollywood's most expensive film productions of all time by 1954.[107]

Critics loved the film. *Variety* praised the original 182-minute cut of *A Star Is Born* for its "filmusical transmutation," which surpassed earlier versions. "Judy Garland glitters with that stardust," which "wastrel star James Mason recognizes ... From the opening drunken debacle at the Shrine benefit to the scandalous antics of a hopeless dipsomaniac when his wife (Garland) wins the Academy Award, there is an intense pattern of real-life mirrorings."[108] As Bosley Crowther of the *New York Times* raved, the "sense of an artificial milieu wraps the whole thing, as in cellophane—all in colors that fill the eye with excitement. It is something to see, this *Star Is Born*." He applauded its spectacle, the Arlen/Gershwin music, especially "The Man That Got Away," a "fine, haunting torch-song." Critics also praised the film's "splendid color on the smartly used CinemaScope screen" as the "finest thing in the show. And a show it is, first and foremost" with lush grand surroundings and poignant performances that "make the heart flutter and bleed." Crowther called it a "brilliantly visualized ... tragic little try at love in an environment that packages the product."[109]

Warner Bros. had the option to cut the picture, however, if costs exceeded $1.5 million. The film was butchered when the studio cut the film to a 154-minute version to enable more screenings per day. Cukor and Garland—and the viewing public—were unhappy about the cuts. Angry filmgoers wrote letters to the studio complaining that they were outraged to be charged expensive roadshow ticket prices for a much shorter film, which they felt had been "butchered," and wanted to see the original version. The cut footage was removed from the picture and unfortunately much of it was destroyed or lost. Cukor was not involved in postproduction or in shooting later musical numbers that were incongruous with the darker, brooding dramatic sequences he had shot.[110] (The film was partially restored in 1983 to 176 minutes.) Despite the cuts, *A Star Is Born* was nominated for Academy Awards for Best Actress, Best Actor, Best Color Costume Design, Best Color Art Direction, Best Song ("The Man That Got Away"), and Best Scoring of a Musical Picture (musical director Ray Heindorf). *A Star Is Born* earned $4,634,000 domestically and $2,176,000 internationally, for a total of $6,810,000—a success, although it barely recouped its huge cost.[111]

Hitchcock's Color Noir Style

Another creative force behind the burgeoning color noir style was Alfred Hitchcock. His earlier gothic and suspense thrillers were steeped in noir visual style, although his murder mysteries and psychological thrillers were quite distinct from more conventional, hard-boiled film noir pictures. Of Hitchcock's noir-style body of work, his black-and-white *roman noir* female gothic thrillers *Rebecca* (1940), *Suspicion* (1941), and *Shadow of a Doubt* (1943) were influential preludes to film noir, albeit not quite as dark in visual style. Hitchcock's darkest black-and-white films were his brooding mid-1940s gothics *Spellbound* (1945) and *Notorious* (1946) (discussed in chapter 1). Both were shot on Hollywood soundstages and studio back lots in expressionistic noir visual style.

In the 1950s, Hitchcock reimagined film noir in a succession of extraordinary color noirs, most notably *Rear Window* (1954) and *North by Northwest* (1959). *Rear Window* was a murder mystery based on a 1942 short story *It Had to Be Murder* by hard-boiled noir writer Cornell Woolrich (using the pseudonym William Irish) and adapted by John Michael Hayes. *Rear Window* was shot to emulate the voyeuristic subjective point of view of temporarily disabled photographer and war veteran, the tormented antihero L. B. ("Jeff") Jefferies (James Stewart), who watches sex, romance, violence, and perhaps a murder from his New York Greenwich Village apartment window—he is confined to a wheelchair, his broken leg in a cast. Gazing across the courtyard with binoculars and a telephoto lens, Jeffries suspects and eventually solves a vicious murder committed on a dark rainy night.

Rather than shoot on location in New York's Greenwich Village, as originally planned, producer-director Hitchcock instead had a huge set built at Paramount studio. He chose to film on enclosed studio soundstages after he was unsatisfied with preliminary lighting and color tests shot on location by his cinematographer Robert Burks.[112] Like Cukor's deliberate color noir approach to *A Star Is Born*, Hitchcock was able to have full control over the set, lighting, shadow, color, visual design, composition, and cinematography for *Rear Window* by filming on enclosed Paramount soundstages. This is key in tracking the evolution of noir as Hitchcock and other filmmakers begin to move back into the studio after gravitating toward location shooting. Hitchcock (and Hayes)

2.12 Black shadows and late-night rain cover Alfred Hitchcock's huge soundstage set as murderer Lars Thorwald (Raymond Burr) dispenses of his wife's body after killing her in *Rear Window*. Paramount, 1954

also enhanced *Rear Window*'s narrative to add strong working women and a romance to Woolrich's story: creating the role of confident Park Avenue fashion goddess Lisa Fremont for star Grace Kelly (who passed up a lead role in Elia Kazan's *On the Waterfront* [1954] to play the part), and casting Thelma Ritter as hard-boiled, no-nonsense maternal nurse Stella.

As early as 1941, Hitchcock had considered using Technicolor to emulate a black-and-white noir milieu. While filming *Suspicion*, he spoke to Phillip Scheuer of the *Los Angeles Times*, who expounded on "Color by Hitchcock," noting Hitchcock's idea as the cinematic master of suspense to "start out in black and white . . . gradually introduce a yellow London fog, and then spring dripping red blood and other violent manifestations of the spectrum." Hitchcock even considered redoing his silent gothic *The Lodger* in color. "The possibilities are endless," he mused. Hitchcock was envisioning a color noir tableau simulating black and white with muted tones and a splash of red already in the early 1940s. In the interview with Scheuer, he painted a picture of a masculine scene permeated with misogynistic gender distress as businessmen are threatened by an independent working woman: "A board room in Wall St.—late afternoon. Shadows on gray walls. Directors' table and chairs of dark mahogany. The men in business suits of gray—light and dark grays. A girl enters. She is wearing a gray tailored suit and a RED hat. It is the only bright color in the room. The message it telegraphs instantly to the audience is: OBTRUSIVE FEMININE INFLUENCE. They can FEEL it."[113]

Like androgynous 1940s wartime noir women, Hitchcock tailored the "very active" character Lisa Fremont in *Rear Window* to be a strong, radiant, vibrant showcase for Kelly, with stunning dresses designed by Edith Head. (He thought other roles like *Dial M for Murder*, where she is nearly strangled, came off cool and did not do her justice.) Hitchcock called Lisa "a typical, active New York woman. There are many of those in New York, work for *Harper's Bazaar*. They're almost like men, some of these women." As in classic film noir, the dialogue in *Rear Window* crackles with hard-boiled wit and deadpan repartee.[114]

Assistant director Herbert Coleman recalled that Hitchcock always worked closely on the script, albeit uncredited, and insisted: "Hitchcock always discussed the scene with the cameraman first. He would tell them what lens to use and what he wanted to include in the scene." Like the claustrophobic confines of film noir, assistant camera operator Leonard South admitted, "Shooting in Jimmy's [James Stewart] apartment" for *Rear Window* "was very difficult, because it was small. It wasn't big. Hitch never liked to use wide-angle lenses. The lens that Hitch liked to use was a 50 mm. That's about what your eyes see."[115]

A powerful hyphenate producer-director, Hitchcock enjoyed tremendous creative control on *Rear Window*—the first film in a multipicture deal with Paramount in which the film's rights and ownership would eventually revert to

Hitchcock. This heightened creative control provided greater latitude for Hitchcock to experiment with the film's visual style. Adapting to new technologies also played a role in *Rear Window*'s color noir aesthetic. Rather than CinemaScope or three-strip Technicolor, *Rear Window* was shot "flat" in nonanamorphic "cropped" (masked) widescreen with single-strip monopack Kodak Eastmancolor negative film, then developed in a Technicolor lab and framed for exhibition with an aspect ratio of 1.66 to 1. Hitchcock and the art department storyboarded all the shots, fine-tuning the film's visual design, lighting, shadows, and color palette. Filming entirely on soundstages also avoided the unpredictable circumstances and erratic weather conditions of location shooting.[116]

In prepping the film *Rear Window*, Hitchcock dispatched four photographers to film Greenwich Village, shooting apartment buildings in all kinds of lighting and weather from different angles. Back in Hollywood, a crew of fifty spent two months working to construct the $75,000 set on the Paramount lot. The massive apartment building set—ninety-eight feet wide, 185 feet long, and forty feet high—had thirty-one individual apartments (twelve completely furnished) and entirely filled Paramount's soundstage 18. In building the set, the crew had to dig into the basement to create the lower courtyard, which was twenty to thirty feet below stage level, and the top of the apartment building across the courtyard soared five stories into the rafters. Hitchcock filmed *Rear Window* from late November 1953 through mid-January 1954 using thousands of huge arc lamps to light the massive set.[117]

Hitchcock lit the enormous set to emphasize color noir style by having different lighting cast the apartment building in the red amber glow of the "magic hour" of dusk, as the sun sets low, and shrouding it in the murky shadows of darkness and rain for night scenes. Hitchcock meticulously visualized his color noir style on the enclosed soundstage set using a color palette of muted tones and ominous dark colors. Like Cukor's *A Star Is Born*, Hitchcock strategically used—and subtracted—color and light to simulate the look of black-and-white film, with the addition of the color red, to enhance the color noir visual style aesthetic technique for *Rear Window*. Because of the multifaceted enormity of the set, Hitchcock had cinematographer Burks fashion an intricate lighting system for *Rear Window* that lit the interiors with noir shadows and backlit individual apartments, often simultaneously, as the exterior of the faux building structure was meticulously illuminated, and prelit in advance to save time and to simulate four different times of the day—morning, afternoon, twilight, and nighttime—with the flip of a switch.[118]

Scenes in *Rear Window* increasingly take place in dim color noir, first bathed in scarlet twilight hues, then ominous shadowy nighttime. As the mystery deepens, Hitchcock visually simulates the look of black-and-white film noir in color with muted tones and splashes of red. Jeff, his beautiful girlfriend Lisa Fremont, and his neighbors move in and out of the shadows. Lisa appears as

Fade to Gray and Color Noir 99

2.13 A color noir shot of Lisa Fremont (Grace Kelly) in black and L. B. Jeffries (James Stewart) looking through binoculars in *Rear Window*. Paramount, 1954

a silhouette and disappears in the darkness. In fact, Hitchcock filmed twenty-seven takes of the famous slow motion color noir shot of Lisa's introduction mysteriously kissing Jeff as her looming shadow crosses his sleeping visage. She appears shrouded in murky doorways, her face hidden when she enters and leaves, turning the lights on, one at a time, to introduce herself.

Rear Window includes violent misogyny when Lisa surreptitiously climbs into suspected murderer Lars Thorwald's (Raymond Burr) window to search his apartment for evidence, then he unexpectedly returns, attacks her, and seems quite ready to get vicious as she screams for Jeff across the courtyard. As in other color noir films *The Red Shoes, Niagara, The Barefoot Contessa,* and *A Star Is Born*, there are strained, distressed gender relations in *Rear Window* between Jeff and Lisa, who wants to get married. (Stella advises reluctant Jeff to wed gorgeous, "perfectly wonderful" Lisa.) Misogynistic violence is certainly evident in Thorwald knocking off and butchering his wife, trekking back and forth at night with saws and suitcases. Considering the grisly misogynistic crime, Stella ponders, "Just where do you think they cut her up?" about the murder. "I'll bet she's scattered all over town. A leg in the East River."

Murder takes place in the dead of night and in the pouring rain as Hitchcock re-creates an iconic film noir milieu with glistening wet streets, nocturnal bars, and stark streetlights in the background. When Jeffries dozes off in his wheelchair on the night of the murder, thunder rumbles as heavy sheets of rain pour down on the stormy courtyard. The moody, blackened nocturnal ambiance is emphasized by the gleaming drenched pavement of the apartment building as a red neon sign flickers from a café through a narrow alley in the distance. A faint gasping scream is heard for a fleeting second through the dark downpour, then disappears as Jeffries sits half asleep in semiconsciousness. In classic Hitchcock-style noir suspense, the audience witnesses, hears, and is provided more cinematic information than the characters on-screen to create narrative tension.

A dim hint of red is also used when murderer Thorwald, after disposing of his wife, kills the neighbors' dog and the only light is the eerie glow of his cigarette in his unlit apartment. Horrified to discover their dog has been slain, one of the owners cries: "He was the only one in the whole neighborhood who liked anybody." Tenants in different apartments—with distinct lamps, ambient source lighting, and shadows within—step onto their patio balconies and lean out their windows to see what happened. Like the murder of Thorwald's wife, the scene occurs in the wee hours of the night. Blackness covers the entire courtyard. As neighbors across the complex express shock, concern, and dismay, the camera simulates Jeffries's point of view as he keenly observes through his own window that Thorwald is the only person who remains indoors—his presence only visibly revealed by the faint orange ember of his cigarette smoldering in the pitch-black room. Thorwald, in fact, dispensed with the dog—digging in his flowerbed—to cover his crime.

Hitchcock projects Jeffries's voyeuristic subjective point of view looking out his window through a viewfinder, binoculars, and a telephoto lens. Burks and the crew developed innovative new camera lenses to emulate Jeffries's point-of-view shots from his apartment, including a ten-inch lens to simulate the view of a telephoto lens on a still camera. Actors in neighboring apartments were given cues with short-wave radios and hidden microphones in flesh-colored headpieces through which Hitchcock delivered instructions. The final, brutal montage climaxes in a violent struggle in Jeffries's pitch-black room. The chaotic action takes place as the screen is entirely cloaked in blackness, heightened by intermittent flashes of red in the dark—as Jeffries uses flashbulbs on his camera to blind his assailant while Thorwald attacks him. In the climactic tussle, Jeffries is thrust out of his rear window and falls to the pavement below, breaking his other leg, as Thorwald is apprehended. Franz Waxman's score plays the song "Lisa" as the film ends.

Rear Window was released in September 1954. Shot for $1 million, it was a huge critical and box office success, grossing $10 million by May 1956, and earning four Academy Award nominations for Best Director (an award Hitchcock never won), Color Cinematography, Sound, and Screenplay.[119] William Brogdon of *Variety* wrote: "Hitchcock combines technical and artistic skills in a manner that makes this an unusually good piece of murder mystery entertainment . . . delivering tense melodrama," noting its Cornell Woolrich story, and praised the "Technicolor camera work by Robert Burks and the apartment-courtyard setting."[120] *Rear Window* rechanneled film noir and Woolrich's 1942 hard-boiled fiction into vibrant, widescreen, color noir visual style. Hitchcock had vividly realized color noir style by designing and filming a huge set on a studio soundstage for *Rear Window*. Even trailers promoting the film featured behind-the-scenes silhouette shadows emphasizing mysterious, low-key noir style in color.

Hitchcock's next major color noir, *North by Northwest*, infused its dangerous, murderous web of espionage with duplicitous intrigue and potentially deadly romantic affairs in a toxic chilling Cold War milieu in 1959. The visual style of *North by Northwest* was darker than his film *Vertigo* (1958, shot on location), and harkened back to his earlier gothic noir films and the color noir shadows of *Rear Window*, albeit slightly lighter in look due to location filming in sunlight. Hitchcock once again emulated noir crime films using color noir imagery in *North by Northwest*—to reenvision black-and-white gothic-espionage films noir, such as his earlier *Notorious*, in widescreen VistaVision color. Ads promoting *North by Northwest* emphasized a stark color noir aesthetic in black, white, and scarlet red. *North by Northwest* was Hitchcock's first and only film for MGM. Hitchcock and screenwriter Ernest Lehman (who penned 1957 noir *Sweet Smell of Success* and *West Side Story*) worked on the script for *North by Northwest* (credited to Lehman, the only original screenplay for a Hitchcock film to date), which revolved around treachery, abduction, lethal crimes, a tormented antihero who is framed and nearly killed, and murder at the United Nations, and culminated in a climactic deadly chase on Mount Rushmore.[121]

2.14 Deep shadows in a color noir image of Eve Kendall (Eva Marie Saint) in a scarlet dress from Roger Thornhill's (Cary Grant) point of view lurking outside the dark cliff house set for *North by Northwest*. MGM, 1959

Hitchcock initially considered star James Stewart, but (perhaps after the failure of *Vertigo*) cast Cary Grant. Hitchcock had worked with Grant on gothic noir films *Suspicion* and *Notorious*, as well as *To Catch a Thief* (1955).[122] In *North by Northwest*, Grant played imperiled advertising executive–turned–wrong man fugitive Roger Thornhill—forcibly abducted, framed for murder, barely escaping death and presumed to be a covert spy—who becomes embroiled in a deadly crime world of duplicity, assassination, false appearances, and international espionage intrigue. Hitchcock cast Eva Marie Saint as Eve Kendall, the "Hitchcock blonde," an undercover spy who initially resembles a noir femme fatale, seducing and betraying the framed antihero as a double-agent, until they are almost assassinated by her lover, enemy agent Jeffery Vandamm (James Mason) and his menacing partner Leonard (Martin Landau).[123] *North by Northwest* was shot in widescreen VistaVision with Eastmancolor, then developed by (and promoted as) Technicolor. Hitchcock used a desaturated color palate of muted tones for *North by Northwest* to simulate the look of a black-and-white film and to achieve a color noir visual style. Even the opening scene, shot in broad daylight on the streets of Manhattan, features drab grays in wardrobe, asphalt, and buildings emulating monochrome. Hitchcock also created massive realistic Hollywood soundstage sets for *North by Northwest* to replicate locations where filming could not take place, which further aided color noir style.[124]

Due to filming restrictions, most shots on and around Mount Rushmore and Vandamm's modern cliff house were shot at MGM on immense studio soundstage sets.[125] As in *Rear Window*, these were re-created with meticulous

2.15 Shadowy shades of indigo color a noir image of Hitchcock's murky soundstage set of late-night Mount Rushmore as a site of a murder scene in *North by Northwest*. MGM, 1959

accuracy, utilizing matte paintings and visual effects. Filming these sequences for *North by Northwest* on studio soundstage sets afforded Hitchcock more latitude and creative control regarding lighting, shadow, and color in filming. Tense dark night scenes of mysterious danger filmed on the set include shadowy interior scenes in a cramped darkened train cabin as Kendall seduces Thornhill and betrays him; and Thornhill climbing precariously up to Vandamm's angular cliff house in the dead of night, hiding in the shadows, and fleeing with Kendall while agents pursue them across the Rushmore monument. Other nocturnal exterior images include shots of an unlit road late at night that becomes a creepy abyss engulfing cars in shadow—after enemy agents kidnap, forcibly intoxicate, and try to kill Thornhill by driving his car off a cliff—and a police car driving on the nocturnal streets of Chicago.[126] All these scenes enhanced the film's color noir visual style. By creatively and strategically utilizing color, lighting, shadow, and set design and employing new technology using Paramount's VistaVision wide-frame system, *North by Northwest* emulated a color variation on film noir. Hitchcock combined a restrained color palette of muted gray and brown and deep indigo tones to simulate black and white (plus splashes of scarlet, burnt orange, and bright red, as in Kendall's stunning red-and-black dress with a plunging backline). In augmenting his VistaVision location filming in *North by Northwest* with massive studio sets, Hitchcock actually benefitted from shooting constraints in reproducing restricted locations he was unable to film, which ultimately aided and enhanced color noir visual style in the film.

2.16 Eve Kendall hangs perilously from the blackened shadowed cliffs of Mount Rushmore in a color noir shot of Hitchcock's nighttime set in *North by Northwest*. MGM, 1959

Hitchcock was inspired by black-and-white film noir style in *North by Northwest*, in this case using widescreen VistaVision to achieve a deft variation on color noir visual design. Hitchcock reenvisioned well-known noir iconography in color and shadowy black-and-white chiaroscuro conventions in a new light for *North by Northwest* as framed antihero Roger Thornhill navigates obstacles and is nearly killed in a waking nightmare. Another scene in *North by Northwest* occurs in the bright sunshine of a rural highway and a farm field, where a crop duster ambushes Thornhill.[127] Shot on location in Wasco, California, which stood in for Indiana (with inserted shots of Grant re-created at the studio), Hitchcock's crop duster scene reimagines film noir in a different context.[128] Hitchcock argued that the crop duster scene in *North by Northwest* reconceived familiar elements of noir style that had been codified in the postwar era and were immediately recognizable, expected, and conventional to filmmakers and audiences by 1959 (which coincided with the end of the black-and-white noir cycle). He compares *North by Northwest* to the archetypal noir crime milieu: shadows, rain-slicked city streets, dark alleys, swirling fog, steam rising from the gutter, streetlights, murky silhouettes, mysterious characters in trench coats, fedoras, cigarette smoke, black sedans screeching out of the darkness, and gunfire. Hitchcock explained in a 1965 interview for the French documentary *Hitchcock s'Explique*, "Now, in every ordinary [noir] film, what is the setting?" Hitchcock described the ominous atmospheric setting of a film noir in vivid detail as an example of what audiences would typically expect from an attempted murder scene in a crime film with a dangerous milieu in a nocturnal metropolis. "The setting is night. The corner of a street in the city. The ground . . . has cobbles washed with water by rain. [The protagonist] stands under the street light." Then a criminal enemy drives by and fires a staccato machinegun. "That is the cliché." In conceiving of the crop duster sequence, Hitchcock noted that he was intentionally straying from these conventions. "I say 'No. Cannot do it that way.' It must be done fresh and new. Therefore, I will do the same scene with nothing. No darkness. No lamp. Nothing at all. All sunlight. Everything."[129] Hitchcock wanted to rework cinematic clichés in the crop duster sequence, creating something unexpected and "out of the ordinary," situating a crime film murder scene in broad daylight in a cornfield, shifting the typical setting from an iconic noir urban jungle to an unlikely but deadly rural locale, updating the bleak remote moors of gothic noir thrillers. Hitchcock called his suspense thrillers "very real," visualizations of a "nightmare," evocative of film noir.[130] Yet he updated conventional noir technique—perhaps feeling that the noir look had run its course—countering the more strategic color noir style he sought and achieved on soundstages with *Rear Window*.[131]

North by Northwest was shot for $4.3 million and earned $9.8 million, a huge success for Hitchcock at the end of the 1950s.[132] Hitchcock drew on his extensive cinematic experience in directing crime, espionage, gothic thrillers, and noir

2.17 A color noir image of a taxicab against a dark nocturnal urban skyline in *North by Northwest*. MGM, 1959

pictures—cinematically conveying subjective prisms of psychological anguish on screen, as in earlier noir films *Suspicion*, *Spellbound*, and *Notorious*. Thus, he intentionally invoked recognizable conventions of film noir in color noir films such as *Rear Window*, but he adopted emergent VistaVision technology with a brighter look shooting on location in color espionage noir *North by Northwest*, adapting its widescreen chromatic visual design to a slightly lighter aesthetic style by the late 1950s.

Chromatic Hues: *West Side Story*

The Red Shoes, *Niagara*, *Rear Window*, *A Star Is Born*, and *The Barefoot Contessa* indicated that color noir visual style had crystallized by 1954, but Hollywood was already adapting to new technology and a lighter, high-key color aesthetic a year later with films like *Oklahoma!*, *Rebel Without a Cause*, *To Catch a Thief*, *Pete Kelly's Blues* (1955), and *Love Me or Leave Me*, as well as the lavish operatic musical adaptation of James M. Cain's *Serenade* (produced in 1955, released in 1956), as *West Side Story* was being prepared for the Broadway stage.[133] And, as we have seen, by the mid- to late 1950s, Hollywood's shift from black-and-white to color film and widescreen technologies now filming outdoors in sunlit locations—along with the industry's move to acetate safety stock (from nitrate) and single-strip Eastmancolor (from three-strip Technicolor), and the influence of bright, high-key, "flat," low-contrast lighting for television—contributed to the decline of noir visual style. Thus, for the most part, Hollywood films from the later 1950s embraced this much brighter, high-key visual style, in both color and black-and-white films as the film industry sought to outshine television. Given the success of television, particularly in the postwar period, as studios grappled with dwindling theatrical attendance and lower box office returns in the post-antitrust era following the Paramount decision, *Variety* observed in 1956:

> There were two ways movies could outflank television: (1) do what television could not do in the matter of spectacle (form) or (2) do what television could not do in the matter of controversial images or narrative (content). In short, "make 'em big or make 'em provocative." During a decade notorious for conservatism and conformity, the motion picture industry, with a vigor born of desperation, became more technically innovative, economically adventuresome, and aesthetically daring than at any time in its history.[134]

West Side Story (1957 on stage, 1961 on screen) grew out of earlier juvenile delinquency film trends that had merged with film noir and social-realist message pictures.[135] Some 1950s widescreen color films would have been made in the more iconic, shadowy noir visual style if they were produced as originally intended. Several postwar color pictures were first slated to be chiaroscuro-style, black-and-white 1940s films noir shot during or just after World War II. These included juvenile delinquent drama *Rebel Without a Cause* and *Serenade*.[136]

A few years later, technology was effectively employed to capture a visually darker color noir style in *West Side Story*. Director-choreographer Jerome Robbins first conceived of what eventually became the stage version of *West Side Story* in 1949. Robbins sought to collaborate with Leonard Bernstein and Arthur Laurents on a tragic modern musical based on Shakespeare's *Romeo and Juliet*, updated to tackle serious issues about ethnic Jewish versus Catholic conflicts, originally called *East Side Story*. Bernstein had scored Elia Kazan's topical social-realist film *On the Waterfront* and was set to compose a Broadway musical stage version of Cain's *Serenade* (to be adapted by Arthur Laurents) in June 1955. Bernstein decided instead to collaborate with Laurents and Robbins on the dark musical tragedy stage production of what would become *West Side Story*: a Broadway play about a contemporary juvenile delinquent couple against the backdrop of civil rights tensions inspired by Chicano gang wars in Los Angeles. They then changed the setting to New York City and the rivalry to Puerto Rican gangs. As East Side tenements were demolished and gang activity moved west, the project became dark Broadway stage musical *West Side Story*, which electrified the American stage in 1957 and the cinematic screen in 1961.

Harold Mirisch paid $350,000 for the screen rights to the 1957 Broadway stage play version of *West Side Story*.[137] "Everyone told us . . . it was suicidal," composer Bernstein noted. "I don't know how many people begged me not to waste my time on something that could not possibly succeed. After all, how could we do a musical where there are two bodies lying on the stage at the end of the first act and everybody eventually dies . . . a show that's so filled with hatefulness and ugliness" and "not even a whisper about a happy ending was heard."[138] It would become one of the great musicals on the stage and a vibrant color noir on the expanded Hollywood screen.

Producer-director Robert Wise was a noir thriller director and proponent of hard-hitting realism; it was his first musical film, and he infused it with color noir style. *West Side Story* used noir cinematic conventions of low-key, high contrast, chiaroscuro lighting (versus bright, thematically upbeat, "flat," high-key musicals), as well as extreme camera angles, especially in the opening shot—a straight down aerial view of an oppressively gray New York City skyline to constrict rather than expand space. Wise's soundtrack uses silence and the ambient traffic sounds in lieu of a symphonic score—more like noir, gangster, and urban crime films than the musical.

West Side Story presented a darker color noir variation on widescreen spectacle trends growing out of the postwar era in its employment of new technology on screen. Color noir aesthetic was impressively reimagined and adapted to large-frame 70mm film technology with a stunning, brooding, chromatic visual style in *West Side Story*, reimagining noir imagery in color. In an effort to compete with television and heighten big screen cinematic spectacle, Hollywood employed an array of emergent new technologies, such as shooting with expanded systems beyond standard 35mm film gauge, moving to large-frame 70mm formats like Todd-AO (used for Zinnemann's musical *Oklahoma!*) in 1955, Panavision in 1956, and Super Panavision 70 introduced in 1959 and used by Robert Wise in *West Side Story*.[139]

West Side Story achieved a gorgeous color noir visual style, shot in Super Panavision 70mm format by Daniel Fapp.[140] It was filmed from early August 1960 through early February 1961 on location in New York City and at Samuel Goldwyn Studios in Hollywood with single-strip Eastmancolor and developed by Technicolor. *West Side Story* featured a gritty visual tableau of dark imagery, muted tones, deep shadows, stark contrast, brooding mise-en-scène, splashes of red (e.g., blood and flashing scarlet lights as sounds of police sirens wail), shrouded concrete freeway underpasses, crisscrossing chain-link fences, enclosed spaces of entrapment, and sites of danger. Violent gangs spar, rumble, and kill—and dead bodies sprawl across late-night streets in an urban jungle. It conveyed an oppressive environment with low-lit cavernous interiors and nocturnal settings, shadowy bedrooms, murky basements, rooftops, and a claustrophobic candy store after hours.

In fact, Robert Burks's color noir cinematography in *Rear Window* inspired cinematographer Daniel Fapp, who won an Academy Award for *West Side Story*, which director Robert Wise described as a "noir musical" with its nocturnal, New York, urban jungle setting that, after opening on location in Manhattan, "could be done [shot] in the studio. Because at night you see what you want to see. You see what you light."[141] The fact that most of *West Side Story* was shot in enclosed Hollywood studios where Wise (like Hitchcock on *Rear Window*) could more readily control lighting, shadow, and color filming with new technologies enhanced the film's color noir visual style.

Fusing the dark shadowy style of film noir with social realism, Wise integrated location shooting of musical dance numbers on the streets of New York with enclosed studio photography on a Hollywood soundstage. "The picture had to open in New York City . . . in its milieu," Wise explained. "Once you got through the rumble at the beginning, the whole antagonism of the two gangs ending up in a fight, the rest of the story onstage and in the film is told at sunset and at night. There was no more daytime stuff in it. The studio wanted me to shoot the entire thing on a soundstage, and you couldn't do it. I finally convinced them that if I could do the whole daytime opening in New York, all the rest could be done in the studio."[142] The milieu is increasingly dark and stylized, and includes flashing neon and reflective surfaces. Chain-link fences repeatedly slice the foreground to represent the fragmentation and splintering apart of romance, the gangs, and their youth. The film's color noir visual style undermines the possibility of a conventional musical happy ending. *West Side Story* shatters utopian innocence as well as classical musical mythology at a time when the studio system, classical musicals, film noir, and more conventional gangster films were in decline. *West Side Story* presented an unlikely

2.18 A color noir shot of young hoodlums in a gang called the Jets dancing to the song "Cool" in a shady parking garage in *West Side Story*. Mirisch/Seven Arts/Beta/United Artists, 1961

convergence of escapist musical style and subversive cynicism inspired by social-realist film noir and crime films. In this early postclassical era, it foreshadowed the inbred dialectical violence that escalated in the United States in the 1960s.

Wise described *West Side Story* as "set in a real background, not a never-never land; a tough side of New York City requiring a good, strong color scheme to accommodate darker areas of the film realistically, but not too flamboyant except in the gym with the red walls," where rival gangs spar on the dance floor. "We tended to use low-key colors." Wise's experience working on earlier noir films enhanced his color noir style on *West Side Story*.[143] Wise collaborated with special effects wizard Linwood Dunn—who developed the optical printer during World War II, won an Academy Award for his technical achievement, and did noir optical effects for *Citizen Kane* (1941) and *Out of the Past*—to create color noir style effects on *West Side Story*.

West Side Story also tackled dark themes and serious social issues, with its Latin jazz-inflected music score and its dynamic athletic dance sequences kinetically conveying death, violence, murder, rape, and emotional turmoil. Lyricist Stephen Sondheim penned caustic lyrics, as gangster antiheroes sang: "Our mothers all are junkies, our fathers all are drunks . . . we're punks; we never had the love . . . every child oughta get. / My parents treat me rough. With all their marijuana, they won't give me a puff. They didn't wanna have me, but somehow I was had . . . that's why I'm so bad." In "Officer Krupke," the lyrics "My father is a bastard, my ma's an S.O.B. My grandpa's always plastered," were censored and changed to "My Daddy beats my Mommy, my Mommy clobbers me. My Grandpa is a Commie." Sondheim's harsh lyrics focus on social issues featured in crime dramas: alcoholism, drug abuse, homosexuality, psychological instability, domestic abuse, and the collapse of the American family with dysfunctional or nonexistent relations, misogynistic gender polemics, and misogynistic sexuality.

The lavish 70mm production had an estimated final cost of $7 million.[144] *West Side Story* was critically acclaimed. It was compared favorably to *On the Waterfront*, for which Bernstein had written the score. Critics called the film a "musical advance" with "drama, dance, and music," a "sparkling" and "moving" "cinematic masterpiece" as well as a "starkly realistic crime film." The *New York Times* described *West Side Story* like a tough noir crime film, writing: "Always there is the palpable frame of a concrete and crushing reality enclosing the action on the screen . . . kids kill one another in a violent rumble" of "mutual hatreds and distrust" of "ethnic groups," and noted its "ironic and tragic" ending, a "piercing and haunting demonstration of social folly and human waste." "[The] juvenile gang feud could not be classed as a musical comedy. It was much too violent and poignant." The color noir musical was called "essentially tragic in mood," with a "gang of tough kids [lounging] in a playground like young panthers in a wire-fenced cage." The *Times* also observed that *West Side Story* makes a "conspicuous advancement of sophistication through the musical film and opens the door to wider expression of more serious and mature themes in this genre."[145]

The color noir style of *West Side Story* was tremendously successful, earning $19.5 million and winning ten Academy Awards, including Best Picture. Fapp's Academy Award–winning cinematography in *West Side Story*, as well as the 1957 stage version, also inspired Janusz Kaminski's atmospheric photography in Steven Spielberg's neo-noir 2021 remake of the film. The motion picture industry's postwar embrace of color film technology revealed filmmakers' and technicians' ability to adapt noir to changing industry conditions as they adopted color noir visual style and created films such as *The Red Shoes, Niagara, A Star Is Born, The Barefoot Contessa, Rear Window, North by Northwest,* and *West Side Story*. The noir impulse continued to evolve, and the legacy and vitality of noir and color noir would be reimagined in neo-noir films in ensuing decades, from *Bonnie and Clyde* (1967) and *The Godfather* (1972) to *Dark City* (1998), and *Bridge of Spies* (2015).[146]

CHAPTER 3

NEO-NOIR

The Legacy of Noir Visual Style

As we have seen, in the evolution of a lighter, grayer acetate look in the 1950s and widescreen color noir in Hollywood's conversion to new technologies, classic film noir ebbed after the chiaroscuro style's zenith in the nitrate era of the 1940s. From the 1960s and 1970s onward, however, neo-noir films nostalgically harkened back to the noir style, although these films were distinct from the earlier cycle. For one thing, they looked different—lighter, more high-key, and often shot on bright sunlit locales without the sharp high-contrast and deep-focus expressionistic cinematography. And they were made in a completely different production environment in which it was very difficult to capture the iconic noir imagery of the 1940s style.

The passing of the classic noir visual style was the result of various factors—from widespread outdoor, daylight location shooting and acetate safety stock replacing nitrate film to antitrust regulation and the film industry's adoption of televisual conventions. The postwar American motion picture industry transformed in the midst of enormous industrial restructuring. As the classical Hollywood studio system (which originally produced film noir and had creatively and economically fostered the style) complied with antitrust regulations, the industry sold off theaters and divested exhibition chains, spurring the postclassical era and a general turn to independent production. As the classical studio system 'dis'integrated during the postclassical era, independent production flourished. In the 1960s and 1970s, amid the Vietnam War, Watergate, and a renewed era of cynicism, neo-noir proliferated in a new Hollywood Renaissance era. (Despite the industry's 'dis'integration and an abundance of independent productions during this period, behind the scenes, Hollywood eventually began to reconsolidate as studios grappled with this new era.) The noir style was thus reimagined and disseminated in these neo-noir films (literally, "new black" films) both in the United States and overseas, paying homage to noir style in a new postclassical era.[1]

This nostalgic harkening back to the original 1940s classic noir style was also seen in 1950s and 1960s 'transnational' noir productions, with shadowy low-key imagery that would influence and provide a cinematic gateway to later neo-noir productions. In April 1958, in "Films Along the Seine," *New York Times* film industry analyst Gene Moskowitz observed that even while France was producing big-budget, color, CinemaScope, costume blockbuster period spectacles, it was also developing a leaner, grittier, black-and-white noir trend, as seen in films like *Rififi* (1955) and *Ascenseur pour l'échafaud* (1958, *Elevator to the Gallows/Lift to the Scaffold*), which were inspired by American crime films. "Gallic producers are continuing to turn out their gangster and murder-suspense films," Moskowitz noted, recognizing the transnational film noir cycle abroad, "which, while also being influenced by American movie makers, now are being deftly done à la Francaise."[2]

Of course, the transnational synergy and transatlantic media production context of film noir had already persisted for decades. Émigré filmmakers (e.g., Alfred Hitchcock, Billy Wilder, Fred Zinnemann, Fritz Lang, and Robert Siodmak) had contributed to the trend after coming to the United States, while classic Hollywood noir filmmakers like Jules Dassin, Edward Dmytryk, and Orson Welles made noir films in Europe during the postwar era. This transnational synergy is seen in noir films shot and coproduced abroad, which included films such as *The Third Man* (1949), *Salón México* (1949), *Night and the City* (1950), *Venetian Bird* (1952), Jean-Luc Godard's *Breathless* (1959), and Alain Resnais's *Hiroshima, Mon Amour* (1959). Stanley Kubrick (director of the 1956 noir *The Killing*) shot *Dr. Strangelove* (1964) at Shepperton Studios in England after the production was moved from New York.[3] Transnational noir persisted with Martin Ritt's *The Spy Who Came in from the Cold* (1965), which was based on John Le Carré's Cold War espionage thriller and was shot in England, Ireland, the Netherlands, and West Berlin. It won British Academy of Film and Television Arts (BAFTA) awards for Best British Film, Best Cinematography, and Art Direction.

As homages to film noir arose overseas, these productions in turn influenced and informed the neo-noir trend in postclassical Hollywood. For instance, early French New Wave films nostalgically reimagined classic 1940s Hollywood film noir, and they were also a transnational influence on later neo-noir films. Twenty-five-year-old French director Louis Malle, for example, earned acclaim for his film noir *Ascenseur pour l'échafaud*, which the *Times* observed was "reminiscent of such noted American thrillers as *Double Indemnity* [1944] and *The*

Postman Always Rings Twice [1946]."[4] Filmed extensively on location on the streets of Paris using mobile equipment that enabled innovative experimental techniques shooting in an elevator shaft and in speeding convertible car chases in the dead of night, *Elevator to the Gallows* anticipated later *Nouvelle Vague* ('New Wave') cinema. Malle's crime film was most famous for its atmospheric jazz score by American musician Miles Davis; its narrative was a James M. Cain–style illicit love triangle gone awry (as a deadly femme fatale conspires with her lover to murder her husband) and a stylized example of the influence of hard-boiled American film noir, pulp fiction, and jazz on early French New Wave crime films. Unlike *Double Indemnity* and *The Postman Always Rings Twice*, however, *Elevator to the Gallows* was a Parisian jazz noir infusing Davis's extraordinary music score in a brooding improvisational theme of pain and loneliness. *Elevator to the Gallows* vividly captured the moody, downbeat spirit of film noir in its nocturnal scenes shot by Henri Decaë, along with Davis's haunting jazz soundtrack. As tendrils of cigarette smoke waft around the tormented femme fatale (Jeanne Moreau) in murky low-key mise-en-scène, she searches in vain for her lover (and murder accomplice) in late-night shadows as rain pours on glistening wet Paris streets.

Decaë also filmed François Truffaut's *400 Blows* (1959) and Jean-Pierre Melville's *Le Samouraï* (1967). Inspired by classic Hollywood films noir, New Wave director Melville shot transnational film noir *Two Men in Manhattan* (1959,

3.1 Femme fatale Jeanne Moreau searches all night for her lover on rainy Paris streets as Miles Davis's bluesy jazz plays in Louis Malle's *Ascenseur pour l'échafaud* (*Elevator to the Gallows/Lift to the Scaffold*). Lux Compagnie Cinématographique de France/Rialto, 1958

3.2 Alain Delon shrouded in color noir shadows in Jean-Pierre Melville's *Le samouraï*. Filmel/Compagnie Industrielle et Commerciale Cinématograp/Fida Cinématografica, 1967

France) in New York at the United Nations (the same year Hitchcock was surreptitiously shooting the UN location for *North by Northwest* [1959]). Melville shot French noir films *Bob le flambeur* (1956), *Le Doulos* (1962), *Le deuxième souffle* (1966), *Le Samouraï* (1967), *Army of Shadows* (1969), *Le cercle rouge* (1970), and *Un flic* (1972). *Le Samouraï* was retitled and released four months after *The Godfather* (1972) as *The Godson* (1972) in the United States.

In these transnational homages to noir, the legacy of film noir style resonated as filmmakers continued to shift from black-and-white to color films and adopted new technologies (for more on the earlier 1950s transition from black-and-white to color film, see chapter 2). Burgeoning incarnations of noir-style films evolved in early transitional neo-noir films such as *A Man Called Adam* (1966), *In Cold Blood* (1967), *Bonnie and Clyde* (1967), *Bullitt* (1968), *The Godfather* (1972), *The Long Goodbye* (1973), *Mean Streets* (1973), and *Taxi Driver* (1976). Later neo-noir films reenvisioned film noir and capitalized on technological advances that enhanced noir-style visual imagery in *Raging Bull* (1980), and transnational films *'Round Midnight* (1986), *Dark City* (1998), and, in the digital era, *Bridge of Spies* (2015).

Early Neo-Noir Style and Homage to Classic Hollywood

Technological innovations such as lighter, more mobile equipment liberated noir filmmaking and had enabled experimental techniques by the late 1950s into the 1960s. *American Cinematographer* reported, "Shooting in natural locations with aid of fast film and portable lighting equipment enhances realism," noting widespread location shooting throughout the film industry, increasing trends in cinematic realism, and advances in brighter, lightweight portable lighting (i.e., improved, higher-wattage filament lamps) and handheld cameras, better lenses, and mobile equipment.[5] By 1968, "more films than ever" were "being filmed in actual locations," *American Cinematographer* observed, contributing to "more creative, more efficient and more economical production" trends.[6] For example, multiple miniature lights (e.g., tiny, bright, quartz-iodine, tungsten-halogen lamps in Sun Gun and ColorTran mini-lights) could be mounted on mobile handheld portable cameras for low-budget location shooting on urban streets.[7] These technical advances enabled filmmakers to shoot with greater mobility using less light and transformed the visual style of films and noir aesthetics, even in low-budget independent productions, both in the United States and overseas.

Mobile equipment liberated the shooting style of *A Man Called Adam*, a low-budget, black-and-white, jazz noir film produced independently by Sammy Davis, Jr. (who portrayed a self-destructive jazz musician) with Trace-Mark Productions and released by Embassy Pictures. *A Man Called Adam* featured brooding low-key cinematography by Jack Priestley shot on location in New York City while it tackled racism in the civil rights era. Its gritty vision and lean independent style was stark, with more obtrusive, disorienting subjective camerawork and disruptive editing to emphasize the antihero's drug-induced downfall, which climaxes when he literally drops dead on stage. The *New York Times* described its visual style: "In the background, as smoke swirls, ice cubes rattle and music throbs sweet, cool or red-hot, is a racial intermingling of black and white as right as the rain." Critic Howard Thompson praised its "small patch of intriguing terrain—the night-blooming world of bandstand performers—sticks to it like glue and plays it, quite literally, from the inside out, which is more than any other jazz drama has tried in years," noting *A Man Called Adam* "dares—that is the only word—to unfold a simple and tender love story" between two Black leads as if "it were the most natural everyday thing in the world. This is rare in the world of film."[8]

In fact, 1966 to 1967 was an important technological milestone for early neo-noir films as Hollywood continued to shift from black-and-white to color film in the postclassical era. During the early 1960s, as film historian Mark Harris notes, "color was reserved for musicals, Westerns, scenic spectacles, and fantasy, while black and white, which was considered more realistic, was used for anything serious, adult, or controversial." He explains that this division was often "forced on filmmakers by the fact that the inconsistencies of color-processing labs were still yielding sloppy, overbright, unrealistic hues [and] was followed by directors until 1966, when the conversion of network television to color (and the refinement of processing techniques) led studios to abandon black and white entirely within a matter of months."[9] Filmmakers increasingly used Eastman Kodak color film rather than black-and-white stock by 1967. Thus, as black-and-white films were being replaced and displaced by color pictures, early neo-noir films shot in color arose from 1967 onward. This 1966–1967 moment was a nexus for early burgeoning neo-noir films such as *A Man Called Adam, In Cold Blood, Bonnie and Clyde, Le Samouraï,* and *Point Blank* (1967).

As Hollywood shifted to color, for instance, director of photography Conrad Hall intentionally shot *In Cold Blood* in gritty black and white to enhance grim cinematic realism. Director Richard Brooks saved money by filming in monochrome and insisted that color was "too romantic."[10] Hall noted, "We wanted to make it real . . . the use of black-and-white . . . heightened [a] sense of truth without making things too lurid." Hall invoked classic noir style in a night shot using artificial rain, a wind machine, and high-contrast backlighting as pouring water streaked a window to create dripping shadows that resembled tears running down a murderer's face just before he is executed. "The light from the prison yard" provided a "dim, moody ambiance" and "we used a wind machine to create some movement in the rain. But the machine blew a mist on the windowpanes . . . so heavy that it started to trail down . . . [and] the light from outside was shining through the water sliding down the window pane and projecting a pattern resembling tears," Hall explained.[11] The *New York Times* described its "potent and atmospheric example of noir-tinged naturalism. Conrad Hall's black-and-white cinematography take us into a shadowy world of irrational evil."[12]

Like classic film noir and color noir, the distinctive, brooding, harsh visual style aesthetic of Hollywood neo-noir films cut across, influenced, and

3.3 Cinematographer Conrad Hall created a backlit image of rain streaking down a window to create noir shadows of tears on the face of a murderer about to be executed in *In Cold Blood*. Columbia, 1967

permeated many different cinematic genres and types of narratives. Like film noir and color noir, neo-noir films were not limited to hard-boiled detective or seedy murder films of lethal adulterous affairs. An array of different post-classical neo-noir films explored darker themes and the visual incarnation of classical film noir style in color during the Vietnam War and the burgeoning Hollywood Renaissance. Most notable perhaps is director Arthur Penn's trend-setting *Bonnie and Clyde*, which reimagined 1930s gangster film outlaws in the spirit of *Gun Crazy* (1950).

For *Bonnie and Clyde*, cinematographer Burnett Guffey strove for cinematic realism, emulating the look of black-and-white film in color. *Bonnie and Clyde* was shot on location near Denton and Pilot's Point, Texas. Guffey achieved dark low-key cinematography to maximize neo-noir visual style in cinematic images of dim, claustrophobic interior spaces and shadowy night shots by using small handheld Arriflex cameras to shoot low-lit sequences inside cramped moving cars, with portable quartz-iodine and Sun Gun lights, and no soft diffuse fill light. Guffey also shot night-for-night gun battles using huge Brute arc lamps with incandescent lighting units to create deep-focus, high-contrast neo-noir visual style.

Guffey tried to minimize the color to emphasize the grim subject matter of *Bonnie and Clyde*. "We tried very hard to subdue the color in this picture mostly through the handling of the sets—dirty motel walls, old bank buildings and that sort of thing," he explained. "Color in itself sometimes detracts from realism ... because it comes out pretty whether you want it to or not." He noted that Penn "attempted to use color without pointing it up as color or glamorizing it in any way, because he felt that this would create a more convincing effect of realism. I think he succeeded because this is one film that can never be called 'pretty.'"[13] *Bonnie and Clyde* portrays a harsh, gritty world of lawless crime and graphic violence, and Guffey's low-lit cinematography is striking in its visual style basking in the red glow of waning "magic hour" sunlight and shadow.

Penn adeptly fused noir visual style with earlier crime conventions, tapping into the contemporaneous social turmoil and the French New Wave, which resonated with a growing new "sex, drugs, and rock 'n' roll" young counterculture audience. As Paul Schrader observed, "Arthur Penn brought the sensibility of '60s European art films to American movies. He paved the way for the new generation of American directors who came out of film schools."[14] Inspired by the transnational vanguard techniques in European cinema, *Bonnie and Clyde* creates an innovative amalgam of genres, paying homage to gangster films, biopics, melodramas, Westerns, fugitive on-the-run films, comedies, road movies, and even Depression-era Busby Berkeley musicals—all with a distinctly noir sensibility. Writer Robert Towne described *Bonnie and Clyde* as "something new in movies, that it may have been putatively a gangster movie, but that it was nothing like *They Made Me a Criminal* [1939] or *I Am a Fugitive from a Chain Gang* [1932] or *You Only Live Once* [1937], all of those movies in which sociological issues were at the forefront and sympathy was enlisted because of the characters' circumstances. This script eschewed that, and it was also a very bold use of what the French had been doing that at the same time transcended mere admiration for them and did something different."[15] Screenwriters David Newman and Robert Benton originally sought French New Wave auteurs François Truffaut and Jean-Luc Godard to direct *Bonnie and Clyde*. Truffaut even insisted Newman and Benton watch *Gun Crazy* and screened the 1950 film noir for *Bonnie and Clyde*'s young writers.[16]

Penn, Benton, Newman, and producer-star Warren Beatty were inspired by film noir.[17] In the late 1960s countercultural era, the renegade couple in *Bonnie and Clyde* is a fascinating reincarnation of a classic 1930s or 1940s gangster and femme fatale. Unlike more masculine, classic gangster films, which relegated women's roles to the periphery, *Bonnie and Clyde* featured a tormented antihero with a strong, bold, sexual, gun-toting, female criminal partner (Faye Dunaway). Like *Gun Crazy*, *Bonnie and Clyde* was a tale about fugitive outlaws that conflated sex, weapons, and violence, a criminal couple on the run blasting their pistols, then meeting their demise in a lethal torrent of gunfire. The deadly finale of *Bonnie and Clyde* reenvisions *Scarface* (1932) to show the outlaw fugitive gangster couple viciously killed in a barrage of machine gunfire, yet it amplified the graphic violence with slow-motion swish pans and elliptical montage editing (shot with multiple cameras running at different frame rates) as they are ambushed in their car in broad daylight. In terms of graphic on-screen violence, *Gun Crazy* and *Scarface* do not even come close to the deadly cinematic slaughter of *Bonnie and Clyde*, itself a commentary on the bloodshed of the Vietnam War.[18]

The success of neo-noir *Bonnie and Clyde* spurred a proliferation of gritty, violent, sexually explicit, neo-noir crime films. Paul Schrader, who wrote Martin Scorsese's iconic neo-noir films *Taxi Driver* and *Raging Bull*, reexamined film noir. In his 1972 *Film Comment* essay, "Notes on Film Noir," Schrader traced noir's development and recognized the wartime 1940s noir, postwar noir, and the 1950s decline of the classic cycle, with Orson Welles's *Touch of Evil* in 1958 providing an epitaph. He also acknowledged the revival of classic noir in nostalgic homages in the new postclassical Renaissance era. Film noir style influenced Penn, and Schrader, Scorsese, and Francis Ford Coppola were the vanguard Hollywood neo-noir stylists. Invoking neo-noir sensibilities, Schrader noted a growing interest in film noir colored by war and postwar "disillusionment."[19]

John Cawelti considered the influence of film noir on experimental Hollywood neo-noir films paying homage to the classic style in his 1978 essay, "*Chinatown* and Generic Transformation in Recent American Films."[20] Roman Polanski visualized noir corruption in the 1937 urban jungle of Los Angeles in the visually lighter, albeit thematically dark, neo-noir *Chinatown* (1974), written by Robert Towne and starring Jack Nicholson, Faye Dunaway, and seasoned noir director John Huston. In *Chinatown*, Polanski plays a hoodlum who viciously slashes the nose of cynical, hard-boiled private detective Jake ("J. J.") Gitts (Nicholson), splattering a scarlet torrent of blood across his face. While the 1974 film *Chinatown* is often considered the iconic neo-noir, its bright glossy cinematography shot in Panavision anamorphic format using Panaflex cameras was not actually very dark in terms of visual style.

Many other early neo-noir films—including *Bullitt*, *The Godfather*, *Mean Streets*, *The Godfather Part II* (1974), and even supernatural neo-gothic *Rosemary's Baby* (1968)—were much more low-key, shadowy, and noir-like in brooding, black, chiaroscuro visual style than *Chinatown*. Many underrecognized films invoked neo-noir style. In particular, 1968 neo-noir *Bullitt*, directed by Peter Yates and independently produced by star Steve McQueen, featured innovative photographic techniques and use of new technology to film on location. *Bullitt* was produced for McQueen's Solar Productions by Philip D'Antoni and released by Warner Bros.-Seven Arts.[21] Cinematographer William Fraker (just after filming *Rosemary's Baby*) achieved a striking neo-noir visual style in *Bullitt*. The film was shot entirely on location in San Francisco using mobile Arriflex cameras. Filming was more difficult because of the limited 400-foot film magazines used for the portable cameras. The logistics for shooting *Bullitt* on location were complicated because shot footage was sent from San Francisco to Los Angeles for processing, and the film dailies were then sent back to Yates and editor Frank P. Keller in San Francisco within 24 hours.

Bullitt is renowned for its dynamic midday car chase, in which high-speed automobiles race from winding San Francisco streets and steep hills to ocean cliffs and highways along the Pacific Coast. A famous high-speed car chase for *Bullitt* was filmed on the Golden Gate Bridge with real-life racer McQueen doing his own 100-mile-per-hour driving across the bridge. Fraker also shot a stunning night-for-night chase sequence on a runway while jumbo jets roar. On-location night shooting was filmed over two weeks on the tarmac at San Francisco International Airport while massive jets taxi and take off on the runways. *Bullitt* used several Pan Am 707 planes and a Pacific Southwest Airlines 727 jet for the sequence. McQueen did his own stunts in *Bullitt*, not only sprinting across the runway along the bay but also running under a departing Pan Am jet in an incredible and dangerous sequence. The huge jet emitted extreme heat and 240-degree-Fahrenheit exhaust fumes as it roared into the night sky.[22] *Bullitt* also featured shadowy low-lit sequences in which McQueen chases a killer through a hospital's dark hallways and cavernous spaces before finally emerging into the harsh contrast of sunlight. The extensive location shooting on *Bullitt* was expensive and time-consuming and caused production delays when the film ran behind schedule. Producers had hoped it would cost much less on location. The production difficulties pushed *Bullitt* over its $4 million estimated budget, and it wound up costing $500,000 more than if the film had been shot at the studio.²³

American Cinematographer called *Bullitt* a "triumph of style." It praised the film's low-key visual aesthetic and inventive, groundbreaking, voyeuristic cinematography that composed and framed images through windows, doorways, and obstructions and used spectacular dynamic photography and editing. Jim Hemphill of *American Cinematographer* applauded how *Bullitt* "impeccably captures the wide tonal range of the piece, which includes dimly lit interiors in scummy hotel rooms as well as some lovely exteriors that showcase the geography and architecture of San Francisco."²⁴ *American Cinematographer* also recognized a trend toward hard-edged detective pictures with a masculine ethos following *Bullitt*, including *Dirty Harry* (1971), *The French Connection* (1971), and *The Long Goodbye*. Other neo-noir crime films included *The Godfather, Mean Streets* and *The Godfather Part II*—dark, gritty, hard-bitten iconic films with fugitive outlaws on the run or in hiding as criminals and assassins face a vengeful bitter end.²⁵

Technological innovations continued in Hollywood into the 1970s as new camera equipment and improved color film stock aided neo-noir visual style in impressive productions, like Coppola's *The Godfather*. Coppola paid homage to classic noir films in his epic neo-noir incarnation of 1940s New York crime mobsters in *The Godfather* and *The Godfather Part II*. Director of photography Gordon Willis achieved moody, high-contrast neo-noir cinematography, shot

3.4 Brooding neo-noir cinematography by Gordon Willis outside the hospital on a pitch-black night in Francis Ford Coppola's *The Godfather*. Paramount, 1972

in 35mm (Eastman 100T 5254) color film (developed in Technicolor) using a Mitchell BNCR camera and a portable Arriflex 35IIC camera with specially designed Bausch & Lomb Super Baltar lenses.

The Godfather boasted shrouded noir visual style. Willis's brooding chiaroscuro imagery is immediately established in the low-lit opening scene as Godfather mob boss Vito Corleone (Marlon Brando), face partially hidden in shadow, holds court in his darkened office, the venetian blinds drawn at midday, creating a claustrophobic, colorless, stark, black-and-white mise-en-scène.[26] The noir stylization adds mystery and heightens tension in *The Godfather*. After Corleone is gunned down and nearly assassinated by rival gangsters, he lies near death. On a dark night, his son Michael (Al Pacino) enters the blackened hallways and cramped unlit rooms of the hospital to find his father's security detail gone. To protect him, Michael waits in the cold on the murky stairs and wet street outside. In the dangerous New York night, mobsters drive by with machine guns ready to kill his father. Film noir veteran Sterling Hayden plays a corrupt cop who viciously beats Michael (for preventing Vito's murder), breaking his jaw in the shadows on the pavement.

The Godfather, filmed for $6.2 million, reaped over $26 million in U.S. ticket sales in the first twenty-six days and earned $86.3 million.[27] *The Godfather* included an ambitious jazz crooner-turned-aspiring Hollywood star (loosely modeled on Sinatra), whose ties to the mob liberate him from a cumbersome big band contract and land him the screen role and fame he desires when Godfather Corleone makes stubborn studio moguls and bandleaders an "offer

3.5 A color noir shot of the front of Jack Dempsey's Restaurant, with red neon reflecting on a black sedan in *The Godfather*. Paramount, 1972

they can't refuse." Nominated for eleven Oscars, *The Godfather* won Academy Awards for Best Picture, Best Actor (Brando), and Best Screenplay (Mario Puzo and Coppola). It was a huge success. Coppola reprised his neo-noir epic two years later in *The Godfather Part II*, the first sequel to win an Academy Award for Best Picture, as well as in subsequent films such as jazz gangster-musical *The Cotton Club* (1984) and *The Godfather Part III* (1990), completing his epic mobster trilogy, shot by the great director of photography Gordon Willis.

In an interview with *American Cinematographer*, Willis recalled "underexposing" *The Godfather* and *The Godfather Part II* for low light levels and shadows. Willis explained his philosophy for using deep shadows and low-key neo-noir lighting to create an ominous "Greek tragedy" zeitgeist by surrounding Al Pacino with darkness as his character transformed into a vicious mobster tainted by a murderous crime environment. By the end of *The Godfather*, former war-hero Michael is corrupted and becomes a mob crime boss, following in Vito's footsteps. He coldly orders the assassination of all the rival gangsters—in an elaborate, noir-style cross-cutting montage—to avenge his father and his older brother Sonny (James Caan), who is murdered. With this brooding, disturbing thematic progression in mind, Willis noted that he made *The Godfather Part II* even darker than *The Godfather*.[28] Like his mob father Vito before him in *The Godfather*, Michael in *The Godfather Part II* is nearly assassinated by rival gangsters. In a shadowy, atmospheric noir-style scene in the dead of night, they shoot up his Lake Tahoe home. In revenge, Michael sends an assassin to try to kill the gangster, Hyman Roth (Lee Strasberg)—as Roth lies in the hospital—in a shrouded night scene.

In designing, lighting, and filming *The Godfather* and *The Godfather Part II*, Willis stressed the importance of using the Technicolor developing process to ensure and preserve the precise chiaroscuro color neo-noir-style visual aesthetic, explaining the significance as cinematic technology was eroding, changing, and deteriorating during this early to mid-1970s period. Willis explained, "I'm a one-light cameraman. I pick a light and a color ratio for the movie, and then ask for one printer at the laboratory." Willis intentionally calibrated the lighting, cinematography, and developing of his neo-noir films to emulate classic noir style. He would underexpose footage and insist that labs not try to correct it. They were obligated to print it exactly the same way every time, hence Willis's term "one light." (Willis's method on *The Godfather* films contrasted with Hall's approach, which involved overexposed footage corrected downward.)[29] Willis sent shot footage for processing and color timing in post-production before printing the film and making film prints from the shot film negative. "The lab just has to do the same thing every day. They don't change anything, although I change things back and forth."[30] Willis noted *The Godfather Part II* "was the last I-B printing to be done in the United States, with dye-transfer work at Technicolor."[31] One of the reasons that *The Godfather* and

The Godfather Part II look so vividly neo-noir is the fact that Coppola and Willis were able to develop the films using Technicolor before the U.S. lab closed in 1975.[32] This abrupt change in the evolving technological situation created an acute filmmaking crisis during the production of *The Godfather Part II* as Willis and Coppola frantically tried to get the film finished, the shot footage developed and color-timed using the Technicolor dye-transfer imbibition process, and the film prints made so the picture could be completed and prints made available to be released before the lab closed.[33] Many Hollywood Renaissance films during this period achieved an enhanced, color noir, visual aesthetic by developing their film (shot in Kodak Eastmancolor) with the Technicolor dye transfer I-B imbibition process to improve the imagery, color, and longevity. Examples include neo-noir films *Bonnie and Clyde, Rosemary's Baby, Bullitt, The Godfather, Mean Streets, The Long Goodbye,* and *The Godfather Part II*. For more on the Technicolor dye-transfer I-B imbibition developing process, see the "Technicolor Dye-Transfer I-B Imbibition Developing Process" box.[34]

New young filmmakers such as Coppola, Scorsese, and Steven Spielberg—as well as film archivists—recognized the technical deterioration of earlier classic color films by the 1970s and 1980s, and were concerned with film restoration and preservation, even as they were filming. In contrast to the earlier Technicolor and color film developing lab process of the classic studio era, the quality of color film lab processing deteriorated during the 1960s and 1970s. For instance, if the yellow color hue on the single strip of Eastmancolor film deteriorated and faded twenty years after filming, the entire film image was ruined and its visual aesthetic was nearly unwatchable. A new generation of Hollywood Renaissance filmmakers even employed shooting techniques such as using low-lighting and deep shadows when making films to cloak low-budget shooting constraints and poor-quality lab work. Willis's insightful comments regarding his work filming *The Godfather* and *The Godfather Part II* stress a series of fascinating technical issues (and creative choices), notably relating to the last days of the dye transfer I-B imbibition process, which further illustrate the continuing evolution of noir visual style and its legacy in color neo-noir films (also relevant in later digital streaming productions) and how these technical issues work cinematically. At a time when film noir becomes a public, fashionable critical construct, directors increasingly reference its style, whatever their generic concern. The neo-noir cycle illustrates how noir was more widely recognized by the 1970s, a trend that would continue into the 1980s and beyond.[35]

The noir legacy was also adapted in *The Long Goodbye, The Parallax View* (1974), *Night Moves* (1975), and *Three Days of the Condor* (1975), often using technical innovations to enhance the color noir aesthetic. Robert Altman's *The Long Goodbye*, for instance, used a creative post-flashing technique. As Edward Lipnick of *American Cinematographer* explained, "Variable flashing after photography was a technique for modifying the characteristics of the color

Technicolor Dye-Transfer I-B Imbibition Developing Process

As in earlier color noir film trends of the 1950s (discussed in chapter 2), Technicolor was typically better for color processing. It provided higher quality color than Eastmancolor because it looked better, lasted longer and was more resistant to fading. This was especially important for long-term archival preservation and film screenings and rereleases years later following initial distribution. The Technicolor dye-transfer developing process—also called the Technicolor I-B imbibition process—simulated the superior look and quality of the original three-strip Technicolor process by deriving three color-separated strips from the use of single-strip monopack Eastmancolor film. The earlier three-strip Technicolor process of the 1930s, 1940s, and early 1950s (which dye-transfer imbibition technique simulated) lasted longer and was more resistant to fading because Technicolor originally filmed, recorded, and encoded color on three separate black-and-white strips of film on more expensive proprietary Technicolor cameras and equipment—where three separate strips of film actually went through the camera, and these three strips of color film separations were then combined during the Technicolor developing process for beautiful, crisp, bright, superior color, as seen, for example, in *The Red Shoes* (1948), *Niagara* (1953), and *The Barefoot Contessa* (1954). This three-strip Technicolor filming and developing process also retained its gorgeous color imagery—and technologically encoded recorded color information—on its separate film strips over time. However, the later single-strip monopack Eastmancolor film used after 1953 was less expensive and easier to use because it did not require special Technicolor cameras or shooting three strips of film, but the lower-quality color film stock drastically faded over time. Yet, as was done with color noir films *A Star Is Born* (1954), *Rear Window* (1954), *North by Northwest*, and *West Side Story* (1961), color films from around 1954 onward that were shot using single-strip Eastmancolor monopack film could more readily retain cinematic color imagery if they were developed using the more expensive higher-quality Technicolor dye-transfer I-B imbibition process to derive three color-separated strips during processing, thus enhancing color (noir) visual style and lasting color longevity, and helping to reduce color fading of films over time.

negative" that "produces results which are esthetically exciting, while solving technical problems." This process, which cinematographer Vilmos Zsigmond utilized at Technicolor Lab for *The Long Goodbye*, involved exposing the film "negative to varying amounts of light after you have shot it and before you have developed it." Flashing was sort of a counter-noir technology. It can produce an image with less contrast, with added light and color in the shadows. It is interesting because it lightened the darker high-contrast look that defined the 1940s and, later, the 1980s and 1990s. It is also interesting because the technology is similar to latensification, a trend in the 1950s. Based on Raymond Chandler's hard-boiled Philip Marlowe novel and adapted by Leigh Brackett, who coscripted the 1946 film noir *The Big Sleep*, *The Long Goodbye* was one of several hard-boiled novels that were remade in the 1970s, including *Farewell, My Lovely* (1975) and *The Big Sleep* (1978).[36]

In the absence of censorship, many neo-noir films amplified screen violence, which was intensified by reimagining brooding noir visual style. Martin Scorsese's gritty neo-noir-style renderings of a vicious New York City in *Mean Streets*, *Taxi Driver* and *Raging Bull* resonated with cinema audiences. Scorsese developed a reputation as a talented auteur of dark masculine crime films about Catholic guilt and grisly graphic cathartic violence, with gritty realism, salacious sex, and disturbing misogyny. Color noir imagery permeated the scrappy urban world where an ill-fated, small-time band of two-bit hoods wind up crashing and being gunned down on the pavement on *Mean Streets*. Scorsese called his early neo-noir films such as *Taxi Driver* "straight

3.6 Stark, scarlet neon lights reflect brooding, shadowy neo-noir style outside the Belmore Cafeteria at night in *Taxi Driver*. Columbia, 1976

low budget pictures," shot for about $1.5 million to $2 million. *Mean Streets* cost a mere $500,000.

In *Taxi Driver*, shot by Michael Chapman and written by Paul Schrader, Scorsese creates a gorgeous color incarnation of a noir tableau that infuses the brooding mise-en-scène surrounding Robert De Niro's volatile, isolated loner Travis Bickle, a Vietnam vet who suffers from what is now recognized to be post-traumatic stress disorder (PTSD), insomnia, and psychological instability. He steers his cab through the rough tawdry New York City streets to the blue strains of Bernard Herrmann's moody jazz score—then strikes out violently.[37] Critics noted the film's distinctive ambiance. "Steam billowing up around the manhole cover in the street is a dead giveaway. Manhattan is a thin cement lid over the entrance to hell . . . full of cracks," Vincent Canby of the *New York Times* observed, describing the film's seedy noir-inflected milieu. "Hookers, hustlers, pimps, pushers, frauds, and freaks . . . form a busy, faceless, unrepentant society that knows a secret litany. On a hot summer night the cement lid becomes a nonstop harangue written in neon."[38] Scorsese's films fostered greater interest in the visual style and cinematic conventions of film noir, and neo-noir films proliferated by the 1970s and continued to gain popularity. In fact, Scorsese called his 1977 jazz neo-noir *New York, New York* (1977) a "musical film noir."[39] He described it as "a mix of *The Man I Love* [1947], Raoul Walsh's forties film noir with music . . . a little touch of *Road House* [1948]" and "Technicolor films" to update conventions "into the obsessive behavior of a noir."[40]

Scorsese's brutal neo-noir masterwork *Raging Bull*, a biopic of boxer Jake LaMotta (Robert De Niro) set in 1940s and 1950s New York (and Miami) and scripted by Paul Schrader and Mardik Martin, was shot in black and white by cinematographer Michael Chapman. In brooding, chiaroscuro, monochrome noir style, LaMotta violently destroys himself and everyone around him in *Raging Bull*. De Niro's powerful performance as LaMotta was filmed to be ominously shrouded in shadow, visually unbalanced, and out of kilter on the edges of the frame as he violently abuses, berates, and beats his two wives and his younger brother Joey (Joe Pesci), all of whom eventually leave and become estranged from him. Noir influenced *Raging Bull*'s stunning black-and-white cinematography, as the volatile LaMotta falls from boxing-ring fame to a blackened jail cell. *Raging Bull* culminates in a devastating scene where LaMotta has hit rock bottom in pitch-black solitary confinement in prison as he faces his demons and beats himself up. In this powerful scene, he repeatedly bangs his head furiously against a wall. In the epilogue, evocative of *On the Waterfront*, he ends up performing with strippers in a shadowy dive nightclub as a bluesy jazz band plays "Night Train," then recites dialogue (to himself) from Elia Kazan's film as he sits looking at himself before a mirror in his backstage dressing room. LaMotta performs as Marlon Brando in the role of boxer Terry Malloy, saying: "It was you,

Charlie," as he reminisces about his estranged brother Joey (Pesci) who will no longer talk to him.

Scorsese strove to emulate chiaroscuro noir style in *Raging Bull*. In response to fading film stock, Scorsese even took advantage of technological limitations to realize his visual design of the film, not only in his decision to film in monochrome but also in purposely incorporating a faded color sequence. Although shot in black and white, *Raging Bull* included a vintage, faded, color home-movie montage with muted tones, where Scorsese pays homage to classic noir *The Postman Always Rings Twice* as self-destructive antihero LaMotta gives his wife (Cathy Moriarty) Lana Turner's white hot-pants outfit. The fight scenes in *Raging Bull* were inspired by James Wong Howe's filming on roller skates for boxing scenes in *Body and Soul* (1947).

In terms of visual style, Scorsese was well aware of the look of nitrate film and classic film noir aesthetic in shooting *Raging Bull*. After filming *New York, New York*, Scorsese recalled that, by 1979, he "decided to make *Raging Bull* in black and white" because he was so angry about and fed up with color film stock fading. He explained that, as a director, "you spend all that time designing in color—because whether it's shades of browns and grays, you still have to design it, and then time it." So it was exasperating "when the color's not going to last." After Technicolor's lab was shuttered, Scorsese observed, "You can't work when one of your major tools is being destroyed, and we have to do something to get a better color stock." Scorsese praised the original nitrate film stock seen in classic 1940s black-and-white film noir, the "lighting style of the Classical Hollywood era, either black and white or color," and three-strip Technicolor pictures like color noirs *The Red Shoes* and *Niagara*. "If you see nitrate on a big screen, there is a difference from 'safety film,'" Scorsese explained. "Black-and-white nitrate was amazing." In explaining his reasoning for filming *Raging Bull* in monochrome, Scorsese emphasized that, in the end, black-and-white film and Technicolor dye transfer color separations are far superior for achieving cinematic aesthetic, lasting color, and noir imagery, as well as for retaining the visual look of a film over time. "The only stable thing ultimately—[is when] you make separation masters and everything onto black and white—[is] celluloid, which supposedly lasts about a hundred years, 70 to 100 years."[41]

Produced by Irwin Winkler and Robert Chartoff, *Raging Bull* cost an estimated $18 million and earned $23 million. Nominated for eight Academy Awards, including Best Picture, Best Director, Best Cinematography, Best Supporting Actor (Pesci), and Best Supporting Actress (Moriarty), it won Academy Awards for Best Actor (De Niro) and Editing (Thelma Schoonmaker). Its noir-style chiaroscuro milieu was acclaimed. Adding a bit of noir-inflected commentary to his review, Joseph McBride wrote, "Martin Scorsese makes pictures about the kinds of people you wouldn't want to know." *Variety* raved about the bravura intensity of Scorsese's boxing sequences, self-destructive characters, and the cinematography, calling *Raging Bull* better than noir films *The Set-Up* (1949) and *Body and Soul*. "Lenser Michael Chapman makes spectacular contributions to the brilliance of the fight scenes... though the film is almost completely in b&w, which fits the subject and time period perfectly, color is used briefly in the home movies sequence... Technicolor did the superb print job."[42] Considered one of the best films of the 1980s, it was a devastating upset when *Raging Bull* was denied the Academy Awards for Best Picture, Best Director, and Best Cinematography.

Although technological limitations during the 1960s and 1970s (such as the closure of Technicolor lab) made it more difficult to create neo-noir visual style, just a few years later the filmmaking climate eventually improved. On the heels of its cinematic revival and popularization by filmmakers like Schrader and Scorsese in the 1970s, the concept and sensibility of film noir gained even more currency and recognition in the 1980s. As Scorsese later noted in 2015, everything finally changed by 1983 and 1984, and continued to get better as film stocks and technical innovation improved and thus aided the ability to create noir-style cinematography in later neo-noir films by the mid-1980s and 1990s.

Evolving Neo-Noir Visual Style and Transatlantic Homage

As technology and the industry evolved, interest in noir continued in a surge of neo-noir productions in the 1980s and beyond. Noir-style visual design—recalling the classic 1940s and 1950s aesthetic—permeated the ambiance, tableaux, mise-en-scène, and shadowy atmosphere of 1980s films such as *Blade Runner* (1982), *'Round Midnight* (1986), *Bird* (1988), and *The Fabulous Baker Boys* (1989), several of which were independent productions.[43] Independent companies like Island Alive, Gladden Entertainment, and Mirage produced stylish neo-noir art films *Choose Me* (1984), *Trouble in Mind* (1985), and *The Fabulous Baker Boys*, while Clint Eastwood's Malpaso (partnering with Warner Bros.) produced *Bird*. By 1984, the *Los Angeles Times* noted the independent companies making hit films on mini-budgets. Low-budget neo-noir films such as *Choose Me* and *Blood Simple* (1984) paid homage to noir in dark, seedy, atmospheric crime milieus, providing an influential template for other lean, independent noir-inflected films that were often the first or second feature from emerging auteurs. For instance, Altman protégé Alan Rudolph shot the low-budget, noir-style *Choose Me* for a mere $835,000 for Island Alive in 1984.[44]

The persistent noir impulse was enabled by further technological advances. Smaller, lighter portable equipment such as the Steadicam in 1975 added even greater mobility and versatility in neo-noir productions like *Body Heat* (1981), *After Hours* (1985), *Goodfellas* (1990), and *Carlito's Way* (1993). Another trend that was common in the 1980s and 1990s was overexposing the negative and then printing down (by using stronger printing lights) to produce thicker blacks on the final print. This development is often associated with Conrad Hall (*In Cold Blood*) and also with Hall's former camera operator Jordan Cronenweth, who shot the moody atmospheric imagery in director Ridley Scott's *Blade Runner*.

Sci-fi neo-noir *Blade Runner* was an incredibly influential film, especially among cinematographers, in the 1980s. The film imagined a blackened futuristic Los Angeles and transformed locales such as the Bradbury building, where *Double Indemnity* was also shot, and the Warner Bros. New York City street backlot, where 1946 classic *The Big Sleep* and iconic crime pictures were filmed, to create a vast, shadowy, neon urban nightscape evoking both film noir and Fritz Lang's *Metropolis* (1927). Cronenweth noted that Scott wanted "the style of photography in *Citizen Kane* [1941]" for the "look" of *Blade Runner*, with "high contrast, unusual camera angles" and "shafts of light." As Cronenweth explained, "We used contrast, backlight, smoke, rain and lighting to give the film its personality and moods" with overcrowded streets "going nowhere. Photographically, we kept them rather colorless." *American Cinematographer* observed how Cronenweth achieved the "classical noir look" for the "futuristic sci-fi masterpiece."[45]

Eastmancolor made improvements in color film stocks in the 1980s, 1990s, and 2000s—with faster, light-sensitive film requiring shorter exposure times and fewer lights, which enabled filmmakers to achieve high contrast in low-light conditions for darker noir visual style aesthetic imagery. New enhanced versions of color film stock—such as Kodak Eastmancolor (1982–1986), EXR (1989–1996), and Vision color (1996–2002), followed by Vision2 color (2002–2007) and Vision3 color (2007 to the present) negative film—enabled deeper shadows and sharper high-contrast cinematography, which contributed to more impressive neo-noir visual style into the new millennium in a wide range of neo-noir films, including transnational productions.

An excellent example of the impact of Eastman's improved color film stock in the 1980s was Bertrand Tavernier's Franco-American neo-noir *'Round Midnight*, which captured the zeitgeist of African American jazz musicians in exile seeking refuge from racism back home in the Paris jazz scene of the late 1950s.[46] Set in Paris in 1959, Tavernier's atmospheric film (its title derived from a Thelonious Monk jazz standard) boasted extraordinary color neo-noir visual design and a moody score by Herbie Hancock. The film centers on the friendship between renowned tenor saxophonist Dale Turner (Dexter Gordon), driven by music but overcome with obsession and addiction in the twilight of his long career, and graphic artist and jazz fan Francis (François Cluzet), two noir antiheroes trying to survive.[47]

For *'Round Midnight*, Tavernier cast legendary real-life tenor sax player Gordon, who brilliantly embodied the role. Like his character in *'Round Midnight*,

Gordon spent fifteen years in Paris and had recorded there with American jazz pianist Bud Powell. The film was inspired by the lives of Powell, saxophonist Lester Young (who died shortly after returning to the United States from France), and French jazz enthusiast Francis Paudras. *'Round Midnight* revealed the downbeat, unglamorous, and exploitative nature of fame and success, exploring the music of postwar bebop jazz while harkening back to noir musicals such as *Blues in the Night* (1941) and Louis Malle's transnational jazz noir *Ascenseur pour l'échafaud* (*Elevator to the Gallows*). In its distinctive noir ambiance of late 1950s Paris, *'Round Midnight* re-created the vibrant live jazz scene of bebop giants Gordon, Miles Davis, and others.[48]

'Round Midnight was beautifully shot using an improved version of Eastmancolor in Panavision 35mm and featured production designer Alexandre Trauner's moody art direction. Trauner—who designed *Le jour se lève* (1939), *The Apartment* (1960) and *Paris Blues* (1961)—described *'Round Midnight*'s color neo-noir visual style and design: "The film's title itself dictates the color style." It opens in stark black and white in an oppressive hotel room that gradually transforms into muted color noir shades of brown. Writer-director Tavernier wanted to poetically convey downbeat themes with exquisite design in "subdued, cold colors, with lots of dark areas, film noir style. This was, in part, in deliberate reaction against the current widespread practice of over-lighting everything, as though theatrical movies were made with television in mind. So much is lost, whole areas of imagination, because of this TV style of lighting. It's often been said television provides a training ground similar to what B movies used to be, but it's not really true. What was so great about B movies were their lighting; that made up for all the weaknesses." Tavernier recalled noir director Jacques Tourneur telling him, "Lighting gives a scene dignity." In conceiving *'Round Midnight*, Tavernier screened noir films shot by John Alton for his cinematographer Bruno de Keyzer to create "shots lit with only one light source" using a "minimal amount of light," as in film noir. *'Round Midnight* achieves extraordinary color neo-noir style. Smoky jazz swirls in shadowy after-hours nightspots, empty rain-slicked Paris streets, dark alleys, and claustrophobic sanitariums. Turner collapses and is arrested, shown in cold steely midnight blue tones with splashes of scarlet red from police cars, an ambulance, neon signs, and a woman's dress. Trauner insisted that "the most important thing" regarding the film's color scheme "is what to leave out." As in George Cukor's color noir design strategy for *A Star Is Born* and Alfred Hitchcock's desaturated palette for *Rear Window* and *North by Northwest*, Trauner tried to eliminate and subtract colors to emphasize certain hues. Tavernier said, "We mapped out very precisely the kind of shapes and colors we wanted, especially the use of blue-gray to make it cold . . . like the color of cigarette smoke. We wanted to evoke the feeling of a black and white photograph, so Trauner painted everything in those cool colors."[49]

3.7 Dexter Gordon and Herbie Hancock play bluesy jazz in noir shadows in a smoky nightclub in Bertrand Tavernier's *'Round Midnight*. Warner Bros., 1986

Nostalgically harkening back to the postwar era of film noir, civil rights, and classic Hollywood, Tavernier insisted he was much inspired by American filmmakers John Ford, William Wellman, Sam Fuller, and Delmer Davies; Howard Hawks's *The Big Sleep*; Michael Powell; French auteur Jean Renoir; and Italian cinema. Tavernier compared Dexter Gordon to Humphrey Bogart and Robert Mitchum, and welcomed Gordon's contributions to his performance and dialogue on the set. "Dexter Gordon was tremendous, very literate with a sharp sense of humor, a great knowledge of film, and incredible admiration for actors like George Sanders, Richard Burton, and James Mason. Dexter said [that] Mason sounded like tenor saxophone. He contributed thirty or forty lines to the film."[50]

The minor key of bluesy jazz is central to this experimental neo-noir with a complex episodic structure that fluidly flows back and forth in time, weaving through different periods—with voice-over narration, time lapses, flashbacks, and flash-forwards reimagining noir sensibility—visually shifting from black-and-white home movies gradually bleeding into color, and audibly drifting between French and English languages. After a drunk passes out on the floor of the club, Turner tells the bartender: "S'il vous plait, I would like to have the same thing he had." Its musical neo-noir ambiance is captured in Lonette McKee's sultry rendition of George and Ira Gershwin's "How Long Has This Been Going On?" evoking Lena Horne and Billie Holiday.

The film's complex, episodic narrative structure, fluidly interwoven across time periods, invokes noir and parallels its music, flowing from one number to another.[51] It is a beautiful, moving filmic homage to jazz and noir cinema. Turner, a tormented musical genius, pursues art for art's sake; he's not selling out his dream, even as it contributes to his suffering. The film's music score, which earned an Academy Award, was filmed and recorded live in jam sessions. Fluid camerawork captured the jazz performances, recorded live in a downbeat milieu replicating Paris's famed Blue Note club in 1959 (shot at Epinay studios north of Paris). Critics applauded *'Round Midnight*'s blue tableau and jazz noir ambiance.[52]

Around this time, Clint Eastwood also directed one of his visually darkest films, the jazz neo-noir *Bird*—a biopic of jazz giant Charlie Parker (Forest Whitaker) produced by Eastwood's Malpaso Productions and released by Warner Bros. in 1988. Shot by Jack N. Green (who later filmed Eastwood's 1993 noir western *Unforgiven*) in fifty-two days for $14.4 million, *Bird* channels film noir aesthetics in its deep shadows and blackened imagery.[53] Evocative of the noir aesthetic, an absence of light permeates the look, feel, and visual style of *Bird*. In fact, *American Cinematographer* observed that in *Bird*, his third film as a cinematographer, Green developed a fascination with "using shadow to shape light" and noted Eastwood's "affinity for very black blacks and deep, dark shadows." Green relished working on a stylish departure for Eastwood. "I knew exactly what kind of visual style Clint wanted before we even got together to discuss it . . . I had grown up in the Bay Area, as he had, and we'd gone to the same jazz bars. I'd read *Bebop* and *Downbeat* and knew what jazz photographs of the period looked like—they were almost silhouettes with very sharp edges of light. I knew that would be what Clint wanted." When Eastwood described that classic noir look, Green decided to shoot a test as a guide to adjust and fine-tune the expressionistic aesthetic of the film. To attain the blue-toned jazz noir style of *Bird*, Green used a Panavision film camera and went with gaffer Tom Stern and star Forest Whitaker to a recording studio at Warner Bros. and shot test footage using "the dark maroon curtains they use as sound dampener as a background." Green noted, "Everything in *Bird* was about hard lighting against dark objects—lots of contrast . . . Throughout the picture, I worked on building strong compositions and strong lighting." To achieve the film's noir imagery in *Bird*, he explained, "We put Forest in front" of dark curtains with "a chair and a saxophone and gave him just a bit of an edgelight, a tiny bounce off the saxophone to give the instrument some reflections." He recalls, "My gosh, it was so pretty. Clint saw it and said, 'That's it!'"

Of one notable sequence, Green observed, "There's a scene where Charlie Parker is at a desk, trying to call his wife on the phone while he's on heroin, and his mistress comes to the door and stands there; it's just a very strong silhouette of her in the doorway and him lit by a little lamp on the desk. Images like that carry so much emotion." Eastwood and Green made conscious choices to emphasize and intensify shadowy chiaroscuro visual style in the film *Bird*. "We did a closer shot of her and put a tiny little light on her eyes," Green recalls, but "Clint wanted to turn that off and just put her in silhouette in her close-up, and that's what ended up in the movie. There's not even a hint of light in her eyes, and it's so powerful because the audience can feel her emotion without seeing more of her face. That's the kind of work I love to do. If I could be remembered for my work on one film, it would be *Bird*."[54] One critic noted the film's noir style in its "studied, shadowy look, at times so striking that the actors' features can't clearly be seen." Another observed that *Bird* "seldom ventures outdoors" and that the film "takes place in the smoky nightclubs where Parker played or in the dimly lighted apartments where his unruly private life unfolded."[55]

The next year, writer-director Steve Kloves and cinematographer Michael Ballhaus shot *The Fabulous Baker Boys* on location in Seattle and Los Angeles. Filmed for $11.5 million, it begins like a rainy film noir with melancholy blue jazz and a one-night stand. The film takes place amid an array of seedy "dark dives," as *American Cinematographer* noted, cramped jazz bars filled with shady visuals, smoke, shadows, and venetian blinds, which the Baker brothers must "resort to for work."[56] Ballhaus emulated noir style to create "garish, unattractive lighting . . . ugly and cheap, and a little sleazy. Some of the places really looked terrible . . . You feel it's kind of a cheap crowd, not a great place to be." Ballhaus recalled that "almost all of the film is set indoors—in lounges, bars, hotels—the places where the Fabulous Baker Boys earn their keep." He explained, "You can still do a lot with light to give the impression that it's an undesirable place."[57] *American Film* applauded *The Fabulous Baker Boys* for its "fierce nostalgia for the romantic scenarios of the '40s" with "new-style romantic fantasies" that "hearken back to the old style," praising Ballhaus's noir-style aesthetic, observing that it "set the standard for modern screen romance . . . some of the most rapturous and moody-blues cinematography around."[58]

Real-life brothers Jeff and Beau Bridges play the Bakers, Jack and Frank, who are lounge musicians performing on piano together in small dive nightclubs. They hire singer Susie Diamond (Michelle Pfeiffer), a cynical, wise-cracking former call girl. The band gets better gigs because of her, but their siren songstress becomes a femme fatale of sorts. She has an affair with hard-boiled, deadpan Jack. Jack is an accomplished jazz musician miserably wasting his talent "Stomping at the Sheraton" on the road and having one-night stands. Susie encourages Jack to follow his dream and play better music. But she breaks up the band, provoking Jack to lash out in a violent explosive fight where he confronts and injures his older brother Frank. Susie leaves to do commercials, Frank becomes a family man teaching piano lessons, and Jack realizes his talent and plays in the hip jazz club downtown with real musicians where he can shine.

Many critics compared *The Fabulous Baker Boys* to film noir and called the picture "slinky," "slangy," "cynical," and "furiously hard-boiled," noting its "smoky, down-at-the-heels glamour." Others recognized the film's smart, nostalgic "passion for Ella Fitzgerald records, film noir and romantic melodrama" like a "beloved movie from the glory days of Hollywood."[59] Elvis Mitchell compared Bridges's jazz musician Jack to noir icon Humphrey Bogart, writing, "It's as if Jack studied Humphrey Bogart's doomed-hero pose from *Casablanca*, tucked the black-and-white glamour into his head and never let it go."[60] Pauline Kael called *The Fabulous Baker Boys* a melancholy "romantic fantasy" that has a "forties-movie sultriness." Critics compared femme siren Michelle Pfeiffer to a "very young Lauren Bacall,"[61] exuding the radiance that was described as "more Bacall than Bacall."[62] Roger Ebert also compared Pfeiffer to a classic noir femme, writing: "Whatever she's doing while she performs that song isn't merely singing; it's whatever Rita Hayworth did in *Gilda*."[63] Its stylish jazzy noir homage made $18.43 million.[64]

The neo-noir aesthetic trend was so pervasive by the late 1980s that it even infused blockbusters like *Batman* (1989). As comic enthusiast Bruce Schwartz told the *Los Angeles Times*, "I like the film noir aspect, where Batman is a creature of the night. They really go back to the comic book."[65] The 1989 *Batman*, shot on elaborate soundstage sets in England, was much darker in visual style and theme than earlier versions, such as the brightly colored comedic 1966 TV show or 1943 low-budget Columbia serial. It was compared to film noir with its brooding expressionistic incarnation of a gothic-styled Gotham City. Its production design by Anton Furst won an Academy Award for its nocturnal cityscape and visual imagery harkening back to the Germanic design of Lang's *Metropolis*.

Reimagining Noir Nostalgia: Late Neo-Noir Homage

The stylish homages to film noir continued into the 1990s, reimagining noir nostalgia in later neo-noir productions. The shadowy visual aesthetic of neo-noir style evolved and flourished in *Mo' Better Blues* (1990), *Miller's Crossing* (1990), *Dead Again* (1991), *Barton Fink* (1991), *L.A. Confidential* (1997), *The Big Lebowski* (1998), and *Dark City* (1998).[66] Harkening back to classic noir cinema in a new Hollywood era, later contemporary neo-noir films experimented with film noir of the classical 1940s nitrate era with irreverent 'post'modernist parody, nostalgia, "demythologizing," and "remythologizing" that embodied generic experimentation and reconceived earlier film noir. This experimentation intensified in the postclassical era. Film scholar John Cawelti considered the self-conscious postclassical transformation of genres from a classical vision to a darker modernist version evincing a changing social, cultural, political, and ideological context that was iconic of neo-noir sensibilities and suggested that "traditional genres" and the "cultural myths" they embody are not "adequate to the imaginative needs of our time."[67]

Especially from the 1980s onward, later neo-noir pictures became increasingly self-reflexive, self-conscious, and self-aware. These films reimagined, nostalgically invoked, and paid homage to classic noir and were often purposely incoherent, more playful, and openly derivative in their experimentation than earlier neo-noir films. This trend is especially evident in the work of the Coen brothers, for instance, in their riff on Raymond Chandler's iconic noir *The Big Sleep* in *The Big Lebowski*. Many later neo-noir films engage in postmodern pastiche, creating a cinematic amalgam, invoking, tapping into, mixing, and combining different styles and historical periods, such as nostalgically paying homage to iconic 1940s noir iconography. This comparatively 'meta' experimental postmodern penchant can be seen in films such as *Blade Runner*, *Dead Again*, *Barton Fink*, *The Big Lebowski*, *L.A. Confidential*, and *Dark City*.

These more recent noir-inflected films emerged during the postmodern era, and they are indeed endemic to it. The stylish proclivity toward paying homage to film noir seen in *The Big Lebowski* and *L.A. Confidential* continued to proliferate, reimagining noir nostalgia in later neo-noir productions like *Dark City*. Neo-noir films nostalgically invoke and reference classic noir visual style and iconic cinematic narratives. Scholar Rodrigo Muñoz-González suggests that contemporaneous film and media companies spurred a burgeoning "production tendency whose main strategies are the continuation and expansion of successful narrative franchises, the adaptation of past media products to contemporary contexts in terms of plot, and the reworking of original material in a different medium." Thus, he argues that a nostalgia economy emerged and created media iterations that mirror older or previous forms. "The nostalgic component is found, narratively, in all the connections with the original material," he explains, and also "economically, in the purpose of engaging past viewers, or fans, with the return of a 'beloved' content and, at the same time, luring younger audiences to consume a product which appears to be new, but it is rooted in a sense of reminiscence."[68]

For example, transatlantic director Kenneth Branagh's *Dead Again* paid tribute to film noir, Hitchcock, Orson Welles, Philip Marlowe, female gothic thrillers, and *Citizen Kane*. *Dead Again* was a romantic murder mystery with flashbacks between two eras, juxtaposing black-and-white images for 1940s scenes, which contrasted with color images set in the present. Branagh and Emma Thompson played dual roles, each appearing as two different characters in the contemporary color sequences and the 1940s black-and-white flashback scenes. In the 1940s flashback, passionate, intense musical composer Rowan Strauss (Branagh) is shown in black and white, framed and imprisoned for the vicious stabbing murder of his pianist wife Margaret (Thompson). These 1940s flashback images contrasted with a lush color look for modern sequences featuring hard-boiled private eye Mike Church (also played by Branagh), who tries to solve the murder mystery, and traumatized amnesiac 'Grace' Amanda

3.8 Noir shadows cloak Kenneth Branagh and Emma Thompson walking on a murky night in *Dead Again*. Paramount, 1991

Sharp (played by Thompson), who tries to regain her memory. The entire film was shot in color; then the 1940s flashback sequences were later desaturated and stripped of their color, emulating shadowy chiaroscuro noir photography. Further invoking the consummate noir couple Bogart and Bacall, Branagh and Thompson were married at the time of filming.

Dead Again was shot in late 1990. In an interview with *American Cinematographer*'s David Heuring, Branagh discussed his creative vision for *Dead Again* and his intended visual aesthetic style working with cinematographer Matt Leonetti. As Branagh explained, "There was something about *Dead Again* that demanded a certain kind of boldness." In particular, he recalled, "Some of my first images of moving pictures are of watching old movies on television, often mainstream movies. For *Dead Again*, which has scenes in 1940s Los Angeles, I wanted to capture the sense that pictures like *Dial M for Murder* [1953] have. There is a noir-ish element—an overused phrase, but pictures like that. *Double Indemnity, Rebecca* [1940]—romantic thrillers that had a style about them." Produced for $15 million, Branagh's stylish neo-noir earned $38 million.[69]

One technological development of the 1990s that influenced neo-noir style was the use of 'bleach-bypass' techniques or ENR. ENR (a proprietary Technicolor silver retention process, developed for Vittorio Storaro in Technicolor Rome by three employees with initials E, N & R) was one of several processes going under the heading of bleach bypass, a chemical effect that involves skipping (part or all of) the bleaching function during the film developing process (thus retaining the silver and resulting in a black-and-white image over the silver) to create darker images that usually have reduced color saturation and exposure latitude. Many cinematographers in the 1990s were very interested in bleach bypass precisely because it could produce two effects associated with the noir style: desaturated colors and deep, deep blacks. Eastman Kodak notes that bleach bypass or ENR was used to increase contrast, darken shadows, and reduce the color saturation of images. This process enhanced noir visual style and was eventually achieved digitally in later productions of the digital era in the 2000s. Director of photography Vittorio Storaro, who shot Coppola's *Apocalypse Now* (1979) and Beatty's *Reds* (1981), was a big influence, as was cinematographer Roger Deakins's photography on *Nineteen Eighty-Four* (1984). A neo-noir film typically associated with this look is David Fincher's *Se7en* (1995), shot by Darius Khondji.[70]

Other innovative reflexive modern neo-noir films included brooding crime pictures such as Coppola's *The Godfather Part III* (1990, which he later reedited as *The Godfather Coda: The Death of Michael Corleone* [2020]), the Coen brothers' *Miller's Crossing*, as well as Spike Lee's jazz infused *Mo' Better Blues*—which critics likened to *'Round Midnight* and *Bird*.[71] As in *'Round Midnight*, later neo-noir films such as *Mo' Better Blues*, *Deep Cover* (1992), *Devil in a Blue Dress* (1995), and *Clockers* (1995) featured Black actors and adapted noir style. These films also featured Black directors and diverse cinematographers while addressing technical issues about exposure, underexposure, and overexposure, and how, like Willis, a director of photography might negotiate with

3.9 Noir shadows and ominous red backlighting cover Denzel Washington in Spike Lee's *Mo' Better Blues*. Universal, 1990

the lab to ensure that details are preserved in the shadows without overcorrecting the footage. For instance, cinematographer Ernest Dickerson stylishly filmed Denzel Washington as a tormented musician antihero in Spike Lee's jazz noir *Mo' Better Blues* using moody shadows, high-contrast composition, in-depth photography, and evocative red lighting to suggest passion, danger, envy, blood, and violence.[72] Director of photography Tak Fujimoto shot director Carl Franklin's *Devil in a Blue Dress* to light Denzel Washington artfully in nighttime situations, adding exposure to highlight dark skin tones. Cinematographer Malik Hassan Sayeed filmed director Spike Lee's *Clockers*, which featured noir lighting, relying on superstrong top lights and backlights with bounce to illuminate faces.

Joel and Ethan Coen's *Miller's Crossing*, shot by Barry Sonnenfeld, was a culmination of the trend of overexposing the negative and then printing down. The Coen brothers' film used strong printing lights (thereby producing deep blacks) to enhance its neo-noir visual style. *Barton Fink* was even darker. John Turturro plays tormented, socially minded antihero Barton Fink, a New York playwright–turned–Hollywood screenwriter who celebrates the common man but suffers from writer's block as he tries to navigate a murky noir milieu of murder after moving to the West Coast. His claustrophobic, dumpy LA hotel room becomes a prison, a "torture chamber of creative desperation," with oozing wallpaper, thin walls, noisy plumbing, and a serial killer next-door neighbor (Charlie Meadows, aka Mad Man Mundt [John Goodman]).[73] The Coen brothers collaborated for the first time with British cinematographer Roger Deakins on *Barton Fink* (they were impressed with his work in the 1988 neo-noir *Stormy Monday*). The Coens and Deakins shot *Barton Fink* for $9 million from late June to August 1990. Set in 1941 Hollywood against the backdrop of World War II and the chaos of Pearl Harbor, *Barton Fink* exuded brooding shadows harkening back to classic 1940s film noir. To achieve the film's low-lit, atmospheric visual style, the Coens meticulously designed and storyboarded *Barton Fink*, working with Deakins, production designer Dennis Gassner, and storyboard artist J. Todd Anderson. In shooting *Barton Fink*, Deakins enhanced the noir aesthetic using multiple cameras and deep-focus photography. Deakins filmed an impressive, ominous tracking shot from a murky cramped hotel bedroom (which becomes a shadowy, blood-soaked murder scene) through the bathroom down a blackened sink drain. Deakins shot another noir-style tracking shot for *Barton Fink*'s fiery climax down a long shady hallway suddenly lit aflame with gas jets in the walls (ignited using a catwalk and perforated wallpaper). In his photography, Deakins noted he was particularly inspired by the visual design of Jean-Pierre Melville's transnational color neo-noir *Army of Shadows*.

American Cinematographer applauded Deakins's exceptionally stylish cinematography, art deco design, muted color palette, and moody low-key lighting

3.10 John Tuturro enters a shadowy 1940s noir hotel lobby in *Barton Fink*. Twentieth Century-Fox, 1991

that created the "painterly beauty of a still life" with illumination to render an atmospheric 1940s milieu combined with the Coens' witty surreal lunacy and "deadpan panache."[74] Vincent Canby of the *New York Times* called *Barton Fink* superb, exhilarating, vivid, and startling, "written in a high old halcyon rush," praising Deakins's remarkably spectacular cinematography.[75] At the Cannes Film Festival, *Barton Fink* won the prestigious Palme d'Or, as well as Best Director and Best Actor (Turturro).

The Coens' 1998 cult classic *The Big Lebowski* reenvisioned Raymond Chandler's *The Big Sleep*. In *The Big Lebowski*, the Coen brothers deftly drew on Chandler, hard-boiled detectives, film noir, Busby Berkeley musicals, singing cowboys, and their own comedic neo-noir legacy in the wake of films such as their influential debut *Blood Simple*, *Miller's Crossing*, *Barton Fink*, and snowy neo-blanc *Fargo* (1996). *The Big Lebowski* and *The Man Who Wasn't There* (2001; an homage to James M. Cain) are less dark in noir style than some other neo-noir films, despite *The Man Who Wasn't There* being shot in black and white.

The Big Lebowski invokes noir in its visual style and flashback structure with voice-over narration in a visual feast of wit, spectacle, and hilarity.[76] It was written on the heels of the Coen brothers' neo-noir films *Miller's Crossing* and *Barton Fink*, and was set during the early 1990s. In the film's noir homage, the 1940s film noir universe of Philip Marlowe in *The Big Sleep* morphs into aging counterculture hippie stoner the Dude (Jeff Bridges), with pop culture references that harken back to film noir, hard-boiled private eyes, classic cinema, and neo-noir films like Robert Altman's *The Long Goodbye*, cinematically reconceiving a noir universe in the iconic City of Angels.

Rather than a classic noir detective antihero recalling his own lethal, urban jungle experience in voice-over narration with a flashback, as in *Out of the Past* (1947) or *Double Indemnity*, *The Big Lebowski*'s narrator is an anonymous deep-voiced cowboy, the Stranger (Sam Elliott), telling the story of the Dude (Jeff Bridges) and pals Walter (John Goodman) and Donny (Steve Buscemi). In the neo-noir zeitgeist of *The Big Lebowski*, the Stranger is the narrative gateway to the Coens' iconic noir world of the Dude and Los Angeles in 1991. Elliott's folksy opening commentary enhances the Dude's mythic legend with voice-over narration as in classic film noir. Invoking reflexive postmodern nostalgia and extratextual critical commentary, drawing the spectator from diegetic immersion in the story, the Stranger seems to break out of the narrative and address the audience directly, inviting viewers to identify with the tale of a "stupefyin'" noir character, story, and setting. He comments on the neo-noir film itself and its reimagining of noir, and admires the Dude's style.

The Coens explained that *The Big Lebowski* is a noir homage to Raymond Chandler–type stories (like *The Big Sleep*) in which style is more important than plot. In *The Big Lebowski*, the Dude functions as a detective trying to solve a crime mystery, meeting unusual characters in an atmospheric milieu harkening back to 1940s Los Angeles.[77] *The Big Lebowski* revolves around noir-style issues of gender, masculinity, and sexuality. As the film parodies film noir with suggestive innuendo and sexual humor, characters in *The Big Lebowski* reimagine classic noir detective antiheroes and femme fatales. The style, tone, and existential spirit of *The Big Lebowski* draw on film noir, and its themes play off provocative issues such as gender distress, misogynism, sexual violence, and empowerment in its elaborate inversion of the seductive, gendered noir landscape. In the Coens' recasting of the jaded elderly General Sternwood in *The Big Sleep*, who enjoys a brandy with Bogart's detective Marlowe while giving him a case (sweating at the orchid hothouse), *The Big Lebowski* is set in motion by wealthy Jeffrey Lebowski (David Huddleston), a wheelchair-bound, paraplegic Korean War vet who shares the Dude's name. Lebowski lives in a mansion in Pasadena, has a trophy wife, and boasts of his charitable Little Lebowski Urban Achievers organization and his connections to Ronald Reagan. As the Dude smokes a joint, he sits with Lebowski in a blackened room at the mansion, pondering masculinity and "what makes a man," their faces low-lit in an eerie glow as flames flicker in the fireplace.

In reframing gender and sexuality, *The Big Lebowski* recasts the noir femme fatale in Maude (Julianne Moore) and Bunny (Tara Reid). Maude and Bunny are outrageous, exaggerated parodies of the famous wild, bad girl, femme fatale sisters, the murderous seductresses Carmen and Vivian Sternwood in *The Big Sleep*, who are embroiled in a mysterious web of lies, blackmail, trouble, scandal,

3.11 Noir shadows cover the Dude and Walter in a late-night bowling alley parking lot with neon signs in *The Big Lebowski*. Gramercy/Polygram, 1998

and deceit. Rather than simply a noir throwback, however, *The Big Lebowski* transcends conventional classic noir tropes in new and different ways, especially in a more lenient contemporary Hollywood era. For instance, Julianne Moore's Maude Lebowski is a dazzling, new, liberated feminist rearticulation of a noir femme fatale. She is an independent woman who is comfortable with her sexuality, and her gender infuses her creativity. An avant-garde feminist artist, she affects a lofty accent; is strong, masculine, and assertive; initiates and enjoys sex; and paints in the nude. Her work is considered "strongly vaginal." She is proud of the sexual nature of her work and her feminist identity. She has money and power, revealing that she holds the purse strings to the Lebowski estate, and gives her father an allowance, thus defying and subverting patriarchy.[78]

These gendered identities also frame the narrative structure of the film and its elaborate blackout fantasy hallucination sequences when the Dude is knocked unconscious, as in the Dude flying over a blackened noir LA cityscape at night. Shot in color noir style, these musical sequences feature black, white, gray, and beige muted tones and shadows to emulate the monochrome noir aesthetic with bold splashes of red and black-and-white sets. The most bizarre of these is his drug-induced nightmare sequence, styled as a musical fantasy called Gutterballs, that he imagines when pornographer Jackie Treehorn (Ben Gazzara) drugs the Dude's White Russian cocktail. Sexual innuendo abounds in this sequence as the Dude blacks out in complete shadow then levitates like a bowling ball in flight. He fantasizes about Maude, placing her in a position of authority, and imagines noir-inspired images of Maude as a sexualized warrior femme fatale with a Viking helmet. Suggestive camera shots visually emulate the point of view of a bowling ball (even from inside) rolling down the lane. The Dude sails by femme fatale "special lady friends," Viking warrior women, and scantily attired dancers (on a black-and-white set) in racy costumes with bowling ball brassieres and pin headdresses. Phallic bowling balls intersect pins, then the Dude flies beneath women's miniskirts between their legs, relishing salacious sexual points of view (evoking Busby Berkeley's pre-Code Hollywood musicals). The Coens filmed the sequence using computer compositing to simulate Bridges's subjective point-of-view flying between dancers' legs with a motorized skateboard camera that followed bowling balls striking pins. The entire subjective point of view in *The Big Lebowski*, like film noir, is thus driven by gender and sexuality.

Another neo-noir, *L.A. Confidential*, cowritten (with Brian Helgeland) and directed by Curtis Hanson, adapted the crime novels of James Ellroy, exploring the seedy world of murder, racism, violence, corruption, misogynism, homophobia, the mob, and crooked cops in the 1950s Los Angeles Police Department (LAPD). Volatile, tormented noir antihero LAPD detectives Bud White (Russell Crowe), Ed Exley (Guy Pierce), and Jack Vincennes (Kevin Spacey) and prostitute Lynn Bracken (Kim Basinger), made to look like Veronica Lake, struggle with their personal demons in an urban jungle where dreams perish. In adapting Ellroy, Hanson noted that he was also influenced by James M. Cain, Raymond Chandler, and Nathaniel West. He wanted to make a noir-inflected period film about the city of Los Angeles "at that magic moment in the 50's when the dream of L.A. was being bulldozed to make way for all the people that were coming here in pursuit of the very dream that was being destroyed." *L.A. Confidential* featured ample glistening night tableaux filtered through what Hanson called the unique look and "layered sunlight of the City of Angels."[79]

Shooting for the neo-noir film began in May 1996 in Los Angeles, with director of photography Dante Spinotti using Panavision Panaflex cameras, lightweight portable equipment, and Panavision lenses. Spinotti wanted to simulate noir-style photographs of Los Angeles, and he recalled nostalgically emulating earlier stills using an expensive, high-quality, hand-crafted Leica still photography camera: "I tried to compose shots as if I were . . . holding a Leica . . . camera." He used darkness to surround and highlight the mise-en-scène and composition of the film's noir tableau. He explained, "I like to shoot dark images. I'm drawn to the mystery of darkness with brightness in the center; that's instinctive to me."[80]

The film initially feels more situated in the 1940s—with call girls getting plastic surgery to look like Rita Hayworth, Lana Turner, and Veronica Lake—but clearly shifts to the 1950s by the end. And it has the paler look and visual style of the 1950s. Hanson strived to make the period film look modern, with

3.12 A color noir image of nighttime silhouettes, headlights, plumes of smoke, shadows, and the red lights of police cars (and a dead body off-screen) in *L.A. Confidential*. Warner Bros., 1997

a unique "quality of light" that would be "bright, sunny, forward looking, but with that noir undercurrent." He screened many hard-boiled noir films for the cast and crew, including many lighter, high-key sunlit 1950s noir films with a brighter, fade-to-gray aesthetic that he sought to emulate, including Robert Aldrich's *Kiss Me Deadly* (1955), Stanley Kubrick's *The Killing*, Nicholas Ray's *In a Lonely Place* (1950) and *The Bad and the Beautiful* (1952), and Don Siegel's *Private Hell 36* (1954) and *The Lineup* (1958). He explained that he "wanted everyone to appreciate what the faces and bodies looked like and how they moved back then, a police force of beefy WWII vets who were used to heavy work but weren't sculpted and trim like today's ideal, instead they smoked and drank too much."[81]

In fact, Manohla Dargis of the *New York Times* called Hanson "A Filmmaker of Sunshine and Noir." Film noir and nostalgia infused the cinematic inception of *L.A. Confidential* as Hanson, a lover of classic Hollywood and previous editor of *Cinema*, pitched the noir project to Warner Bros. using photos rather than a script:

> I had some photos of some jazz musicians of the time, like Chet Baker and Jerry Mulligan, and I'd say, "This is the way the movie is going to sound." I'd have a shot of a couple actors of the period—old publicity stills—one was a guy named Aldo Ray. "This is what Bud White looks like." And then some shots of some houses. "These are the houses our characters live in." It's not the houses you see in *The Big Sleep*. They're houses that were designed after World War II, and they're modern looking. The idea being, it was true to the '50s, but putting the accent on the forward looking '50s."[82]

Ellroy had referred to his novel *L.A. Confidential* as a 'hard-boiled historical romance.' Invoking the look, feel, and jazz of the postwar era, Hanson also intended to update the look of the noir picture to reflect the "Light of Los Angeles" in its atmospheric setting. "The light is very much what this place is about," he explained, describing his intention to re-create the "palette of the desert landscape," and acknowledging that he considered smoke and film noir visuals to be clichéd. As a result, Hanson's brighter visual look is not quite as shadowy in its visual style compared to other neo-noir films. In capturing this look, Spinotti sought greater mobility, shooting with a Steadicam and portable equipment while making some technical choices to enhance the low-key noir style. "I suggested that we shoot in the Super 35 widescreen format; I wanted to use spherical lenses," he recalled, because "we also knew we would be shooting a lot at night" in low-light situations, and wanted to get sharp, deep-focus images. He was thus able to set and adjust the camera lenses to capture more light with greater visible detail in the dark night-for-night filming. The ability to capture more light was achieved by using the f-stop (a measure of the light gathering ability) of the camera lenses in relation to the focal length divided by the diameter of the aperture to allow shooting in darker conditions—the smaller number means it gathers more light; for example, an f2 gathers four times as much light as an f4. "With anamorphic zoom lenses . . . you are limited to a stop of f5.6; with spherical lenses you can open up to f2.8, 2.3 or more and still get a very sharp image," Spinotti explained. "We also wanted to have the ability to move around and use a Steadicam, which is easier with spherical lenses."[83]

As Davis Williams of *American Cinematographer* observed, the film reinvented and visually updated the "classic film noir style" with a somewhat lighter aesthetic, but Spinotti also included some traditional noir motifs in his photographic approach, such as "menacing, exaggerated shadows, or shadows cast on walls by venetian blinds." He noted, "One of the more notable visual aspects of the picture is the cinematographer's use of darkness to surround and highlight the most important aspect of each tableau, much in the way that early filmmakers actually vignetted the edges of a scene to emphasize its vital elements."[84] Revealing the ongoing popularity of noir-style neo-noir productions by the late 1990s, *L.A. Confidential*, filmed for $35 million, was an impressive commercial and critical success. It was unveiled at the Cannes Film Festival in May 1997 and nominated for the prestigious Palme d'Or award. The acclaimed neo-noir film earned over $64 million in the United States, and $126 million worldwide. Nominated for nine Academy Awards, including Best Picture, Best Director, Best Cinematography, Production Design, Editing, Sound, and Music, *L.A. Confidential* won Academy Awards for Best Writing (Hanson and Helgeland) and Best Supporting Actress (Basinger).

Another, even blacker neo-noir production was underway overseas, one that was shrouded in shadowy visual style. Initially called *Dark World*, the moody picture was described as a "noir-ish tale set in the '30s–'40s-style City That Never Was." It was a city that artificially manufactured film noir, appropriating its visual iconography and nostalgic 1940s period as illusory synthetic nocturnal urban sights, sounds, crimes, and fabricated memories. Retitled *Dark Empire*, it was eventually known as *Dark City*, a spectacular cinematic noir homage noted for its murders, detectives, low-key color mise-en-scène, and stunning "tour of darkness."

Like *The Big Lebowski*, it would also continue to gain a following as an influential cult classic.[85] The Australian American picture, jointly produced by Warner Bros.' New Line Cinema and Australian director Alex Proyas's independent company Mystery Clock Cinema, the 1998 transnational sci-fi neo-noir *Dark City* is steeped in the shadowy late-night milieu of 1940s film noir. Like the classic style, it was filmed on enclosed soundstages: shot by cinematographer Dariusz Wolski with production designers George Liddle and Patrick Tatopolous at Fox Studios in Sydney, Australia. Proyas and Wolski deftly created a brooding, labyrinthine noirscape in *Dark City* where night never ends. In fact, it is so dark that the film's noir fugitive John Murdoch (Rufus Sewell) asks the hard-boiled police detective (William Hurt), "When was the last time you saw the sun out?" It becomes a self-reflexive 'meta' analysis of *Dark City*'s noir visual style: by having the framed noir antihero intentionally include postmodern commentary in the dialogue for viewers (as well as the detective) that refers to the shadowy, pitch-black look of the film as well as the manufactured urban jungle setting that always take place in the dead of night, evoking classic film noir.

Murdoch suffers from amnesia and is framed for a series of vicious murders of young women, many of them prostitutes. He is pursued by cops and mysterious killers. His wife Emma (Jennifer Connelly) performs in a dark jazz

3.13 Fugitive antihero John Murdoch (Rufus Sewell) moves through deep neo-noir shadows in Alex Proyas's *Dark City*. Mystery Clock/New Line Cinema, 1998

nightspot. The cityscape is intentionally blacked out and frozen in time on unlit, late-night, rain-slicked streets. The visual noir tableau in this *Dark City* underworld is actually a false façade of manufactured nostalgia. The blackened metropolis is a synthetic reproduction created on a planet by menacing alien strangers who black out the city, stop the clocks and 'tune' everyone to sleep at midnight every night—implanting artificial memories with new lives, identities, and criminal pasts in its inhabitants—visually morphing the murky urban landscape where reality itself is a perceptual construct of postmodern pastiche, an amalgam and mixing of different styles and historical periods, combining iconic nostalgic 1940s noir iconography with futuristic dystopian sci-fi images. Produced for $27 million, *Dark City*'s 1940s-style film noir milieu, vintage Technicolor memories, dreams, billboards, postcards, and movie theaters invoked classical Hollywood. The studio even insisted on adding a noir-like voice-over narration to the film for its 1998 release, adding to its noir ambiance (à la *Blade Runner*, which also included voice-over narration as an homage to classic noir in its original release).

Dark City created an impressive noir aesthetic in its visual stylization, production design, and cinematic milieu steeped in blackened expressionism. *American Cinematographer* applauded the unique look of its dense noir-style city and eerie subterranean underworld inhabited by alien strangers. Wolski filmed streetlights using sodium-vapor lights to create a "yellow-green palette for the city streets and then metal-halide fluorescent tubes to produce a blue-green look for the underworld in *Dark City*." Both "realms"—the shadowy "urban jungle" and underworld—"display a dark noir sensibility that also glows intensely with unhealthy hues."[86] *Dark City* anticipated future developments in

3.14 Murdoch gazes upon iconic noir-style wet city streets, dim streetlights, and bright (red) neon signs of an automat amid deep neo-noir shadows in Alex Proyas's *Dark City*. Mystery Clock/New Line Cinema, 1998

fusing noir cinema shot on film with emergent digital computer graphic imagery (CGI) and visual effects (VFX).

Technicolor visual colorist Peter Doyle recalled the excitement in fusing film noir and German expressionism on *Dark City*, working as a visual effects producer/supervisor consultant for Kodak and using hybrid digital special effects produced on Silicon Graphics Inc. (SGI) computers and Cineon digital intermediate systems, which were being developed in Victoria, Australia, and in Rochester, New York.[87] In the digital intermediate process, filmmakers shot on film, which was then digitized in order to manipulate the color, shadow, lighting, saturation, and other characteristics of images digitally using a computer in post-production that enhanced noir style in the digital era. As seen in *Dark City*, the digital intermediate motion picture finishing process, for example, would revolutionize the look and style of neo-noir productions and anticipated the later digital era: by allowing the fine-tuning of images digitally (using lookup tables [LUTs] color grading) to enhance noir style, adding an aesthetic look to an image, and allowing digital footage to look more like film by dropping filters on images during the post-production process. For cinematographers, the adoption of the digital intermediate was immensely consequential—and seen as something of a threat to their careers. Filmmakers would increasingly shoot noir-style productions digitally in the new millennium, and new technologies enabled visual style to be changed, tweaked, and manipulated digitally.

The critics applauded *Dark City* for the extraordinary rendering of its noir-style milieu, and the neo-noir film was quite influential. Visual effects and animation *Vfxblog* journalist Ian Failes and colorist Peter Doyle note how *Dark City* "surprised many by instantly becoming a neo-noir sci-fi classic."[88] It recalled, reimagined, and paid homage to classic noir visual style in its exquisite black 1940s aesthetic, and other films were inspired by it. For instance, sci-fi neo-noir *The Matrix* (1999) was heavily influenced by *Dark City*, and it was filmed the following year at the same studio, the new Fox Film Studios in Sydney, Australia. Filmmakers screened *Dark City* before making *The Matrix*, and they emulated *Dark City*'s simulation of black-and-white imagery and use of computer graphics special effects, although *Dark City*'s noir visual style is much darker.

Reviewers such as Roger Ebert recognized the visual stylization, cinematography, iconic setting, and production design of *Dark City* in its spectacular, moody incarnation of film noir. Todd McCarthy of *Variety* observed that *Dark City* was set in a "hostile urban environment defined by late '40s noir" but is shot with a "futuristic element that vastly increases the visual opportunities beyond dark shadows on slick city streets." The film is significantly darker than other neo-noirs like *L.A. Confidential* and *The Big Lebowski*, and critics praised *Dark City*'s imaginative noir design with its startling, threatening underworld; glowing street signs; low ceilings; and cramped rooms capturing the style, look, and feel of 1940s New York in its "perennially nocturnal city." Some critics even compared the dark urban film to German expressionism and Lang's *Metropolis*, which also anticipated the expressionistic chiaroscuro look of classic film noir and inspired the aesthetic of *Blade Runner*.[89] The *New York Times* called *Dark City* a nightmare that transforms noir, where in its "most visually striking sequences, buildings shift, and the entire metropolis heaves into a different configuration."[90]

Dark City was named the top film of 1998 by Roger Ebert, who celebrated its distinctive look as a "great visionary achievement" and compared it to film noir, *Metropolis, Blade Runner, M* (1931), *The Cabinet of Dr. Caligari* (1919), *Batman*, comic books, and Edward Hopper's 1942 painting *Nighthawks*. Ebert praised the "vast noir metropolis" in *Dark City*, which seemed to exist in an alternate time line, combining elements of the past and present with visions from the future as it "presents a city of night and shadows, but it goes far beyond *Batman* in a richness of ominous, stylized sets, streets, skylines and cityscapes. For once a movie city equals any we could picture in our minds." He noted *Dark City*'s fusion of science fiction and film noir in a city of dank flophouses where "villains, in their homburgs and flapping overcoats, look like a nightmare inspired by the thugs" with pale faces, commending the new noir world that *Dark City* creates.[91]

Dark City was a fitting culmination of impressive postclassical films paying homage to classic noir imagery, as we have seen in notable productions such as *'Round Midnight, Barton Fink, The Big Lebowski*, and *L.A. Confidential*. *Dark City* reenvisioned film noir on the cusp of a digital era. Notable new developments such as emergent digital technologies in the new millennium would transform noir visual style and affect cinematography. These developments would also accelerate the shift to streaming cinematic content, which would eventually transform media production, distribution, and reception in the streaming era.

CHAPTER 4

FROM NOIR TO NETFLIX

Streaming Darkness in the Digital Era

The fascinating evolution of film noir style, particularly in terms of changing technologies and new forms of delivery, consumption, and reception, endured into the digital era. As with earlier noir, color noir, and neo-noir, digitally streaming noir in the new media era reveals the continuing influence of the evolving noir aesthetic, which ties back to classic noir, and again we see how the persistent noir style is informed by shifting technology, narrative, and thematic elements as well as the industrial and material conditions of production. The evolution of noir style since the 1940s provides insight into the way aspects of classic film noir—itself a range of styles, fashions, and associated thematic tropes—relate to key developments in the technical apparatus of cinema regarding cinematography and creative decisions with regard to available technology. Film noir style persisted—after shifting from nitrate to acetate and color film stocks—through the digital revolution and the move to streaming. In fact, chiaroscuro imagery of classic visual style continues to be reimagined cinematically in later neo-noir films and digital iterations of noir darkness.

Archival research and contemporaneous industry trade discourse reveal what happens to noir visual style and the legacy and influence of noir in the digital streaming era. The shadowy color noir style and brooding thematic narratives seen in transnational neo-noir film productions such as *'Round Midnight* (1986) and *Dark City* (1998) anticipated later neo-noirs like *The Aviator* (2004), *Bridge of Spies* (2015), *The Irishman* (2019), *Rebecca* (2020), and *Nightmare Alley* (2021). In the new millennium, the convergence of aesthetic style and evolving technology has spawned a noir revival where viewers around the world binge films steeped in digital darkness on streaming platforms such as Netflix. New media harkens back to the influential iconic shadowy imagery of classic 1940s cinema in an array of long-form productions—for example, *House of Cards, Daredevil, Jessica Jones, Babylon Berlin, Ozark*—serial episodes telling a longer story in distinctive evocations of noir visual style.[1]

The dissemination of noir style across an array of media platforms has occurred over many years. In April 1997, as *L.A. Confidential* was set to be unveiled at the Cannes Film Festival and as *The Big Lebowski* (1998) was finishing production, a new company called Netflix began operations, with subscribers renting movies by mail, and competed with video stores like Blockbuster.[2] Netflix started streaming in 2007 (continuing mail-order DVD rentals until 2023), made key series deals with AMC in 2011 (streaming *Breaking Bad* and *Mad Men*), and moved into original programming in 2012 and 2013. Since then, streaming media has proliferated, and companies like Netflix and Amazon's Prime Video have reshaped the film/media industry. For example, Netflix has become an extremely successful streaming media company known for producing noir-style content and has created its own mode of digital neo-noir programming in a rapidly changing media landscape.[3] Its enormously successful subscription video on demand (SVOD) streaming service has also spurred other media companies to create competing streaming services (e.g., Disney+, HBO Max, Amazon Prime Video, and Peacock)—and remains the foremost digital streaming media platform and producer of noir media.

In this remarkable new digital era, streaming media companies—predominantly Netflix and Amazon Prime Video—continue to channel the ongoing noir impulse in a different form by paying homage to classic film noir style from 1940s and 1950s films via cinematic digital media and transferring nostalgia from older classic film noir and neo-noir to newer forms of digital darkness, such as noir-style, original, long-form serial programs that allow viewers to relive and binge-watch an immersive film noir past. Key to streaming media companies' house style are long-form digital dramas (*House of Cards*, Netflix's first in-house original production dropped in 2013 and was very noir in visual style) that simulate extended movies—with six to twelve to several dozen serial episodes telling a longer noir story—and pay homage to the iconic visual style of the classic noir cycle.

Original long-form, noir-style programming (especially on Netflix) is more akin to an expanded cinematic motion picture, with its entire extended duration available for binge-watching. Netflix typically releases its seasons all at once and commercial-free—playing the next episodes automatically when they are watched in sequence—to create an immersive, intensified, dark filmic experience telling a longer noir story. Such new noir-style, long-form media productions are designed to be binge-watched over many serial dramatic installments that are spread out to emulate an extended movie rather than a conventional episodic television series. These digital noir productions differ strikingly from random, disparate, self-contained, narratively resolved television episodes interrupted by commercials—episodes that are watched once a week and rerun in any order. A long-form noir narrative is also created when watching shows from other networks on Netflix, such as AMC's *Breaking Bad*, with many seasons of episodes streamed sequentially and available to watch all at once. Note that *House of Cards* comprised seventy-three episodes (over six seasons), and *Breaking Bad* had sixty-two (over five seasons); both were heavily binged as long-form noir on Netflix.[4]

The streaming model and an emerging era with the ability to create digital darkness rely heavily on new technologies—digital cameras; superior higher definition 4K and 8K ultra-high-definition (UHD) digital camera technology; image processing; visual effects; digital projection; enhanced screens for home viewing; and faster 5G capability with greater speed, quality, and reliability for streaming video. Netflix programs have used these technological advances to update and reinvent film noir visual style and aesthetic technique. Enhancements in digital technology contributed to the production of original neo-noir feature films and long-form noir serial dramas. Netflix has also become a major distributor and exhibitor of independent neo-noir films such as *Come and Find Me* (2016), *Furie* (2019), *The Ghost Who Walks* (2019), and *Official Secrets* (2019), and invited global audiences to binge noir visual style in a plethora of films and long-form dramas from around the world in a single sitting. In an evolving convergent culture, such developments have accelerated transnational cinematic digital media reception and overseas coproduction. Netflix has produced over fifty long-form noir narratives since 2012 and over twenty noir-style, feature-length films since 2016.[5]

The persistence of the noir impulse continues in this rapidly evolving digital landscape in an emergent era of what I call digital noir or streaming noir. Netflix's rise has been an exercise in nostalgia as well as creative disruption as its original programming reboots noir in both features and long-form series.[6] When Netflix first moved into streaming as an aggregator, a vast array of titles, including classic films noir like *Double Indemnity* (1944), independent films, and foreign films, was available on Netflix. Netflix originally got streaming rights relatively cheaply because studios saw it as an ancillary revenue source and did not view Netflix as a competitor. As streaming took off in the early 2010s, however, availability of classic films noir became more limited as studios began to view Netflix as a threat when over-the-top (OTT), direct-to-consumer (DTC) streaming revenues increased and cord cutting contributed to declining cable television viewership. As Netflix became a media powerhouse, the established global media conglomerates (which own the major studios, film production, distributors, and television companies) moved into streaming on platforms emulating Netflix. But Netflix had already reinvented classic noir as new content. Noir content has proliferated as digital media streaming became even more dominant in the wake of the COVID-19 global pandemic, when conventional theatrical viewing was halted because of the dangerous virus. Video-on-demand (VOD) streaming offered a safer mode of viewing films and long-form media.

Digital Noir in the Streaming Era

Billy Wilder's iconic transitional film noir *Sunset Boulevard* (1950), one of the last major features shot on nitrate, recently reappeared as an SVOD offering on Netflix, and once again fading silent cinema star Norma Desmond prophetically proclaimed, "I am big. It's the pictures that got small." This classic noir film was prescient about the changing convergent media landscape, from television to home video, to digital streaming.[7] Netflix has prospered in its move to create new original programming such as noir feature films and long-form serial dramas. Netflix joined the Motion Picture Association of America (MPAA) in 2019, officially designated a major Hollywood studio. By then the company had established its brand and a veritable house style keyed to film noir.

Netflix is a consummate example of a programming strategy designed to exploit our nostalgic yearning for classic noir films. From its earliest years, Netflix featured noir and neo-noir classics like *Double Indemnity, Laura* (1944), *The Stranger* (1946), *Sunset Boulevard,* and *The Godfather* trilogy (1972, 1974, 1990). Netflix has since created new original noir-style content and offers fewer older classic noir films via VOD media streaming. As video stores and art cinemas disappear, classic noir films have been more difficult to find and see as they too disappear from many streamers, art house theaters, and Netflix screens. With streaming, the age of video stores, movie rentals, and Netflix mailing classic films on DVD seems like a distant memory.[8]

The melding of noir and nostalgia on Netflix is also evident in its noir-style long-form and original series period programs set in the past, such as *Babylon Berlin* and *Narcos*. Netflix openly references and actively invokes nostalgia in its contemporary programming, for example, *House of Cards*, and in Marvel coproductions *Daredevil* and *Jessica Jones* (Disney+ later rebooted them with less noir style). *House of Cards* even includes a screening of classic film noir *Double Indemnity*, incorporating images into its atmospheric, shadowy, noir visual design as the movie projects in the background and characters recite dialogue from the film in the dark. (Netflix's version of *Daredevil* and *Jessica Jones* are much more shrouded and expressionistic than many series on other platforms like Disney+, and *House of Cards* is shadier in visual style than the earlier 1990 British series.) Netflix original noir productions have complemented their streaming of independent and neo-noir films like *Dark City, Barton Fink* (1991), and *Bridge of Spies*.[9]

As a producer and streaming company of noir content, Netflix also created a short neo-noir film, *Meridian* (2016), to help train developers, engineers, and filmmakers to re-create noir visual style while testing technical capabilities handling smoke, fog, shadows, storm clouds, lightning bolts, night rain, and high-contrast chiaroscuro lighting techniques, which are particularly challenging to achieve in digital streaming and image compression. Paying homage to classic noir, *Meridian* opens with color images of Hollywood that resemble old Technicolor archival stock footage shot on film from the 1940s, with black sedans on Los Angeles streets as period music plays and a caption reads 1947. It juxtaposes this retro cinematic look with interiors digitally shot in sharp, high-contrast chiaroscuro style with shadows obscuring faces of police detectives in fedoras and light through venetian blinds splintering the rooms. A mysterious series of disappearances seem to be murders on the cliffs high above the ocean as a sudden raging thunderstorm and a phantom femme fatale appear, resulting in doom for the detectives in an eerie pitch-black sea cavern. Netflix has even embraced the shadowy aesthetic and referenced film noir and neo-noir, and explained how to create noir visual style in the company's corporate branding on social media. The official Netflix Film Twitter account tweeted in November 2020: "happy Noirvember everybody!" Netflix's account included a dark, moody noir-style video visually explaining film noir, chiaroscuro cinematography, and high-contrast expressionistic lighting. It described neo-noir and various Netflix noir films, such as Netflix original *Earthquake Bird* (2019), and neo-noir films *Drive* (2011) and Scorsese's *Taxi Driver* (1976), also available to stream on Netflix.[10]

Netflix and noir have an important connection and an unlikely synergy that goes beyond the streaming service's offering of noir titles. Noir as a 1940s–1950s period style was founded on the emergence of an intensified form of spectatorship that was initially stratified by gender as men served in World War II and women held down the home front in the United States and Allied cinema-viewing markets for the duration.[11] Netflix nostalgically harkens back to the kinds of film connoisseurship that gave rise to noir as an important cultural and critical distinction when viewers overseas, for example, originally discovered noir films by engaging in a form of intensified spectatorship as these wartime Hollywood films from 1940–1946 were released all at once in France after the war. In an evolving digital media era, streaming companies are ultimately introducing a new generation to noir aesthetics and triggering a curiosity and interest that is keeping the noir style alive. As seen in the company's noir short *Meridian*, Netflix has technical specifications for its filmmakers, developers, engineers, and digital new media producers that requires original films and series to be shot in 4K UHD, thus determining how viewers see noir content and enhancing a digital noir aesthetic. In this way, classic noir anticipated the current emphasis on transmedia convergence, and Netflix has appropriated noir as an important part of its hybrid business model.

Binge-watching digital noir-style streaming media is an immersive noir viewing experience. In the wake of COVID-19, streaming companies like Netflix provided a home-viewing environment for binge-watching noir, which illustrates how viewers can enter the dark, disturbing nocturnal world of noir cinema and noir long-form serial drama by submerging themselves in a solitary or communal experience of intense media immersion. Analyzing the distinctive formal-aesthetic look, mise-en-scène, and extraordinary film noir style of chiaroscuro lighting, shadowy design, and expressionistic cinematography is especially important and requires sharp clarity; high contrast; and crisp, deep-focus cinematic images with enhanced audio quality for optimal visuals and sound design. Netflix has offered optimal sound and picture quality, and user interface and streaming reliability to view and experience noir cinema/media, and the company's streaming success demonstrates that as technology has improved and as faster computing led to higher speeds and better quality, so has the company's SVOD capability to create and harken back to noir visual aesthetic in streaming films and media.[12] As streaming capabilities advanced, so did the ability to deliver digital darkness in brooding noir-style original content, from series like *Daredevil* and *Jessica Jones*, to theatrical features like *Bridge of Spies* and original neo-noir film *The Irishman*.

Long-Form Streaming Noir: *Daredevil*

Netflix originals *Daredevil* (2015–2018), *Jessica Jones* (2015–2019), and *Luke Cage* (2016–2019) are steeped in shadowy noir cinematography, cloaking a dangerous urban underworld in a New York cityscape in the black of night. Technological innovations, such as Netflix's ultra-high-resolution 4K camera requirement, have enhanced the ability to create and visualize noir style in an emergent digital production and viewing environment. The style has been so aggressively noir that some of Netflix's programming is considered "too dark," particularly by television critics more accustomed to conventional television. But more recent long-form dramas, on HBO as well as Netflix, are increasingly shot and visualized as extended noir-style movies in UHD rather than as conventional low-resolution television.[13] HBO's *Game of Thrones*, *Perry Mason*, and *Tokyo Vice*, for instance, were indicative of the convergence of noir style and technology in the digital streaming era.[14]

A prime example of noir-style long-form digital drama is *Daredevil*, a 2015 Netflix original coproduced with Marvel Television and based on the comic book. It later moved from Netflix to Disney+ in 2022. Matt Murdock, a blind lawyer by day, is a vigilante by night. He investigates crimes like a hard-boiled noir private eye. Starring as Murdock is Charlie Cox, recognizable from his appearance as a bootlegging Irish gangster in *Boardwalk Empire*, HBO's

4.1 A color noir shot as crime-fighting vigilante by night Matt Murdock (Charlie Cox) looks out at the urban jungle metropolis in *Daredevil*. Netflix/Marvel, 2015

nostalgic Prohibition-era neo-noir. The shadowy noir visual style of *Daredevil* was so striking that its cinematographer Martin Ahlgren (who also worked on Netflix's *House of Cards*) was asked if the brooding imagery was too dark. Ahlgren was also asked if *Daredevil*'s darkness related to its being shot in ultra-high resolution with 4K cameras (required by Netflix), and whether the 4K requirement affected the lighting of the Netflix noir long-form cinematic series. "I don't think it is a 4K versus regular HD problem necessarily, although if you watch it in HDR you certainly get a fuller range of colors and detail in the shadows." Ahlgren insisted, however, "I think you have to watch it like you would a movie in a theatre—in a dark room. The show lives in the shadows and if you watch it in a sunlit environment, you're going to have a problem seeing all the nuance of what happens in the dark. We light and color grade with this viewing environment in mind, and just hope that the audience will pull down the blinds before watching."[15]

Daredevil's first season was so dark—often featuring inky blacks juxtaposed with amber streetlights—that Ahlgren lightened the New York cityscape in the second season. "Netflix wanted the second season to be a little less dark than the first one," he explained. "While they loved the gritty and dark feeling that had been established, they wanted to see a little more into the shadows and have more definition to the many scenes that take place at night."[16]

Neo-noir visual style is becoming darker than ever as digital technology improves and advances. But in order to stream, the image must be digitally compressed, and this compression process can often compromise the look of a film or series, degrading the image quality of its noir visual style

4.2 A nearly pitch-black interior shot of Murdock clad in black and standing in the shadows. He is backlit by fire in *Daredevil*. Netflix/Marvel, 2015

4.3 A shadowy shot of Murdock in black crouching on a rooftop in the dead of night in *Daredevil*. Netflix/Marvel, 2015

on-screen—especially with dark shadows and fog, and with slow internet connections. Thus, the look of media digitally shot and streamed—or projected with digital technology—is often less cinematic or filmic in its appearance because digital technology compresses images. Digital photography is much harsher in the way it handles optical light and contrast, which is completely different than the cinematic look of film. This is one reason why watching noir on film in theaters—particularly when theatrical exhibition venues screen actual celluloid (or nitrate) 35mm (or 70mm) film—offers vastly superior quality for viewing noir style versus smaller digital and televisual devices with lower resolution. Thus, many films and long-form dramas, especially Netflix original noir programming, are shot in UHD 4K in a new digital production and media streaming era. This enhances noir images. Digital technology also advanced noir style in feature films combining special effects with shooting on film.

Digital Darkness in Feature Films: *Bridge of Spies* and *The Irishman*

Noir visual style flourished in the new millennium, projecting digital darkness as seen in neo-noir films such as *The Aviator, Bridge of Spies*, and *The Irishman*. Many feature films combined noir style with cultural critique and innovative uses of new technologies. Digital (and transnational) production and reception would also proliferate in a wider digital post-production, filming, and global streaming media environment in feature films in a new streaming era. Netflix furthered its noir-style programming portfolio with original feature films—financing and producing impressive neo-noir period films *The Irishman* in 2019 and *Da 5 Bloods* in 2020, following neorealist *Roma* in 2018. Filmed in Vietnam and Thailand, Spike Lee's Netflix original *Da 5 Bloods* reenvisions the 1948 noir classic *The Treasure of the Sierra Madre* and includes graphic shadowy imagery as it flashes back to the Vietnam War overseas amid the soulful, mournful strains of Marvin Gaye's powerful "Inner City Blues" and songs from his iconic *What's Going On* album painfully enunciating the chaos and lethal bloodshed of the Vietnam era. *Da 5 Bloods* theatrical release was affected by the COVID-19 pandemic and thus relied heavily on streaming distribution via Netflix. Other neo-noir feature films screened theatrically, then enjoyed wide popularity on streaming platforms. Many also enhanced noir imagery with digital technology.

As technological advances enhanced neo-noir imagery, filmmakers increasingly invoked the noir aesthetic. Some combined shooting on film with digital effects to achieve and re-create noir visual style. For example, Martin Scorsese paid homage to classic Hollywood and film noir, and used digital special effects to emulate the look of two-color and three-strip Technicolor noir in his neo-noir masterwork *The Aviator*, shot on six different Kodak 35mm film stocks using Panaflex Platinum cameras with Primo lenses in various locations and on Hollywood soundstages. Color noir style permeated the film as tormented, psychologically unstable antihero, the tycoon, filmmaker, and recluse Howard Hughes (Leonardo DiCaprio) sits naked, brooding in the dark. He is visually consumed in blackness. Deep shadows are pierced by pulsating flashes of red light signaling danger and distress as he sits backlit by projected images that flicker across his visage while he compulsively screens his films over and over—and goes crazy—in a locked room. The stark noir images of the pitch-black projection room visually recall classic noir style reminiscent of Orson Welles's *Citizen Kane* (1941) and Wilder's *Sunset Boulevard*. Images in *The Aviator* shift from desaturated two-color tones to deep, rich, moody color noir hues emulating three-strip Technicolor over the course of the film. Scorsese continued his noir penchant with a grayer tableau in the corrupt cop neo-noir *The Departed* (2006, adapting the 2002 Hong Kong film *Infernal Affairs*), in the expressionistic *The Cabinet of Dr. Caligari* (1919)–like psychotic labyrinthine *Shutter Island* (2010), and in the innovative fusing of film with new digital special effects techniques to create the mob world of *The Irishman*.

Such iconic noir style showcasing technical innovation was also seen in other impressive productions, such as director Steven Spielberg's neo-noir film *Bridge of Spies*. It was released theatrically then streamed on Netflix in the United States and the United Kingdom, and was shot on film with digital special effects. The film harkened back to the Cold War of the late 1950s and early 1960s, reimagining and paying homage to film noir visual style. Scripted by Matt Charman and the Coen brothers, *Bridge of Spies* deploys film noir visual style to reenvision the divided cities of East and West Berlin. Shot on both sides of the Atlantic in three different countries, Spielberg filmed on location in New York, California, Poland, and Germany, including at Studio Babelsberg in Potsdam, Berlin, and Glienicke Bridge crossing the Havel River, which was the site of prisoner exchanges of spies between the East and West. *Bridge of Spies* cinematically replicated the harsh imagery of Cold War film noir style in a color neo-noir. Polish cinematographer Janusz Kaminski and production designer Adam Stockhausen re-created the Cold War climate amid the rise of the Iron Curtain, showing the building of the Berlin Wall, and reconceived the brooding, paranoid zeitgeist and shadowy visual aesthetic of 1940s and 1950s film noir.

Kaminski, Spielberg, and Stockhausen used noir visual style imagery to transform locations in Wroclaw, Poland, and re-create the stark, menacing Eastern German milieu of the Cold War behind the Berlin Wall in *Bridge of Spies*. The filmmakers created and used noir visual style to engage in and accentuate cultural critique regarding the harsh, deadly climate of the Cold War and escalating social and geopolitical tensions between East and West Berlin during this

4.4 Cinematographer Janusz Kaminski creates neo-noir style with noir silhouettes in deep shadows as rain pours on wet city streets in Steven Spielberg's *Bridge of Spies*. DreamWorks/Amblin/Disney, 2015

period. Kaminski first worked with Spielberg on *Schindler's List* (1993), and this noir master has shot *every* Spielberg film since then.[17] Film stocks had further improved in the new millennium, thus enhancing the noir visual style of neo-noir films like Spielberg's *Bridge of Spies* and Scorsese's *The Irishman*.

Kaminski shot *Bridge of Spies* on 35mm Kodak Vision3 250D 5207 and Vision3 500T 5219 color film stocks with anamorphic lenses using two different film crews for the U.S. and Germany shoots, which contributed to distinct looks for each locale, with deepening shadows for different dangerous Cold War settings. "The lighting style is very much film noir. I was going for shadows, wanting the lighting to reflect the shadowy world of the Cold War, and I was definitely using a lot more hard light," Kaminski explained. "It's more of a stylized look . . . I wanted a bit of distortion around the edges of the frame" with a "warmer look for the scenes in America, cooler in West Germany, even cooler in East Germany." Evocative of the film adaptation of John Le Carré's noir spy thriller *The Spy Who Came in from the Cold* (1965), *Bridge of Spies* powerfully deployed its atmospheric noir visual style to convey and emphasize the horrifying violence of people being shot as they desperately try to climb up the wall and cross to West Berlin. Gunfire and searchlights pierce the blackened night shadows in a perilous Cold War era marked by bloodshed, the Berlin Wall, and the Iron Curtain.

Kaminski explained how he wanted to emphasize a bleakness in the images of *Bridge of Spies*, making them "void of color," with darkness and a harsh, desaturated look to simulate black-and-white photography and film noir imagery. He used cold, bluish hues to create a color noir variation on what he called "classical film noir" to create a "shadowy world." To achieve this noir visual technique in

4.5 Tom Hanks crouches by a car and is soaked in rain, with stark backlighting emulating classic noir imagery in *Bridge of Spies*. DreamWorks/Amblin/Disney, 2015

night scenes, Kaminski shot "all sorts of shadowy figures" using "rain, umbrellas, people coming out of the shadows, following footsteps" to heighten cinematic tension, maximize suspense, and suggest the danger of the world of espionage with brooding low-lit noir visual style.[18] Such iconic tableaux captured the dark, menacing spirit of film noir's shady chiaroscuro cinematic spaces while amplifying images of disturbing Cold War cultural tensions and violence.

The noir film's protagonist, American lawyer James Donovan (Tom Hanks), is sent to Berlin to negotiate prisoner exchanges. He witnesses civilians being killed on the Berlin Wall and is shocked and saddened—he is also robbed, betrayed, and imprisoned in the East. The film projected, emulated, and critiqued Cold War tensions and was an exemplar of the neo-noir style. It was also a transnational production reimagined in the new millennium digital era as streaming media platforms proliferated online across the globe. *Bridge of Spies* underscores the persistence of the noir impulse in mainstream Hollywood production as well as the concurrent development of that impulse in theatrical features and in streaming content.[19] Innovative departures in filmmaking, technology, and reception are evident as noir style is readily deployed in the digital streaming media era: another example is Scorsese's *The Irishman*.

Martin Scorsese's acclaimed Oscar-nominated film *The Irishman*, a period epic of postwar racketeering and the murder of Jimmy Hoffa, deliberately harkens back to iconic noir visual style and employs new digital techniques to de-age its characters—nostalgically visualizing the more youthful images of

4.6 A color noir shot of cars in deep shadows on a blackened, late-night city street in Martin Scorsese's *The Irishman*. Netflix, 2019

famed neo-noir actors Robert De Niro, Al Pacino, Joe Pesci and Harvey Keitel. Scorsese was inspired by Jean-Pierre Melville's earlier noir pictures, which he showed to cinematographer Rodrigo Prieto to create the shadowy look and tone of *The Irishman*. "The tone of the movie, it had to be contemplative and an epic, but it had to be an intimate epic," Scorsese observed. "I showed a couple of Jean-Pierre Melville films, *Le Doulos* [1962] and *Le deuxième souffle* [1966; aka *Second Breath*], with Jean-Paul Belmondo, both of those pictures. It's a very different world, but I liked the understatement of it," Scorsese explained. "Then I showed a film called *Touchez pas au grisbi* [1954], which means 'Don't touch the loot,' which is a very famous early '50s French gangster film with Jean Gabin ... Another one was Jules Dassin's *Rififi* [1955]," the classic French heist film. "There was a period there where a lot of those films were coming over here," said Scorsese of the transnational influence of noir cinema on the style of *The Irishman*.[20]

The Irishman was shot on film and digitally enhanced, with certain scenes digitally shot to create the special visual de-aging effects.[21] Film stocks and digital technology improved in the new millennium, and Scorsese and Prieto shot scenes that did not require de-aging visual effects with Kodak 5219 and 5207 35mm film stocks using Arricam LT and ST cameras to create a stunning noir aesthetic. Then they fine-tuned the look of the film and made it darker, with deeper shadows and a desaturated color palette depending on the decade. For instance, Scorsese and Prieto digitally enhanced the scenes for *The Irishman* shot on film to emulate the look and feel of different historical periods—using

Figure 4.7 Bright red neon sign for the Villa Di Roma Restaurant and murky silhouette figures on glistening wet city streets in *The Irishman*. Netflix, 2019

the more colorful aesthetic of Kodachrome color film for the 1950s, for instance, and Ektachrome for the 1960s. Scorsese and Prieto also desaturated color using the ENR (a proprietary Technicolor silver retention process, developed for Vittorio Storaro in Technicolor Rome by three employees with initials E, N & R) lab process to reduce color saturation, create darker images, and add contrast for scenes set in the 1970s and later, which further emphasized the shadowy noir look of the film. The digital visual effects (VFX) scenes were shot with a complicated three lens rig, the "three-headed monster" (with a Red Helium camera as the main camera) so visual effects artists at Industrial Light & Magic could de-age the actors digitally.[22]

Other films available to stream on platforms also used digital technology to enhance a noir-style aesthetic and create a more "filmic" cinematic rendering of its visual look. For example, French cinematographer Bruno Delbonnel convinced director Joe Wright to use the Arri Alexa digital camera with Cooke lenses to capture the "darkness" and blackouts of 1940 wartime in low-light photography for *Darkest Hour* (2017).[23] As seen in original neo-noir films *The Irishman* and *Da 5 Bloods* and long-form noir *Daredevil*, as well as period films available to stream like *Darkest Hour*, noir style harkening back to an earlier time was definitely a strategy employed by Netflix in its production endeavors and corporate branding—as well as in the film titles available to stream on the platform. The streaming company has strategically channeled noir visual style and cinematic conventions into its original long-form digital programming, as in *Jessica Jones, Ozark, House of Cards, Daredevil*, and an array of noir.[24]

Noir Aesthetics in *Jessica Jones*

The Netflix original series *Jessica Jones, Daredevil, Luke Cage, Iron Fist, The Punisher*, and *The Defenders* reimagine the brooding shadowy visual style of classic 1940s hard-boiled film noir crime movies, Marvel Cinematic Universe (MCU) superhero film franchises, and graphic novels. Characters move between long-form serial programs and feature films to create a long-form meta noir narrative series harkening back to the classic noir aesthetic.

Jessica Jones includes abundant noir shadows and venetian blind bars of entrapment. The digital noir even interjects a screening of Orson Welles's 1958 film noir *Touch of Evil* into an episode as the main characters watch the movie projected onto the side of a building from a New York City rooftop one night. *Jessica Jones* star Krysten Ritter is also recognizable from *Breaking Bad*, and she reappears in Netflix neo-noir film *El Camino* (2019). Ritter's cynical, hard-boiled private eye hitting the bottle in *Jessica Jones* is evocative of classic film noir; tough women survivors solve crimes overcoming sexual violence, abuse, and assault. In this meta noir universe, Jessica Jones also has a fling with Luke Cage. And Jessica Jones, Daredevil, and Luke Cage appear together in *The Defenders*. These noir productions are more immersive when binge-watched as long-form neo-noirs on Netflix without commercials rather than as weekly

4.8 Krysten Ritter as a hard-boiled femme private eye in harsh color noir shadows with slashes of light in *Jessica Jones*. Netflix/Marvel, 2015

episodes or with commercial interruptions, as on conventional television or on some other streaming platforms.²⁵

Improvements in digital technology also helped to enhance neo-noir imagery in *Jessica Jones*. The distinctive, blackened, cinematic shadowy aesthetic in *Jessica Jones* was achieved by shooting digitally with a Red Epic Dragon camera with Panavision PVintage lenses to intensify the chiaroscuro neo-noir visual style. *Jessica Jones* cinematographer Manuel Billeter, who also worked on *Luke Cage* and *Iron Fist*, treated the noir-style Netflix Marvel coproductions not as typical comic book superhero source material but rather as brooding, dramatic, psychological character studies. For *Jessica Jones*, Billeter explained, "Instead of following the look specifically set in the printed comics, we developed a fresh, but coherent and authentic look for the motion picture version. It was important we stay true to the 'feel' of the original ideas, but in following our own intuitively creative approach, I feel we succeeded in making the show look great for modern audiences." It is certainly worth noting that Billeter refers to noir long-form *Jessica Jones* as a "motion picture."²⁶ *Jessica Jones* filmmakers and producers specifically sought this cinematic noir aesthetic.

Billeter emulated what he described as a "film noir look" with lighting, shadow, color, and production design to create a cold, stark visual palette in his gritty, dark, "minimalist" approach to lighting and photography. Billeter used Panavision lenses with the high-resolution digital RED Dragon camera to heighten the noir look of *Jessica Jones* and give the visual imagery more of

4.9 Cinematographer Manuel Billeter creates brooding chiaroscuro noir style with stark contrast; neon signs; and rain-soaked, late-night New York City streets in *Jessica Jones*, shot on location. Netflix/Marvel, 2015

a crime-and-suspense look (rather than the look of fantasy or science fiction). Billeter wanted the imagery to visually convey the psychologically damaged, traumatized people in the noir narrative. As Billeter explains of the characters in *Jessica Jones*: "They had a flawed look to them . . . they aren't perfectly flat, they're not perfectly sharp all across the image, but that's what I thought would help tell the story better, this story of a broken-down, former super-hero with PTSD [post-traumatic stress disorder]." To achieve a retro noir aesthetic in 4K UHD, Billeter merged filmic and digital equipment, using Panavision PVintage prime lenses, newly rehoused, and Ultra Speed lenses from the 1970s, and an organic construction of the classic line of glass (of the 1970s lenses) counterbalanced with the high-resolution digital sensor of the RED Dragon camera, thus modifying and customizing technology to create a more cinematic noir look for *Jessica Jones*.[27]

Jessica Jones conveys feminist concerns about the oppression of women in the dangerous New York cityscape. Hard-boiled detective Jessica Jones has been raped, traumatized, and psychologically gaslighted by a sadistic manipulative male predator, Kilgrave (David Tennant), who is a psychopath. Like a classic noir antihero, evocative of Humphrey Bogart in *The Big Sleep* (1946) and *Dead Reckoning* (1947) or Robert Mitchum in *Out of the Past* (1947), she is a tough resilient survivor, suffering PTSD while solving crimes and bloody murder mysteries in the urban shadows with hard-drinking, chain-smoking deadpan panache. Women, including the cynical heroine, in *Jessica Jones* are

4.10 Cinematographer Manuel Billeter created dim lighting using lightweight portable equipment to punctuate pitch-black interiors and thus emulate classic noir style in *Jessica Jones*. Netflix/Marvel, 2015

repeatedly told to smile by misogynistic abusers who inflict physical, sexual, and psychological violence upon them.

Jessica Jones was also distinctive as a long-form (Netflix and Disney+) series featuring women with greater creative control and power on-screen and behind the camera. *Jessica Jones* was created by Melissa Rosenberg and featured women stars, writers, executive producers, and directors like S. J. Clarkson and Liz Friedman. Ritter's gritty portrayal of Jessica Jones as a survivor who fights back against violence, rape, and abuse in images on-screen and in Netflix publicity, and resiliently spars with hard-boiled, deadpan wise-cracking dialogue, is summed up in the tagline: "Fight like a woman."

The nocturnal world of *Jessica Jones* uses noir to articulate feminist concerns as the down-and-out private eye is gaslighted (by Kilgrave) like an abused victim of violence in a female gothic narrative. *Jessica Jones* comments on these feminist issues.[28] The film reimagines and is evocative of classic noir critical discourse. For instance, Raymonde Borde and Étienne Chaumeton recognized the eroticization of violence, especially sexual violence, and provocative gender polemics in films noir.[29]

Jessica Jones projected noir screen images of women facing harassment, misogynistic violence, aggressive coercion, assault, brutality, murder, imprisonment, and rape. The issues portrayed in *Jessica Jones* are even more resonant in the digital Me Too era and in light of Hollywood's recent revelations of sexual harassment, assault, and coercion behind the scenes in the motion picture and media industries, which are in turn incredibly influential in shaping social ideas associated with gender, sex, and power. Noir women in classic era, gothic noir films such as *Spellbound* (1945), *Gilda* (1946), *Phantom Lady* (1944), *Scarlet Street* (1945), *Notorious* (1946), and *Whirlpool* (1950) in many ways anticipate neo-noir heroines like the traumatized private eye who has been raped in *Jessica Jones*.

The oppressive milieu Jessica Jones faces is visually realized in the brooding, disturbing noir cinematography. In filming *Jessica Jones*, cinematographer Billeter preferred a desaturated tone when shooting nighttime exteriors; he shot wide to incorporate city backdrops, emphasizing the urban jungle with color gels and multiple light sources to showcase the glistening, shrouded neon underworld at night—stark street signs, lampposts, storefronts, and traffic lights—and used Super White Flame gels to match practical sodium-vapor lights and achieve a signature shadowy look. To create the iconic dark alleys and murky, dimly lit, late-night streets of film noir, Billeter utilized the New York City location to add ambiance to *Jessica Jones*. "I'm always striving to use whatever is present at the locations, like streetlights . . . not just to use them but to integrate them into the shot, and using wide lenses especially to be able to see the city and embrace it instead of trying to hide it." When filming *Jessica Jones*, he used abundant shadows with color gel backlights in the background to create a noir aesthetic that blended into existing locations and moody lights in the "urban-scape of New York."[30]

Emulating the constrained confines and the feeling of entrapment of classic film noir, Billeter created claustrophobic noir-style interior spaces by photographing in cramped New York City locations for *Jessica Jones*. Billeter also used wide shots indoors, which can be a problem because he preferred to work with full ceilings on interiors rather than open overheads. Working on a tight schedule added shooting constraints and limited the use of specialized lighting, but Billeter emphasized and evoked the realism of classic noir in visually framing the composition of shots of indoor location sets. Despite budgetary, scheduling, and spatial restrictions, Billeter was able to create impressive noir style using portable equipment; Chimera lighting; rich incandescent lamps; and small, mobile, Cineo, large-output, light-emitting diode (LED) lighting systems. Technological advances in lighting also aided the long-form noir's look and aesthetic in shooting cramped spaces. Billeter was able to achieve what he called a "gritty, fairly dark, noirish cinematic" aesthetic in filming *Jessica Jones* to emphasize the "crime-and-suspense feel" imagery with a "cold, stark" desaturated color palette. Billeter explained how he achieved low-lit noir style using the Cineo LED as a tiny 'booklight,' bouncing slivers of light into crevices and containing it with an "8 × 8 frame with egg crates" to create stark shadows. This flexibility enhanced noir style in illuminating the set. Billeter noted that LED lights were very versatile for the noir style of *Jessica Jones* because they could be shaped in any way and were flat, so lights could be hidden very quickly yet produced a lot of output to create high-contrast images with slashes of light, which aided emulating the striking chiaroscuro of film noir. "LED technology has had a tremendous impact on lighting," he explained, enabling cinematographers "to hide these small units behind little nooks and crannies" and are "much cooler, so if you're on smaller sets or even in the studio, the heat factor can be very important." The fact that LED lights generated much less heat output on set was crucial to creating noir style because heat was often trapped in the cramped, low overhead of *Jessica Jones* interior sets used on location in New York City.[31]

The look of *Jessica Jones* becomes a kind of living breathing character. The brooding, low-key chiaroscuro mise-en-scène is especially dark in the first season and, like *Daredevil*, gradually lightens in later seasons of the long-form serial drama. But it was still quite pronounced and created a defining aesthetic. The noir influence is also evident in other competing media conglomerates, such as HBO and Disney+, and their noir-style variations on noir programming, such as HBO's *Perry Mason, Boardwalk Empire, Game of Thrones*, and *Tokyo Vice*, and Disney's *The Mandalorian*.

Noir Competitors

New media technologies enabling enhanced digital noir visual style and streaming companies like Netflix and Amazon have transformed media viewing and propagated noir visual style in the digital era, and other major media companies have responded, producing original content and streaming nostalgia in cinematic, long-form dramas, including noir style content.[32] This digital streaming climate has accelerated the production of long-form noir dramas across platforms. The noir impulse (including its narrative aspects and tropes) is impressive in its ability to carry over into new kinds of narratives even in this new digital incarnation of noir seen in long-form noir in the streaming era. The noir aesthetic, with its brooding shadows, is certainly featured at many media companies, such as Disney+ and HBO Max (renamed Max in 2023), and their variations on noir programming. The ephemeral nature of Netflix's long-form neo-noir has been encouraged by media competitors ending their deals with Netflix and pulling their media content (including classic noir film titles) from Netflix's delivery platform. Chuck Tryon observes how, in an era of digital streaming, conglomerates often constrict access and availability of media to develop "better mechanisms for controlling when, where, and how content is circulated."[33] New incarnations of noir style were adapted, displaced, redeployed, and disseminated on an array of streaming platforms in the digital era. In many cases, however, competitors impede the immersive digital noir viewing experience (i.e., the ability to binge-watch serial long-form noir sequentially, all at once) with commercial interruptions or by releasing shows once a week.[34]

Netflix faces competition from fellow nostalgia merchant Disney, which launched its Disney+ streaming service in November 2019. Although streamers do not release specific expenditures for noir content, Disney budgeted approximately $1.5 to $1.75 billion for original Disney+ content and $3 billion for its subsidiary, Hulu, in 2020, spending an estimated $15 billion on streaming in 2021. Netflix spent over $17 billion in 2021; Amazon spent $13 billion on Prime video and music in 2021; and Warner planned to spend $18 billion in 2022 on HBO, HBO Max, Turner networks, and Warner Bros. theatrical releases.[35] Disney had previously partnered with Netflix on original long-form Marvel coproductions *Daredevil, Jessica Jones, Luke Cage, Iron Fist, The Punisher,* and *The Defenders,* and two years after these series ended, the rights to use the characters reverted to Marvel.[36] In March 2022, these noir-style productions moved from Netflix to Disney+, which further illustrates the ephemeral nature and circulation of noir in the streaming era between evolving collaborators-turned-competitors.

Encouraged by the success of Netflix, other competing media conglomerate entities such as HBO, BBC, ITV, PBS, Amazon, Hulu, Apple, and Disney also compete and offer different strains of noir, coinciding with their unique corporate brands and other media content. This is perhaps not so surprising for noir, evocative of distinctive 'house styles' during the classic studio era, where studios offered their "brand" of films, contract stars, styles, and various strains of noir pictures. These new variations on noir style emerge now in the digital streaming era, and as seen in the classic 1940s and 1950s noir era, the resilient adaptable noir visual style permeated a vast array of different genres. For instance, Amazon's original offerings include jazz-infused music noir *Sylvie's Love* (2020) and *One Night in Miami* (2020); long-form dramas *Jack Ryan*, *The Collection*, and *The Man in the High Castle*; and neo-noir films like Tom Clancy espionage thriller *Without Remorse* (2021, starring Michael B. Jordan), *Lansky* (2021), and the Swedish Nordic noir trilogy of *The Girl with the Dragon Tattoo* (2009). Hulu streams noir gothics *The Handmaid's Tale*, *Top of the Lake*, and *The Old Man*, and jazz noir musical biopic *The United States vs. Billie Holiday*. Apple TV+ includes *Shining Girls*, *Black Bird*, and Tom Hanks's neo-noir films *Greyhound* (2020) and *Finch* (2021). Starz features stylish long-form noir *Magic City*; TNT includes moody 1940s period noir *I Am the Night*; FX presented *The Shield* and *The Americans*; Paramount produced espionage thriller *Berlin Station*, *The Offer*, and *Rabbit Hole*; and Disney+ offered Netflix/Marvel coproductions (i.e., *Daredevil*, *Jessica Jones*, *Luke Cage*, *Iron Fist*, *The Punisher*, and *The Defenders*), as well as *The Mandalorian*, *Obi-Wan Kenobi*, *Andor*, *Echo* and *Moon Knight*.[37]

HBO, of course, had its own stylish version of noir. Notably, HBO was distinctly known for its signature brand of high-quality, prestige noir-style programming, as seen in an array of gritty series like *Oz* (1997–2003), *The Sopranos* (1999–2007), *The Wire* (2002–2008), *Boardwalk Empire* (2010–2014), *The Night Of* (2016), *Vinyl* (2016), *Game of Thrones* (2011–2019), *Perry Mason* (2020–2023), *Watchmen* (2019), and *Tokyo Vice* (2022), and even the stark, grisly, visually dark combat series *Band of Brothers* (2001) and *The Pacific* (2010). HBO also featured indie-style original films like Fine Line Features/HBO Film's quirky jazz-infused noir docu-comedy *American Splendor* (2003), and showed neo-noir films like parent company Warner Bros.' *Motherless Brooklyn* (2019), noir-style sci-fi *Dune* (2021), and *The Batman* (2022), and noir productions from other companies such as Searchlight's *Nightmare Alley*, which was released theatrically, then streamed on HBO Max. The global pandemic and digital streaming era certainly transformed the reception context for noir across the industry. In retrospect, films increasingly moved to streaming, along with original and long-form noir programming. HBO also made licensing deals to stream noir titles like *The Batman*, *Dune*, and *Band of Brothers* on Netflix in 2023.[38]

The cinematography of these long-form HBO dramas is cloaked in noir shadows—*Boardwalk Empire*, *Game of Thrones*, *Perry Mason*, and *Tokyo Vice* revel in neo-noir darkness. The noir impulse and superior quality of shooting on film was noted in 2010 by cinematographer Jonathan Freeman while shooting *Boardwalk Empire*: "It's certainly a relief to be shooting film—the dynamic range and highlight detail in film is so far superior to HD." Like *Bridge of Spies* and *The Irishman*, shadowy noir visual style was enhanced in *Boardwalk Empire* by shooting on improved Super 35mm Kodak Vision3 500T 5219 and Vision3 250D 5207 film stocks. In striving to achieve a more cinematic look by shooting on actual film rather than shooting digitally, Freeman acknowledged the influence of Gordon Willis's work on *The Godfather* movies.[39] Although often considered comparatively inferior in look, style, and aesthetic to film, digital technology would eventually improve years later, as seen in the ability to enhance digital darkness in the wake of Netflix's requiring the use of more advanced 4K UHD cameras for productions to create cinematic images emulating the superior film aesthetic so essential for noir visual style (evident in *Daredevil, Jessica Jones,* and *Meridian* by 2015 and 2016).

Revealing the influence, legacy, and proliferation of noir style in a convergent digital era, Matthew Dessem of *Slate* noted that technological innovations and filmmakers' creative choices and intentions contributed to television shows being darker—in *Game of Thrones* and other long-form series.[40] The aptly titled *Game of Thrones* episode "The Long Night" was so dark it resembled a blackout. "Why is *Game of Thrones* so dark?" Chris Stokel-Walker of *Wired* pondered. The director, cinematographer, creators, showrunner, and visual special effects producer on *Game of Thrones* all acknowledged they were aiming for a cinematic experience of long-form, high-quality film noir in a digital arena. (Full disclosure: One of the visual special effects producers was formerly an avid student in my first university film noir class.) Like the cinematographer for *Daredevil* championing shadowy noir-style blackened cinematic imagery, filmmakers produced long-form noir drama with the filmic style in mind—made possible by new advances and improvements in UHD digital technology, digital projection, enhanced screens for home viewing, and faster 5G streaming capability—rather than designing productions for an antiquated array of reception viewing devices or conventional television. "We asked the cinematographer. Fans complained that the Battle of Winterfell was too dark to see properly. But cinematographer Fabien Wagner defends the gloom," Stokel-Walker explained.[41] In a 2019 *Indiewire* article entitled, "*Game of Thrones* Cinematographer Defends Battle of Winterfell Against Complaints It's Too Dark to See," Zack Sharf observed, "Fabian Wagner was behind the camera for 'The Long Night' and says the evolution from dark to light was important to play out in the cinematography."[42]

Perry Mason featured a moody noir visual aesthetic that permeated its expressionistic photography in a much darker, hard-boiled incarnation of the earlier CBS 1957–1966 television courtroom series starring Raymond Burr, a film noir veteran of *Raw Deal* (1948), *Pitfall* (1948), *Walk a Crooked Mile* (1948), *The Blue Gardenia* (1953), and *Rear Window* (1954) fame. Directed and executive-produced by Emmy-winning *Boardwalk Empire/The Pacific/Sopranos* HBO alum Tim Van Patten, *Perry Mason* is shot in noir style by David Franco and produced by star Matthew Rhys. Rhys's dark, brooding Perry Mason is a hard-boiled private eye prone to heavy drinking who suffers from PTSD after fighting in World War I. Mason's noir style antihero even functions as a detective solving murder mysteries while shifting his talents to arguing lethal crime cases in the courtroom. He ends up behind bars amid shadows by the end of season 2. The opening of the first season was especially dark, visually lightening as the latter part of the season progressed. Noir visual style continued to pervade the second season, especially in stunning elaborate patterns of shadows through venetian blinds backlit through windows, although the second season was a bit visually lighter overall than the first.

Based on actual crimes in Depression-era Los Angeles, *Perry Mason*'s gritty, disturbing atmospheric images flash back to the violent horrors of the combat trenches in World War I; the graphic deaths during the conflict convey Mason's psychological torment.[43] In this new reimagining of *Perry Mason*, reconceiving the central character as a down-on-his-luck, alcoholic private eye solving crime in the shadows while battling his demons from the war certainly invokes classic film noir. The source of Mason's PTSD, shown in nightmarish flashbacks, is evocative of the subjective point of view in classic film noir montages. Rhys recalled being inspired by Raymond Chandler and Humphrey Bogart in preparing for the role.[44]

HBO's *Perry Mason* was distinctive for its expressionistic aesthetic and exceedingly self-aware of the classic style and ethos. It was much darker in visual style and thematic tone than the original network television series. Critics repeatedly compared *Perry Mason* to film noir and praised the long-form drama for reenvisioning its imagery and artistic technique. *Perry Mason* harkens back to the gritty Depression era with stunning chiaroscuro cinematography evoking the ambient visuals and existential zeitgeist punctuated by Terence Blanchard's atmospheric jazz score to emphasize its blue-toned mood. Blanchard's pensive music was evocative of classic noir and his moody scores for Spike Lee films, including *Mo' Better Blues* (1990) and *Da 5 Bloods*, as well as Showtime's television series *Homeland*.

Critics applauded HBO's *Perry Mason* as a "swank noir," a "stylish, Depression-noir reboot" of the earlier lighter show, and "one of the most beautiful series ever made."[45] They also praised Franco's cinematography as a feast of great "cinematic noir works, evoking the Depression-era timeframe by way of sepia filters and bluesy shading."[46] "Like so many great noirs before it," wrote media critic Ben Travers in *IndieWire*, *Perry Mason* is an "exquisitely rendered crime noir." He praised the series' shadows, night shoots, and impeccable lighting, which together create an "ambiance akin to the best black-and-white noirs, only in color."[47] Graham Fuller of *Sight and Sound* called *Perry Mason* an "impressively murky Depression-era retro-noir," commending its visual style, and compared it to Netflix's *Babylon Berlin*.[48] The fact that its cinematic style was compared to noir in the British Film Institute's *Sight and Sound*, a renowned cinema journal,

4.11 Elaborate backlighting, venetian blinds, and shadows surround Matthew Rhys, who stars as the gritty noir detective antihero fighting crime and PTSD in *Perry Mason*. HBO, 2020

is noteworthy: cinephiles loved the aesthetic. Other conventional television critics were less appreciative of noir style in these dark long-form dramas.

A distinctively noir look and style also pervaded streaming rival Disney+'s long-form *Star Wars* spinoff series *The Mandalorian*. The chiaroscuro imagery in *The Mandalorian* was dark. It sported impressive noir visual design, especially in the darker first season, which is cloaked in shadows and many nighttime scenes. In fact, some television critics complained that *The Mandalorian*—like *Jessica Jones*, *Daredevil*, and *Game of Thrones*—was too dark. Disney was criticized for not offering actual high-dynamic-range (HDR) cinematography for *The Mandalorian*, resulting in darker contrast digital streaming images. The second season of *The Mandalorian* (like *Daredevil* and *Jessica Jones*) is much brighter visually than the first season—set in sunlit deserts and frozen, white, snow-covered ice caves. Nonetheless, *The Mandalorian* was supremely enjoyable as a visually dark, long-form episodic *Star Wars* adventure series with an adorable baby Yoda, nostalgically invoking the original films.

Filming for *The Mandalorian* used innovative new technologies. *American Cinematographer* marveled at how Lucasfilm's Industrial Light & Magic digitally created and produced the entire noir-style setting of *The Mandalorian* in studio using new enhanced Stagecraft visual effects screen technology, which enabled the series to shoot digitally to replicate actual locations and used footage from Iceland and Chile. Filming for season 2 of *The Mandalorian* was completed right before the COVID-19 lockdown in early spring 2020, and

Stagecraft also allowed filmmakers to resume some shooting despite the pandemic. In particular, *The Mandalorian* cinematographers Greig Fraser and Barry Idoine and showrunner Jon Favreau employed new Stagecraft technologies to frame images for *The Mandalorian* that emulated the look of "exotic, picturesque locations," which was invaluable because it allowed them to film the series virtually in studio without having to travel to remote locales. They admitted that "it simply wasn't plausible to take a crew to the deserts of Tunisia or the salt flats of Bolivia on a short schedule and limited budget" (or to do anything like that during the COVID-19 pandemic, for that matter).

These new technologies resulted in exquisite virtual locales all shot in the studio, which added to the shadowy noir visual style of *The Mandalorian*. Filmmakers used more sophisticated virtual digital special effects to render images and allow shooting on soundstages, not unlike the rear projection so often used in 1940s films noir. As explained in an interview with *American Cinematographer*, digital "technology had to advance enough that the epic worlds of *Star Wars* could be rendered on an affordable scale by a team whose actual production footprint would comprise a few soundstages and a small back lot." In explaining the production techniques and special effects used for shooting *The Mandalorian*, filmmakers applauded the invaluable "ability to do real-time, in-camera compositing on set . . . so that the actors were in that environment in the right lighting—all at the moment of photography," which was accomplished using Stagecraft volume motion capture compositing.[49]

Unlike edgier original noir programming (i.e., HBO, Netflix and Marvel coproductions) aimed at adults, Disney/Lucasfilm's *The Mandalorian* targeted families and teens with PG-13 content. Its episodes are a mere thirty minutes each, and they are not released all at once to binge like an extended movie. Instead, they are programmed once a week like a family-oriented network television show, reimagining a high-concept blockbuster for an adolescent audience. Despite the gorgeous cinematic imagery and cutting-edge effects technology, *The Mandalorian* was criticized as being too shadowy. For instance, television critics such as Dan Clarendon of *TV Insider*, Matthew Dessem of *Slate*, and Matt Mitovich of *TV Line* objected to shadows in *The Mandalorian* and other noir long-form dramas. Clarendon complained that the dark aesthetic was marring these shows: "For many viewers, television is too dark these days—not in subject matter, necessarily, but actual cinematography. Even with expensive televisions, some viewers can't make out the action of their favorite shows, let alone those who try watching programs on smaller screens." Critics took issue with what Mitovich described as "directors—and more often showrunners/producers—trying to get too cinematic" with "dimly-lit," "prestige television," low-light cinematography. Dessem attributed this growing dark, cinematic, long-form noir phenomenon to being "naturally modeled on Gordon Willis' famous low-light work on *The Godfather*."[50]

The fact that this enhanced cinematic noir style is so widespread in the digital streaming universe across an array of platforms—from Netflix to HBO Max, Amazon, and even Disney+—shows how pervasive, powerful, influential, and persistent the noir visual style is. It is impressive that long-form noir productions are using new technology to heighten visual artistry and emulate Willis's low-lit cinematography in *The Godfather*. Noir has remarkable longevity and adaptability. These shadowy long-form productions simulate extended episodic noir movies rather than traditional, conventional television (or even prestige television).

Transnational Noir in the Streaming Era

Noir style was also evident overseas in transnational coproductions, such as the Netflix original production *Babylon Berlin*. Transnational production, noir visual style, and cultural critique evolved in the digital era in international, long-form, noir digital content and neo-noir films. Streaming companies continue to create and reenvision a noir-style past by invoking visual conventions in a global context. Netflix does this through international partnerships, overseas productions, and coproductions, as seen in transnational productions such as *Babylon Berlin*. Set in prewar Berlin, *Babylon Berlin* was shot in Germany with an atmospheric, stylish noir narrative that engaged in cultural critique. *Babylon Berlin* was coproduced by X Filme Creative/ARD/Sky, which partnered with Netflix on the production. Like an extended cinematic movie on an epic scale, *Babylon Berlin*, was touted as the most expensive German television series ever made. It engages in social commentary as it re-creates the strife and free-wheeling hedonism of Weimar Berlin. In a smaller version of cameras used for *Darkest Hour*, neo-noir visual style was enhanced in *Babylon Berlin* by shooting with advanced portable digital equipment using lightweight Arri Alexa mini cameras and Panavision PVintage lenses to accentuate its chiaroscuro aesthetic. The series uses ominous visual cues in its stylish, shadowy imagery to warn of the troubling signs of fascism in the rise of the Third Reich while invoking film noir, Weimar cinema, *Cabaret* (1972)–style noir musicals, hard-boiled detectives, jazz, showgirls, gritty crime, and political intrigue.

In *Babylon Berlin*, Volker Bruch plays traumatized World War I veteran Gereon Rath, a hard-boiled, drug-addicted detective investigating murder, blackmail, and porn films. He is aided by a prostitute-turned-stenographer and aspiring female detective, Charlotte Ritter (Liv Lisa Fries). Rath and Ritter are fabulous dancers in Weimar nightclubs, and they perform in surreal dream sequences reminiscent of Bob Fosse's *Cabaret* and Dennis Potter's *The Singing Detective* (1986), and *Pennies from Heaven* (1978, 1981). While recalling film noir, *Babylon Berlin* is also evocative of other Netflix international coproductions: *Generation War*, also starring Bruch and harkening back to World War II Germany, and Cold War espionage drama *The Same Sky*, set in 1970s East and West Berlin.[51]

4.12 A color noir shot of traumatized hard-boiled detective Gereon Rath (Volker Bruch) in *Babylon Berlin*. X Filme Creative Pool/Netflix, 2017

4.13 Shadows cover prostitute-turned-stenographer (and aspiring female detective) Charlotte Ritter (Liv Lisa Fries) as she moves through a color, noir-style Weimar nightspot in *Babylon Berlin*. X Filme Creative Pool/Netflix, 2017

Babylon Berlin's brilliant noir-style postmodern re-creation of the Weimar-era metropolis is the centerpiece of the long-form drama. Berlin is the star of the show, the *New York Times* observes. "The lavish production lovingly recreates the city's 1920s streets, cafés, and nightclubs. Around 70 percent of the series was shot on location." Yet the brooding series sported a decidedly expressionistic, chiaroscuro, noir aesthetic (rather than lighter shades of gray 'film gris' tones). Recreating the Weimar era in classic noir style, *Babylon Berlin* was also filmed on a massive soundstage set created at the historic Babelsberg studios. The huge production was shot in 180 days and cost €38 million (about $44 million) to produce. The ambitious series had three different crews, and its writer-directors Tom Tykwer, Achim von Borries, and Henk Handloegten had all sought to work together on a project based on the prewar Weimar period and disturbing rise of the Nazis.[52] *Babylon Berlin* conjures cinematic, film noir-style memories, films, and documentaries about World War I and Weimar Germany, capturing the creative zeitgeist of UFA studio and Weimar cinema in its modernist opening credits, which pay homage to the German expressionism that was so influential to film noir, avant-garde experimentation, and Walter Ruttmann's 1920s films *Opus I* and *Berlin: Symphony of a Great City*. The first two seasons of *Babylon Berlin* were released all at once on Netflix to enable binge-viewing. *Babylon Berlin* star Liv Lisa Fries also opened Netflix's original neo-noir film *Munich: The Edge of War* (2021), which offers social critique regarding the 1938 Munich Agreement and the dangerous rise of fascism and anti-Semitism. Long-form espionage noir *The Defeated* (2020), set in 1946 Berlin, examined the aftermath and devastation of the war in Europe.

In this evolving digital era, transnational noir streaming media also included an array of Nordic noir films such as *The Girl with the Dragon Tattoo* (Sweden 2009; United States 2011) and *The Snowman* (2017, shot in Oslo, Norway). Netflix's first original long-form was a Nordic noir, *Lilyhammer* (2012), a Norwegian Rubicon/Renegade TV production, a gangster comedy yarn with music, starring Steven Van Zandt from HBO's *The Sopranos* and Bruce Springsteen's E Street Band. Other productions include stylish long-form dramas like *Marcella* (2016–2021), described as a "Nordic noir set in London." It reimagined classic noir and neo-noir style. Swedish actor Stellan Skarsgård starred as a menacing homme fatale serial killer in *The Girl with the Dragon Tattoo*. He played a brooding, psychologically tormented detective antihero in moody long-form noir *River* (2015). Skarsgård also portrayed a Russian mafia money launderer in the John Le Carré British spy thriller neo-noir film *Our Kind of Traitor* (2016).

Neo-noir productions continue to proliferate as Netflix aggressively moves into expanding its streaming service globally and making international production deals for original long-form dramatic noir programs, while acquiring other series from overseas for its diverse offering of Netflix originals such as *Babylon Berlin*, *Kleo* (2022–), and *The Witcher* (2019–, shot in Hungary, Poland,

Austria, and the Canary Islands); BBC coproductions *Giri/Haji*, *River*, and *Collateral*; and ITV coproduction *Marcella*. The streamer partnered with *Blade Runner* filmmaker Ridley Scott, who produced the moody neo-gothic noir film *Earthquake Bird* (shot in Tokyo), and with John Woo, who directed neo-noir *Manhunt* (2017) in Osaka and around the Kansai region of Japan. Other long-form noirs such as Netflix neo-Gothic *Maid* (2021, shot in Victoria, Vancouver Island, Canada) engaged in cultural critique and highlighted the disturbing gender polemics and distress of domestic abuse. Long-form noir *The Journalist* (2022), also filmed on location in Tokyo, Japan, involved a tenacious maverick reporter investigating dangerous political and institutional corruption. Stylish espionage noir *Kleo* was shot in Berlin, Germany, and Mallorca, Spain. Gritty crime noir *AKA* (2023) was filmed in Île-de-France and in locations around Paris, France. Shadowy spy thriller *Traitors* (2019, coproduced by Channel 4) was shot in Cardiff and South Wales (standing in for 1945 London), and *The Diplomat* was filmed around London and the Cotswolds in the United Kingdom. In this changing media production and distribution climate, streaming companies such as Netflix are increasingly producing and offering noir.[53] Darkness pervaded other noir-style Netflix original programming, such as low-lit serial long-form dramas *Ozark* and *The Chilling Adventures of Sabrina*.

Digital Darkness and Noir Imagery: *The Chilling Adventures of Sabrina* and *Ozark*

Netflix clearly has thrived offering original noir-style, long-form dramas such as *The Chilling Adventures of Sabrina* (2018–2020), a coproduction between Netflix and Warner Bros. Starring Kiernan Shipka of *Mad Men* fame as Sabrina Spellman, the series was based on Archie Comics and developed by Roberto Aguirre-Sacasa. It was shot in Vancouver, Canada. To create the brooding, noir-style, supernatural underworld visual effects, Netflix and Warner Bros. collaborated with acclaimed visual effects company Zoic Studios, best known for the special effects work on *Game of Thrones*, *Firefly*, and *Buffy the Vampire Slayer*.

The Chilling Adventures of Sabrina is steeped in blackened imagery, and the show self-reflexively comments on its absence of light. It projects noir narratively and visually while characters exist in the shadows; murderous underworld gangs destroy lights and black out a city; and tormented antiheroes experience nightmares flashing back to the 1940s, then meet their demise in an existential abyss. Like *Daredevil* and *Jessica Jones*, *The Chilling Adventures of Sabrina* created an unlit world that was significantly darker visually than its earlier comic book, graphic novel, or other incarnations. Zoic executive and creative director Andrew Orloff noted, "When I started talking to Lee Krieger, the director of the first two episodes, who kind of set the look for the show with Rob [Seidenglanz], the other directing producer, it became clear that they were doing something that was aesthetically and visually different."

The entire milieu of the long-form noir series is dramatically shrouded in low-lit shadows. Filmmakers also used cinematic lenses to create visual effects, such as blurring backgrounds in the style of a vignette. "The lenses they used for those scenes are specialty, vintage lenses," Orloff explained. "They were basically museum pieces that they retrofitted to the digital cameras they use on the show to give it that filmic look. This is still being shot digitally with all the modern technology, but the glass they put it through—literally the lens that the show is being viewed through—is of that time." In other words, as in *Jessica Jones*, retro equipment was used for *The Chilling Adventures of Sabrina* to create a more cinematic look. "They're anamorphic and have a very specific type of distortion and feel, and create a very specific look they use to communicate when there's heavy magic being used on the show. It creates a very unique and specific effect, and it's a cool visual signature."[54]

In an interview with *Digital Trends*, Orloff discussed Zoic and the visual effects studio's work on *The Chilling Adventures of Sabrina*. "It was going for this very specific look that referenced a lot of horror films from the '70s and the early '80s—Roman Polanski films, Dario Argento films, Romero, et cetera. They wanted to make it look like it was an artifact from that time and from that space, plucked out of that whole genre, and that was exciting."[55] This visual retro gothic look further enhanced the deep chiaroscuro, noir-style aesthetic. *The Chilling Adventures of Sabrina* even mocked the bright, high-key visual conventions of broadcast television sitcoms (e.g., the earlier, lighter ABC sitcom television series *Sabrina*, even recasting its characters and actors in a darker undertone) in favor of a more cinematic look resembling film noir saturated in murky blackness. Four seasons of *The Chilling Adventures of Sabrina* were cloaked in stunning, brooding, chiaroscuro noir visual style.

Technical innovation and a noir style also permeated Netflix's long-form neo-noir *Ozark*, executive-produced and (occasionally) directed by its star Jason Bateman. Producer-star Bateman directed the first two episodes of seasons 1, 2 and 3 as well as the final two episodes of season 1 and the finale of season 4. Bateman won an Emmy in 2019 for his direction in season 2. *Ozark* received eighteen Emmy nominations in 2020 for season 3.[56] *Ozark* was recognized by Matt Grobar of *Deadline* for its "highly cinematic, extremely dark realism" in the gritty tone and aesthetic that "visually shape a world" of "brutal psychological and physical violence" involving a tormented antihero who launders money for—and whose family becomes dangerously embroiled in—a murderous drug cartel. *Ozark* features nightmarish spaces and low-lit nocturnal imagery shot by cinematographers Ben Kutchins (in the first two seasons), Armando Salas (in the third season), and Shawn Kim (in the final fourth season) to achieve what filmmakers called "a coolness, a cold color palette" that "felt like it was shot on old Fuji film, like an old European movie."[57]

For instance, Kutchins employed stark noir visual style in the cinematography for *Ozark* to enhance the realism and intimacy, paying homage to Orson Welles's classic noir technique and stylized mise-en-scène in *The Lady from Shanghai* and *Citizen Kane*. "Orson Welles was one of the first people to really play with that idea that putting a wide lens right up next to an actor's face really brings you into their world," Kutchins observed. As in classic Welles cinematography, an unsettled camera reveals information and perspective to heighten psychological tension.[58] Kutchins explained that because Netflix required original films and series to be shot in ultra high definition 4K UHD, the first two seasons of *Ozark* were shot using a Panasonic VariCam digital camera to achieve gritty, low-key, dimly lit chiaroscuro noir imagery in ultra high definition. "We shot the show on a Panasonic VariCam, and the reason we chose that is a combination of needing to shoot on 4K, but also the camera really performs well in low light, and that's something we knew we were going to be doing a lot of," emphasizing the filmmakers' desire to make digital photography look more cinematic and emulate the visual style of a classic film noir motion picture. He added, that in particular, "the Panasonic performs" impressively "in low light and there's a [visual] grittiness to it…that I think is filmic." In emulating noir style, Kutchins noted that there is an effort on the show to use the least amount of light possible. He explained that the cold visual color palette accentuating noir style in *Ozark* is digitally achieved using just enough light to barely see the actors' eyes.[59]

The pitch-black night scenes, long narrow claustrophobic hallways, shadowy interiors, reflective voyeuristic glass windows, subjective point-of-view shots, and depressing blue-gray tint of daytime images accentuated the ominous tension and eerie noir visual style in *Ozark*. A brooding darkness permeated the visuals of the Netflix drama, especially in seasons 1, 2, and 4. In the first two seasons, for example, Kutchins noted that he sought to create "the subtlest version of a really hostile and dangerous environment" and used a wide lens to capture the isolating atmosphere. "A wider lens more replicates the human perspective. I'm going to feel more presence of the environment . . . Not a mushy background completely out of focus, but to always feel like the actors are really a part of the environment. The shadows on their faces are a part of their environment and they could disappear into the shadows at any point."[60]

Filled with blues and blacks, *Ozark* is extremely dark in its noir style and aesthetic. To intensify the color blue in the images, filmmakers used an in-camera cyan tilt with practical and single-source lights, then made sure episodes were precisely color-corrected in digital post-production. In creating this distinctive visual style that paid homage to classic film noir, filmmakers wanted to do something that was unique to *Ozark* to create a distinct look. When asked

4.14 Pitch-black shadows cloak murderous crimes in *Ozark*. Netflix, 2017–2022

why *Ozark* is so dark, Kutchins explained that he and Bateman intended the visual design of the show to "emulate the disturbing world the Byrd family has to navigate." They achieved this effect by color-correcting the imagery to emphasize what is lurking in the shadows.[61] Kutchins also enhanced the noir look of *Ozark* by digitally touching up images to darken certain areas of the frame in post-production to add mysterious shadows. Kutchins collaborated with colorist Tim Stipan to transfer the images digitally into a harsh and inhospitable blue hue to capture the displaced visceral feeling and experience of *Ozark*. "The look is very much like an old Fujifilm," he said. "This very cold world, cyan look . . . is a replication of an old Fujifilm stock that I used to use."[62] These techniques intensified the brooding noir style of *Ozark*. The Netflix noir was so dark that, yet again, critics and viewers complained about the shadowy look.[63]

In this new digital production and binge-watching reception climate, it is worth noting the difficulty of analyzing and critically appraising long-form noir series versus classic noir feature films. One observation, in general, is how many long-form streaming noir productions begin steeped in darker, brooding, shadowy noir style and then are visually lightened in subsequent seasons. This gradual lightening of long-form noir often occurs after critics complain about how dark these series are, as with *Daredevil, Jessica Jones, Perry Mason, Game of Thrones, The Mandalorian, The Chilling Adventures of Sabrina,* and *Ozark*. Nevertheless, filmmakers have noted that streamers, particularly Netflix, have a recognizable aesthetic, evident in the distinctively dark noir look, style, and ethos of Netflix originals. Many television critics, apparently preferring low-resolution, high-key, flat televisual sitcom lighting, complained that noir series were too dark and "filmed in unrelenting noir shadows." I would argue that it is precisely because these stunning, dark, extended filmic productions are actually more accurately simulating long-form noir cinema, meant to be binged all at once in sequence like an expanded movie, rather than a conventional low-resolution television show. Filmmakers on long-form noirs such as *Ozark, Jessica Jones, Daredevil, Game of Thrones,* and *Perry Mason* maintained that their objective was a cinematic experience more like an extended movie soaked in shadowy, low-key, high-contrast visual style instead of the visually constrained, low-contrast imagery of earlier broadcast television. These long-form productions are steeped in blackened noir imagery and pay homage to the visual aesthetic of classic film noir style. As is evident in many international coproductions, cinematic noir visual style also permeated Netflix original long-form series like *Babylon Berlin.* Like *Daredevil,* television critics criticized *The Chilling Adventures of Sabrina* and *Jessica Jones* for exuding visual darkness. Kathryn VanArendonk of *Vulture* insisted "TV Shows Are (Literally) Too Dark," arguing, "Periods of darkness are vital visual tools, which do so much to create mood and delineate space and time," but complained that *Jessica Jones* was too dark. Many television critics—apparently preferring lighter televisual conventions designed for brightly lit living rooms—virulently objected to "an entire episode" of *Jessica Jones* being "filmed in unrelenting noir shadows." Television critics evidently seemed to miss the point of the cinematic noir style of *Daredevil, Jessica Jones, The Chilling Adventures of Sabrina, Ozark,* and even HBO's *Game of Thrones* and *Perry Mason.*[64] Yet I would argue it is precisely this very darkness—so evocative of classic film noir—that makes these digital long-form noir productions so stunning, remarkable, and worthy of critical recognition.

It is worth considering a notable feature of long-form noir: whether the recurrent gradual lighting of visually dark noir series in later seasons is related to critic/viewer fatigue (audiences getting tired of the dark style); capitulation to technical limitations (i.e., not everyone watching on an HD television); or television critics and viewers (accustomed to bright, flat, high-key television lighting) not appreciating cinematic dark style, just as classic noir was later criticized for not showing stars' faces when brightly lit television conventions became popular. As seen in *Daredevil* and Warner Bros.' original conception for *Act of Violence* (1949), it is worth pondering whether digital-era media conglomerates and streaming noir producers insisted on eliminating shadowy night scenes and dark cinematography style. With this in mind, it was very encouraging to see the brooding, blackened noir visual style shadows revived for the final season of Netflix's *Ozark* and intentional creative choices again paying homage and harkening back to the classic noir aesthetic.

As seen in the critical reception for *Perry Mason,* some film critics were more appreciative of—and familiar with—cinematic conventions of noir visual style cinematography in long-form drama than many television critics. For example, Kelle Long of the *Motion Picture Association* observed that *Ozark* is "relentless" with "gruesome death" and "grisly torture . . . the camera offers no relief. You cannot look away. . . . The show's cinematography is compelling and immersive," adding, "*Ozark* benefits from committing to the darkness. Some of the plot points can be surreal, but the style carries a weight and realism."[65] Later, after critics complained of its extremely dark visual style, *Ozark* shifted from using a Panasonic Super 35 VariCam to a full-frame Sony Venice camera in the third season, and used a different cinematographer, Armando Salas, which contributed to the series adopting a slightly lighter, "softer," less shadowy look.[66]

By 2020, the reception climate was upended—both for digital noir media streaming and the theatrical film exhibition market—and completely transformed by COVID-19. Netflix initially announced that Bateman would likely not direct any episodes for *Ozark*'s final season 4. However, the fierce brooding shadows and ominous tones returned in season 4 of *Ozark* (with many episodes directed by women, including star Laura Linney), and Bateman indeed directed a stunning atmospheric series finale.[67] Emulating noir style, Bateman and Linney are often shot in total blackness (except for a slight glimmer of light reflected in their eyes), especially in their dark claustrophobic bedroom as they plot their next move and try to avoid being killed by the Mexican drug cartel they work for. The lethal matriarch (who assassinates her kingpin brother and takes over the cartel) coolly appears in a black dress and stilettos smoking a cigarette, borrowing the iconography of a classic femme fatale. A huge storm moves in as imperiled characters drive on slick slippery roads and run through the pouring rain on a blackened night evocative of so many classic noir films. A new cinematographer, Shawn Kim, shot season 4 to emphasize an even darker "sense of danger in the shadows" and used "negative space" to visually intensify "alienation and entrapment" in the later episodes of the series.

Filmmakers compared *Ozark* to classic film noir technique and explained how they strived to make the final season darker than ever. In shooting the final episodes, "in terms of light," Kim explained, "it's mostly about denser shadows, elevated contrast—a bit more noir." To create such pervasive darkness even on bright sunny days filming on location in Georgia, Kim and camera operator Ari Issler had to literally block and "blot out" the sun to create blackened images and cloak characters in murky shadows when shooting.[68] As in *Ozark, Daredevil, Jessica Jones, Perry Mason, Game of Thrones, The Mandalorian, Babylon Berlin*, and *The Chilling Adventures of Sabrina* and in feature films *Bridge of Spies* and *The Irishman*, filmmakers' cinematic objectives to create noir style are now enhanced by new advances and technological improvements. Filmic long-form serial noirs are clearly conceived with cinematic production aims and sophisticated cinematography accentuated by new digital technology reimagining the look and visual style of classic noir films, even remaking them as in *Nightmare Alley* (1947/2021), the female gothic *Rebecca* (1940/2020), and the noir musical *West Side Story* (1961/2021).

EPILOGUE

THE PERSISTENCE OF NOIR IN THE COVID-19 ERA

2020 and Beyond

The persistence of film noir throughout American film history and its continuing influence and contemporary resonance are truly remarkable. The profound transnational legacy of the shadowy visual style lives on, evolving from its origins in the 1940s blackened chiaroscuro of nitrate film through the grayer 1950s film gris aesthetic style to widescreen color noir productions intended to heighten spectacle and compete with the high-key, low-contrast look of television. Noir then spread overseas in transnational productions that influenced and anticipated later postclassical neo-noir films in a new Hollywood era. The noir vision eventually shifted to a new media proliferation of neo-noir productions streaming—and binge-viewing—darkness in the digital era, a trend that was enabled by emergent technology and aesthetic technique in a global convergent culture. Viewers far and wide now regularly stream and binge-watch noir content, paying homage to the classic style.

The 1940s film noir impulse has evolved, transformed, and persisted in new and different iterations in a digital streaming media era. Noir had come a long way from the 1940s to 2020. The legacy of Alfred Hitchcock's iconic gothic noir film has endured to inspire a new cinematic version of *Rebecca* (1940), remade eighty years later in glorious color noir style by Ben Wheatley and streamed digitally via Netflix in late 2020. "In 50 years, the dawn of the streaming broadcasters might be remembered as another golden age of cinema," *American Cinematographer* observed of *Rebecca* in January 2021. Despite a global pandemic, noir continued to be reimagined in the digital streaming era as the words from

Alfred Hitchcock's classic 1940 adaptation of Daphne du Maurier's 1938 novel *Rebecca*, "Last night I dreamt I went to Manderley again," were heard in the opening voice-over narration of a new gothic noir iteration echoing across screens. *Rebecca* (2020) was shot to achieve noir visual style with digital technology, revealing how new productions reimagine classic noir style in the new digital streaming era, particularly in the wake of COVID-19. The use of new advanced digital technology, which enabled noir style in the new neo-gothic incarnation of *Rebecca*, was recognized and praised in industry trade journals. *American Cinematographer* noted, "Right now, the fight for dominance is funding a huge range of productions that demand carefully applied craft and also, increasingly, the big guns of modern production technology," such as "larger sensors, HDR [high dynamic range], 4K and beyond. Sometimes, though, that drive for high-spec moviemaking meets a simultaneous desire for classical pictures that evoke a period setting," as in noir-style *Rebecca*—streaming as an original film on Netflix.[1]

The 2020 Netflix version recalled classic noir with a sense of nostalgia. Hitchcock's classic film and the new Netflix digital incarnation opened with the same moody voice-over narration and subjective point of view, flashing back in time to evoke nightmare memories. The shadowy chiaroscuro imagery, ominous themes, dark stylized mise-en-scène, and flashback narrative structure in the remake (as in Hitchcock's version) recall more masculine hard-boiled films noir—but with a woman narrator. Rather than an urban jungle, the film has the menacing sights, eerie sounds, and black silhouette of a haunted mansion in ruins and overrun by tendrils of swirling fog and a tangled labyrinth of clutching vines. These feminized strains of gothic noir films—a more woman-centered noir variation compared to the tormented hard-boiled antihero and dangerous femme fatale seductress in masculine iterations of hard-boiled noir, as indicated by the elusive female narrator describing the gothic noir scene in *Rebecca*—targeted a female audience and centered on a woman's point of view, as a naïve, ingénue-redeemer-everywoman protagonist encountered an older, mysterious, potentially deadly homme fatale.

Phil Rhodes of *American Cinematographer* noted the ominous, blackened low-lit ambiance and dark secrets pervading the digital remake of *Rebecca*. After marrying a widower, tormented noir-style gothic heroine Mrs. de Winter (Lily James) finds that her husband is being investigated for murdering his first wife Rebecca, then obsessively takes matters into her own hands and emulates a female detective investigating the murder in the dark shadows of an after-hours, claustrophobic locale to solve the crime (and attempt to clear her husband's name). The assertive actions of the heroine make this remake more contemporary and perhaps more noir than the original. "A small corner of London had been taken 80 years into its own past," *American Cinematographer* recalled, and in a new digital technological era, "simulating the historically

E.1 Cinematographer Laurie Rose creates deep shadows and indigo blue color noir style in *Rebecca*. Netflix/Working Title, 2020

warm glow of receding streetlights." Cinematographer Laurie Rose observed the "wetter, dreary, more Gothic" milieu created for the *Rebecca* remake, in which forbidding housekeeper Mrs. Danvers (Kristin Scott Thomas) menaces the new Mrs. de Winter, who is trapped in the shadows of Manderley in a "kind of ghost story." Thus, the traumatized noir heroine eventually gathers her wits and becomes a resilient gritty survivor.

Netflix's transnational noir *Rebecca* (coproduced with Working Title) was shot at numerous old mansions across the United Kingdom, in the south of France, and on a location off Tudor Street in London. *Rebecca* was shot digitally with night-for-night photography to emulate classic gothic noir period style. Rose, like many digital cinematographers, strove for shooting and lighting to create a filmic look harkening back to film noir on celluloid. Shooting with a large-format 65mm version of the cameras used in *Darkest Hour* (2017), Rose captured the shadowy noir interiors and stunning sweeping locations of the Mediterranean and UK countryside using an Arri Alexa 65 digital camera with a huge 6.5K sensor and Arri Prime DNA lenses to provide an atmospheric canvas of period imagery based on "vintage optics from different historical periods." He also filmed using a Steadicam, which enabled a more fluid mobile style of digital darkness. Rose noted how thematic narrative concerns informed the film's visual style as a neo-gothic noir, accentuating the subjective mood of the tormented heroine as she "undergoes an emotional change, grows up and develops a darker side." Noting the influence of noir on the gothic, he observed, "It's the detective story where she takes control of her destiny, for good or bad." To achieve this noir visual aesthetic style in *Rebecca*, Rose explained that "[m]ore and more, with bigger sensors and higher resolutions," he wanted to create "vintage" cinematic images using a digital camera.[2]

The noir impulse has endured as Netflix and other streaming media have evolved, transforming amid rapid growth, while Netflix continues its noir-style offerings.[3] What a difference seventy years and the global COVID-19 pandemic made to alter filmmaking and filmgoing reception conditions since *Sunset Boulevard* (1950) signaled the twilight of nitrate cinema in 1950 after the earlier 1940s pinnacle of expressionistic film noir visual style. By 1950, Hollywood executives sought to avoid downbeat cinematic depictions of noir violence, extreme brutality, disease, sickness, sordid underworld backgrounds with unsympathetic characters and overemphasized suffering on screen. At the time, Darryl Zanuck warned all directors and producers at the Fox studio in 1950 about films such as Elia Kazan's viral disaster noir *Panic in the Streets* (1950), Billy Wilder's *Sunset Boulevard*, John Huston's *Asphalt Jungle* (1950), Otto Preminger's *Where the Sidewalk Ends* (1950), and other noir films with psychopathic characters who have "outlived their usefulness"—as a "shocking disappointment" and a "very high risk."[4]

In contrast, the popularity of digital noir soared in 2020 and 2021 as streaming services saw a huge spike in viewership, with a particularly high viral demand for disease-oriented disaster productions, evocative of toxic disaster noir *Panic in the Streets*, with *Contagion* (2011), *Outbreak* (1995), *Outer Banks* (2020–), and *Chernobyl* (2019) becoming top-viewed streaming titles in the spring of 2020. *IndieWire* observed, "Many people are opting not for escapism, but for movies that imagine just how bad pandemics can get."[5] While the rapidly spreading coronavirus devastated communities worldwide and closed theaters, workplaces, schools, and universities; shuttered film and television production; and canceled cinema conferences and film festivals in an era of social distancing, cineastes in quarantined isolation increasingly streamed cinema and media, including noir, online in surging numbers in 2020 and 2021. COVID-19 radically transformed film and media production and reception contexts, with exhibition and filmmaking halted and distribution shifted to streaming. Not only were viral disease disaster noir films popular during the pandemic, Netflix original long-form drama *Outer Banks*, a post-hurricane, crime-murder-mystery disaster noir, was one of the most-watched Netflix titles in the United States (in the top ten) when it appeared on April 15, 2020. Season 2 of *Outer Banks*, shot amid the epidemic from August 2020 through April 2021, was also the highest-viewed (number-one Netflix title) when it was released on July 30, 2021.

There was even a circulation of noir titles swapped between streamers of digital noir in the wake of the pandemic and the surging demand for noir streaming content, as seen in *Daredevil* (2015–2018), *Jessica Jones* (2015–2019), and other noir-style Marvel coproductions moving from Netflix to Disney+, reinforcing the ephemeral nature of digitally streaming noir as productions appear and disappear online. Italian producer Gianni Nunnari, who executive-produced neo-noir films such as David Fincher's *Se7en* (1995) and Martin Scorsese's *The Departed* (2006) and *Shutter Island* (2010), co-executive-produced the atmospheric long-form noir *StartUp* (2016–2018), starring *Sherlock*'s Martin Freeman as a crooked cop and Adam Brody embroiled in cybertech, murder, and drug money laundering, for Sony's Crackle streaming service. *StartUp* was shot on location in San Juan, Puerto Rico (although it was set amid the nightscape, corruption, gang wars and tough streets of Miami), and ran three seasons before it was canceled, then was picked up and acquired a few years later by Netflix, which breathed new life into the long-form digital noir series, released in October 2020 in the midst of the pandemic to soaring popularity, then later disappearing in 2022.[6]

Yet media analysts expressed concern that the pandemic would permanently transform the industry as film and media productions struggled to resume shooting operations in the wake of the global COVID-19 outbreak. For instance, it was initially not clear when digital noir *Ozark* or other noir series would resume production (*Ozark*'s final season eventually aired in 2022). There were casualties of the virus: one of the actors in *Outer Banks* died of COVID-19 during production. Netflix canceled the 2020 original long-form neo-noir *Queen Sono*, reversing the renewal of the South African series because of the difficulty of shooting in thirty-seven different locations across four countries in Africa during the pandemic.[7] The pandemic also interrupted production midseason on Showtime's long-form neo-noir *Billions*, leading to its release as a partial incomplete season 5, and the loss of tormented noir antihero Ax (Damian Lewis) until the final season 7 of the series. Production for HBO Max original Yakuza noir series *Tokyo Vice* was shut down and delayed eight months because of the virus, which complicated shooting on location in Tokyo, although the crew was able to film in less-accessible areas of the city with fewer crowds after the lockdown.

Warner Bros.' noir-style *The Batman* (2022) feature suspended production for six months because of a widespread outbreak on set, which included star Robert Pattinson, and the death of its vocal coach from COVID-19 while filming on location in London and Liverpool, England, and Scotland. *The Batman* exuded and reveled in noir visual style. Filmmakers acknowledged the influence of classic film noir and Gordon Willis's cinematography in *The Godfather* (1972) on the moody, shadowy look of *The Batman*. Directed by Matt Reeves, *The Batman* was shot by cinematographer Greig Fraser, who shot *Rogue One* (2016), won an Academy

Award for *Dune* (2021), and won an Emmy for *The Mandalorian*. Filming began in January 2020 and wrapped in March 2021 following the COVID shutdown. Fraser photographed *The Batman* with Arri Alexa LF digital cameras, using digital capture and custom ALFA anamorphic lenses, and also used Stagecraft "volume" digital CGI effects technology to intensify the brooding noir aesthetic.

Fraser and Reeves created a vast, urban noir, nighttime Gotham cityscape of darkness, corruption, rain, and violence lurking in the shadows in *The Batman*'s blackened atmospheric milieu with slashes of light and red in its color noir design. They sought a darker incarnation of *The Batman* that projects a subjective noir point of view from the perspective of a younger, psychologically scarred orphan: like the dangerously flawed detectives and criminals of classic noir, an antihero, Bruce Wayne (Pattinson), is a traumatized vigilante lost in darkness and shadows, functioning as a detective solving crimes.[8]

Of course, COVID-19 also added losses and huge costs to productions. Numerous feature film theatrical releases were affected by the pandemic. Many films were delayed, including *Nightmare Alley* (2021), *The Batman*, *Dune*, and *West Side Story* (2021), as the theatrical market tried to recover from the pandemic in 2021 and 2022. For instance, the release of *The Batman* was pushed back a full year. Despite filming challenges, the brooding $200 million *The Batman* eventually scored box office earnings of over $750 million globally in its theatrical release, making it one of the highest grossing films of 2022.[9] In this case, viewers came out for the noir-style film despite the epidemic. (Many other recognizable intellectual properties, with so-called large, built-in audiences, were flops, especially during the pandemic.)

The release of Steven Spielberg's gritty, epic remake of the noir musical *West Side Story* was rescheduled. After plans to open in theaters in December 2020 were scrapped, the film was eventually released a year later in December 2021 to an extended theatrical run through early 2022. *West Side Story* was shot on film from July through September 2019 on location in New York City; at Steiner Studios soundstages at Brooklyn Navy Yard; and in Paterson, Newark, and Essex County, New Jersey. Cinematographer Janusz Kaminski and production designer Adam Stockhausen had also filmed and designed Spielberg's neo-noir *Bridge of Spies* (2015). Spielberg's new version of *West Side Story* opens with stark realism and empty silhouette shadows of destroyed concrete rubble, emulating the black-and-white style of combat newsreels showing a war zone and the devastation of postwar Europe as it visually presents the setting of warring youth gangs. Its location shooting undercut some of the soundstage-bound noir style of the earlier version. Film historian Mark Harris of *New York* magazine appealed to people to see *West Side Story* on Twitter. Paul Schrader even expressed his concern regarding dim prospects for the theatrical feature market in *The New Yorker*.[10] In a dicey COVID-era theatrical reception context, *West Side Story*, shot for $100 million, earned $72.6 million theatrically before streaming on Disney+ and HBO Max in March 2022.

A smaller, more intimate streaming variation on noir visual style infused the lean Netflix original indie film *Malcolm & Marie* (2021). Noir was adapting to the pandemic: *Malcolm & Marie* was the first Hollywood film written and produced since the COVID-19 outbreak. Directed by Sam Levinson, *Malcolm & Marie* featured moody monochrome cinematography by Marcell Rév, intentionally harkening back to classic noir cinema with chiaroscuro shadows shot on Kodak Double-X 35mm black-and-white film stock using Zeiss Super Speed lenses. Rév explained that filmmakers shot with two actors on one location to "evoke a lot of classics. It was made consciously with a respect to those classics or like a classical kind of filmmaking with the knowledge that we were in 2020. That was paying tribute to these old movies, and we were playing with this kind of style in a modern way." John David Washington played a young emerging film director, Malcolm, with Zendaya as his girlfriend Marie, in a personal story confronting and grappling with harsh truths about their relationship. *Malcolm & Marie* was shot during the outbreak, with filming entirely contained to the Caterpillar House, a glass home in Carmel-by-the-Sea, California. The 35mm black-and-white film was the most-watched title on Netflix when it appeared in February 2021—set, filmed, and streamed at home.[11]

Several black-and-white productions were shot or released during the pandemic, including *Malcolm & Marie*, a monochrome version of *Nightmare Alley: Vision in Darkness and Light* (2022), *Belfast* (2021), and *Mank* (2020). Along with the stunning, impressive, black-and-white cinematography of *Malcolm & Marie*, shot on monochrome film to capture the noir visual style of somber expressionistic spaces more vividly, these films continued the evolving noir style on screen and on streaming services. Instead of shooting on film,

E.2 Director of photography Marcell Rév shot *Malcolm & Marie* on 35mm black-and-white film to produce stunning noir cinematography with moody chiaroscuro shadows. Netflix, 2020

Mank featured stylized, extreme-contrast, electronic photography using a specially designed Red 8K Ranger digital camera with a black-and-white Helium sensor. The look was a very harsh visual aesthetic. For example, a noir-style scene of a shadowy walk through Hearst castle and zoo following a conversation moving from claustrophobic interiors to the outdoor garden in shady chiaroscuro was shot digitally using a day-for-night filter. Director of photography Erik Messerschmidt, who won an Academy Award, acknowledged, "*Mank* is not a gumshoe noir thriller," noting he sought to emulate other styles rather than noir but praised the fast monochrome digital sensor for shooting and preferred the "added range in the shadows" to control subtly the lighting, shadow, highlights, color hue or black-and-white shading, exposure, and contrast in high-dynamic-range (HDR) cinematography.[12]

An even more notable recent neo-noir film is *Nightmare Alley*, an impressive 2021 remake of a classic noir filmed in 1947 by director Edmund Goulding and director of photography Lee Garmes, adapting a 1946 William Lindsay Gresham novel of the same name. The stunning new Searchlight Pictures version of *Nightmare Alley*, directed and cowritten by acclaimed Academy Award–winning Mexican auteur Guillermo del Toro (coscripted by Kim Morgan), was filmed by Danish cinematographer Dan Laustsen, who also shot del Toro's *Crimson Peak* (2015) and Academy Award–winning *The Shape of Water* (2017). It features extraordinary color noir visual style using digital technology. Searchlight also released a black-and-white version of the film, entitled *Nightmare Alley: Vision in Darkness and Light* in Los Angeles. (The original 1947 version was, of course, shot in black and white.) The chiaroscuro imagery in del Toro's neo-noir remake was equally impressive in black and white in the monochrome version of the noir-style film released in Los Angeles theaters in early 2022.

Set in the late 1930s and 1940s prewar and wartime period, the picture is also evocative of classic noir. (Tyrone Power played the noir antihero in the 1947 version.) The film pays visual homage to Orson Welles's *The Lady from Shanghai* (1948); Hitchcock's *Spellbound* (1945); and to *Detour* (1945), *Double Indemnity* (1944), and *The Cabinet of Dr. Caligari* (1919). The film opens in a stark shadowy inferno. Volatile noir antihero Stan Carlisle (Bradley Cooper) murders his father, burns the house down, then joins an eerie carnival. Carlisle rises to fame as a fraudulent mentalist, manipulating and deceiving everyone he meets, until he is betrayed by seductive femme fatale psychologist, Dr. Lilith Ritter (Cate Blanchett). He then becomes a desperate, ruined sideshow geek whose life and livelihood are destroyed.

The new *Nightmare Alley* consciously and visually harkens back to film noir style, and the film is self-reflexively promoted as a noir picture. Publicity even featured what was described as a "neo-noir featurette," a behind-the-scenes trailer in which del Toro discusses his love of film noir and classic Hollywood and his desire to revive its stylish imagery, shadowy deep-focus cinematography, and expressionistic production design. Del Toro articulated his artistic vision for *Nightmare Alley*, which related to the film's ominous, disturbing thematic and narrative concerns, as well as its biting cultural critique. He explained, "*Nightmare Alley* is a look and a very specific strand of the underbelly of America. It is the flip side of the American dream. It's a nightmare." Del Toro underscored his desire to recall film noir. "I love noir as a mood, as an emotion, as a sentiment." Regarding the film's aesthetic design, he added: "I tried to study the [stylistic] language of the period" to emulate classic Hollywood noir cinema visually. "I want this to be the modern equivalent to the movies that people complain they don't do anymore. It's a movie that celebrates cinematic style," del Toro emphasized, and "we wanted it to feel real." He admitted, "It was a monumental endeavor."[13]

In an interview with *American Cinematographer*, cinematographer Laustsen explained how he and del Toro shared a distinctive dark vision for the film and sought to use optics, lenses, and cameras that would accentuate close-up, deep-focus shots. The filmmakers shot *Nightmare Alley* using the Alexa 65 6K digital camera as their main unit for principal photography and Alexa LF digital cameras for Steadicam shots. They used Arri Signature Prime camera lenses and added diffusion to the back of the lens to soften the images and to make them look more cinematic and filmlike. Laustsen described how he and del Toro also used filters on the front of the lens to create a misty, diffused "filter flare" ("not a lens flare") using custom Tiffen Pro Mist filters. In shooting and lighting the picture, Laustsen noted that, throughout filming, he maintained the same T stop—in this case, a 2.8/4 split ("a T3.5") at ISO 800—to maintain a consistent feel to the images.[14]

The filming of *Nightmare Alley* was, like other productions, affected by the pandemic. Laustsen and del Toro began shooting the film on location in Toronto, Canada, and Buffalo, New York, for several weeks in January 2020. Production was then halted for six months because of COVID-19, shutting down in March 2020 until August 2020. When shooting resumed in September, extensive portions of the huge, elaborate, outdoor tent set for the carnival on location in Ontario had blown away and had to be reconstructed. Cooper had lost weight during the pandemic, which worked out well because they had shot the later snowy winter scenes for the end of the film first before resuming shooting the stormy, rain-drenched sequences where tormented drifter Carlisle is emaciated when he initially joins the carnival at the beginning of the film. These developments over the course of the film's production would eventually further enhance the noir style of *Nightmare Alley*.

The lengthy six-month hiatus because of the pandemic provided Laustsen and del Toro more time to come to an even better understanding of how they wanted to continue shooting their noir story when they returned to work with safety protocols in place after the lockdown. Production wrapped in December 2020. Shot for $60 million, the critically acclaimed noir *Nightmare Alley* was

E.3 Bradley Cooper's noir antihero steps onto jet black night streets with red neon signs as shadows permeate the moody nocturnal ambiance in Guillermo del Toro's *Nightmare Alley*. Searchlight/TSG, 2021

released theatrically in December 2021, and in black and white in January 2022, and earned $36.8 million worldwide. It was nominated for Best Picture, Cinematography, Director, and Production Design, then digitally streamed on HBO Max and Hulu in February and March 2022. Martin Scorsese penned an editorial, "Why Martin Scorsese Wants You to Watch *Nightmare Alley*," in the *Los Angeles Times*, praising Guillermo del Toro's ambitious film for its "power," "resonance," "haunted, [and] doomed" characters, noir style, and biting cultural critique; commenting allegorically on the current dystopian COVID-19 climate; and begging viewers to see the noir film.[15]

In 2021 through 2022, as feature film production and theatrical releases resumed after the pandemic lockdown was lifted and as the Academy Award nominations were announced, the profound legacy of the classic noir visual style was strikingly evident. Noir aesthetics permeated many 2022 Academy Award–nominated films across an array of genres, studios, and streaming platforms. Such films included not only *Nightmare Alley* (Searchlight/TSG) but also Steven Spielberg's noir musical *West Side Story* (Amblin/TSG/20th Century), Denis Villeneuve's sci-fi neo-noir *Dune* (Legendary/Warner Bros.), Jane Campion's noir Western *The Power of the Dog* (2021; New Zealand Film Commission/BBC/Netflix), and Kenneth Branagh's black-and-white social realist film *Belfast* (Northern Ireland Screen/TKBC/Universal). In fact, Branagh admitted that the pandemic and global production lockdown inspired him to write and direct the more personal and intimate semiautobiographical story *Belfast*. The solid theatrical box office of Warner Bros.'s *The Batman* also underscored the popularity of noir in 2022.

The legacy of film noir has thrived in the digital new media age of convergent culture. As noir-style productions proliferated on theatrical screens and on streaming platforms, the persistence of the noir impulse endured. The noir style featured prominently as digital streaming continued to transform the industry, and media companies retooled and shifted to streaming—especially in the wake of the COVID-19 era. As we have seen, these noir images permeate a digital streaming media era, and the strategy of producing, programming, and disseminating noir visual style was prominent on streamers like Netflix.[16] Productions such as *Jessica Jones*, *Daredevil*, and *The Irishman* resonated during the pandemic, and an array of gritty noir survivors overcame seemingly insurmountable obstacles on digital screens at home and in theaters, as seen in *Nightmare Alley*, *Belfast*, *The Batman*, *Rebecca*, *Malcolm & Marie*, *Da 5 Bloods* (2020), *Ozark*, *The Night Agent* (2023–), and *The Queen's Gambit* (2020).

Another huge hit in the COVID-19 era was Netflix's atmospheric, original, streaming serial drama *The Queen's Gambit*. The long-form noir featured extensive filming in Germany. It was shot mostly in Berlin and, like *Bridge of Spies* and *Babylon Berlin* (2017–), its impressive noir-style visual aesthetic was created and enhanced by shooting on elaborate soundstages at Babelsberg Film

E.4 Anya Taylor-Joy, in impressive color noir shadow, as self-destructive chess champ Beth Harmon in *The Queen's Gambit*, shot at Babelsberg Film Studio. Netflix, 2020

Studio. *The Queen's Gambit* was expressionistic in its use of light and shadow. Because they were shooting in Germany and there was not much natural sunlight on location, filmmakers set up lights outside the windows to create greater chiaroscuro high contrast in the images. Cinematographer Steven Meizler shot *The Queen's Gambit* using Red Ranger digital cameras with Zeiss Supreme lenses to accentuate its noir visual style.[17]

The Queen's Gambit conveyed a stylish, gendered noir universe on-screen in its moody aesthetic. Like a classic noir antihero, Anya Taylor-Joy was especially memorable in her acclaimed Golden Globe Award–winning performance as a scrappy survivor shrouded in murky shadows with drug-induced hallucinatory nocturnal visions of chess matches. Brooding, rebellious, self-destructive, drug- and alcohol-addicted orphaned chess champ Beth Harmon (Taylor-Joy) spirals into an obsessive dance to Shocking Blue's "Venus" (compulsively drinking in front of the television). She brilliantly defied conventions with her independent noir heroine fighting to survive—and nearly perishing (and overdosing)—in a man's world. *The Queen's Gambit* was a massive success when it streamed on Netflix in the fall of 2020 during the COVID-19 pandemic, winning eleven Emmy Awards and two Golden Globe Awards.

Like the critical acclaim of theatrical features *Nightmare Alley*, *The Batman*, *Dune*, *Belfast*, and *West Side Story*, the popularity of streaming noir-style productions such as *The Irishman*, *Malcolm & Marie*, *Rebecca*, *The Power of the Dog*, *Da 5 Bloods*, *Tokyo Vice*, *Perry Mason*, *Ozark*, *Jessica Jones*, *The Queen's Gambit*, *AKA*, and espionage thriller *The Night Agent* reveal the ongoing legacy of noir visual style content in a digital new media era. Many noirs were especially popular and widely viewed via digital streaming. Scorsese's neo-noir film *The Irishman*; Spike Lee's *Da 5 Bloods*; brooding noir-style neo-gothic *Rebecca*; *The Old Guard*; and noir-inflected long-forms *Ozark*, *Jessica Jones*, *The Queen's Gambit*, *The Night Agent*, and *AKA* were top titles on Netflix in the United States in the weeks that they were released. In fact, Netflix reported a record-setting 62 million households watched long-form noir *The Queen's Gambit* in its first twenty-eight days, making it one of the streamer's biggest scripted limited series to date. *The Queen's Gambit* hit the top ten in ninety-two countries and was number one in sixty-three countries; *The Night Agent* reached Netflix's top ten in ninety-three countries, premiering with 168.71 million hours viewed; 27 million households streamed *Da 5 Bloods*; and 72 million households binge-watched *The Old Guard*.[18]

The industry ultimately transformed during the COVID-19 pandemic in 2020 through 2022, and we have seen how the noir impulse continued. Noir productions are increasingly streamed at home or watched remotely on myriad devices rather than—or in addition to—being projected and screened at a theater.[19] Streamers like Netflix led the charge in the era of media convergence in programming noir content. By 2022, well into the pandemic, theatrical releases also indelibly invoked noir conventions (prior to streaming digitally), as evident in *Nightmare Alley*, *The Batman*, *Dune*, *Belfast*, and *West Side Story*. Noir's legacy and persistent influence is also seen in original long-form noir dramas in the digital streaming era. Such evolving conditions and technological advances are fascinating to consider vis-à-vis the emergent technological and industrial production, distribution, and reception context and the evolution of the noir visual style. Producing and streaming classic film noir, color noir, neo-noir, and long-form neo-noir worldwide reimagines classic noir style and aesthetic technique in the new millennium. It is extraordinary how the noir impulse persists as we look forward to new incarnations of the iconic look and feel of film noir in the future.

NOTES

Introduction

1. Nino Frank, "Un nouveau genre 'policier': l'adventure criminelle," *L'Écran Francais* 61 (August 28, 1946): 8–9, 14; Jean Pierre Chartier, "Les américains aussi font des films noirs," *Revue du Cinema* 1 (November 3, 1946): 66–70; Sheri Chinen Biesen, *Blackout: World War II and the Origins of Film Noir* (Baltimore, MD: Johns Hopkins University Press, 2005), 1–2.
2. John Alton, *Painting with Light* (Berkeley: University of California Press, 1995), 44–45, 56.
3. John Lingan, "Film from the Ashes: A Beautiful but Deadly Art Is Reborn at the Nitrate Picture Show," *The Verge*, June 17, 2015.
4. Dave McNary, "Netflix Closes Deal to Buy Hollywood's Egyptian Theatre," *Variety*, May 29, 2020. The Egyptian reopened in November 2023.
5. *The Irishman* and *Roma* screened theatrically before streaming digitally on Netflix. Lee's *Da 5 Bloods* was supposed to premiere theatrically at the Egyptian in 2020, but the COVID-19 pandemic disrupted plans, necessitating a virtual event instead. L. M. Harnisch, "Noir City Hollywood: CANCELED," *LA Daily Mirror*, March 12, 2020.
6. Thomas Brady, "Big Color Rush On," *New York Times*, June 17, 1951.
7. Mark Harris, *Pictures at a Revolution* (New York: Penguin, 2008), 101, 422.
8. Janusz Kaminski interview on *Bridge of Spies* in ASC Staff, "The cinematographers on *Sicario, Bridge of Spies, Carol* . . . ," *American Cinematographer* 97, no. 1, January 2016.
9. Kathryn VanArendonk, "TV Shows Are (Literally) Too Dark," *Vulture*, August 2016; Kayla Cobb, "'Ozark' Cinematographer Ben Kutchins Explains Why the Hell the Show Is So Dark," *Decider*, August 30, 2018.
10. Raymonde Borde and Etienne Chaumeton, *Panorama du film noir américain (1941–1953)* (Paris: Minuit, 1955); see also Raymonde Borde and Etienne Chaumeton, *A Panorama of American Film Noir*, trans. Paul Hammond (San Francisco: City Lights, 2002).

1. Film Noir Visual Style from Wartime to the Postwar 1940s Nitrate Era

1. Philip Scheuer, "Film History Made by 'Double Indemnity,'" *Los Angeles Times*, August 6, 1944.
2. Contemporaneous American industry trade and critical discourse recognized a psychologically violent Hollywood crime trend spurred by *Double Indemnity* by 1944–1945. Fred Stanley, "Hollywood Crime and Romance," *New York Times*, November 19, 1944; Fred Stanley, "Hollywood Shivers: The Studios Are Busily Stirring Up a Grade A Witches' Brew," *New York Times*, May 28, 1944; Lloyd Shearer, "Crime Certainly Pays on Screen: The Growing Crop of Homicidal Films Poses Questions for Psychologists and Producers," *New York Times*, August 8, 1945; Sheri Chinen Biesen, *Blackout: World War II and the Origins of Film Noir* (Baltimore, MD: Johns Hopkins University Press, 2005), 1–2. (Soon to be coined "film noir" in 1946 as dark crime films *Double Indemnity*, *The Big Sleep*, *Gilda*, and *The Postman Always Rings Twice* were screened for French critics abroad.)
3. Along with blackouts and air raid drills, for instance, war-related shooting constraints included national security restrictions on filming outdoor locations near coastlines and rail lines—especially in the Los Angeles basin, which was considered a "theater of war" after Pearl Harbor; set construction limitations; and rationing of film, lighting and set materials (nails, lumber, rubber, tires [essential for transportation], fabrics necessary for set dressing and wardrobe costumes), as well as electricity, all of which contributed to the development of classic film noir style in wartime. Recycled sets on enclosed studio soundstages were thus cloaked in shadows, smoke, and mirrors, and backlot streets glistened with water from rain machines. For further reading, see Biesen, *Blackout*; Thomas Schatz, *Boom and Bust: American Cinema in the 1940s* (New York: Scribners, 1997).
4. Robert Mitchum interviewed by Arthur Lyons in *Death on the Cheap* (New York: DaCapo, 2000) 2.
5. Mark Robson, interviewed in *The Velvet Light Trap* 10 (1973).
6. Jack Warner letter to Peter Lorre, Jack Warner Collection, USC Cinematic Arts Library, University of Southern California, Los Angeles, California, September 27, 1943.
7. Fred Stanley, "Hollywood Crime and Romance," *New York Times*, November 19, 1944.
8. Shearer, "Crime Certainly Pays on the Screen."
9. Shearer, "Crime Certainly Pays on the Screen."
10. USC Pressbook Collection, USC Cinematic Arts Library, University of Southern California, Los Angeles, California, 1943–46; Raymonde Borde and Étienne Chaumeton, *Panorama du film noir américain (1941–1953)* (Paris: Minuit, 1955); *A Panorama of American Film Noir*, trans. Paul Hammond (San Francisco: City Lights, 2002). See also Biesen, *Blackout*.
11. Stanley, "Hollywood Shivers."
12. Schatz, *Boom and Bust*, 236; Diane Waldman, "Horror and Domesticity: The Modern Gothic Romance of the 1940s" (PhD diss., University of Wisconsin, 1981); Diane Waldman, "'At Last I Can Tell It to Someone!': Feminine Point of View and Subjectivity in the Gothic Romance Film of the 1940s," *Cinema Journal* 23, no. 2 (1984): 29–40.
13. Helen Hanson, *Hollywood Heroines* (London: I.B. Tauris., 2007), 67–68.
14. Stanley, "Hollywood Shivers;" Sheri Chinen Biesen, *Film Censorship: Regulating America's Screen* (New York: Columbia University Press, 2018); Waldman, "Horror and Domesticity;" Waldman, "'At Last I Can Tell It to Someone!;'" Thomas Schatz, *The Genius of the System* (New York: Pantheon, 1988, 1996); Schatz, *Boom and Bust*; Biesen, *Blackout*; Hanson, *Hollywood Heroines*; Sheri Chinen Biesen, *Music in the Shadows: Noir Musical Films* (Baltimore, MD: Johns Hopkins University Press, 2014). See also

Sheri Chinen Biesen, "Manufacturing Heroines: Gothic Victims and Working Women in Classic Noir Films," in *Film Noir Compendium*, ed. Alain Silver and James Ursini (New York: Applause/Hal Leonard, 2016); Alain Silver and James Ursini, eds., *Film Noir Reader 4* (New York: Limelight, 2004-2005).

15. "$5,000 Production: Hitchcock Makes Thriller Under WPA Order on New Sets," *Life* 14 (January 25, 1943): 70-73; Joseph Valentine, "Using an Actual Town Instead of Movie Sets," *American Cinematographer* 23 no. 10 (October 1942): 440-462.
16. Dan O'Shea, letter to Fox president Joe Schenck, David O. Selznick Archive, University of Texas at Austin Harry Ransom Humanities Research Center, Austin, Texas, July 15, 1943, 1; Publicity and Script Files for *Jane Eyre*, Twentieth Century-Fox & USC Pressbook Collections, USC Cinematic Arts Library, University of Southern California, Los Angeles, California, 1943-1944; Schatz, *The Genius of the System*, 331.
17. James Wong Howe, "Visual Suggestion Can Enhance 'Rationed' Sets," *American Cinematographer* 23 no. 5 (June 1942): 246-247.
18. James Wong Howe, "Documentary Film and Hollywood Techniques," 1943 Hollywood Writers Mobilization and University of California Conference Proceedings, presented at UCLA 1943 (published by Berkeley: University of California Press, 1944), 94-96, reprinted as "Documentary Technique in Hollywood," *American Cinematographer* 25 no. 1 (January 1944): 10, 32.
19. George Stevens, quoted in Patrick McGilligan, *Film Crazy* (New York: St. Martin's Press, 2000), 87-88.
20. John Seitz, quoted in Ella Smith, *Starring Miss Barbara Stanwyck* (New York: Crown, 1973), 177.
21. Billy Wilder, interviewed by Cameron Crowe in *Conversations with Wilder* (New York: Alfred Knopf, 1999), 53; Billy Wilder, interviewed by Gene D. Phillips, *Literature/Film Quarterly* (Winter 1976), repr. Robert Horton, ed., *Billy Wilder: Interviews* (Jackson, MS: University Press of Mississippi, 2001), 103.
22. Joseph Breen, MPAA/PCA File, Academy of Motion Picture Arts and Sciences Margaret Herrick Library, Beverly Hills, California, May 25, 1945; J. Edgar Hoover, *Hollywood Citizen-News*, September 6, 1946, 5.
23. Herb Lightman, "Cameraman's Director," *American Cinematographer* 28, no. 4 (April 1947): 124-25, 151. *Notorious* was photographed through January 1946, with retakes in April.
24. For further reading on rear projection, see Sheri Chinen Biesen, "Filming on Location in the Classical Hollywood Studio System: From the Sound Era Through World War II," in *Hollywood on Location: An Industry History*, ed. Joshua Gleich and Lawrence Webb (New Brunswick, NJ: Rutgers University Press, 2019).
25. "Alfred Hitchcock Disclaims Art in Mystery Films," *Ogden Standard Examiner*, May 5, 1946; "Director Says Women Create Sweater Girls," *New Castle News*, September 13, 1946. See also Lizzie Francke, *Script Girls: Women Screenwriters in Hollywood* London: (London: British Film Institute, 1994); Schatz, *Boom and Bust*; Biesen, *Blackout*; J. E. Smythe, *Nobody's Girl Friday* (Oxford: Oxford University Press, 2018); Shelley Stamp, "Film Noir's 'Gal Producers' and the Female Market," *Women's History Review* 29, no. 5 (2019): 801-821.
26. Richard B. Jewell, "RKO Film Grosses, 1929-1951: The C. J. Tevlin Ledger," *Historical Journal of Film, Radio and Television* 14, no. 1 (1994): Appendix 1, 1-11. Like *Notorious*, other films noir *Spellbound, Double Indemnity, The Lost Weekend, Mildred Pierce, The Big Sleep, The Postman Always Rings Twice, Scarlet Street, Gilda, The Blue Dahlia,* and *The Stranger* enjoyed strong box office earnings by 1946, with many making

approximately $5 million. "60 Top Grossers of 1946," *Variety* 165, no. 5 (January 8, 1947): 8; William Schaefer Collection, USC Cinematic Arts Library, University of Southern California, Los Angeles, California, 1944–1946; H. Mark Glancy, "MGM Film Grosses, 1924–1948: The Eddie Mannix Ledger," *Historical Journal of Film, Radio and Television* 12, no. 2 (1992): Appendix 1, 12; Paramount Collection Production Budget File, Academy of Motion Picture Arts and Sciences Margaret Herrick Library, Beverly Hills, California, 1944–1946.
27. Mitchell camera ad, *American Cinematographer* 27, no. 8 (August 1946): 273; Kodak film ad, *American Cinematographer* 28, no. 4 (April 1947): 155.
28. Fred Stanley, "An Old Hollywood Costume," *New York Times*, October 21, 1945, X1, 3; Schatz, *Boom and Bust*; Biesen, *Blackout*.
29. Orson Welles in Stanley, "An Old Hollywood Costume," X1, 3.
30. Shearer, "Crime Certainly Pays on the Screen."
31. Daniel Mainwaring (aka Geoffrey Homes), Frank Fenton, and James M. Cain (uncredited), *Out of the Past*, RKO screenplay, story files and production correspondence, UCLA, 1945–1946.
32. George Turner, "Out of the Past," *American Cinematographer* 65, no. 3 (March 1984): 32–36.
33. RKO Pressbook for *Out of the Past*, USC Pressbook Collection, USC Cinematic Arts Library, University of Southern California, Los Angeles, California, 1947; Daniel Mainwaring (aka Geoffrey Homes), Frank Fenton, and James M. Cain (uncredited), *Out of the Past*, RKO screenplay, story files and production correspondence, UCLA, 1945–1946; Richard B. Jewell, *Slow Fade to Black: The Decline of RKO Radio Pictures* (Berkeley: University of California Press, 2016), 73–74.
34. Joseph Breen, Transcript of Conference Between Executives, Producers and Joseph Breen, RKO Studios, Los Angeles, California, April 11, 1946; Jewell, *Slow Fade to Black*, 44. (Breen had served as RKO production chief in 1941 and 1942 during final filming and release of Hitchcock's gothic noir *Suspicion*.)
35. Joseph Breen, Letter to RKO's William Gordon, MPAA/PCA File, Academy of Motion Picture Arts and Sciences Margaret Herrick Library, Beverly Hills, California, June 12, 1946.
36. Joseph Breen, MPAA/PCA File, Academy of Motion Picture Arts and Sciences Margaret Herrick Library, Beverly Hills, California, June 5–August 23, 1946.
37. "Out of the Past," *Variety*, November 19, 1947, 8.
38. "Out of the Past," *Hollywood Reporter*, November 14, 1947, 3.
39. Bosley Crowther, "Out of the Past," *New York Times*, November 26, 1947, 18.
40. Earning $1,240,000 domestically and $625,000 overseas. Jewell, "RKO Film Grosses."
41. Breen, MPAA/PCA File, Academy of Motion Picture Arts and Sciences Margaret Herrick Library, Beverly Hills, California, June 5–August 23, 1946.
42. "Top-Drawer Industry Leaders Accent Staggering Production Costs but Fear No B.O. Dip," *Variety* 165, no. 5 (January 8, 1947): 5–6.
43. Breen, MPAA/PCA File, Academy of Motion Picture Arts and Sciences Margaret Herrick Library, Beverly Hills, California, June 5–August 23, 1946.
44. Columbia Pressbook for *Dead Reckoning*, USC Cinematic Arts Library, Los Angeles, California, 1947.
45. Columbia Pressbook for *Dead Reckoning*, USC Cinematic Arts Library, Los Angeles, California, 1947.
46. Columbia Pressbook for *Dead Reckoning*, USC Cinematic Arts Library, Los Angeles, California, 1947.
47. "Dead Reckoning," *Hollywood Reporter*, May 29, 1946, 20.

48. T.M.P., "At Loew's Criterion: 'Dead Reckoning,'" *New York Times*, January 23, 1947.
49. *Variety* Staff, "Dead Reckoning," *Variety*, January 29, 1947, 8.
50. Like *Dead Reckoning* and *Out of the Past*, gangsters inhabited the postwar noir *Kiss of Death* (1947). Directed by Henry Hathaway and shot by Norbert Brodine, 20th Century-Fox's *Kiss of Death* starred Victor Mature as a brooding ex-con, Nick Bianco, pressured into working for the police to investigate notorious hoodlum Tommy Udo (Richard Widmark, in his film debut). Udo is a vicious psychopathic killer who cackles while he pushes an old woman in a wheelchair down the stairs as she pleads for her life. *Kiss of Death* publicity invoked horror conventions, including a dead body in posters while displaying a stylized chiaroscuro-lit Mature as the film's tortured antihero. However, Fox did not promote or highlight breakout star Widmark, who steals the picture as the menacing psychotic killer. *Kiss of Death* was filmed on location in New York, although the hard-boiled film had a lighter, more high-key, sun-soaked look because of the extensive location shooting. Fox pressbooks promoted the noir filming on actual locations and outdoor daylight throughout the city. Widmark reprised his murderous psychopath persona in low-lit noir *Road House* (1948) opposite Ida Lupino and Cornel Wilde. The postwar hard-boiled trend continued with other macho noir films such as Robert Wise's shady atmospheric *Born to Kill* (1947), featuring Lawrence Tierney as a brutal killer, promoted with a smoldering cigarette hanging from his grim lips, with Claire Trevor as a dangerous sexualized femme; they were called: "Bullet-Man and Silken Savage." Wise's masculine boxing noir *The Set-Up* (1949) was touted as "Sensational" and "Muscular."
51. Herb Lightman, "The Lady from Shanghai: Field Day for the Camera," *American Cinematographer* 101, no. 8 (June 1948): 200–201, 213.
52. Promoted as three quarters of a mile long.
53. Lightman, "The Lady from Shanghai."
54. Lightman, "The Lady from Shanghai;" Columbia Pressbook for *The Lady from Shanghai*, USC Cinematic Arts Library, University of Southern California, Los Angeles, California, 1948.
55. Lightman, "The Lady from Shanghai," 201.
56. Columbia Pressbook for *The Lady from Shanghai*, USC Cinematic Arts Library, University of Southern California, Los Angeles, California, 1948.
57. Lightman, "The Lady from Shanghai," 213.
58. Publicity, Production and Budget Files for *Dark Passage*, William Schaefer & USC Pressbook Collections, USC Warner Bros. Archive, USC Cinematic Arts Library, University of Southern California, Los Angeles, California, 1947. See also Joshua Gleich, *Hollywood in San Francisco: Location Shooting and the Aesthetics of Urban Decline* (Austin: University of Texas Press, 2018).
59. Documentary style realism infused the visual aesthetic and topical cultural critique of *The Naked City* and hard-hitting social realist noir "message" pictures such as *The Lost Weekend, Body and Soul, Crossfire*, and *Act of Violence*. (Writer-producer Charles Brackett collaborated with Wilder on *The Lost Weekend* after refusing to adapt *Double Indemnity*.) For further reading on *The Naked City*, see Schatz, *Boom and Bust*.
60. This cycle of social problem films gained critical and box office success in Hollywood after World War II. Some were produced independently. Others were produced at studios such as RKO and 20th Century-Fox. In particular, a run of postwar Academy Award Best Picture winners were message pictures—Wilder's *The Lost Weekend* in 1945, William Wyler's *The Best Years of Our Lives* in 1946, Elia Kazan's *Gentleman's Agreement* in 1947, Robert Rossen's *All the King's Men* in 1949. For example, Wyler's *The Best Years of Our Lives* (shot by Gregg Toland, independently produced by Samuel Goldwyn) was the highest grossing

film of the 1940s (since *Gone with the Wind*), earning $11.5 million by 1947, and Kazan's *Gentleman's Agreement* made $7.8 million. Many of these message pictures were championed by socially minded executives such as Dore Schary and Darryl Zanuck during this period just after the war. *The Best Years of Our Lives* made over $10.7 million in its initial release, according to "All-Time Top-Grossers," *Variety*, January 18, 1950, 18.

61. "Body and Soul," *Daily Variety*, August 13, 1947.
62. "Body and Soul," *New Yorker*, November 15, 1947.
63. Jewell, "RKO Film Grosses."
64. USC Pressbook Collection, USC Cinematic Arts Library, University of Southern California, Los Angeles, California, 1947.
65. "Crossfire," *New York Times*, March 1947.
66. American Film Institute; *Ebony*, December 1947.
67. James Wong Howe was graylisted. Dmytryk eventually returned to directing years later, following his agreeing to "name names" in the second HUAC hearings. Murray Schumach, *The Face on the Cutting Room Floor: The Story of Movie and Television Censorship* (New York: Da Capo, 1975), 139; Brian Neve, *Film and Politics in America* (New York: Routledge, 1992, 2004); Thomas Doherty, "Reflections on Hollywood's Infamous Blacklist 70 Years Later," *Hollywood Reporter*, November 24, 2017.
68. Fred Zinnemann quoted in Brian Neve, "A Past Master of His Craft: An Interview with Fred Zinnemann," *Cineaste* 23, no. 1 (1997): 15–19.
69. Schumach, *The Face on the Cutting Room Floor*, 139.
70. Fred Zinnemann, "The Story of *The Search* by Fred Zinnemann," *Screenwriter* 4, no. 2 (August 1948): 12–13, 30; Neve, "A Past Master of His Craft," 15.
71. Zinnemann and Surtees filmed the boat scenes on location at Big Bear Lake in California, outside Los Angeles.
72. His cold, anguished recounting of events is chilling. "It doesn't make any difference why I did it. I betrayed my men." Frank explains to her what he did in Germany, describing how he secretly cut a deal with the Nazi commandant of the prison camp, who lied to him—claiming to spare the lives of his starving men when they tried to escape—and then ordered his men to be murdered. "They were dead. The Nazis even paid me a price. They gave me food and I ate it." He shamefully admits: "I hadn't done it just to save their lives. I talked myself into believing it, that he would keep his word. But in my guts from the start I think I knew he wouldn't. And maybe I didn't even care." Miserable, he adds: "They were dead and I was eating, and maybe that's all I did it for, to save one man—me. There were six widows. There were ten men dead. And I couldn't even stop eating," recalling the barbed wire fence where his men perished when the Nazis starved them, bayoneted them, and sicced dogs on them, then left them to die. Frank is ashamed. When Joe tries to kill him, Frank refuses to call the police, insisting to his wife Edith: "You don't know what made him the way he is. I do."
73. Robert Surtees, "The Story of Filming *Act of Violence*," *American Cinematographer* 29, no. 8 (1948): 268.
74. Fred Zinnemann, *A Life in the Movies: An Autobiography* (New York: MacMillan, 1992), 74.
75. Zinnemann conveys the veteran antihero's tortured state of mind and anguished survivor's guilt by using noir visuals and sound design to project his terror. Frank remembers in horror how his men died trapped in the tunnel in the Nazi prison camp during the war after he betrayed them. Frank hears voices—of Joe, the sounds of his men, the Nazis who killed them—then shouts to warn them not to go into the tunnel, to try to escape, as his hallucinations overwhelm him. We realize Joe—seemingly a menacing antagonist—was actually his best friend, a disabled victim of Frank's betrayal.

76. He gravitates toward the blaring siren of an oncoming train, crossing the tracks of a railyard in a plume of smoke, then stands in its path. He loses his nerve and jumps out of the way as the train passes, just missing him. In an explosive climactic finale, the late-night wind howls at the train station as we witness the transformation and ultimate redemption of both antiheroes, as Frank sacrifices his own life to save Joe from assassination by a hit man. Frank suffers and is punished for his betrayal that led to the death of his men, yet Frank courageously takes a bullet and does the right thing to prevent Joe's murder—humanizing his friend in the process—before he dies. (Shot by the assassin, Frank and the hit man perish in a fiery car crash.) Joe survives, is redeemed, and wants to tell Edith that Frank died saving his life.
77. Women play an important role in humanizing *Act of Violence*. Frank's wife Edith (Janet Leigh) is youthful, innocent, and idealistic. Yet she's already married with a baby to a mysterious older man (like a gothic noir) whom she has idolized but doesn't really know. The film's shady imagery reveals his disreputable past: he's been secretly on the run, hiding and trying to escape his past for years, ever since the war ended, perhaps the entire time she has known him. They packed up suddenly and moved 3,000 miles from Syracuse, New York, to California without collecting his last paycheck. She realizes something deeply unsettling is going on. She has married a stranger. Not only has he been living a lie, but he can only find solace in this masculine world of male camaraderie—at work, at a builder's convention, at war, even fishing on the lake with the guys—while she stays with the baby in their comfortable middle-class home, oblivious to his dark secrets (as the suburbs are being built and the baby boomers are being born after the war). After fleeing Joe (and unable to face his wife Edith), Frank stays with a washed-up prostitute, Pat (Mary Astor), who is looking for kicks and sets him up with several sleazy, disreputable scam artists and assassins. They hustle Frank, ask him for money, get him drunk and convince him to hire a hit man to kill Joe. Pat regrets the whole dirty business—despite the fact that she and her disreputable cronies are all on the take. She offers her cheap, simplistic dime philosophy to Frank, insisting that all the problems in the world can be summed up as either "love trouble" or "money trouble." She has no conception of how Frank's grave, complex situation, moral dilemma, and suffering have absolutely nothing to do with troubled romance or a shortage of cash.
78. Zinnemann, *A Life in the Movies*, 74.
79. Surtees, "The Story of Filming *Act of Violence*," 268.
80. Mary Astor, *A Life on Film* (New York: Doubleday, 1959).
81. MGM Publicity and Script Files for *Act of Violence*, MGM & USC Pressbook Collections, USC Cinematic Arts Library, University of Southern California, Los Angeles, California, 1949.
82. William Brogdon, "Act of Violence," *Variety*, December 22, 1948, 6.
83. Bosley Crowther, "*Act of Violence* (1949)," *New York Times*, January 24, 1949, 16.
84. Eddie Mannix Ledger & Fred Zinnemann Collections, Academy of Motion Picture Arts and Sciences Margaret Herrick Library, Beverly Hills, California, 1949.

2. Fade to Gray and Color Noir

1. Dana Polan, DVD commentary for *The Naked City* (2007; New York: Criterion Collection). Free from earlier shooting constraints, the prevalent postwar trend toward documentary realism and location filming outdoors in sunny broad daylight often mitigated against the moody shadows of noir style. Black-and-white film noir was changing,

adopting a new look and style in response to postwar industrial and cultural challenges, shifting gender roles and themes, and adapting to changing filmmaking conditions and new emergent technologies. *American Cinematographer* recognized *The Naked City*, shot entirely in New York City, as a remarkable posthumous "tribute in celluloid" to independent producer Mark Hellinger, who had produced noir films *The Killers* and *Brute Force*. Herb Lightman, "The Naked City: Tribute in Celluloid," *American Cinematographer* (May 1948): 152–153, 178–179. See also Thomas Schatz, *Boom and Bust: American Cinema in the 1940s* (New York: Scribner's, 1997).

2. In fact, these assorted disparate films merely reveal how noir was splintering, becoming more diffuse and dispersed even at the onset of the decade. Noir would lose its iconic look after the shift from nitrate in 1951. As films increasingly faded to gray, they strayed from the original noir aesthetic style altogether. These later films were no longer truly noir, as the cycle eventually unraveled, coming apart over the course of the 1950s. With this in mind, to what extent are lighter grayer, gris films still considered noir? As noir moved away from its dark shadowy World War II 1940s stylistic technique, later films were visually brighter and less noir after 1950 than existing accounts would typically have it. For further reading on *In a Lonely Place*, see Dana Polan, *In a Lonely Place* (London: British Film Institute, 1994).

3. Paul Schrader, "Notes on Film Noir," *Film Comment* 8, no. 1 (1972): 8–10, 12.

4. Bosley Crowther, "Du Pont Makes Tough Film Base," *New York Times*, November 2, 1955, 1. See also "Air Force Tests du Pont's New Photo Film," *New York Times*, December 23, 1951, F6. *American Cinematographer* announced Eastman Kodak's research development and testing of professional "nonflammable" "safety" (acetate) film print stock, which would eventually replace 35mm nitrate film stock. The U.S. government had used safety stock for films (with portable 16mm mobile cameras and shorter release runs) and combat filming during the war. The film technology for 35mm safety acetate stock eventually improved durability to supplant nitrate, thus avoiding risking print damage and higher costs for the industry. "Eastman Kodak Explains Research Status of Professional Safety Film," *American Cinematographer* 27, no. 2 (February 1946): 54. As Hollywood shifted from nitrate to acetate 'safety' film stock in the 1950s, a less shadowy semi-documentary location-based style was seen in noir films.

5. Brodine shot noir crime films *The House on 92nd Street* (1945), *Somewhere in the Night* (1946), *Boomerang!* (1947), *Kiss of Death* (1947) and *Road House* (1948 [uncredited]). Norbert Brodine quoted in Herb Lightman, "*13 Rue Madeleine*: Documentary Style in the Photoplay," *American Cinematographer* 28, no. 3 (March 1947): 89.

6. Herb Lightman, "Sleep My Love: Cinematic Psycho-Thriller," *American Cinematographer* 29, no. 2 (February 1948): 46–47.

7. Leigh Allen, "Filming the *I Love Lucy* Show," *American Cinematographer* 33, no. 1 (January 1952): 22–23, 34–36.

8. Raymonde Borde and Étienne Chaumeton, *Panorama du film noir américain, 1941–1953* (Paris: Minuit, 1955; trans. Paul Hammond [San Francisco: City Lights, 2002]), 6–29. Earlier noir films about criminals and focused on narratives told from an antiheroic point of view were eventually superseded by Cold War films that revolved around crime-fighting cops enforcing the law and projected an all-powerful federal government. For further reading, see Raymond Borde and Étienne Chaumeton, "Towards a Definition of Film Noir," in *Film Noir Reader*, ed. Alain Silver and James Ursini (New York: Limelight, 1996); Robert Sklar, *Movie-Made America* (New York: Random House, 1975, 1994), 253; Alain Silver and Elizabeth Ward, *Film Noir: An Encyclopedic Reference to the American Style* (Woodstock, NY: Overlook, 1979, 1993); Frank Krutnik, *In a*

Lonely Street: Film Noir, Genre, Masculinity (New York: Routledge, 1991); Schatz, *Boom and Bust*, 204–206, 232–239; James Naremore, "Film Noir: The History of an Idea," *Film Quarterly* 49, no.2 (Winter 1995–1996): 14–17, repr. in *More Than Night* (Berkeley: University of California Press, 1998, 2008); Sheri Chinen Biesen, *Blackout: World War II and the Origins of Film Noir* (Baltimore, MD: Johns Hopkins University Press, 2005); Alain Silver and James Ursini, *The Noir Style* (New York: Abrams, 1999, 2013).
9. No crime films earned $4 million by 1949. Jerry Wald quoted in Thomas Brady, "Uneasy Hollywood," *New York Times*, March 5, 1950, 101.
10. Joseph Breen, MPAA/PCA File, Paramount Collection Production File, Academy of Motion Picture Arts and Sciences Margaret Herrick Library, Beverly Hills, California, April 21–24 May 1949. Industrial and censorial pressures from the MPAA persisted in response to noir production by the late 1940s into the 1950s.
11. Wilder mocks Hollywood myths; he ridicules romance, glamour, fame, stardom, and starry-eyed couples. Norma brags: "I'm richer than all this new Hollywood trash! I've got a million dollars." Unimpressed, Joe replies, "Keep it." Undeterred, she boasts, "Own three blocks downtown, I've got oil in Bakersfield, pumping, pumping, pumping! What's it for but to buy us anything we want!" But she can't buy Joe's love, a career comeback, or public adulation. She is lonely, desperate, suicidal, egomaniacally yearning for her silent-era accolades. Norma's butler and former husband Max, played by Eric von Stroheim (who directed a few of Swanson's silent films), admits: "I could have continued my career, only I found everything unendurable after she had left me." (In real-life, Swanson fired Stroheim from the uncompleted *Queen Kelly*.) Everything is a sham, a front, a façade like hollow Hollywood soundstage sets creating false illusions. Max sends fake fan letters to Norma. Even script girl Betty had plastic surgery to seek stardom, then stopped pursuing fame: "What's wrong with being on the other side of the cameras?" Betty prefers the phony back lot because she was raised by a "picture family": her parents and grandparents worked at the studio for generations, which is why she has a job.
12. Herb Lightman, "Old Master, New Tricks," *American Cinematographer* 31, no. 9 (September 1950): 309, 318, 320.
13. Lightman, "Old Master, New Tricks," 309, 318, 320; Jeffrey Couchman, "A Pair of Aces: Cinematographer John F. Seitz, ASC Teamed with Director Billy Wilder to Create Some of American Film's Most Indelible Images," *American Cinematographer* 84, no 3 (March 2003): 78–86; Jeffrey Couchman, "Restoring *Sunset Boulevard*," *American Cinematographer* 84, no 3 (March 2003): 83); Rachael Bosley, "*Sunset Boulevard*," *American Cinematographer* 84, no 4 (April 2003).
14. Lightman, "Old Master, New Tricks," 309, 318, 320.
15. Lightman, "Old Master, New Tricks," 309, 318, 320; Hollis Moyse, "Latensification," *American Cinematographer* 29, no 12 (December 1948): 409, 426–427.
16. Paramount Collection Production Budget File, Academy of Motion Picture Arts and Sciences Margaret Herrick Library, Beverly Hills, California, 1950; American Film Institute; "Top-Grosses of 1950," *Variety* 181, no. 4 (January 3, 1951): 58.
17. David Freeman, "*Sunset Boulevard* Revisited," *The New Yorker*, June 21, 1993, 72–79.
18. Zanuck called *Sunset Boulevard* "a masterpiece until it was released throughout the country and failed to do business. It is not so big a masterpiece today." In fact, he dispatched a confidential memo to "All Producers and Directors" at Fox, criticizing *Sunset Boulevard* and other 1950 noir films, adding: "the theatre-going public has been saturated with pictures of violence and films with underworld or 'low' backgrounds." In a revealing admission about the decline in popularity of noir crime films, Zanuck

explained, "Audiences today, particularly in America, do not want pictures of violence or extreme brutality . . . In spite of the high quality of such pictures as *Panic in the Streets, Asphalt Jungle, Where the Sidewalk Ends*, etc., etc., these films and all films in this category have proved to be a shocking disappointment . . . particularly, if they are 'downbeat' in nature or deal with sordid backgrounds, unsympathetic characters and over-emphasized 'suffering'" with "psychopathic disorders." His conclusion: "Pictures in this category are certainly a very high risk." Darryl F. Zanuck correspondence, Twentieth Century-Fox Collection, USC Cinematic Arts Library, University of Southern California, Los Angeles, California, June–December 1950; Biesen, *Blackout*; Rudy Behlmer, *Memo from Darryl F. Zanuck* (New York: Grove Press, 1993), 174–194.
19. Wilder's *Ace in the Hole* slams media, reporters, TV, radio, even the American public. The crew constructed a huge cliff dwelling set in stark rural New Mexico near ancient indigenous Native American ruins. The darkest moments are chiaroscuro tunnels in a mine where Tatum shines a flashlight for eerie facial lighting. His reporter-antihero is a failed writer (in an extraordinary cold-hearted performance by Douglas) who is caustic and unsympathetic, toying with a philandering married blonde femme. Lorraine tells sleazy Tatum: "I've met a lot of hardboiled eggs in my time, but you're twenty minutes." Wilder refers to his earlier noir films in *Ace in the Hole*, which opens with Tatum riding up in a convertible on a tow truck (suggesting Joe's car being towed in *Sunset Boulevard*), paying homage to the illicit affairs in *The Postman Always Rings Twice* and *Double Indemnity*, whose Medford, Oregon, witness "Jackson" Porter Hall returns as Tatum's disapproving editor.
20. In his guilt, Tatum nearly strangles Lorraine, who stabs him in the stomach with scissors. Instead of getting a doctor for his wound, Tatum gets a priest for Leo's last-rites dying wish. Neff also had the perfect fall guy but couldn't let him take the blame, returning to his office to confess when he could still get away; Joe redeems himself driving away Betty for her own good, although he plans to leave Norma.
21. The industry executives' criticism of *Sunset Boulevard* paled in comparison to the response to *Ace in the Hole*, which bombed and did not enjoy the critical acclaim or financial return of *Sunset Boulevard*.
22. Wilder's definitive noir-styled aesthetic and vanguard cultural commentary of societal corruption and exploitative profiteering were oddly prophetic, and his noir vision and dark sensibility continue to resonate.
23. Hollywood's postwar B films related stories of actual gangsters and topics that had been censored during the war years. When notorious real-life gangster Al Capone died (after serving prison time), Frank J. Wilson wrote "Undercover Man: He Trapped Capone" for *Collier's* magazine, which was the basis for Lewis's *The Undercover Man* as well as his later noir *The Big Combo*, also based loosely on events surrounding the arrest of Capone. Critics complained about its "dreary" gray visual mise-en-scène, arguing that it "looks so much like so many films of the cops-and-robbers formula, in the new semi-documentary style, that it offers nothing refreshing in the way of pictorial surprise . . . for all its explosive flurries of gun-play and passing of violent threats." They even rejected hard-boiled fiction by 1949–1950 in *Gun Crazy*. Bosley Crowther, "The Undercover Man, with Glenn Ford as Federal Agent," *New York Times*, April 21, 1949, 30.
24. *Gun Crazy* was copyrighted as *Deadly Is the Female* in December 1949 by Pioneer Pictures. "Gun Crazy," *Hollywood Reporter*, March 4, 1949, 10.
25. Breen, MPAA/PCA File, Paramount Collection Production File, Academy of Motion Picture Arts and Sciences Margaret Herrick Library, Beverly Hills, California, 1949.

26. Joseph H. Lewis in Peter Bogdanovich, *Who the Devil Made It?* (New York: Ballantine, 1997), 675–679; Lewis in Francis Nevins, *Joseph H. Lewis* (London: Scarecrow, 1998), 38–39.
27. As indicated by its alternate title, *Deadly Is the Female*, publicity was all about targeting men (from World War II veterans to those preparing for the Korean conflict) with sex and violence and a strong, independent, androgynous female. As in earlier censorable red-meat wartime crime films, it promoted the film's ruthless femme fatale as a blonde bombshell—"The Flaming Life and Loves of the Most Infamous of All Female Outlaws! From Her Crimson Lips . . . to the Blazing Tips of Her Gun . . . She's *Boxoffice!* Blazing, Blasting Life Story of Laurie Starr the Lethal Blonde! Wanted In A Dozen States! Hunted by the FBI! *Gun Crazy*. Daring! Devastating! Men Were A Dime A Dozen to Laurie Starr!" The publicity also noted the outlaw couple's "tempestuous love affair," a fusion of sex and violence.
28. Howard Thompson, "Episodic and Familiar," *New York Times*, August 25, 1950, 17. Yet the film's improvised dialogue was a far cry from the crisp hard-boiled repartee, tight writing, and brilliant innuendo heightening witty double-entendre to get by Code censors in the earlier red-meat noir cycle of the war years, especially in yarns penned by Cain, Chandler, and Wilder. If it had more clever hard-boiled banter and chiaroscuro style, it undoubtedly would have been even more noir. Some critics did appreciate the film. *Hollywood Reporter* gave high praise to Lewis in October 1949. *Gun Crazy* is a "shoot-'em-up story of desperate love and crime. After a slow beginning, it generates considerable excitement" about an antihero who "turns criminal to keep the love of a girl with no scruples. It's not a pleasant story . . . it is curiously cold and lacking in genuine emotions," *Variety* wrote, noting the outlaw couple's physical attraction and fascination with guns. While criticizing the writing and direction "staying on the surface and never getting underneath the characters," the finale "races along" under Lewis's direction, a "continual chase broken only by new holdup jobs pulled by Dall and Cummins." The *New York Times* admitted the script was "fairly literate," the dialogue "quite good," the photography "first-rate," and Lewis's direction "kept the whole thing zipping along at a colorful tempo which deserves a much better outlet." Critics complained its "young desperadoes" are not motivated beyond "grim appreciation of money" and "restlessness," but not "sentimentalized" as "luckless tools of society." Regarding the film's gun-toting outlaws and their erogenous proclivities, its "clean-cut youngster" stars "look more like fugitives from a 4-H Club than from the law," saying the femme fatale appeared "fragile as a Dresden doll," but "Cummins bites into her assignment like a shark." However, "it takes more than crime and the King Brothers to make sows' ears out of silk purses." Variety staff, "Gun Crazy," *Variety*, December 31, 1949; "Deadly Is the Female," *Variety*, November 2, 1949, 10; "Deadly Is the Female," *Hollywood Reporter*, October 31, 1949, 4.
29. Lewis worked on projects like sunlit crime film *A Lady Without Passport* (originally, *Visa*, a documentary-style story of Cuban immigrants). With the postwar popularity of Italian neorealism, the *New York Times* announced in May 1952 that Vittorio Gassman, a "film star in Italy before coming here a few months ago," would play an "escaped convict who is eventually straightened out by an understanding warden" in *Cry of the Hunted* (1953), Lewis's best noir at MGM. *Cry of the Hunted*, which cost $544,000, was a low-budget endeavor at MGM. It is a riveting underrecognized film noir, one of the best pictures produced by the studio's B unit supervised by Charles Schnee. Written by Jack Leonard and produced by William Grady, Jr., it featured bright high-key outdoor sunlit settings and a jaded law enforcement official who chases an escaped fugitive from

a prison cell through a murky tunnel and a Louisiana swamp. Lewis claimed he shot the film on the lot, although sequences included locations filmed in September 1952 at Louisiana bayous and Angel's Flight Railway in Bunker Hill in downtown Los Angeles. *Cry of the Hunted* was a tight masculine swamp noir that, unlike his earlier *My Name Is Julia Ross*, exuded muscular macho virility. Its working title was *Men Don't Cry*. The crime narrative traced the rugged outdoor survival in the wilderness and the relationship between two men on opposite sides of the law. Yet *Cry of the Hunted* humanized its ethnic fugitive from justice who was running for his life. Lewis shot a striking noir sequence in a pitch-black prison cell where the law officer brutally beats and tries to force the criminal-inmate (Gassman with a Russian/Eastern European accent) to inform and name the names of his coconspirators. *Cry of the Hunted* can be seen as a fascinating allegory for Red Scare xenophobia and the Hollywood blacklist. It traces the fugitive fleeing and hunted by the tenacious law officer obsessed with his capture. It included rugged, manly fistfights; alligators; turbulent quicksand; drug-induced, swamp fever, hallucination sequences; an opportunistic, ladder-climbing cop; and a shady sheriff who shoots first and asks questions later. Women were relegated to the periphery. Despite being a fine example of Lewis's low-budget B noir work, when *Cry of the Hunted* was released, the *New York Times* didn't even review it. In retrospect, Lewis lamented: "I think I recognized I had made a mistake at MGM by accepting the Hedy Lamarr picture and then after that nothing but smaller pictures. I wanted bigger things and I screwed up. But maybe I didn't, because I'm alive." Thomas M. Pryor, "Vittorio Gassman in New Metro Film—Italian Actor Named to Star in *Cry of the Hunted*, Story of a Convict and His Warden," *New York Times*, May 27, 1952; Nevins, *Joseph H. Lewis*, 44.
30. "3 Groups Ready to Film *Big Combo*—Allied Artists Joins Theodora Productions and Security Pictures in Melodrama," *New York Times*, July 28, 1954.
31. Many filmmakers were moving into independent production in this changing postwar era. Allied Artists grew out of Poverty Row studio Monogram Pictures, which foresaw a waning future for low-budget films and established Allied Artists in 1946 to make costlier B-plus films with higher production values, and Monogram renamed itself Allied Artists in 1953.
32. Thomas Doherty, *Hollywood's Censor* (New York: Columbia University Press, 2007), 6. For further reading, see Sheri Chinen Biesen, *Film Censorship* (New York: Columbia University Press, 2018).
33. Lewis also suggested oral sex and homosexuality in the noir film. "The Big Combo," *Hollywood Reporter*, June 23, 1954, 2; William Brogdon, "The Big Combo," *Variety*, February 16, 1955, 16; Howard Thompson, "The Big Combo," *New York Times*, March 26, 1955, 13. The *Los Angeles Times* wrote on June 23, 1954, that Yordan had "turned down offers of as high as $75,000 plus a percentage" for his original screenplay for *The Big Combo*. The script "was in great demand with reported bidders, including United States Productions, Russ-Field, Frank P. Rosenberg and Edward L. Alperson." Edwin Schallert, "'Big Combo' Will Star Cornel Wilde," *Los Angeles Times*, June 23, 1954, B7.
34. "The Big Combo," *Hollywood Reporter*, 2.
35. PCA censors were appalled and wanted to omit a scandalous shot suggesting oral sex as too explicit, but Lewis's crafty sexual innuendo remained in the film. Bogdanovich, *Who the Devil Made It?*, 685–686, and Nevins, *Joseph H. Lewis*, 44.
36. David Raksin's jazz soundtrack music was scored at Samuel Goldwyn Studios.
37. Nevins, *Joseph H. Lewis*, 44–45.
38. Nevins, *Joseph H. Lewis*, 44–45.
39. Publicity for *The Big Combo*, USC Pressbook Collection.

40. Many critics admonished salacious cinematic activity in the absence of departing censor Breen, slamming the *The Big Combo*'s brutal crime theme, violence, and shadowy visual style—not even mentioning John Alton nor appreciating the stunning photography. *Motion Picture Herald* called *The Big Combo* "very good." *Variety* called it "hard-hitting," a "grim meller of honest cop . . . smashing a crime syndicate and its leader . . . cut out to order" for the crime fan who "likes his action rough and raw." "Since Philip Yordan's original screenplay doesn't follow a credible line, there's not much sense to the torture scene, not to most of the motivations used to plot the course of this shocker." Calling for law and order, *Variety* complained, "Even after Wilde has been subjected to the indignities by Conte and his strongarm boys . . . pic has you believe he still can't bring the hood to justice." "*The Big Combo*," *Motion Picture Herald*, July 16, 1955, 329; Brogdon, "*The Big Combo*," 16; Thompson, "*The Big Combo*," 13.
41. Thompson, "The Big Combo," 13.
42. Kenneth Turan, "Some Real Eye-Openers: Preservation fest at UCLA," *Los Angeles Times*, July 20, 2006.
43. Crowther, "*The Undercover Man*," 30.
44. For further reading, see Christopher Anderson, *Hollywood TV* (Austin: University of Texas Press, 1994).
45. Robert Frasier quoted in Norman Keane, "Films for Television," *American Cinematographer* 30, no. 4 (April 1949): 125–126, 138.
46. Charles Loring, "Some Do's and Don'ts for TV Film Photography," *American Cinematographer* 30, no. 8 (August 1949): 283, 294.
47. *The Enforcer* publicity clamored: "The Hero of this story is the Fighting District Attorney of this City—and Every City!" Lobby cards proclaimed: "They called him The Enforcer . . . Here is the story of the man who matched himself against a nationwide network of 'killers-for-hire' . . . the first story of the Double-Fisted D.A. who Tore Apart the Evil Dynasty that peddled Murder for a Price!" As Bogie raises his arm and fires a gun, captions read: "If you're smart you'll come in—If you're dumb you'll be dead." Lobby cards pictured swaggering tough-guy DA Bogart next to a cop, arresting mobsters, punching criminals, grabbing and collaring crooks, and protecting society streets while a girl witness looks away to avoid hoodlums.
48. Bosley Crowther, "The Enforcer," *New York Times*, January 26, 1951.
49. Herb Lightman, "'The Thief'—A New Trend in Films?," *American Cinematographer*, 33, no. 10 (October 1952): 432–433. *The Thief* production notes/publicity, USC Pressbook & United Artists Collections, University of Southern California, Los Angeles, California, 1952; Dupont film ad, *American Cinematographer* 34, no. 1 (January 1953): inside cover. It was shot in standard Academy aspect ratio (widescreen debuted in 1953).
50. Publicity for *The Big Heat*, USC Pressbook Collection, University of Southern California, Los Angeles, California, 1953. The film was shot in standard Academy aspect ratio. The main character is also a returning vet.
51. Kenneth Sweeney, "*The Big Heat* (1953)," *American Cinematographer* 93, no. 8 (August 2012). See also Patrick McGilligan, *Fritz Lang: The Nature of the Beast* (New York: St. Martin's, 1997).
52. Publicity for *Kiss Me Deadly*, USC Pressbook Collection, University of Southern California, Los Angeles, California, 1955.
53. For more on *Kiss Me Deadly*, see Schrader, "Notes on Film Noir," 8–9; Alain Silver, "*Kiss Me Deadly*: Evidence of a Style," in *Film Noir Reader*, ed. Alain Silver and James Ursini (New York: Limelight, 1996), 209–235.

54. The reverse roll of the credits, of course, anticipated the later style of *Star Wars*' iconic "A long time ago, in a galaxy far, far away . . ." Hammer gives Christina a lift, dryly commenting that she uses her whole body rather than just her thumb to get a ride. He asks if she always runs around wearing no clothes, assuming she is fleeing an over-amorous lover. Breathless, clad in a trench coat, and running barefoot, she apparently has nothing on underneath. Over the credits, as they drive down the long expanse of the road in the dark, we hear loud sounds of Christina's heavy panting, suggesting racy sexual exertion rather than arduous running. Her winded gasping drowns out the faint strains of Nat King Cole singing "Rather Have the Blues" on the radio. When they stop at a gas station, the attendant implies that they have been having sex on the side of the road. After they bypass a roadblock, however, it is revealed that she is fleeing an insane asylum and being pursued. The night and low-angle lighting below their faces cast harsh, ominous shadows across their features. She tells him, if they don't make it, to "remember me." Mysterious thugs suddenly intercept them, knock Hammer out, and viciously beat the girl, whose screams pierce the air. The violence occurs off-screen, only showing her legs kicking wildly until they go limp when she blacks out. They push Mike and Christina, unconscious in the convertible, over a mountain cliff, and the car crashes engulfed in flames. It is not clear who these violent terrorizing entities are: gangsters, the government, authorities from the asylum, or a Cold War enemy? It is a dangerous, disturbing, widescreen noir world that is out of order, where no one is safe and anyone can die on the spot. In a blurring, subjective, point-of-view dissolve shot, Hammer awakens in the hospital to find that Christina has been killed. Mike and his secretary-girlfriend Velda (Maxine Cooper) leave the hospital into the much brighter sunshine outside.
55. Publicity for *Kiss Me Deadly*, USC Pressbook Collection, University of Southern California, Los Angeles, California, 1955.
56. As Hammer pursues leads all over Los Angeles trying to find out who murdered Christina and why, he encounters a duplicitous femme fatale, Lily Carver/Gabrielle (Gaby Rodgers), who opens—and detonates—a deadly atomic Pandora's box in the process. The famous, explosive, atomic apocalyptic finale of *Kiss Me Deadly* is recognized by film critics as projecting nuclear fears in the Cold War era.
57. MPAA/PCA Files for *Kiss Me Deadly*, MHL, AFI, USC, 1954–1955.
58. MPAA/PCA Files for *Kiss Me Deadly*, MHL, AFI, USC, 1954–1955.
59. "Cult Classic Mystery: A new video release of 'Kiss Me Deadly' . . . ," *Los Angeles Times*, August 12, 1997, F1, F10.
60. For Hecht-Hill-Lancaster/Norma-Curtleigh Productions.
61. It featured feisty dialogue such as Lancaster's hard-boiled barb: "I'd hate to take a bite outta you. You're a cookie full of arsenic." Consumed with ego, toxic masculinity, entitlement, and jealous rage, Hunsecker endeavors to destroy Steve Dallas (Marty Milner), a jazz musician engaged to his younger sister, nineteen-year-old Susie (Susan Harrison). When Dallas ridicules Hunsecker as a "national disgrace" full of "phony patriotism," Hunsecker coldly retaliates like a mob boss calling in favors: he has corrupt cop Harry Kello (Emile Meyer) plant drugs on, brutally beat, frame, and arrest Dallas on false charges, then has Sidney Falco plant false stories in the press that Dallas is a Communist who smokes marijuana—which gets him fired from the jazz club. Suggesting a potentially incestuous relationship with his sister, Hunsecker plans a vacation with Susie after destroying Dallas and breaking off her engagement. "You're all I've got in this whole wide world," Hunsecker tells Susie before betraying her and arranging to ruin her fiancé. When Susie finds out what they have done, she lets her brother and Falco destroy each other, then in cold disgust declares she would rather die than live with her

brother and walks out to join Dallas at the hospital. The film's expanded widescreen mise-en-scène is accentuated in the final overhead shot as she walks away across the New York City streets.

62. The film included Chico Hamilton, Fred Katz, Paul Horn, Carson Smith, John Pisano, and bassist Buddy Clark sitting in, with jazz music composed by Chico Hamilton and Fred Katz. A. H. Weiler, "The Screen: Sweet Smell of Success," *New York Times*, June 28, 1957, 29.
63. Its ending and negative depiction of police lieutenant Harry Kello was allowed, after an honorable police officer was added.
64. Ernest Lehman Collection, USC Cinematic Arts Library Special Collections, 1955–1957; Ernest Lehman Collection, Harry Ransom Humanities Research Center at the University of Texas, 1955–1957; "Sweet Smell of Success," American Film Institute, 1957; "Sweet Smell of Success," *Hollywood Reporter*, August 10, 1955; Sam Kashner, "A Movie Marked Danger," *Vanity Fair*, April 2000, 415–432; Ann Hornaday, "Sweet Smell of Success: A Film With Staying Power," *Los Angeles Times*, December 25, 2000.
65. *Sweet Smell of Success* Pressbook, USC Pressbook Collection, 1957.
66. One of eighty-two films. *Time*, USC, MHL, AFI, 1957–1959; *New York Herald-Tribune*, January 6, 1958; *New York Times*, May 24, 1959. *Sweet Smell of Success* was later celebrated as a bold gutsy film criticizing the Hollywood blacklist. It has since been deemed a noir classic.
67. Welles wanted to shoot in Tijuana, Mexico.
68. Universal unfortunately butchered, reedited, and reshot the film against Welles's wishes, although it was later restored many years after his death. The studio did not promote the film extensively, and it was a commercial failure. Welles later directed the 1965 Spanish-Swiss coproduction *Chimes at Midnight*. Universal Collection, USC, MHL, AFI, 1957–1958.
69. Schrader notes film noir "ground to a halt" after 1953. Schrader, "Notes on Film Noir," 8–10, 12. Alain Silver, Elizabeth Ward, James Ursini, and Paul Schrader note that film noir is a style. Robert Sklar and Thomas Schatz note that film noir arose as a period style growing out of the wartime and postwar eras. David Bordwell also notes that film noir is not a genre in "The Bounds of Difference" in David Bordwell, Janet Staiger and Kristin Thompson, *The Classical Hollywood Cinema: Film Style and Mode of Production to 1960* (New York: Columbia University Press, 1985), 74-75. Robert Sklar describes film noir as the "psychological thrillers that emerged at the time of the war," observing the noir cycle's "claustrophobia," "psychology," "look" and "pervasive tone" in "1940s films where a dark and constrictive mood derives in part from the material limitations of wartime filmmaking: restrictions on travel virtually eliminated location shooting where interior sets could serve, and stringent budgets seem to have cut down on lighting as well. Yet the gloom and constriction were not merely an accommodation to forced economies; their film-makers intended them that way . . . fascination with guilt and the ambiguous play of identities," the "hallmark of *film noir* is its sense of people trapped—trapped in webs of paranoia and fear, unable to tell guilt from innocence, true identity from false. Its villains are attractive and sympathetic, masking greed, misanthropy, malevolence. Its heroes and heroines are weak, confused, susceptible to false impressions. The environment is murky and close, the settings vaguely oppressive. In the end, evil is exposed, though often just barely, and the survival of good remains troubled and ambiguous." Robert Sklar, *Movie-Made America*. (New York: Random House, 1975, 1994), 253. See also Thomas Schatz, *Boom and Bust: American Cinema in the 1940s*. (New York: Scribners, 1997), 204-206, 232-239.

70. Myriad factors during the 1950s contributed to this new, lighter, less shadowy look, both in monochrome and vis-à-vis the surge in color film production after the war, which also factored in and contributed to noir's evolving visual style after the war. The increasing use of location filming in outdoor sunlight and studio industry adoption of brighter, low-contrast televisual conventions in films during this period was extremely important, influential, and significant to noir's evolution and aesthetic. While the unique production environment of World War II fostered noir's original style in the nitrate era, the industry's adoption of brighter televisual conventions, increased location shooting, and changes in the film stock itself contributed to a lighter noir aesthetic style in the 1950s.
71. In the wake of brighter, high-key, low-contrast television conventions; sunny daytime outdoor location shooting; and the shift from nitrate film to acetate safety stock.
72. Abel Green, "All Pix in Color Within 5 Yrs," *Variety*, 169, no 5 (January 7, 1948): 3 (top front-page headline), 158. Green announced the new technology in 1948, noting, "For best exhibition purposes, a prism reflector, costing $500–$750, would entail minor conversion to the standard projection equipment."
73. Crime films would indeed not vanish altogether either.
74. Philip Scheuer, "Movie Realism at Peak in 1948: But Signs Begin to Hint That Postwar Hardness Is Cracking," *Los Angeles Times*, December 26, 1948, D1, 4. Regarding the motion picture industry's postwar conversion from nitrate to acetate safety film initiated in 1948, Anthony L'Abbate, George Eastman Museum Head of Preservation, observed, "When the transition came in 1950–51, it was most likely using up what stock they had on hand at the studio and then when they ordered more it was acetate rather than nitrate . . . some 1951 films that were shot on nitrate negative had acetate release prints [e.g., color musicals *An American in Paris* and *Show Boat*] . . . it seems that Kodak stopped producing nitrate stock by the middle of 1950." George Eastman Museum Head of Preservation, Anthony L'Abbate (per film preservation archival intern Robert Boddingham), research correspondence, January 2020. By October 1950, *Variety* also reported that theater owners were pushing studios and the film industry to convert to "total and exclusive use of acetate-based stock" in lieu of nitrate film due to "economy of operations" savings and lower costs, transportation and insurance risk because it was "non-flammable" and posed "no fire hazard," writing: "Actually all major companies use the acetate at the studios but some releases to exhibs are nitrate. Newsreels are also nitrate. Kodak adopted a program of switching to acetate two years ago [in 1948] and completed the full conversion several months ago." Variety Staff, "Acetate-Based Stock Also Sought at TOA Meet," *Variety*, October 18, 1950. Innovative technology contributed to the emergence of a color noir style aesthetic. To compete with television, Hollywood used new technologies to distinguish itself as a bigger, more spectacular, more elite leisure activity.
75. Thomas Brady, "Big Color Rush On," *New York Times*, June 17, 1951, X5.
76. Color film capability, such as color tinting and an array of chromatic processes, certainly appeared even in the early silent era. Technicolor, for instance, had been around for years. For example, two-color Technicolor films included *The Black Pirate* (1927), *Doctor X* (1932), and *Mystery of the Wax Museum* (1933). Three-strip Technicolor films appeared in Hollywood in the 1930s. The first three-strip Technicolor film was Walt Disney's animated short *Flowers and Trees* (1932); the first live-action, three-strip Technicolor feature film was *Becky Sharp* (1935)—which required so much light that the huge arc lamps damaged the eyes of actors. The first three-strip Technicolor animated feature film was Disney's *Snow White and the Seven Dwarfs* (1937). David O. Selznick's production of *A Star Is Born* (1937) and *Gone with the Wind* (1939), as well as *The Wizard of Oz* (1939) and *Blood and Sand* (1941), were early Technicolor breakthroughs.

77. For further reading on noir musicals and color noir films, see Sheri Chinen Biesen, *Music in the Shadows: Noir Musical Films* (Baltimore, MD: Johns Hopkins University Press, 2014). See also Tino Balio, ed., *Hollywood in the Age of Television* (Boston: Unwin Hyman, 1990); *The Century*, Season 1, Episode 5, part 2, "Coming Apart: Picture This," produced by ABC News, executive produced (directed) by Tom Yellin, originally aired April 8, 1999, ABC; Peter Lev, *The Fifties* (New York: Scribner's, 2003); Drew Casper, *Postwar Hollywood* (Malden, MA: Blackwell, 2007).
78. Philip Scheuer, "Coproducer Explains 'Red Shoes' Success," *Los Angeles Times*, December 19, 1948, 19; USC.
79. Alan Wood, "Inside Story of Mr. Rank," *Everybody's Weekly*, February 23, 1952; For further reading on noir musicals and color noir films, see Biesen, *Music in the Shadows*.
80. Boris asks Vicky: "Does he know what he is asking?" and entices her to return. Lermontov says to Vicky, as Julian appears in ominous black, insisting she leave before the performance, "Would you make her a great dancer?" Boris explodes at Julian. "Never. Why do you think I have waited day after day since you snatched her away from me? For a chance to win her back!" Lermontov disgustedly dismisses Vicky's "infatuation" with Julian as adolescent nonsense. "If you go with him now, I will never take you back. Never!"
81. *The Red Shoes* was filmed in the summer and fall of 1947 on location in London and at Pinewood Studios (in Iver, west of London), and in Paris, Monte Carlo, and Villefranche in the South of France.
82. Herb Lightman, "The Red Shoes," *American Cinematographer* 30, no 1 (March 1949): 82–83, 99–100.
83. After working at UFA (Universum-Film Aktiengesellschaft), Walbrook had played a murderous sadistic homme fatale in the British gothic *Gaslight* (1940), remade by George Cukor in 1944.
84. Moira Shearer quoted in Brian McFarlane, *An Autobiography of British Cinema* (London: Methuen/BFI, 1997), 532–535. Albert Basserman, who played ballet designer Sergei Ratov, died after the filming.
85. "TECHNICOLOR ALTERS PRACTICE ON OUTPUT," *New York Times*, March 13, 1953, 23; "TECHNICOLOR AGREES TO LET PATENTS," *New York Times*, February 25, 1950, 11; Thomas F. Brady, "BIG COLOR RUSH ON," *New York Times*, June 17, 1951, X5; "COLOR FILM BOOM SEEN," *New York Times*, December 23, 1954; Thomas M. Pryor, "COLOR STANDARDS SET…Motion Picture and TV Engineers Soc sets standards for color photography," *New York Times*, October 22, 1954; Thomas M. Pryor, "COLOR IS REQUIRED FOR CINEMASCOPE; Restriction in Fox Contract Forces 2 Studios to Change Black-and-White Plans," *New York Times*, April 5, 1955, 33; Richard W. Haines, *Technicolor Movies: The History of Dye Transfer Printing* (Jefferson, NC: McFarlane, 1993), 51–52.
86. The shift from black and white to color, and from three-strip Technicolor in *The Red Shoes*, *Niagara*, and *The Barefoot Contessa* to widescreen with Eastmancolor, enabled filmmakers to create distinctive color noir visual style in *A Star Is Born*, *Rear Window*, and *West Side Story* and a sunlit variation in *North by Northwest*. By the mid- to late 1950s, a lighter, high-key color aesthetic was also seen in *Rebel Without a Cause* (1955), *Love Me or Leave Me* (1955), *Pete Kelly's Blues* (1955), and Hitchcock's *To Catch a Thief* (1955), *Vertigo* (1958), and *North by Northwest* (1959). Color noir was adapted to large-frame 70mm film technology in a stunning homage to the visual style in *West Side Story* (1961).
87. Darryl F. Zanuck, Twentieth Century-Fox Collection, USC Cinematic Arts Library, University of Southern California, Los Angeles, California, March 12–May 7, 1953; Behlmer, *Memo from Darryl F. Zanuck.* 234, 238–39.

214   2. Fade to Gray and Color Noir

88. Eastmancolor was more compatible with the CinemaScope widescreen anamorphic process than three-strip Technicolor, as seen in *The Robe* and *How to Marry a Millionaire* in 1953.
89. Patrick McGilligan, Backstory 2: Interviews with Screenwriters of the 1940s and 1950s (Berkeley: University of California Press, 1991), 236–237.
90. "Niagara," *Hollywood Reporter*, January 20, 1953.
91. A. H. Weiler, "Niagara Falls Vies with Marilyn Monroe," *New York Times*, January 22, 1953, 20.
92. "Niagara," *Variety*, January 21, 1953, 6.
93. The film cost $1.67 million according to Aubrey Solomon, *Twentieth Century Fox: A Corporate and Financial History* (Lanham, MD: Scarecrow Press, 1989) 248; "The Top Box Office Hits of 1953," *Variety*, January 13, 1954; USC Cinematic Arts Library, American Film Institute, Los Angeles, California, 1953–1954.
94. Stunning color noirs *The Red Shoes*, *Moulin Rouge*, *Niagara*, and *The Barefoot Contessa* were filmed in three-strip Technicolor.
95. *A Star Is Born* was independently coproduced by Garland and husband Sid Luft's Transcona Enterprises with Edward L. Alperson and Warner Bros. Studio, which also released and provided financing for the film.
96. An inebriated Norman hits Vicki in the face, interrupting her speech and humiliating himself and his wife on live TV in front of Hollywood industry brass when she receives an Oscar. Like Maine's self-destructive actions in *A Star Is Born*, Libby later vengefully beats Norman up at a racetrack. Esther looks in the mirror, overcome with anxiety after averting an onstage calamity with drunken Norman, as she applies red lipstick, which he cynically uses to draw on the wall.
97. Alain Silver and Elizabeth Ward, *Film Noir: An Encyclopedic Reference to the American Style* (Woodstock, NY: Overlook, 1979), 2.
98. Schrader, "Notes on Film Noir," 12.
99. Many films in his period were shot in single-strip, monopack Eastmancolor and were developed in Technicolor using the dye transfer I-B imbibition process; then they were promoted as being filmed in Technicolor.
100. Leavitt worked with director of photography (DP) Harry Stradling to film John Berry's *Tension* and *The Pirate*. Hoch had previously replaced *A Star Is Born*'s original photographer Harry Stradling after production delays caused a scheduling conflict with another film.
101. Al Harrell, "The Making of *A Star Is Born*," *American Cinematographer*, 65, no. 2 (February 1984): 36.
102. Ronald Haver, *A Star Is Born: The Making of the 1954 Movie and Its 1983 Restoration* (New York: Knopf, 1988; Applause, 2002), 125; George Cukor Collection, University of Southern California, Los Angeles, California, 1953–54; Harrell, "The Making of *A Star Is Born*," 36.
103. WarnerColor was Warner's version of single-strip Kodak Eastmancolor monopack film stock. Haver, *A Star Is Born*, 135.
104. Gene Allen quoted in Haver, *A Star Is Born*, 125.
105. Haver, *A Star Is Born*, 125; George Cukor Collection, University of Southern California, Los Angeles, California, 1953–54; Harrell, "The Making of *A Star Is Born*," 36.
106. Haver, *A Star Is Born*, 125; George Cukor Collection, University of Southern California, Los Angeles, California, 1953–1954; Harrell, "The Making of *A Star Is Born*," 36.
107. George Cukor Collection, USC Warner Bros. Archive, 1953–1954.
108. Abel Green, "Film Reviews: 'A Star Is Born,'" *Variety*, September 29, 1954, 6.

109. Bosley Crowther, "The Screen: 'A Star Is Born' Bows," *New York Times*, October 12, 1954, 23.
110. George Cukor Collection, USC Warner Bros. Archive, 1953–1954. At the end of principal photography, Cukor left for Europe. Dance director Jack Donahue and choreographer Richard Barstow later directed musical numbers with Roger Edens [uncredited] in Cukor's absence, some of which were eventually cut from the film for general release after its premiere.
111. *A Star Is Born*'s cost was advertised as $6 million. William Schaefer Collection, George Cukor Collection, USC Warner Bros. Archive, USC Pressbook Collection, USC Cinematic Arts Library, University of Southern California, American Film Institute, Los Angeles, California, 1953–1954; Haver, *A Star Is Born*; Lev, *The Fifties*.
112. Hitchcock simulated the visual style, lighting, and iconography of noir in color. They made the protagonist a famous war-turned-magazine photographer. Burks also shot Gjon Mili's jazz noir *Jammin' the Blues* (1944).
113. Alfred Hitchcock quoted in Phillip K. Scheuer, "Color by Hitchcock," *Los Angeles Times*, March 2, 1941, 52.
114. Lisa announces, "It's opening night of the last depressing week of L.B. Jeffries in a cast." Jeff mutters, "I haven't noticed any big demand for tickets." "That's because I bought out the house," she smoothly replies. As Lisa has dinner delivered for a romantic evening, she asks, "What would you think of starting off with dinner at 21?" Jeff dryly responds, "You have, perhaps, an ambulance downstairs?" When she shows him a sheer nightdress and negligee, Lisa coyly says, "Preview of coming attractions." Stella, another strong assertive woman, thinks people "ought to come together—*wham*—like a couple of taxis on Broadway." She suspects neighbor Miss Lonely Hearts across the way is contemplating suicide because she's handled enough red pills to put everybody in Hackensack, New Jersey, to sleep for the winter.
115. "*Rear Window* Ethics: Remembering and Restoring a Hitchcock Classic," DVD production notes and documentary on the making of *Rear Window* (2001; Universal City, CA: Universal Studios Home Entertainment); *Rear Window* correspondence in Alfred Hitchcock Collection, Paramount Collection Production File, Academy of Motion Picture Arts and Sciences Margaret Herrick Library, Beverly Hills, California, 1953–1954; USC Cinematic Arts Library, University of Southern California, American Film Institute, Los Angeles, California, 1953–1954; Arthur Gavin, "*Rear Window*," *American Cinematographer*, 35, no. 2 (February 1954): 77–78, 97; David Atkinson, "Hitchcock's Techniques Tell *Rear Window* Story," *American Cinematographer*, 71, no. 2 (January 1990): 34–40; Scott Curtis, "The Making of *Rear Window*," in *Alfred Hitchcock's Rear Window*, ed. John Belton (Cambridge: Cambridge University Press, 2000), 21–56.
116. Hitchcock's decision to film entirely on soundstages at Paramount rather than on location in New York afforded him far greater creative control over *Rear Window*'s visual design, lighting, shadow, and color palette. Filming on studio-bound soundstage sets more closely resembled the war-related 1940s shooting constraints amid blackouts and location restrictions, which originally contributed to the look and style of film noir in the first place. Hitchcock wanted to transcend the failure of his earlier high-key, one-set gimmick in *Rope* (1948), also set in a Manhattan apartment, with a more dynamic elaborate visual rendering in *Rear Window*. Alfred Hitchcock Collection, Paramount Production File, Margaret Herrick Library, 1953–1954; USC Cinematic Arts Library, University of Southern California, American Film Institute, Los Angeles, California, 1953–1954; Gavin, "*Rear Window*," 77–78, 97; Atkinson, "Hitchcock's Techniques Tell *Rear Window* Story," 34–40; Curtis, "The Making of *Rear Window*," 21–56 John Belton, *Alfred Hitchcock's Rear Window*, 18.

117. There were problems lighting the huge set, especially when filming Stewart in the foreground while the camera focused on action taking place in the apartments across the courtyard. Given the amount of light necessary to illuminate the set and the limited speed of color film emulsions at that time, Hitchcock's crew had to use every available light at Paramount Pictures at one point, plus additional lights borrowed from Columbia and MGM. Stewart and other cast and crew members—especially in the upper stories at the top of the set—had to endure extreme heat due to the lights. In fact, lighting challenges on the set unexpectedly created a noir milieu on and off camera: it got so hot that the lights set off the sprinkler system and drenched and blacked out the soundstage set. "Suddenly, in the middle of [shooting], the lights set off the sprinkler system," Stewart remembered. "Not just a section of [the set], but on all the stages, and we're not talking about little streams of water but torrents." All filming had to stop as the entire set and production was plunged into wet darkness. It became a very noir milieu. However, Stewart recalled that Hitchcock was unfazed. "He sat there and told his assistant to get the sprinklers shut off and then to tell him when the rain was going to stop, but in the meantime to bring him an umbrella." Alfred Hitchcock Collection, Paramount Production File, Margaret Herrick Library, 1953–1954; USC Cinematic Arts Library, University of Southern California, American Film Institute, Los Angeles, California, 1953–1954; Gavin, "*Rear Window*," 77-78, 97; Atkinson, "Hitchcock's Techniques Tell *Rear Window* Story," 34–40; "Making of *Rear Window*" and "*Rear Window* Ethics: Remembering and Restoring a Hitchcock Classic," [DVD features] (2001; Universal City, CA: Universal Studios Home Entertainment); Curtis, "The Making of *Rear Window*," 21–56; "James Stewart" [DVD feature], *Rear Window* (2001; Universal City, CA: Universal Studios Home Entertainment).

118. Alfred Hitchcock Collection, Paramount Production File, Margaret Herrick Library, 1953–1954; USC Cinematic Arts Library, University of Southern California, American Film Institute, Los Angeles, California, 1953–1954; Gavin, "*Rear Window*," 77-78, 97; Atkinson, "Hitchcock's Techniques Tell *Rear Window* Story," 34–40; "Making of *Rear Window*" and "*Rear Window* Ethics: Remembering and Restoring a Hitchcock Classic," [DVD feature] (2001; Universal City, CA: Universal Studios Home Entertainment); Curtis, "The Making of *Rear Window*," 21–56.

119. Hayes won an Edgar Allan Poe Award from the Mystery Writers of America for the screenplay. Alfred Hitchcock Collection, Paramount Production File, Margaret Herrick Library, 1953–1954; USC Cinematic Arts Library, University of Southern California, American Film Institute, Los Angeles, California, 1953–1954; Gavin, "*Rear Window*," 77-78, 97; Atkinson, "Hitchcock's Techniques Tell *Rear Window* Story," 34–40; "Making of *Rear Window*" and "*Rear Window* Ethics: Remembering and Restoring a Hitchcock Classic," [DVD features] (2001; Universal City, CA: Universal Studios Home Entertainment); Curtis, "The Making of *Rear Window*," 21–56.

120. William Brogdon, "*Rear Window*," *Variety*, July 14, 1954, 6.

121. Lehman's dialogue included memorable witty hard-boiled barbs such as: "I'm an advertising man, not a red herring. I've got a job, a secretary, a mother, two ex-wives and several bartenders that depend upon me, and I don't intend to disappoint them all by getting myself slightly killed," "No. No, Mother, I have not been drinking. No. No. These two men, they poured a whole bottle of bourbon into me. No, they didn't give me a chaser," "Something wrong with your eyes? Yes, they're sensitive to questions." "I don't like the way Teddy Roosevelt is looking at me."

122. *North by Northwest* reimagines earlier black-and-white gothic-espionage noir films, shifting the earlier female-centered context to a more male-centric one, shot in widescreen color: as a masculine star vehicle revolving around charismatic Grant.

123. Eve eventually redeems and marries Roger, with Hitchcock's phallic innuendo as a train enters a tunnel. Eva Marie Saint replaced Grace Kelly in *On the Waterfront* and won an Oscar. Hitch's favorite blonde, Kelly, had already left her Hollywood acting career to become princess of Monaco following filming of *Rear Window* and *To Catch a Thief*. PCA censors objected to enemy agent Jeffery Vandamm's (James Mason) menacing partner Leonard (Martin Landau) being portrayed as effeminate and repeatedly insisted that his character's "flavor of homosexuality" be subdued. They were also concerned about Eve being openly depicted as Vandamm's mistress and racy lines of dialogue suggesting Eve's promiscuity, all of which remained in the film—although when Roger meets Eve on a train and asks, "Is that a proposition?" her suggestive reply "I never make love on an empty stomach" was rerecorded with "make" replaced with "discuss."
124. Principal photography took place from August to December 1958 on location in New York City; Chicago; Rapid City, South Dakota. The famous, higher-key crop-dusting scene was shot in Wasco, California, northwest of Bakersfield. Hitchcock noted that Lehman and production designer Robert Boyle were permitted to tour and sketch the inside of the United Nations building, although no shooting was permitted outside or in the interior. Despite this prohibition, Hitchcock managed to shoot Grant and his assailants—leaving cabs and briskly sprinting upstairs to the UN building entrance—with a camera hidden in a van.
125. There were also legal issues securing rights to shoot on Mount Rushmore because the National Park Service objected to filming at the monuments, informing Hitchcock: "No scenes of violence will be filmed near the sculpture, on the Talus Slope below the sculpture, or any simulation or mockup of the sculpture or Talus Slope, or any public-use area of Mount Rushmore." Hitchcock was permitted to film establishing long shots of the monument and outdoor balcony of the tourist cafeteria. *North by Northwest* correspondence in Alfred Hitchcock Collection, MGM Production, Budget/Legal Files, MPA Files, Margaret Herrick Library, Beverly Hills, California, 1958–1959; MGM Collection, Ernest Lehman Collection, USC Cinematic Arts Library, University of Southern California, Los Angeles, California, 1958–1959; Ernest Lehman Collection, Harry Ransom Humanities Research Center, University of Texas at Austin, Austin, Texas, 1958–1959; "Destination Hitchcock: The Making of *North by Northwest*," DVD production notes and documentary feature on the making of *North by Northwest*, Turner Entertainment Co. and Warner Home Video, 2000.
126. Roger makes a scene and disrupts an art gallery auction—as spies try to kill him—and learns that Vandamm is smuggling secret microfilm in a statuette. As Roger is arrested, driven in the police car through the city at night, and spirited to a plane by an intelligence officer, Hitchcock plays with sound, preventing the audience from hearing an explanation of what is going on as the loud noise of the engine on the tarmac drowns out the dialogue. Amplifying gothic-style noir gender distress, Roger ridicules Eve for bedding and betraying him for lover Vandamm, and nearly getting him killed by a crop duster firing a machine gun in a cornfield. After Roger nearly blows Eve's cover as a double-agent, Eve pretends to shoot Roger at Rushmore. *North by Northwest* is laced with misogynism: upon discovering that his mistress Eve is a spy, Vandamm plans to murder her. As the aircraft lands on the dark runway in the dead of night on the cliffs of Rushmore, he plots to dispose of her by throwing her from a plane flying at an altitude of great height.
127. Although distinct from much of the film, which takes place in the city or on a train.
128. Seemingly the antithesis of film noir, the sequence was quite different than the iconic dark, nocturnal, urban jungle, wet streets of film noir, with its barren landscape of

sunlit crops wide open in the middle of nowhere rather than the typical shadowy noir nightscape as a setting of a murder crime scene.
129. Alfred Hitchcock, *Hitchcock S'Explique* [French documentary interview], André S. Labarthe, 1965. Hitchcock's description was evocative of Hollywood's noir-style crime cycle. Mysterious atonal sounds of jazz (iconic of film noir) are even heard on the soundtrack.
130. Hitchcock, *Hitchcock S'Explique*, André S. Labarthe, 1965.
131. *North by Northwest* does not have as much noir style in its color design as it could have had because Hitchcock purposely made it that way. It does offer more color noir aesthetic than *Vertigo* and many other of his color films, however, given his intention and locations and high-key preference by the late 1950s. The industry's postwar shift from chiaroscuro to brighter, high-key interiors and sunlit outdoor locations shot on acetate film (replacing nitrate)—as well as adoption of lighter, low-contrast televisual conventions—countered noir aesthetics, seen in some other Hitchcock films. For instance, *Rope* featured bright, higher-key interiors despite being filmed indoors on Technicolor nitrate. *Dial M for Murder* (1953), was shot in 3D on acetate with light interiors. *I Confess* (1953) was shot in sunlit Montreal. *Strangers on a Train* (1953) included an array of high-key outdoor locales. Location filming basking in the bright sunlight on the colorful, high-key beaches of the French Riviera mitigated against noir stylistics in Hitchcock's *To Catch a Thief* (1955), shot for $2.5 million and earning $4.5 million in the United States. One exception is the stunning scene with Grace Kelly and Cary Grant cast in silhouette indoors in her blackened, unlit hotel room at night, backlit by fireworks exploding in the dark nocturnal sky through the window. Hitchcock remade *The Man Who Knew Too Much* in 1956 for $1.2 million, which made $11.3 million, his biggest hit of the decade and a somewhat more conventional big-budget spectacle, filmed in bright, high-key widescreen VistaVision color and shot on location in Morocco, in London, and at Paramount Studios. Hitchcock would soon reimagine his 1940s gothic and espionage thrillers (such as *Notorious*) in color films *Vertigo* and *North by Northwest*, which achieved a widescreen VistaVision variation on color noir style despite more extensive filming on location. A few years after *Rear Window*, Stewart reteamed with Hitchcock for another classic, *Vertigo* (1958). Stewart played a tormented, psychologically afflicted antihero, retired police detective Scottie, who suffers from vertigo. He becomes obsessed with ill-fated gothic femme heroine Madeleine/Judy (Kim Novak), who perishes from the top of a bell tower. Shot in large frame VistaVision, *Vertigo* featured crime; murder; and toxic, obsessive fatal attraction impressively set against spectacular locations in San Francisco; Mission San Juan Bautista; Big Basin Redwoods State Park; Mission Dolores; and Watsonville, California. The extensive location shooting in *Vertigo* consequently offset much of its noir imagery. A covered bridge resembled a tunnel cloaked in silhouette and blackened shadow. Interiors, including a noirish cavernous stairwell and shrouded bell tower at Mission San Juan Bautista, and brighter locales such as Ernie's restaurant with its red walls and Ransohoff's department store, were created then shot at Paramount Studios. In fact, the bell tower in *Vertigo* was "painted in on glass for the exterior shots [of already shot footage of the existing mission] and the interior of the Tower was built on the set." The real Mission San Juan Bautista location does not have a bell tower. The mock-up of the tower was seventy feet tall. The most striking interior was the dark, noir-style, claustrophobic stairwell with a steep, narrow climb winding high to the top: opening to a cramped murky balcony shrouded in shadow, from which the heroine climactically plunges to her demise. Shot for $2.5 million, *Vertigo* was a disappointing failure at the box office in 1958. However, that did not

stop Hitchcock from creating another color noir masterwork with spy thriller *North by Northwest*. *Vertigo* was scarcely a commercial crowd-pleasing hit picture, and his next effort was thematically much more upbeat. While *Vertigo* was shot in large-frame VistaVision, it was shown theatrically in widescreen 35mm—reduced to a smaller film gauge (i.e., reduction printed) for exhibition—and thus was not shown in its proper format until its later Super VistaVision 70mm restoration in 1996–1997. *The Wrong Man* (1958) used abundant, gray, semidocumentary location photography. *Psycho* (1960), shot with his television crew, was more of a high-key postclassical gothic horror picture rather than a classic film noir. The television series *Alfred Hitchcock Presents* (1955–1962) utilized significant outdoor location filming in California and was comparatively lighter and higher key in visual style. Paramount memos for *Vertigo*, Paramount Production, Budget/Legal Files, Paramount Collection, Margaret Herrick Library, Beverly Hills, California, March 31, 1958; *San Francisco* magazine, July 1982, 51–57.

132. Eddie Mannix Ledger, MGM Budget Files, Alfred Hitchcock Collection, Margaret Herrick Library, Beverly Hills, California, 1959.
133. As well as Hitchcock's later films *The Man Who Knew Too Much*, *Vertigo*, and *North by Northwest*. Many postwar films shot outdoors on exterior locations basked in the bright sunlight comparatively void of shadowy noir imagery.
134. Gene Arneel, "Pix' Big and Bold Bid for Gold," *Variety*, August 8, 1956, 3.
135. The young gang members in *West Side Story* resembled teen derelicts in *Are These Our Children?* (1931), *Reefer Madness* (1936), the Dead End Kids in *Dead End* (1937), *Crime School* (1938), *Angels with Dirty Faces* (1938), *Hell's Kitchen* (1939), *They Made Me a Criminal* (1939), Jackie Cooper in *Where Are Your Children?* (1943), and Bonita Granville in *Youth Runs Wild* (1944, produced in Val Lewton's RKO noir B unit when filmmaker Robert Wise was there). Many films were discouraged by PCA censors and, like gangster pictures, banned by the Office of War Information (OWI) and Office of Censorship during World War II as controversial social topics and potential fodder for anti-American Nazi propaganda. After the conflict, noir B films like *They Live by Night* (1949) were channeled into juvenile delinquency films to capitalize on the emerging postwar youth market, as seen in *The Wild One* (1954), *Rebel Without a Cause* (1955), *Blackboard Jungle* (1955), and *Jailhouse Rock* (1957).
136. For instance, James M. Cain's *Serenade* was initially a shady noir project, but it was instead made into a bright, lavish, operatic, widescreen, WarnerColor musical sanitized of censorable noir content and visual style. This was also the case with Warner Bros.' suburban teen-angst color melodrama *Rebel Without a Cause*. Originally intended for a young Marlon Brando as a lean, monochrome, socially conscious B noir crime film about a young murderous psycopath in prison in 1947 (subtitled: *The Hypnoanalysis of a Criminal Psychopath*), it was ultimately stripped of its hard-boiled noir scenes, expressionistic visual style of blackened chiaroscuro, and lethal psychotic criminality a decade later in 1955. It became a visually brighter, high-key, big-budget color film, publicized as being about "problem kids from well-to-do homes," with a much more polished, glossier, widescreen color look than its original, low-budget, monochrome serial killer conception. While shooting the widescreen color film on location near Griffith Park Observatory, director Nicholas Ray also faced many challenges, complaints from residents and interruptions halting filming of night scenes—many of which were cut—which further reduced the noir style of *Rebel Without a Cause*. Ray instead emphasized the new widescreen CinemaScope technology, with its 2.55:1 aspect ratio, by composing shots with an abundance of light in multiple frames within a frame—using glass partitions of windows and doorways to split the screen and feature different characters—to

220   2. Fade to Gray and Color Noir

maximize the expansive width of the image. *Rebel Without a Cause* correspondence in Jack Warner Collection, USC Warner Bros. Archive, USC Pressbook Collection, University of Southern California, AFI, Los Angeles, California, 1946–1955; WB Press Book for *Serenade*, WB story files for *Serenade*, WBA, WSC budget figures, USC, 1956; Roy Hoopes, *Cain: The Biography of James M. Cain* (New York: Holt, Rinehart and Winston, 1982), 467.

137. *West Side Story*'s racially charged narrative of urban corruption, ethnic tensions, and self-destructive gang members was indicative of noir films. Tormented Jets gang antihero Tony (Richard Beymer) falls in love with Puerto Rican immigrant Maria (Natalie Wood), the sister of rival Sharks gang leader Bernardo (George Chakiris), which leads to tragedy. New York street gangs dance as they prepare for a rumble, where they beat and kill each other to Bernstein's riveting music. There is no chance of escape from the urban violence. Bernardo kills Tony's best friend, Jets leader Riff (Russ Tamblyn). Tony kills Bernardo in revenge. The Jets misogynistically harass (and metaphorically gang rape) Bernardo's girlfriend Anita (Rita Moreno). Bernardo's friend Chino (who desires to marry Maria himself) jealously guns down Tony in vengeance. It was a dark violent vision for a musical directed and choreographed by Robbins, written by Laurents, produced by Hal Prince and Robert E. Griffith, and with riveting music composed by Bernstein and lyrics by Stephen Sondheim in a downbeat musical reworking of *Romeo and Juliet* highlighting racial prejudice in the civil rights era. Like the original stage version, the screen production of *West Side Story* infused film noir style and youth-oriented gangster antiheroes to create a dark color noir musical film. On stage and screen, *West Side Story* revealed contemporary social realist interracial tensions and cultural critique in a moody variation on Shakespeare's *Romeo and Juliet*. Produced and directed by Robert Wise in collaboration with choreographer-director Jerome Robbins, the film version of *West Side Story* was adapted by Ernest Lehman. *West Side Story*'s screen adaptation was independently produced by Mirisch Company (with Seven Arts, Beta Productions, and B & P Enterprises), and released through United Artists in 1961. Harold Mirisch, Robert Wise Collection, University of Southern California, Los Angeles, California, September 12, 1960.

138. Leonard Bernstein quoted in Craig Zadan, *Sondheim and Co.* (New York: DaCapo, 1994), 17; Leonard Bernstein in Howard Taubman, "A Foot in Each Camp," *New York Times*, October 13, 1957, 129.

139. 70mm formats were shot in 65mm and projected in 70mm. Panavision designed MGM's Camera 65, and Super Panavision 70 had a 2.20:1 aspect ratio using spherical lenses, unlike anamorphic systems such as Ultra Panavision 70, or CinemaScope's earlier 35mm anamorphic system used for noir musicals like Cukor's *A Star Is Born*.

140. Using Super Panavision 70mm large-frame format as well as 35mm, with second unit photography by Robert Relyea.

141. Robert Wise quoted in Jerry Kutner, "Interview, Robert Wise," *Bright Lights* 10–11 (1993) 33; Daniel Fapp, "Personal Favorite: *Rear Window*," *American Cinematographer*, 67, no. 3 (March 1985): 104; Robert Wise Collection, Ernest Lehman Collection, University of Southern California, Los Angeles, California, 1961; Ernest Lehman Collection, Harry Ransom Humanities Research Center, University of Texas at Austin, Austin, Texas, 1961.

142. Robert Wise quoted in Jerry Kutner, "Interview, Robert Wise," *Bright Lights* 10–11 (1993) 33; Robert Wise Collection, University of Southern California. Like Hitchcock with *Rear Window*, *West Side Story* attained and heightened its chiaroscuro color noir visual style because Wise intentionally chose to shoot most of the film as night interiors on shadowy enclosed soundstage sets.

143. Wise became a seasoned director of noir films such as *Born to Kill* (1947), *The Set-Up* (1949), and *Odds Against Tomorrow* (1959). Wise had edited Orson Welles's *Citizen Kane* (1941). Russ Tamblyn, playing gang leader Riff, had played a juvenile delinquent in the 1949 noir *Gun Crazy*. Wise in Kutner, 33; Robert Wise, "West Side Story: Problems of Style," Robert Wise Collection, University of Southern California, Los Angeles, California, January 21, 1960, 1–2; Robert Wise, interview by Sheri Chinen Biesen, 1998.
144. Wise estimated the final cost at $7.5 million, Mirisch at $6.75 million. *West Side Story* was initially budgeted at $4,029,600. Robert Wise, interview by Sheri Chinen Biesen, 1998; Walter Mirisch, *I Thought We Were Making Movies, Not History* (Madison: University of Wisconsin Press, 2008), 127; Budget, Robert Wise Collection, USC, 1960–61.
145. "Crowther, Musical Advance: *West Side Story* Expands on Screen," *New York Times*, October 22, 1961, Section 2, 1.
146. Joel Finler, *The Hollywood Story* (New York: Crown, 1988; Columbia University Press, 2003), 277. The evolution of the noir aesthetic is seen in later iterations of the visual style in a new postclassical era in Hollywood and overseas, in such films as *Le Samouraï* (1967), *Bullitt* (1968), and *'Round Midnight* (1986).

3. Neo-Noir: The Legacy of Noir Visual Style

1. For further reading on New Hollywood, see Mark Harris, *Pictures at a Revolution: Five Films and the Birth of New Hollywood* (New York: Penguin, 2008); Thomas Schatz, "New Hollywood" in *Film Theory Goes to the Movies*, ed. Jim Collins, Hillary Radner and Ava Preacher Collins (New York: Routledge, 1993); Peter Biskind, *Easy Riders, Raging Bulls* (New York: Simon and Schuster, 1999); Thomas Schatz, "Film Industry Studies and Hollywood History" in *Media Industries*, ed. Jennifer Holt and Alisa Perren (Malden, MA: Wiley-Blackwell, 2009); J. Hoberman, "Ten Years That Shook the World," *American Film* (June 1985): 34–59; Thomas Schatz, "The Studio System and Conglomerate Hollywood" in *The Contemporary Hollywood Film Industry*, ed. Paul MacDonald and Janet Wasko (Malden, MA: Wiley-Blackwell, 2008); Robert Kolker, *A Cinema of Loneliness* (Oxford: Oxford University Press, 1988, 2000, 2011); Thomas Schatz, "New Hollywood, New Millennium" in *Film Theory and Contemporary Hollywood Movies*, ed. Warren Buckland (London: Routledge, 2009).
2. Gene Moskowitz, "Films Along the Seine," *New York Times*, April 20, 1958, X7.
3. This noir trend was also seen overseas in *Drunken Angel* (1948), *The Barefoot Contessa* (filmed abroad), and color noir sci-fi film *The H-Man* (1958). Don Siegel's *The Killers* (a 1964 color remake of Siodmak's 1946 noir) was originally intended for television but was deemed too violent for a TV movie and was instead released theatrically in Europe and the United States.
4. Moskowitz, "Films Along the Seine," X7.
5. Walter Strenge, "Realism in Real Sets, and Locations," *American Cinematographer* 38, no. 10 (October 1957): 650; George Howard, "Design Improvements in High-Wattage Filament Lamps Respond to Studio Needs," 39, no. 4 (April 1958): 228.
6. Andrew Lazlo, "Recent Trends in Location Lighting," *American Cinematographer* 49, no. 9 (September 1968): 666.
7. Lazlo, "Recent Trends in Location Lighting," 666–668, 696–697; "The Evolution of Motion Picture Lighting," *American Cinematographer* 50, no. 1 (January 1969): 94–97, 108, 119, 177.
8. Howard Thompson, "Movies: Out of Tune with the World of Jazz," *New York Times*, August 21, 1966, 108. For further reading on jazz noir, see Sheri Chinen Biesen,

Music in the Shadows: Noir Musical Films (Baltimore, MD: Johns Hopkins University Press, 2014).

9. Harris, *Pictures at a Revolution*, 101, 422.
10. Based on Truman Capote's book of an actual crime (with music by Quincy Jones). Richard Brooks quoted in Peter Bart, " 'In Cold Blood' On the Firing Line," *New York Times*, October 16, 1966, 123.
11. Conrad Hall quoted in Stephen Pizzello, "Wrap Shot: *In Cold Blood*," *American Cinematographer* (March 22, 2019).
12. "While Quincy Jones's score provides a hint of human warmth to the bleak landscape." A. O. Scott, "Critic's Choice: *In Cold Blood*," *New York Times*, November 4, 2005.
13. Burnett Guffey quoted in Herb Lightman, "Raw Cinematic Realism in the Photography of *Bonnie and Clyde*," *American Cinematographer* 48, no. 4 (April 1967).
14. Paul Schrader quoted in Dave Kehr, "Arthur Penn, Director of *Bonnie and Clyde*, Dies," *New York Times*, September 30, 2010, A1; Patrick Goldstein, "Blasts from the Past," *Los Angeles Times*, August 24, 1997; Harris, *Pictures at a Revolution*, 2008. Although set in the stark, dusty Great Depression era and harkening nostalgically to classic 1930s gangster movies and 1940s films noir, *Bonnie and Clyde* invoked the existential cynicism, violence, sexual revolution, and countercultural dissention of the late 1960s Vietnam War era. In addition, *Bonnie and Clyde* was made just as Hollywood's Production Code censorship eroded and was scrapped—replaced with a ratings system in 1968. Arthur Penn's fugitive couple forged a new breed of American cinema: defying established conventions with the film's modernistic experimentation, social commentary, and climactic montage.
15. Robert Towne quoted in Harris, *Pictures at a Revolution*, 152.
16. Goldstein, "Blasts from the Past;" Harris, *Pictures at a Revolution*, 2008, 195. *Bonnie and Clyde* consciously paid homage to earlier crime antiheroes and gritty iconography in its neo-noir style. See also Sheri Chinen Biesen, "Arthur Penn's *Bonnie and Clyde* as Counterculture Gangster Film: Reimagining Classic Gangster Pictures and Film Noir," in *Critical Insights Film: Bonnie and Clyde*, ed. Rebecca Martin (Ipswich, MA: Salem Press, 2016).
17. As the films opens, Penn cuts to a stylized close-up of Bonnie Parker (Faye Dunaway) shot at an oblique Dutch angle through the bars of her head board. She grips, pounds, and shakes it as if imprisoned as she lies naked on the bed in her room. Then she descends the stairs, shot at an extreme low angle and backlit so she is practically a silhouette with a transparent dress (to suggest a racier, censorable variation on 1944 noir *Double Indemnity*'s lethal femme fatale Phyllis descending stairs). Veteran cinematographer Guffey had shot films since the Prohibition era, winning an Oscar for *Bonnie and Clyde*. (Guffey's imagery in *Bonnie and Clyde* captures the look and feel of another tragic ill-fated Depression-era journey of survival: John Ford's film adaptation of John Steinbeck's *The Grapes of Wrath* [1940], shot in noir style by Gregg Toland.) Warren Beatty bought the *Bonnie and Clyde* script for $10,000. When Benton and Newman expressed their desire for Truffaut or Godard to direct, Beatty replied, "You've already written a French New Wave film. What you need is a good American director." Penn rejected the project three times before agreeing to direct *Bonnie and Clyde*. David Newman, Arthur Penn, and Robert Benton quoted in Goldstein, "Blasts from the Past;" Harris, *Pictures at a Revolution*, 195. Guffey was a veteran film noir photographer.
18. The final montage sequence of *Bonnie and Clyde*, in which birds and bullets fly, recalls and transcends the fugitive *Gun Crazy* couple's demise, gunned down in a foggy swamp, or the violent death of the gangster in *Scarface*.

19. Paul Schrader, "Notes on Film Noir." *Film Comment* 8, no. 1 (1972): 8–13.
20. John Cawelti, "*Chinatown* and Generic Transformation in Recent American Films," in *Film Theory and Criticism*, 4th ed., ed. Gerald Mast, Marshall Cohen, and Leo Braudy (New York: Oxford University Press, 1992), 498–511.
21. Achieving neo-noir visual style with portable equipment, and executive-produced by Robert Relyea (who shot second unit photography on *West Side Story*).
22. The dark night visually punctuated by runway lights in *Bullitt* recalled stark neon on noir streets.
23. Even the film company's wardrobe was stolen while shooting on location. Variety Staff, "Bullitt...," *Variety*, October 23, 1968, 9; Variety Staff, "Bullitt," *Daily Variety*, February 23, 1968, 2; Variety Staff, "Bullitt," *Daily Variety*, March 13, 1968, 2; Variety Staff, "Bullitt," *Daily Variety*, April 23, 1968, 2; Variety Staff, "Bullitt," *Daily Variety*, October 16, 1968, 3; Special Collections, USC Cinematic Arts Library, American Film Institute, Los Angeles, California, 1968. See also Joshua Gleich, *Hollywood in San Francisco: Location Shooting and Aesthetics of Urban Decline* (Austin: University of Texas Press, 2018).
24. Jim Hemphill, "*Bullitt* (1968) Special Edition," *American Cinematographer* 49, no. 10 (October 2005); Variety Staff, "Bullitt," *Daily Variety*, March 18, 1968, 12.
25. Edward Lipnick, "Creative Post-Flashing Technique for *The Long Goodbye*," *American Cinematographer* 54, no. 3 (March 1973): 278.
26. Coppola wrote and directed the renowned screen crime saga in collaboration with author Mario Puzo, and produced the sequel (the first was produced by Albert Ruddy), for executive Robert Evans at Paramount. After working on *Bonnie and Clyde* (before writing *Chinatown*), Robert Towne famously wrote the patio scene between mobster Vito Corleone (Marlon Brando) and his son Michael (Al Pacino), where he passes the reins of power and his crime empire to him in Coppola's postclassical gangster picture, *The Godfather*.
27. Joel Finler, *The Hollywood Story* (New York: Crown, 1988; Columbia University Press, 2003), 277. John H. Allan, "Profits of *The Godfather*," *New York Times*, April 16, 1972, F3.
28. Willis noted, "I made [*The Godfather Part II*] even darker than the first movie for that reason." However, Willis noted the cinematic imagery "doesn't work . . . when you run it in a theater with below-standard projection. In order to be at a standard for viewing film, a theater screen and projector must produce 16 foot-lamberts . . . if it's not, you're not going to see what you're supposed to see." Gordon Willis quoted in [American Society of Cinematographers] ASC Staff, "Gordon Willis, ASC Interview at AFI [American Film Institute]," *American Cinematographer* 59, no. 9 (September 1978).
29. Conrad Hall shot *In Cold Blood, Cool Hand Luke, Black Widow, American Beauty*, and *Road to Perdition* and won an Oscar for *Butch Cassidy and the Sundance Kid*.
30. "I'm a one-light cameraman. I pick a light and a color ratio for the movie, and then ask for one printer at the laboratory. The lab just has to do the same thing every day. They don't change anything, although I change things back and forth." Willis used the Technicolor dye-transfer I-B imbibition developing process on shot footage as a technique to enhance neo-noir visual style for *The Godfather* and *The Godfather Part II*. Willis explained that "from those dailies—after everything has been cut—they [i.e., Technicolor lab] make separations (which are the matrices) and then finally the print." Willis noted that the Technicolor film processing and printing for *The Godfather* took much longer than for *The Godfather Part II*. "*The Godfather* took eight weeks to print, but we printed *Part II* in 10 days." Production, developing, and postproduction flew at a frenzied furious pace on the sequel film because Coppola "kept making changes. He kept re-cutting." As Willis admitted, "I was getting tired of shooting during the day and

spending the evenings at Technicolor" while finishing reshooting and printing the film as the Technicolor lab was shutting down. "They kept it open for us," Willis breathed. "There was a lot of hysteria, because they'd already had so many advances of money, and where was the movie?" Willis recalled Technicolor's commitment to finish the picture. He noted, "They said, 'We've got to get this out; we're closing down the plant.' And I won't tell you what I said, because you can't print it. But I got Francis [Ford Coppola] on the phone, and we kept the plant open, and got more of the materials needed for printing out of Eastman and finished off the initial run—which in itself was an accomplishment." Willis added, "I went home and got drunk after I heard that they were ready to punch out a thousand prints of a half-timed movie." Gordon Willis quoted in [American Society of Cinematographers] ASC Staff, "Gordon Willis, ASC Interview at AFI [American Film Institute]," *American Cinematographer* 59, no. 9 (September 1978).

31. He emphasized: "This was the last I-B printing to be done in the United States, with dye-transfer work at Technicolor." This is one reason these films look so great. Willis explained, "Every time you make a cut in an I-B roll you have to redo the matrices. That's 2,000 feet. So every time he'd make a change they'd have to make new matrices, and he kept cutting right up to the very last minute. I finally got him on the phone and said: 'Are you going to make any more cuts? This is impossible. We can't get it together.' He finally finished, and that gave us a week before the film went into release. So we did the best we could." Gordon Willis quoted in [American Society of Cinematographers] ASC Staff, "Gordon Willis, ASC Interview at AFI [American Film Institute]," *American Cinematographer* 59, no. 9 (September 1978). Richard W. Haines, *Technicolor Movies: The History of Dye Transfer Printing* (Jefferson, NC: McFarlane, 1993), 168.

32. Willis and Technicolor scholar Richard Haines note that Coppola's *The Godfather Part II* was one of the last films to use the Technicolor dye-transfer imbibition (I-B) process. In 1975, Technicolor shut down its U.S. lab, which developed film using the dye-transfer imbibition process. *The Godfather Part II* was released on December 18, 1974. Wide releases [e.g., Spielberg's *Jaws*] demanded much larger runs of release prints than Technicolor could provide, and the U.S. lab shut after the Technicolor company misjudged the market and positioned itself for smaller regional print runs. Gordon Willis quoted in [American Society of Cinematographers] ASC Staff, "Gordon Willis, ASC Interview at AFI [American Film Institute]," *American Cinematographer* 59, no. 9 (September 1978); Haines, *Technicolor Movies*, 168.

33. Gordon Willis quoted in [American Society of Cinematographers] ASC Staff, "Gordon Willis, ASC Interview at AFI [American Film Institute]," *American Cinematographer* 59, no. 9 (September 1978).

34. Others films were shot and developed in Eastmancolor rather than the Technicolor process. The films shot in Eastmancolor included the 1971 blaxploitation neo-noir *Shaft*, which was shot and developed in Metrocolor, MGM's branding of Eastmancolor. For further reading see Haines, *Technicolor Movies*, 168. Kodak Eastmancolor film stock had improved as the industry shifted away from three-strip Technicolor during the 1950s. In 1954, however, Technicolor was dissatisfied with Eastman Kodak's inferior new acetate safety stock (which the film industry switched to in the early 1950s) and even used Dupont film for a brief period until Eastman improved its safety stock. Improvements in Kodak's Eastmancolor stock with the introduction of new, "faster," light-sensitive, higher-speed color negative and print films earned Kodak a scientific/technical achievement Oscar in 1952. For example, color negative film 5248 was introduced in 1952 and 1953 and became an industry standard for six years, increasing the rate of Hollywood's conversion to color film production after 1953 and 1954. After that,

increasingly high-speed improvements allowed more rapid, light-sensitive exposure times in 1959 (i.e., faster color negative 5250) and again in 1962 (even better color negative 5251). These color film improvements had contributed to Hollywood studios shifting to color films over the course of the 1950s into the 1960s. In 1962, as the industry moved to color, Norwood Simmons of *American Cinematographer* praised the "New Eastman Color Negative and Print Films" that allowed "better color reproduction" and "less graininess due to significant improvements in emulsion characteristics," which made it possible for filmmakers to shoot with less light, thereby lowering production costs. As a result, films shot with the same amount of light looked brighter and needed less illumination with fewer lights for cinematic images to be exposed. Other developments included improved Tri-X panchromatic negative film 5233 in 1954, and better Plus-X/Tri-X reversal film in 1955. Norwood L. Simmons, "The New Eastman Color Negative and Print Films," *American Cinematographer* 43, no. 6 (June 1962): 362–363, 385; Thomas F. Brady, "BIG COLOR RUSH ON," *New York Times*, June 17, 1951, X5; Thomas M. Pryor, "COLOR STANDARDS SET…Motion Picture and TV Engineers Soc sets standards for color photography," *New York Times*, October 22, 1954; "COLOR FILM BOOM SEEN," *New York Times*, December 23, 1954; Thomas M. Pryor, "WIDE-SCREEN FILM WILL DROP COLOR," *New York Times*, March 24, 1955, 39; Thomas M. Pryor, "COLOR IS REQUIRED FOR CINEMASCOPE; Restriction in Fox Contract Forces 2 Studios to Change Black-and-White Plans," *New York Times*, April 5, 1955, 33; "COLOR FILMS," *New York Times*, November 20, 1955. See also Biesen, *Music in the Shadows*; Eastman Kodak, *Chronology of Motion Picture Films*, https://www.kodak.com/US/en/motion/About/Chronology_Of_Film/default.htm.

35. In fact, noir visual style was so pervasive in the postclassical era that even films that we don't typically associate with neo-noir included distinctive color noir imagery that simulated black and white with splashes of red. Examples include *The Graduate* (shot by Robert Surtees, who filmed *Act of Violence*), and the original theatrical versions of *Star Wars* (1977) and *The Empire Strikes Back* (1980), prior to their brighter, more colorful special editions with added digital effects.
36. Edward Lipnick, "Creative Post-Flashing Technique for *The Long Goodbye*," *American Cinematographer* 54, no. 3 (March 1973): 278.
37. Herrmann also scored *Citizen Kane, Jane Eyre, The Ghost and Mrs. Muir, Vertigo, North by Northwest*, and *Psycho*.
38. Vincent Canby, "Movie Review: 'Taxi Driver,'" *New York Times*, February 8, 1976, 36; see also Vincent Canby, "Film View: Scorsese's Disturbing 'Taxi Driver,'" *New York Times*, February 15, 1976, Section D, 1; Guy Flatley, "Martin Scorsese's Gamble," *New York Times*, February 8, 1976, 36.
39. Martin Scorsese quoted in Mary Pat Kelly, *Martin Scorsese* (New York: Thunder's Mouth, 1991), 102; Martin Scorsese, DVD Introduction for *New York, New York* (2005) and BBC interview (1995); Martin Scorsese and Carrie Rickey, DVD commentary for *New York, New York* (2005; Santa Monica, CA: Metro Goldwyn Mayer Home Entertainment).
40. Scorsese quoted in Mary Pat Kelly, *Martin Scorsese* (New York: Thunder's Mouth, 1991), 102; Vincent LoBrutto, *Martin Scorsese* (Westport, CT: Praeger, 2008), 204. For further reading, see Scorsese quoted in David Thompson and Ian Christie, *Scorsese on Scorsese* (London: Faber & Faber, 1989), 69; Jonathan Kaplan, "Taxi Dancer," *Film Comment* 13, no. 4 (July–August 1977): 41–43; Richard Glatzer, *Magill's* (Englewood Cliffs, NJ: Salem Press, 1984), 567–569; *Dialogue*, 1984 in Les Keyser, *Martin Scorsese* (New York: Twayne, 1992), 85–89; Tom Milne, "New York, New York," (Martin Scorsese: a Sight and Sound special), *Monthly Film Bulletin* 44, no. 524 (September 1977): 194–195.

41. Kent Jones, interview with Martin Scorsese, transcript from the 53rd New York Film Festival, "NYFF: Martin Scorsese on Film Preservation," *Film Comment* 51 no. 5 (October 27, 2015).
42. Joseph McBride, "*Raging Bull*," *Variety*, November 12, 1980, 26.
43. Other early-1980s neo-noir films included *Body Heat* (1981), *The Postman Always Rings Twice* (1981), and *Cutter's Way* (1981).
44. Dale Pollock, "Film Company Makes Hit Movies on Mini-Budgets," *Los Angeles Times*, December 29, 1984, SD C1.
45. Jordan Cronenweth quoted in Herb Lightman, "*Blade Runner*: Cronenweth's Cinematography," *American Cinematographer* 63, no. 7 (July 1982, repr. August 14, 2020).
46. '*Round Midnight* was coproduced by French independent companies Little Bear and P.E.C.F., written and directed by French director Bertrand Tavernier, cowritten by David Rayfiel, produced by Irwin Winkler (*New York, New York*; *Raging Bull*), and funded and distributed by Warner Bros. The film began in a conversation one evening between Bertrand Tavernier, Martin Scorsese, and Irvin Winkler. Scorsese asked what the French filmmaker would want to direct as his dream movie if he had total freedom and creative control, and Tavernier responded: "A story about American jazz musicians in Paris in the late 50s." Winkler offered to produce the film and Warner Bros. agreed to finance the transatlantic picture with a $3.5 million budget, although Tavernier recalled there was reluctance from studio executives to do a story about jazz or "an old Black guy." It's quite remarkable that Tavernier achieved such a gorgeous color noir visual aesthetic style in jazz neo-noir '*Round Midnight* and still managed to keep its final cost at just $3 million—$470,000 below budget. Bertrand Tavernier, Irvin Winkler, USC Pressbook Collection, University of Southern California, Los Angeles, California, 1986; Richard Phillips, "An Interview with Bertrand Tavernier," Sydney Film Festival, USC Special Collections, USC Cinematic Library, University of Southern California, Los Angeles, California, July 10, 1999.
47. Winkler noted, "When I did *New York, New York* with Scorsese, we had a hard time finding the proper ending for the film . . . One of the endings we discussed was DeNiro's character going to Paris to play because his music was never appreciated in America." Tavernier noted the affinity blacklisted filmmakers had with American jazz musicians in exile in Paris. '*Round Midnight* even starred blacklisted director John Berry as the Blue Note club's bartender. '*Round Midnight* first opens in New York, in a claustrophobic 52nd Street hotel room where jazz musician Dale gazes out the window as his friend Hershell lies in bed, dying, before moving to Paris. (In real life, Hershal Evans was a sax player with Lester Young in Count Basie's band.) As sax legend Dale (Gordon) struggles with addiction, he performs jazz with remarkable skill, playing "sweetly" at the Blue Note nightspot in Paris. Despite his fame, genius, and musical virtuosity, he is haunted by demons as he feeds his addiction, like Ray Milland in *The Lost Weekend*. Dale is reduced to stealing tips to score his next drink. Gordon told Tavernier: "I would steal, but never beg." In a detox effort, he is locked in his room by his handler Buttercup (Reaves-Phillips) and denied drinks, money, or his passport. When he escapes, binges, and passes out on the dark late-night streets, he's arrested, locked up, and sent to a hospital. His addiction nearly destroys him, but he finally gets clean. When Dale leaves Paris and comes back to New York City, his old haunts return him to a harsh dangerous world of seedy drug dealers (who sell heroin and threaten and pull switchblades on anyone interfering with their score) preying on jazz musicians—and he ultimately dies (it is intimated that he overdoses). All the while, extraordinary strains of jazz music envelop and permeate the film. '*Round Midnight* was evocative of Miles Davis's

poignant blue-toned jazz score of isolation and loneliness in *Ascenseur pour l'échafaud* (*Elevator to the Gallows*). Tormented antiheroes in *'Round Midnight* are overcome by their obsessions and passions. Even the music and jazz artistry are all-consuming and overpowering. "My life is music. My love is music. And it's twenty-four hours a day," Dale tells the French hospital psychologist, who is moved to tears. Critic Michael Dempsey of *Film Quarterly* noted, "That's a heavy sentence to face. It's like something that will not turn off . . . not let go of you." Seeking beauty, playing jazz, and performing are painful endeavors for Tavernier's protagonists, not unlike those in *The Red Shoes*, as are Dale's struggles. He recollects the physical violence, abuse, and trauma of racism and war. *'Round Midnight* even mentions *The Red Shoes*, as jazz musicians quote impresario Lermontov during a recording session. Dale's pain becomes more understandable when he powerfully recounts his memories of World War II brutality and racism: "I remember it rained pitifully that day . . . I found myself in the Camp Polk stockade where they started to do drum paradiddles on my head—for some time . . . You know, it just occurred to me that bebop was invented by the cats who did get out of the army." The scene evokes the heartbreaking personal demons and trauma depicted in European art cinema, punctuated by a haunting tracking shot across World War II army barracks, recalling Alain Renais's *Night and Fog* (1955), a stark documentary of Nazi concentration camps. In a decisively noir milieu, obsessive jazz fan Francis, soaked in the late-night pouring rain outside the club, crouches on the ground, straining to hear Dale play jazz (through an air duct), after abandoning his little girl at home alone. He later desperately, angrily begs his estranged wife for cash for a larger flat so Dale can move in with him. "I think the scene is very important because it brings out the dark side of [Francis's] character," Tavernier explains. "It's a very [emotionally] violent scene. It's somebody who is so childish and immature that he is telling the woman whom I think he still loves that he has never been inspired by her. So he *hurts* her all the time." Walking along New York's East River, Dale says to his friend, "You know, Francis, there is not enough kindness in the world." It is the last time we see Dale alive. Gordon came up with the line after a musician on the set quoted the 1944 film noir *The Mask of Dimitrios*. Bertrand Tavernier and Irvin Winkler, "'Round Midnight," USC Pressbook Collection, USC Cinematic Library, University of Southern California, Los Angeles, California, 1986; Jean-Pierre Coursodon, "*'Round Midnight*: An Interview with Bertrand Tavernier," *Cineaste* 15 no. 2 (1986): 18–23; Michael Dempsey, "All the Colors," *Film Quarterly* 40 no. 3 (1987): 2–5.

48. Bud Powell and Lester Young by casting an incomparable ensemble of real-life jazz musicians, including Herbie Hancock, Bobby Hutcherson, Wayne Shorter, Ron Carter, Tony Williams, Freddie Hubbard, John McLaughlin, Billy Higgins, and Cedar Walton and bluesy jazz vocals by Lonette McKee and Sandra Reaves-Phillips. Jazz bassist Ron Carter exclaimed: "It took a damn Frenchman to finally make a serious movie about us!"

49. Bertrand Tavernier quoted in Coursodon, "*'Round Midnight*," 18–23. See also Bertrand Tavernier quoted in Dempsey, "All the Colors," 2–5; Bertrand Tavernier quoted in Richard Phillips, "An Interview with Bertrand Tavernier," Sydney Film Festival, USC Special Collections, USC Cinematic Library, University of Southern California, Los Angeles, California, July 10, 1999.

50. Tavernier recalled the jam sessions recorded live as musicians Gordon, Higgins, and Hancock improvised jazz solos and performances in blue-toned noir musical numbers on film. "'Round Midnight," USC Pressbook Collection, USC Cinematic Library, University of Southern California, Los Angeles, California, 1986; Coursodon, "*'Round Midnight*," 18–23; Richard Phillips, "An Interview with Bertrand Tavernier," Sydney Film

Festival, USC Special Collections, USC Cinematic Library, University of Southern California, Los Angeles, California, July 10, 1999; Dempsey, "All the Colors," 2–5. Tavernier was a second-generation French New Wave director.

51. Tavernier recalled, "In the musical sequences, the camera work *had* to adapt to the music constantly because the music was improvised, and all of it was recorded directly while filming—which no one thought we could manage to do. We never knew in advance what the musicians [would play in their solos] . . . how many choruses they were going to take. A number that went on for four minutes in one take might go on for seven in the next." The deep shadows and brooding low-key lighting surrounded the musicians as they played, while cigarette smoke swirled around the stage. "I was lucky to get a wonderful camera operator who is a musician himself and who patterned his camera moves after the harmonic structure of the compositions," Tavernier explained, "so that he could smoothly track along a musician playing a solo and move past him just as he completed it." Coursodon, "*'Round Midnight*," 18–23; "'Round Midnight," USC Pressbook Collection, USC Cinematic Library, University of Southern California, Los Angeles, California, 1986; Richard Phillips, "An Interview with Bertrand Tavernier," Sydney Film Festival, USC Special Collections, USC Cinematic Library, University of Southern California, Los Angeles, California, July 10, 1999; Dempsey, "All the Colors," 2–5.

52. Critics raved about *'Round Midnight*. It was a critic's choice at the New York Film Festival. Janet Maslin of the *New York Times* called it "masterly," and insisted that "no actor could do what the great jazz saxophonist Dexter Gordon does" in Tavernier's "glowing tribute to the golden age of bebop." She also applauded its "tremendous depth of feeling," real-life inspiration, and "lovely, elegiac" pacing. Gordon's performance was praised as the "very embodiment of the music" with "heavy-lidded eyes," "smoky voice," and "long, graceful fingers" that "seem to be playing silent accompaniment to his conversation." *Variety* praised the film's visual style and "atmosphere" as a "rare example of Franco-American filmmaking in the truest sense of the term," with color images that flow forward and harken back to the past to "turn into the black-and-white, home-movie memories they will someday become." Sheila Benson of the *Los Angeles Times* applauded the film's evocative milieu with lonely Paris streets and stark hotel rooms filled with "humbling" minor key music, calling it the "first film about jazzmen to be made in their own rhythms; it's a ballad, with repeated themes, long sustained passages and a perfect, delicate gravity . . . With consummate tact, intelligence and passion, Tavernier lets us understand the cost of such exploration." *'Round Midnight* reveals "civilized rage" at the "beauties and horrors of a musician's life," writes Sheila Benson, as Dale, "complex and magnificent," moves "serenely to his own inner rhythms, ironic, unexpectedly sweet, utterly aware of both his powers and his demons." *'Round Midnight* grossed $3,250,000. Besides its Oscar for Best Original Score, newcomer Gordon was nominated for Best Actor. Tavernier recalled, "When the film was released in America, Marlon Brando sent a letter to Dexter in which he said that for the first time in fifteen years he learnt something about acting. Dexter read me the letter over the phone and said, 'After that who needs an Oscar?'" Gordon died just four years after his acclaimed performance (he did not receive the award). "*'Round Midnight*," *Variety*, April 16, 1986, 14; "'Round Midnight," USC Pressbook Collection, USC Cinematic Library, University of Southern California, Los Angeles, California, 1986; Richard Phillips, "An Interview with Bertrand Tavernier," Sydney Film Festival, USC Special Collections, USC Cinematic Library, University of Southern California, Los Angeles, California, July 10, 1999; Janet Maslin, "Film Festival; Dexter Gordon Stars in ''Round Midnight,'" *New York Times*, September 30, 1986, 11; Variety Staff, "''Round Midnight," *Variety*, April 16, 1986, 14;

Sheila Benson, "Movie Review: Taking a Sublime Look at a Jazz Musician's Life," *Los Angeles Times*, October 16, 1986, 1, 8.
53. Eastwood cited the film's cost at $9.1 million. Although it was critically acclaimed, *Bird* overran an estimated $9 million budget and grossed only $2,181,286 in the United States. USC Pressbook Collection, University of Southern California, Los Angeles, California, 1988.
54. Jack Green, ASC interview in John Silberg, "A Cut Above," *American Cinematographer* 90, no. 1 (January 2009): 1–3.
55. Eastwood's neo-noir was praised as the "most concerted effort to capture the spirit of Parker's music." Janet Maslin of the *New York Times* observed, "Until Bertrand Tavernier's *'Round Midnight*, in which Dexter Gordon served as the purest imaginable embodiment of jazz and its attendant way of life, it might have seemed impossible to convey these things on screen," adding that *Bird* reinforces "jazz's elusiveness." Although distinctive and critically praised for its noir visual style, it was Parker's jazz music in *Bird* that won an Academy Award for Best Sound, and Whitaker earned Best Actor at the Cannes Film Festival. Janet Maslin, "Charlie Parker's Tempestuous Life and Music," *New York Times*, September 26, 1988, C, 19.
56. David Heuring, "*The Fabulous Baker Boys*: Lounge Lizards in Love," *American Cinematographer* 70, no. 11 (November 1989): 50.
57. Michael Ballhaus quoted in Heuring, "*The Fabulous Baker Boys*: Lounge Lizards in Love," 50.
58. "The Fabulous Bakers Boys," *American Film* [magazine of the American Film Institute], June 1990, 50.
59. Rita Kempley, "The Fabulous Bakers Boys," *Washington Post*, October 13, 1989; Janet Maslin, "Review/Film; Pfeiffer and 2 Bridges Brothers in 'The Fabulous Bakers Boys,'" *New York Times*, October 13, 1989, C, 14.
60. Elvis Mitchell, "Sibling Ivories," *LA Weekly*, October 27–November 2, 1989, 55.
61. Pauline Kael, "The Fabulous Bakers Boys – Review," *New Yorker*, October 16, 1989; Rita Kempley, "The Fabulous Bakers Boys," *Washington Post*, October 13, 1989; Maslin, "Review/Film; Pfeiffer and 2 Bridges Brothers in 'The Fabulous Bakers Boys,'" *New York Times*, October 13, 1989, C, 14.
62. Rita Kempley, "The Fabulous Bakers Boys," *Washington Post*, October 13, 1989; Janet Maslin, "Review/Film; Pfeiffer and 2 Bridges Brothers in 'The Fabulous Bakers Boys,'" *New York Times*, October 13, 1989, C, 14.
63. Roger Ebert, "The Fabulous Bakers Boys," *Chicago Sun-Times*, October 13, 1989.
64. USC Pressbook Collection, USC Special Collections, USC Cinematic Library, University of Southern California, Los Angeles, California, 1989.
65. Jack Mathews, "Batman, the Gamble,'" *Los Angeles Times*, June 18, 1989, 7; Paul Dean, "The New Batmobile," *Los Angeles Times*, June 12, 1989, D1. Neo-noir visual style would continue to proliferate, accelerated even further by technological advances that enhanced noir imagery. A slew of new productions nostalgically paid homage to the classic noir aesthetic during the 1990s, a trend that persisted into the new millennium.
66. Other 1990s neo-noir films included *The Player* (1992), *Reservoir Dogs* (1992), *Red Rock West* (1993), *Pulp Fiction* (1994), and *Donnie Brasco* (1997).
67. Cawelti, "*Chinatown* and Generic Transformation," 498–511.
68. The nostalgia trend seen in neo-noir films also persisted in the later digital streaming era. Rodrigo Muñoz-González, "The Nostalgia Economy: Netflix and New Audiences in the Digital Age," Ph.D. Abstract, Department of Media and Communications, London School of Economics and Political Science, London, United Kingdom, 2017, 3;

see also Rodrigo Muñoz-González, "Consumerism, Nostalgia, and Geek Culture...," Ph.D. Thesis, Department of Media and Communications, London School of Economics and Political Science, London, United Kingdom, 2021.
69. Branagh added, "I was also drawn to the fullblooded style" of Leonetti's cinematography on modern thrillers *Jagged Edge* and *Eyewitness*. Kenneth Branagh quoted in David Heuring, "The Director—Cinematographer Connection," *American Cinematographer*, 72, no. 11 (November 1991); USC Pressbook Collection, USC Special Collections, USC Cinematic Library, University of Southern California, Los Angeles, California, 1991.
70. See "Technicolor Decades 1975–2015" at eastman.org; https://www.eastman.org/technicolor/decades; https://www.eastman.org/technicolor/decades/1975–2015; George Eastman Museum and Technicolor Online Research Archive; "Motion Picture Processing Techniques" at kodak.com. https://www.kodak.com/US/en/motion/page/processing techniques/; The American Society of Cinematographers, ASC Staff, "Technicolor's ENR" and "SILVER RETENTION," in "Soup du Jour," *American Cinematographer* 98 (2017): 2 at theasc.com; https://theasc.com/magazine/nov98/soupdujour/pg2.htm. See also Alexis Van Hurkman, "Bleach Bypass Looks," in *Color Correction Look Book: Creative Grading Techniques for Film and Video*, ed. Alexis Van Hurkman (San Francisco, CA: Peach Pit Press/Pearson Education, 2013); Eastman Kodak, *Chronology of Motion Picture Films*; https://www.kodak.com/US/en/motion/About/Chronology_Of_Film/default.htm.
71. Scorsese's brutal gangster neo-noir *Goodfellas* (1990) featured a stunning, fluid, subjective point of view, long-take shot introducing mafia "made men." It was followed a few years later by *Casino* (1995), with a deadly crime world of sudden violence.
72. Dickerson also shot Lee's *Do the Right Thing* and *Malcolm X*.
73. Stephen Pizzello, "DVD Playback: Barton Fink," *American Cinematographer* 84, no. 8 (August 2003): 2; "A League of His Own," *American Cinematographer* 92, no. 1 (January 2011).
74. Pizzello, "Barton Fink," 2; "A League of His Own."
75. Vincent Canby, "'Barton Fink,' a Dark Comedy from Joel and Ethan Coen," *New York Times*, August 21, 1991, C-11.
76. Raised in Minnesota, which the Coens pay homage to in *Fargo*, Joel Coen studied film at New York University and Ethan Coen studied philosophy at Princeton before pursuing their filmmaking career with a series of stylish, offbeat independent films laced with their surreal, darkly comedic point of view.
77. *The Big Lebowski* opens at night on a dark nocturnal cityscape. The distinctive ambiance in *The Big Lebowski* is reinforced by the Coens' convoluted Chandler-like plot and grab-bag of quirky LA ingredients—night streets, neon signs, the Dude's dive apartment, continuous break-ins, robberies, assaults, smashed cars, late-night Ralph's Market and bowling (rather than a nightclub), driving with a broken windshield, and eating In-N-Out Burgers as Santana's "Oye Como Va" (in lieu of jazz) blares on the radio to create a labyrinthine crime mystery-parody. The nightspots and lifestyle are familiar as these seemingly random locales suggest an early 1990s rendering of the Southern California noir milieu: iconic and instantly recognizable, deftly embodying the Angeleno experience and spirit of LA for those who lived there during that period. Its cult appeal further resonates with most viewers who haven't but know LA mainly through movies. *The Big Lebowski* was shot from January through April 1997 on a $15 million budget. It initially had a lukewarm reception during its original six-week theatrical release in 1998. Scott Timberg, "The Achievers: The Story of the Lebowski Fans Explores The Dude Phenomenon," *Los Angeles Times*, July 30, 2009, A-4.
78. These strong, sexual, transgressive women are not romantic, sentimental, or feminine. Neither are they weak victims. They are quite active in driving and propelling the story.

Their narrative agency is even more remarkable because it is often considered a masculine buddy movie. Gold-digging, nymphomaniac, trophy wife and porn star Bunny is Maude's young stepmother (rather than her sister), who offers sexual favors for money and mysteriously disappears while her misogynistic, nihilist, adult film costar colleagues wreak havoc, demanding ransom and engaging in vicious threats and violence.

79. Curtis Hanson quoted in Alex Simon, "Curtis Hanson—Confidentially," *Venice Magazine*, September 1997.
80. Davis Williams, "Wrap Shot: *L.A. Confidential*," *American Cinematographer* 99, no. 5 (May 3, 2018); ASC Staff, "L.A. Confidential," *American Cinematographer* 78, no. 10 (October 1997).
81. Simon, "Curtis Hanson;" Manohla Dargis, "Curtis Hanson: A Filmmaker of Sunshine and Noir," *New York Times*, September 24, 2016, C4.
82. Simon, "Curtis Hanson;" Dargis, "Curtis Hanson," C4; Williams, "Wrap Shot;" ASC Staff, "L.A. Confidential," *American Cinematographer* 78, no. 10 (October 1997).
83. Simon, "Curtis Hanson;" Dargis, "Curtis Hanson," C4. Williams, "Wrap Shot;" ASC Staff, "L.A. Confidential," *American Cinematographer* 78, no. 10 (October 1997).
84. Williams, "Wrap Shot;" ASC Staff, "L.A. Confidential," *American Cinematographer* 78, no. 10 (October 1997).
85. Chuck Wagner, "Dark World," *Cinefantastique* 29, no. 3 (September 1997): 7.
86. Kenneth Sweeney, "DVD Playback: *Dark City* (1998)," *American Cinematographer* 89, no. 10 (October 2008).
87. Doyle was known for his digital color grading on *Dark City*, as well as on Peter Jackson's *The Lord of the Rings* trilogy and Joe Wright's *Darkest Hour*.
88. Ian Failes, "*Dark City* at 20: A Conversation with Colorist Peter Doyle," *Vfxblog*, February 25, 2018.
89. In its "desperate search through a labyrinth of time, memory and sinister manipulation." Todd McCarthy, "*Dark City*," *Variety*, February 20, 1998, 73.
90. Stephen Holden, "Film Review; You Are Getting Sleepy: Who Are You, Anyway?," *New York Times*, February 27, 1998, 8.
91. Roger Ebert, "*Dark City*," *Chicago Sun-Times*, February 27, 1998. Ebert called its gorgeous, blackened noir style an original, exciting, and innovative triumph of atmospheric visual stylization, art direction, set design, cinematography, and special effects that stirred the imagination in its brooding noir-styled city of the future and leaps into the unknown.

4. From Noir to Netflix: Streaming Darkness in the Digital Era

1. While some of these more recent digital productions may not prove to be as timeless, classic, or iconic as quintessential 1940s nitrate films noir *Double Indemnity, Out of the Past*, and *Act of Violence* or neo-noir films like *The Godfather, 'Round Midnight*, or *Dark City*, they nevertheless intentionally harken back to earlier noir productions and exude abundant noir style.
2. Before video rental chains went out of business. Netflix was initially a subscription DVD-by-mail service of older classic and contemporary films, outcompeting Blockbuster for rentals, a great bargain. The continuing evolution and legacy of the noir style is seen in the importance of *The Sopranos* and *The Wire* era at HBO (originally Home Box Office) and the convergence of film and television, which is widely recognized to have changed the relationship of cinema and TV in the film/media industry. The impact of HBO on TV is equivalent to Netflix's on the film industry. When HBO

produced *The Sopranos*, Home Box Office was still a premium, subscription, cable movie library company offering new theatrical releases on the air. In 1999 *The Sopranos* was a pivot, a turning point, because HBO's production of original series soared to over 60 percent of its offerings and original noir-styled, long-form serial dramas like *The Sopranos* became more profitable than legacy networks as they shifted away from quality TV. As long-form dramas became respectable, this development changed the business and set the stage for streaming companies like Netflix.
3. In 2011, Netflix was still getting most of its revenue from movie rentals. Netflix shifted to original programming, however, and much of it was noir-styled, with 17 hours in 2012 rising to stream over 2,700 hours of original programming in 2019. So this pivot was as important as the one at HBO. Thomas Schatz, "HBO and Netflix—Getting Back to the Future," *Flow* 19 (January 20, 2014), 7. See also Henry Jenkins, *Convergence Culture: Where Old and New Media Collide* (New York: New York University Press, 2006), 104, 114.
4. For years, Netflix has insisted that its programming would remain ad-free, and for most users, content continues to be ad-free, although a lower-tier, ad-supported version was provided in 2023 for users wanting a cheaper option.
5. Netflix original long-form noir serial dramas include *Lilyhammer* (2012), *House of Cards* (2013), *Daredevil* (2015), *Jessica Jones* (2015), *River* (2015), *Narcos* (2015), *Bloodline* (2015), *Marcella* (2016), *Luke Cage* (2016), *Four Seasons in Havana* (2016), *Secret City* (2016), *Babylon Berlin* (2017), *Ozark* (2017), *The Punisher* (2017), *Iron Fist* (2017), *Bad Blood* (2017), *Mindhunter* (2017), *Collateral* (2018), *Gun City* (2018), *Narcos Mexico* (2018), *Giri/Haji* (2019), *Shadow* (2019), *Traitors* (2019), *High Seas* (2019), *Queen Sono* (2020), *The Eddy* (2020), *Lost Bullet* (2020), *Cursed* (2020), *The Defeated* (2020), *Outer Banks* (2020), *StartUp* (2020), *The Queen's Gambit* (2020), *The Club* (2021), *Lupin* (2021), *Maid* (2021), *Shadow and Bone* (2021), *In from the Cold* (2022), *The Journalist* (2022), *Kleo* (2022), *The Night Agent* (2023), and *The Diplomat* (2023). Netflix original neo-noir feature films include *Message from the King* (2016), *Crooked House* (2016), *Manhunt* (2017), *Curtiz* (2018), *Outlaw King* (2018), *The Irishman* (2019), *Earthquake Bird* (2019), *The Coldest Game* (2019), *El Camino* (2019), *The Highwaymen* (2019), *The King* (2019), *Da 5 Bloods* (2020), *Rebecca* (2020), *Mank* (2020), *Rogue City* (2020), *Malcolm & Marie* (2021), *Munich: The Edge of War* (2021), *The Stronghold* (2021), *Operation Mincemeat* (2022), and *AKA* (2023).
6. Netflix excelled as a rental outfit delivering classic noir and neo-noir titles to its subscribers and as a producer of original noir programming.
7. In 2009, as Netflix became a popular way to rent movies, it was considered the ultimate virtual video store. Just five years later, James Surowiecki of the *New Yorker* maintained, "Though Netflix still streams plenty of great films, no one really thinks of it as a dream video store in the sky anymore" (James Surowiecki, "What's Next for Netflix?," *New Yorker*, October 20, 2014. Some liken Netflix to a pay-television company, but I would argue Netflix has become much more.
8. In its earlier incarnation as a DVD rental company, Netflix was not unlike Turner Classic Movies (TCM), although TCM featured a wider array of classic Hollywood films, and Criterion, which specialized in independent/international cinema or art house programming. Conglomerate cutbacks also threatened the TCM cable channel and there was an uproar and backlash over how cutbacks to TCM would affect viewers (and the legacy of film history) and make it more difficult to see classic films (including classic noir films). In the past, Netflix had featured noir films such as Billy Wilder's *Ace in the Hole*, Orson Welles's *Touch of Evil*, and Carol Reed's *The Third Man*; Curtis Hanson's neo-noir *LA Confidential*, the Coen brothers' *Barton Fink* and *The Big Lebowski*, Steven

Spielberg's *Schindler's List* and *Bridge of Spies*, Scorsese's *The Aviator*, and Peter Jackson's noir-styled *Lord of the Rings* trilogy to stream and as DVD rentals. Netflix has also moved beyond American Movie Classics (AMC), Home Box Office (HBO) or Showtime, shifting from a cinema library to a producer of new original content. Netflix maintains its vast film (and TV series) library, which is accessible to watch, stream, pause, or binge as immersive long-form cinema à la Netflix's new re-envisioned noir digital content at any time, in any way, at any locale rather than on a live TV channel with continuous programming or in a movie theater. Sheri Chinen Biesen, "Binge Watching the Past: Netflix's Changing Cinematic Nostalgia from Classic Films to Long Form Original Programs," in *Netflix Nostalgia: Streaming the Past on Demand*, ed. Kathryn Pallister (Lanham, MD: Lexington Books, 2019).

9. Netflix also streamed noir-styled series from other networks, such as AMC's *Breaking Bad* and *Better Call Saul*; BBC's *Sherlock*, *London Spy*, and *Top of the Lake*; international coproductions *The Same Sky*, *Narcos*, and *Generation War*; and CW's *In the Dark* and *Arrow*. Patty Jenkins inked a deal with Netflix after helming *Wonder Woman* and the TNT noir series *I Am the Night*. In July 2020, Netflix original neo-noir superhero blockbuster *The Old Guard* reached 72 million household views in four weeks, making Gina Prince-Bythewood the first Black female director in Netflix's top ten most popular films.

10. Netflix Film (@NetflixFilm), "happy Noirvember everybody!," Twitter, November 1, 2020, https://twitter.com/netflixfilm/status/1322956623300587520?s=21. *Tweeted as Netflix Film (@NetflixFilm) in 2020; Netflix Film (@NetflixFilm) was later converted/changed to Netflix Tudum (@NetflixTudum), and Twitter was renamed X, in 2023.

11. Sheri Chinen Biesen, *Blackout: World War II and the Origins of Film Noir* (Baltimore, MD: Johns Hopkins University Press, 2005), 1–2. See also Thomas Schatz, *Boom and Bust: American Cinema in the 1940s* (New York: Scribner's, 1997).

12. Netflix's array of neo-noir programming includes many transnational noirs, including *Earthquake Bird* (2019, produced by *Blade Runner*'s Ridley Scott, shot in Japan), *Furie* (2019, the first Vietnamese film released in the United States, produced by Veronica Ngo) and *Manhunt* (2017, a Chinese–Hong Kong coproduction shot in Japan, directed by John Woo). The long-form Netflix original noir BBC coproduction *Giri/Haji* (2019) was shot in London and Hastings, England, and in Tokyo, Japan. Netflix has also prominently featured noir originals *Shadow* (2019) and *Queen Sono* (2020), which were shot in South Africa; *The Eddy* (2020) and *Lost Bullet* (2020), which were shot in France; original BBC coproductions *Collateral* (2018) and *River* (2015); BBC's *Sherlock* (2010–2017); original ITV coproduction *Marcella* (2016), shot in the United Kingdom; original films *Curtiz* (2018, shot in Hungary) and *The Coldest Game* (2019, shot in Warsaw, Poland); original series *Narcos* (2015) and *Narcos Mexico* (2018), which were shot in Colombia; *Four Seasons in Havana* (2016, shot in Cuba); *High Seas* (2019, shot in Spain); and *Bad Blood* (2017, shot in Montreal, Canada). Netflix has developed several strategies to balance the financial constraints of licensing newer or premium Hollywood content. It has had its greatest success in striking this balance with its shift to original long-form drama and films, many of which have either explicit or implicit ties to noir aesthetics. This is most evident in its signature series *House of Cards*, which follows the shady dealings of a corrupt politician, but it is also prominent in recent series like *Babylon Berlin*, *Jessica Jones*, *Giri/Haji*, *Daredevil*, *Luke Cage*, *Shadow*, *Collateral*, *Marcella*, and *River* and in original films *The Irishman*, *Earthquake Bird*, *Curtiz*, *The Coldest Game*, *Rebecca*, and *Da 5 Bloods*. The connection to noir is also evident in some of the serial dramas for which cable networks like AMC and FX have been praised and which Netflix has prominently featured. AMC's hit shows *Mad Men* (2007–2015) and *Breaking Bad*

(2008–2013) have strong noir elements: flawed or corrupt protagonists, elaborate overlapping plot lines, and a distinct visual style. Sun-scorched New Mexico runs counter to general assumptions about noir, but *Breaking Bad* uses this as a kind of character element that informs its story world with striking cinematography shot on location in harsh barren deserts, evocative of *Ace in the Hole*. *Breaking Bad* was a noir-inspired AMC basic cable series that really became a huge hit after it was picked up by Netflix in later seasons and binged via online streaming. Becoming a major progenitor of binge viewing long-form neo-noir drama, *Breaking Bad* had especially high viewership during the fifth season, which premiered in August 2013 with an impressive 5.9 million viewers, more than double its previous season premiere. Its finale drew 10.3 million viewers a few months later due to its release and availability on Netflix. In this and other cases, Netflix has fueled the success and increased the popularity and ratings of certain shows. Thomas Schatz writes, "The veritable partnership with AMC in the marketing and dual launch (on cable and the Internet) of its hit series has been crucial to Netflix's climb in recent years." (Schatz, "HBO and Netflix—Getting Back to the Future, 7.") Netflix original neo-noir film *El Camino*, a sequel to *Breaking Bad*, premiered in 2019 and was available to stream on Netflix the same day as its limited release in theaters. The film appeared on Netflix and opened in selected independent theaters on October 11, 2019, before airing on AMC in 2020. Like its original neo-noir production *House of Cards*, as well as those produced by other networks such as AMC's *Mad Men* and *Breaking Bad*, it was aided by the addictive viewing habits of binge watching. Joe Otterson, "'Breaking Bad' Movie Sequel With Aaron Paul Will Air on Netflix and AMC," *Variety*, 13 February 2019; Schatz, "HBO and Netflix—Getting Back to the Future, 7;" Sheri Chinen Biesen, "Binge Watching 'Noir' at Home: Reimagining Cinematic Reception and Distribution via Netflix," in *The Netflix Effect: Technology and Entertainment in the 21st Century*, ed. Kevin McDonald and Daniel Smith-Rowsey (New York: Bloomsbury Academic, 2016); Andrew Wallenstein, "Netflix Flexes New Muscle with *Breaking Bad* Ratings Boom: Should Netflix Be Paying Studios for Content or the Other Way Around?," *Variety*, August 12, 2013; James Poniewozik, "'Breaking' Record: What Boosted Walter White's Ratings?," *Time*, August 13, 2013, 11.
13. TV critics even complain of noir-styled shadows and call long-form noir dramas "too cinematic," relegating serial neo-noir to so-called quality television marred by chiaroscuro aesthetics, when in fact these cinematic noir productions should be thought of as extended, long-form, noir-styled films.
14. As seen in Netflix/Marvel's *Daredevil* and *Jessica Jones*, and HBO's *Perry Mason* and *Game of Thrones*, amid the convergence of film noir style cinema and streaming video on demand in the digital era, many cinematographers have tried recently to emulate a cinematic experience of a long-form, multi-hour movie shot in neo-noir style with higher quality. Noir on film on the big screen in a theater or on a large, high-quality, high-definition (HD) or ultra high-definition (UHD) viewing screen on Netflix (as with *The Irishman, Roma*) offers superior quality to other competing digital compression streaming services, including HBO and Amazon.
15. Martin Ahlgren quoted in Kuljit Mithra, "Interview with Martin Ahlgren (June 2018)," Daredevil: The Man Without Fear, June 2–2018, https://manwithoutfear.com/daredevil.shtml.
16. Mithra, "Interview with Martin Ahlgren."
17. Collaborating for two decades, including filming *Saving Private Ryan* in 1998.
18. Janusz Kaminski on *Bridge of Spies*, quoted in The American Society of Cinematographers, ASC Staff, *American Cinematographer* 97, no. 1 (January 2016): https://theasc

.com/articles/ac-january-16-online-articles; USC Pressbook Collection, USC Special Collections, USC Cinematic Library, University of Southern California, Los Angeles, California, 2015.

19. In relation to nostalgic digital variations on noir, it is fascinating to consider how later iterations of noir harken back to the past as the noir style and its technological underpinnings persist and whether noir style becomes an approach for certain stories and a reflection of current cinematographic technology and practice. One could also ponder whether noir style becomes increasingly more aligned with cultural critique in an era of cynicism. I think noir certainly does continue to resonate even more intensely and compellingly in this downbeat cynical cultural climate. As the influence of the noir style continues and evolves, can noir survive as a sensibility as well as a style? Are neo-noir films like *'Round Midnight* in this sense much more noir than *Paris Blues*? Or is *Bridge of Spies* more noir than *The Spy Who Came in from the Cold*, for all the difference in look? I would argue yes, that transnational neo-noir films *'Round Midnight* and *Bridge of Spies* are stylistically more noir looking in their visual aesthetic than pictures like *Paris Blues* or *The Spy Who Came in from the Cold*, although these earlier films engage more fully in social critique. However, earlier classic 1940s noir films *Double Indemnity*, *Out of the Past*, and *Act of Violence* offer a more definitive nitrate noir aesthetic in terms of visual style, which was highly influential to later productions. For that matter, it will also be interesting to see how long-form noir productions like *Daredevil*, *Jessica Jones*, *Babylon Berlin*, *Game of Thrones*, *Breaking Bad*, and *Ozark* hold up over time.
20. Scorsese interviewed in Jordan Raup, "Martin Scorsese on the Films and Books That Influenced *The Irishman*," *The Film Stage* (October 27, 2019): https://thefilmstage.com/martin-scorsese-on-the-films-and-books-that-influenced-the-irishman/.
21. VFX for seasoned actors De Niro, Pacino, Pesci, and Keitel in *The Irishman*.
22. Valentina I. Valentini, "*The Irishman* DP Shares How He Mixed Media to Define the Movie's Different Eras," *Variety*, October 30, 2019; For more on the ENR process, see "Technicolor Decades 1975–2015" at eastman.org; https://www.eastman.org/technicolor/decades; https://www.eastman.org/technicolor/decades/1975–2015; George Eastman Museum and Technicolor Online Research Archive; "Motion Picture Processing Techniques" at kodak.com. https://www.kodak.com/US/en/motion/page/processing techniques/; The American Society of Cinematographers, ASC Staff, "Technicolor's ENR" and "SILVER RETENTION," in "Soup du Jour," *American Cinematographer* 98 (2017): 2 at theasc.com; theasc.com/magazine/nov98/soupdujour/pg2.htm. See also Alexis Van Hurkman, "Bleach Bypass Looks," in *Color Correction Look Book: Creative Grading Techniques for Film and Video*, ed. Alexis Van Hurkman (San Francisco, CA: Peach Pit Press/Pearson Education, 2013); Eastman Kodak, *Chronology of Motion Picture Films*; https://www.kodak.com/US/en/motion/About/Chronology_Of_Film/default.htm.
23. Matt Grobar, "Cinematographer Bruno Delbonnel on His Feeling-Based Approach to *Darkest Hour*," *Deadline*, January 5, 2018.
24. Like *Daredevil* and *The Irishman*, a cinematic experience pervaded other productions and Netflix originals. *Boardwalk Empire* producer Steve Kornacki also coproduced the 2019 third season of the Netflix long-form noir drama *Jessica Jones*, coproduced with Marvel. Nostalgia even infuses and informs the way in which Netflix is conceived and how media analysts define the nature of the company. Tim Wu, "Netflix's War on Mass Culture: Binge-Viewing Was Just the Beginning," *New Republic*, December 4, 2013, 1; "Thinking Outside the Set-Top Box," *The Economist*, December 14, 2013, 69.
25. *Jessica Jones* anticipates the deadpan, chain-smoking blind female detective in the CW's *In the Dark*, who references *Daredevil* in the first episode. Like *Jessica Jones*, the *In the*

Dark female detective is a rape survivor. In this fluid, ephemeral, digital streaming environment, even the Marvel coproduction series eventually move from Netflix to Disney+.

26. Manuel Billeter quoted in "A Marvel DP: A Discussion on Cinematography with Manuel Billeter on Lighting *Jessica Jones* for Netflix," Chimera Lighting blog, 2016. https://chimeralighting.com/marvel-dp-discussion-cinematography-manuel-billeter-lighting-jessica-jones-netflix/
27. Billeter quoted in "A Marvel DP." https://chimeralighting.com/marvel-dp-discussion-cinematography-manuel-billeter-lighting-jessica-jones-netflix/.
28. As does *Luke Cage* on gender and racism, and Jenkins's TNT noir *I Am the Night*.
29. Raymonde Borde and Étienne Chaumeton, *Panorama du film noir américain (1941–1953)*, trans. Paul Hammond (San Francisco: City Lights, 2002).
30. Billeter quoted in "A Marvel DP." https://chimeralighting.com/marvel-dp-discussion-cinematography-manuel-billeter-lighting-jessica-jones-netflix/.
31. Billeter. https://chimeralighting.com/marvel-dp-discussion-cinematography-manuel-billeter-lighting-jessica-jones-netflix/
32. Competitors promised to "look a lot like Netflix," for example, TV networks (HBO, Showtime, NBC, CBS, TCM, Starz, ABC, PBS, FOX), film studios (Disney, Warner Bros., Universal, Paramount, Sony, Amazon Films, Apple, Google/YouTube), satellite services (Dish/SlingTV), and streaming services (Hulu, Roku, Vudu, PlayStation). Emily Steel, "Cord-Cutters Rejoice," *New York Times*, October 16, 2014; Emily Steel, "HBO Plans New Streaming Service," *New York Times*, October 15, 2014.
33. As Chuck Tryon suggests, in an age of cord cutting amid the growth of Netflix and media streaming options, "digital distribution raises new questions about how, when, and where we access movies and what this model means for entertainment culture." Digital media "seem to promise that media texts circulate faster, more cheaply, and more broadly than ever before," but Tryon argues that, despite the "promises of ubiquitous and immediate access to a wide range of media content, digital delivery has largely involved the continued efforts of major media conglomerates to develop better mechanisms for controlling when, where, and how content is circulated." Chuck Tryon, *On-Demand Culture: Digital Delivery and the Future of Movies* (New Brunswick, NJ: Rutgers University Press, 2013), 3–4.
34. Media conglomerate companies and networks that previously had joint-partnership deals with Netflix (such as Starz and Disney) increasingly viewed Netflix as a rival competitor and ended their agreements, opting instead to pull their film libraries and remove media content from Netflix to offer their own proprietary media streaming services and create or show films and programs to compete with Netflix. For instance, media conglomerate competitors such as Starz, Disney, and Warner Bros. terminated distribution deals and pulled media content from Netflix to set up proprietary streaming services (Disney+, HBO Max, etc.) and thus compete with the streaming company, then ironically complained that Netflix no longer offered classic cinema to binge on its media programming platform. When Hulu struck a deal with Criterion, pulling Criterion art cinema from Netflix, Hulu streamed Criterion's art cinema, such as noir films and international classics like Akira Kurosawa's masterwork *Ran*, interrupted by commercials. Criterion and TCM later made deals to stream classic films and art cinema on FilmStruck commercial-free as on Netflix, then Criterion started its own streaming channel after FilmStruck was shuttered when AT&T acquired WarnerMedia. Even Amazon and HBO insert ads for other shows and interrupt so-called commercial-free programming in the midst of binge viewing. HBO/Warner Bros. later made a deal with

4. From Noir to Netflix   237

Netflix to stream some HBO/Warner Bros. programming on Netflix in 2023. For further reading, see Sheri Chinen Biesen, "Nostalgia, Remembrance and Crises in an Evolving Streaming Media Industry," *Film Criticism*, 47(1), 2023. https://doi.org/10.3998/fc.5174

35. Disney spent approximately $15 billion on streaming, $16 billion for linear, and $2 billion on theatrical—$25 billion in all in 2021—expecting to rise to $33 billion in 2022. Tony Maglio, "From Disney to Peacock," *IndieWire*, March 8. 2022; Sergei Klebnikov, "Streaming Wars Continue," *Forbes*, May 22, 2020; Elain Low, "Netflix Reveals $17 Billion in Content Spending in 2021," *Variety*, April 20, 2021. By comparison, Netflix spent $13.9 billion on original content in 2019, $11.8 billion in 2020 (it had planned to spend $16 billion but then the pandemic occurred), and over $17 billion in 2021. Netflix and other streamers such as Amazon were considered pacesetters in an emerging digital streaming media production, distribution, exhibition, and reception climate, and especially savvy conveyors of noir nostalgia. To put Netflix's production expenditure in context, Netflix spent $8 billion on original content in 2018. Hollywood's entire output for 2015 was $7 billion to produce 109 films—versus Netflix's 2018 output of eighty films and 620 original series. Todd Spangler, "Netflix Eyeing Total of About 700 Original Series," *Variety*, February 27, 2018; David Ng, "Netflix Saw Record Subscriber Growth in Fourth Quarter," *Los Angeles Times*, January 22, 2018; Meriah Doty, "US Film Production Spending Increased 11 Percent to $7 Billion in 2015," *The Wrap*, June 15, 2016.

36. *Daredevil, Luke Cage, Iron Fist*, and *The Defenders* reverted in late 2020; *Jessica Jones* and *The Punisher* reverted in early 2021.

37. One could recognize the noir influence in shadowy long-form productions such as HBO's *Perry Mason, Boardwalk Empire, The Night Of, Tokyo Vice*, and *Game of Thrones* and in Disney's *The Mandalorian*. Like Netflix, they were striving to achieve a cinematic noir-styled aesthetic in a digital streaming era. Such long-form dramas excelled at remarkable film noir imagery.

38. There was also a huge industry dustup when Warner Bros. announced they would release their entire 2021 film slate simultaneously on HBO Max and in theaters on the same "day and date" because of COVID-19. I would argue that the original noir programming and dominance of long-form media streamed on digital platforms such as Netflix have also been accelerated by competing conglomerate studios and media companies pulling films, including classic film (noir) content from Netflix over the past decade.

39. Jonathan Freeman quoted in David Heuring, "Shooting *Boardwalk Empire* on Super 35mm," *Studio Daily*, September 30, 2010.

40. Matthew Dessem, "Why TV Shows Are Darker Than Ever. Literally," *Slate*, June 29, 2016; Matthew Dessem, "Why You Couldn't See a Damn Thing on This Week's *Game of Thrones*," *Slate*, April 29, 2019.

41. Chris Stokel-Walker, "Why Is Game of Thrones So Dark? We Asked the Cinematographer. Fans Complained That the Battle of Winterfell Was Too Dark to See Properly. But Cinematographer Fabien Wagner Defends the Gloom," *Wired*, April 30, 2019.

42. Anna Tingley, "'Game of Thrones' Cinematographer Defends Lighting Choices for Battle of Winterfell Episode," *Variety*, April 30, 2019; Zack Sharf, "'Game of Thrones' Cinematographer Defends Battle of Winterfell Against Complaints It's Too Dark to See," *Indiewire*, April 30, 2019; Stokel-Walker, "Why Is Game of Thrones So Dark?;" Dessem, "Why You Couldn't See a Damn Thing."

43. Flashbacks and PTSD sequences in *Perry Mason* recall earlier noir films, *Babylon Berlin*, and HBO prestige neo-noir combat series *The Pacific* and *Band of Brothers*.

44. Rhys's antihero in *Perry Mason* harkened back to classic noir, crime films, *Boardwalk Empire* and his Cold War espionage antihero in FX neo-noir series *The Americans*.

Likewise, Rhys's *The Americans* partner Keri Russell continued noir intrigue in Netflix's 2023 espionage thriller *The Diplomat*. Gabriella Paiella, "Matthew Rhys on the *Perry Mason* Finale, What Happened to His *Americans* Character, and His Big *Columbo* Moment," *GQ*, August 10, 2020.

45. Ben Travers, "*Perry Mason* Review: HBO's Swank Noir Is One of the Most Beautiful Series Ever Made," *IndieWire*, June 18, 2020; Melanie McFarland, "*Perry Mason* Is a Stylish, Depression-Noir Reboot," *Salon.com*, June 21, 2020; Paiella, "Matthew Rhys on the *Perry Mason* Finale."
46. Travers, "*Perry Mason* Review;" McFarland, "*Perry Mason* Is a Stylish, Depression-Noir Reboot;" Paiella, "Matthew Rhys on the *Perry Mason* Finale."
47. Travers, "*Perry Mason* Review."
48. Graham Fuller, "Perry Mason Review: Matthew Rhys Stars in a Convoluted Reboot," *Sight and Sound*, August 14, 2020. https://www.bfi.org.uk/sight-and-sound/reviews/perry-mason-review-matthew-rhys-stars-convoluted-reboot
49. Jay Holben, "*The Mandalorian*: This Is the Way," *American Cinematographer* 101, no. 2 (February 6, 2020).
50. Dan Clarendon, "9 TV Shows Viewers Think Are Literally Too Dark," *TV Insider*, March 1, 2020; Matt Mitovich, "Dear TV: Lighten Up! Poorly Lit Scenes Confuse Viewers, Can Frustrate Actors," *TV Line*, February 7, 2018; Dessem, "Why TV Shows Are Darker Than Ever." See also Kathryn VanArendonk, "TV Shows Are (Literally) Too Dark," *Vulture*, August 2016.
51. *Generation War* was produced by ZDF German public broadcasting UFA/TeamWorx, and *The Same Sky* was produced by UFA Fiction/Beta Film/ZDF/Czech TV.
52. Tykwer also made *Run Lola Run*. Siobhán Dowling, "Ahead of the Third Reich, a Dizzying Metropolis: Sex, Drugs and Crime in the Gritty Drama *Babylon Berlin*," *New York Times*, November 7, 2017, C11.
53. Noir style permeated transnational productions overseas as Netflix original German film *All Quiet on the Western Front* (2022) won Oscars for its shadowy cinematography and production design, as well as Best International Film (and music score). Given its transnational reception and global production strategy, it is not surprising that Netflix collaborated with the BBC to produce exceptional neo-noir, long-form dramas such as *Giri/Haji*, *River*, and *Collateral*. Other noir-inflected international coproductions include the Netflix original neo-noir film *Message from the King*, as well as the brooding period dramas *The King* and *Outlaw King*. In fact, *Outlaw King* opens with an eight-minute continuous shot (candlelit à la Gothic noir *Jane Eyre*) that ends in an explosion, paying homage to Orson Welles's famous long-take opening shot in the film noir *Touch of Evil*. And these were truly international and transnational neo-noir coproductions, as seen in Netflix/BBC's *Giri/Haji*, which was filmed in Tokyo and London; *Message from the King*, which was shot in Los Angeles and South Africa; *Outlaw King*, which was filmed in Scotland; *Babylon Berlin*, which was shot in Germany; *River* and *Collateral*, which were filmed in London; Spanish noirs *High Seas* and *Gun City*; Turkish noir *The Club*; and *The King*, which was shot in Hungary with some filming in England. Netflix's acclaimed 2018 black-and-white neorealist film *Roma* was shot in Mexico. Netflix also collaborated with Sony on period epic *The Crown* (2016–2023), which stylishly reimagines Gothic noir, which was filmed in the United Kingdom and South Africa. Programs that were traditionally produced by other major media companies are now to be viewed, binge-watched, and consumed in a way that streamers have made more popular and pervasive. For example, the BBC lamented that it was not involved in the transnational Netflix production *The Crown*.

Netflix's serial filmed adaptation of Mark Harris's *Five Came Back* (coproduced by Steven Spielberg) is a quality, long-form dramatic documentary of the 1940s era that would typically be an HBO miniseries; however, it is shown in a way ideally suited for binge-watching on Netflix, and it is accompanied by other related programs (the original World War II documentaries discussed in the Netflix original program) available to view on Netflix, all shown in a way that they would not have been seen on conventional television. Another example of the recent trend toward cord cutting and competition is the Netflix American noir-styled reboot of the original series *House of Cards*, which is commended as a quality prestige production nostalgically invoking the earlier celebrated BBC series *House of Cards*. Both are written and coproduced by Andrew Davies, and both are on par with high-brow British television and with international art cinema productions.

54. Rick Marshall, "Peek Behind the Magic and Monsters of *The Chilling Adventures of Sabrina*," *Digital Trends*, December 1, 2018, https://www.digitaltrends.com/movies/chilling-adventures-of-sabrina-visual-effects-vfx/.
55. Marshall, "Peek Behind the Magic and Monsters."
56. Tied for the most of any drama series, *Ozark* has been one of Netflix's most-watched original programs.
57. Matt Grobar, "*Ozark* Cinematographer Ben Kutchins Wades into Highly Cinematic, Extremely Dark Realism with Netflix Crime Drama," *Deadline*, August 20, 2018.
58. Ben Kutchins quoted in Grobar, "*Ozark* Cinematographer Ben Kutchins."
59. Grobar, "*Ozark* Cinematographer Ben Kutchins."
60. Kelle Long, "Emmy Nominated *Ozark* Cinematographer on the Show's Bleak & Immersive Style," *Motion Picture Association*, August 22, 2018.
61. Kayla Cobb, "*Ozark* Cinematographer Ben Kutchins Explains Why the Hell the Show Is So Dark (Literally, Not Figuratively)," *Decider*, August 30, 2018.
62. Long, "Emmy Nominated *Ozark* Cinematographer."
63. Kayla Cobb of *Decider* recognized the brooding look of the noir *Ozark* when she pondered "why the hell the show is so dark." Cobb, "*Ozark* Cinematographer Ben Kutchins."
64. VanArendonk, "TV Shows Are (Literally) Too Dark."
65. Long, "Emmy Nominated *Ozark* Cinematographer."
66. Adam Chitwood, "*Ozark* Cinematographer Armando Salas Explains Why Season 3 of the Netflix Series Is Brighter," *Collider*, August 19, 2020.
67. Netflix released *Ozark*'s final season 4 in a longer fourteen-episode run form, in two separate seven-episode "seasons." Some of the final episodes of *Ozark* were directed by Robin Wright, who also directed episodes of *House of Cards*. With its Motion Picture Association (MPAA renamed MPA in 2019) designation as a major motion picture feature filmmaking production company, Netflix has increasingly emulated a Hollywood studio producing films and long-form noir (as does Amazon with its purchase of MGM). Many criticized the murky milieu in long-form noir, including *Ozark*. With this recurrent critique of visual darkness in mind, it is important that filmic long-form serial noir be regarded and conceptualized vis-à-vis filmmakers' and the noir series' obvious cinematic production aims paying homage to noir rather than as conventional low-resolution television. As is evident in these new incarnations of blackened imagery in long-form, noir-styled crime, such dramas digitally streamed and binged on Netflix and HBO are closer to extended noir cinematic movies than they are to more conventional TV shows broadcast on television.
68. Catherine Springer, "How *Ozark* Cinematography Put a 'Sense of Danger in the Shadows' for Season 4," *Variety*, April 29, 2022.

Epilogue. The Persistence of Noir in the COVID-19 Era: 2020 and Beyond

1. Phil Rhodes, "*Rebecca*: Revisiting Manderley," *American Cinematographer* 102, no. 1 (January 16, 2021).
2. Rhodes, "*Rebecca*." Rose admitted that visually: "I want character, texture and soul. I do that with a bit of onboard ISO. I shot *Rebecca* at 1,280 or 1,600, because the big sensor has so much latitude. It can handle that high-ISO approach, which puts a bit of grit into the images." On a balmy night in August 2019, a SkyPanel S360-C lighting rig created "steely" artificial moonlight perched atop a cherry picker and an array of PAR cans. Although some of these recent digital, noir streaming productions (including *Rebecca*) were criticized as not being on par with classic nitrate noir (including the original Oscar-winning Hitchcock picture), classic 1940s film noir visual style was reimagined, paid homage to, and invoked in the new digital production and streaming media era.
3. Jon Swartz, "Netflix Has Biggest Quarter with Nearly 16 Million New Subscribers Signing On," *Marketwatch*, April 22, 2020.
4. Zanuck admitted high cost and location filming hurt profits. Twentieth Century-Fox Collection, USC Cinematic Arts Library, June–December 1950.
5. (We even binged HBO disaster noir *Chernobyl* during the pandemic.) Chris Lindahl, "Beyond *Contagion*: Interest in Outbreak Movies, Podcasts, and More Surges Across the Internet," *IndieWire*, March 17, 2020.
6. YouTube original production *Cobra Kai* was also picked up by Netflix (after three seasons and being canceled) and became a huge hit, surging in popularity during the pandemic, with later seasons produced by Netflix. Netflix also acquired BBC's grittier noir period epic *The Last Kingdom*.
7. Popular supernatural noir fantasy *Cursed* was canceled because of COVID-19, Netflix also canceled feminist noir comedy *Glow*, retracting season 4 renewal of the series for safety reasons to avoid physical contact of women wrestling in its large female ensemble cast.
8. Zack Sharf, "Matt Reeves: 'The Batman' . . . ," *Variety*, March 7, 2022.
9. "The Batman," *Box Office Mojo*, April 20, 2022.
10. Paul Schrader goes so far as to speculate that, in the future, long-form media streamed on platforms such as Netflix will supplant traditional, two-hour, feature film viewing in theaters, a trend that was exacerbated in the wake of COVID-19, and that half of the theaters in New York City will not reopen after the pandemic. Arclight and Pacific theaters in Los Angeles, including the famous Cinerama Dome theater in Hollywood, announced they would not reopen (investors later offered to enable the reopening of the historic landmark exhibition site). Richard Brody, "Paul Schrader on Making and Watching Movies in the Age of Netflix," *The New Yorker*, April 22, 2021.
11. Carolyn Giardina, "How *Malcolm & Marie* Cinematographer Pays Tribute to Classic Filmmaking in a Modern Way," *Hollywood Reporter*, January 19, 2021.
12. Stephen Pizzello, "*Mank*: A Writer in Exile," *American Cinematographer* 102, no. 2 (February 24, 2021). In a sense, *Mank* attempts to appropriate black-and-white noir and *Citizen Kane*, although it is nowhere near as striking or as compelling as 1940s noir or Welles's definitive masterwork. *Mank* does, however, digitally refigure black-and-white noir in its noirish inclinations, despite its egregious historical inaccuracies and revisionism. Yet it does not do justice to Welles's *Citizen Kane* or classic black-and-white noir cinematography shot on nitrate film. The noir proclivity is especially acute in a global convergent digital streaming era, particularly because of technological advances

in an era of high-definition Ultra HD 4K/8K, more powerful 5G streaming, enhanced projection, binge-watching, and the prevalence of cord cutting. New digital media technologies enhanced neo-noir visual style in the digital streaming era. *American Cinematographer*'s Jay Holben observed that "Netflix helps drive the creative vision with high-dynamic-range content." For instance, David Fincher's *Mank* (shot digitally in black and white to emulate Welles's *Citizen Kane*) and gritty Netflix noir-styled period procedural *Mindhunter* were shot by Erik Messerschmidt. Fincher also directed several episodes of *House of Cards*, serial killer neo-noir film *Se7en*, and the 2011 version of Nordic noir *The Girl with the Dragon Tattoo*. Jay Holben, "Netflix Helps Drive the Creative Vision with High-Dynamic-Range Content," *American Cinematographer* 100, no. 12 (December 22, 2019).

13. Guillermo del Toro, "Neo-Noir" featurette (publicity trailer) for *Nightmare Alley* (2021; Los Angeles: Searchlight Pictures).
14. Steven Fierberg, "Clubhouse Conversations—*Nightmare Alley*" (interview with cinematographer Dan Laustsen), *American Cinematographer* 102, no. 1 (January 19, 2021). https://theasc.com/videos/clubhouse-conversations-nightmare-alley
15. Martin Scorsese, "Why Martin Scorsese Wants You to Watch *Nightmare Alley*," *Los Angeles Times*, January 21, 2022.
16. It will be interesting to see how the strategy of programming noir evolves vis-à-vis streamers' earlier noir programming strategy and whether companies continue or back away from a governing noir aesthetic (and ethos) due to the increased competition as they diversify offerings. The proliferation of digital noir is all the more remarkable because a streamer that was once a meager start-up company—that is, Netflix—is now a Motion Picture Association member. It joined Hollywood studios and acquired the Egyptian Theater in 2020 and partnered with American Cinematheque as it continues to churn out noir-styled neo-noir content. Julia Alexander, "Streaming was part of the future—now it's the only future: Four major entertainment conglomerates undergo big restructures," *The Verge*, October 28, 2020, https://www.theverge.com/21536842/streaming-disney-hbo-max-peacock-cbs-all-access-warnermedia-viacom-nbcuniversal?utm_campaign=theverge&utm_content=entry&utm_medium=social&utm_source=twitter; Dave McNary, "Netflix Closes Deal to Buy Hollywood's Egyptian Theatre," *Variety*, May 29, 2020. https://variety.com/2020/film/news/netflix-hollywood-egyptian-theatre-1234619985/
17. Tomris Laffly, "Why *The Queen's Gambit* Looks so Damn Good," *Vulture*, November 25, 2020.
18. The noir trend continued with neo-noir films *Marlowe* (2023), the shadowy visuals of *All Quiet on the Western Front* (2022), Christopher Nolan's brooding World War II/Cold War atomic thriller *Oppenheimer* (2023, shot on newly developed Kodak black-and-white 70mm film stock combined with color and digital effects), and Martin Scorsese's noir western *Killers of the Flower Moon* (2023). "Netflix Releases Second-Quarter 2020 Financial Results," [Press Release on Second-Quarter 2020 Earnings Letter To Shareholders], Netflix, Inc. (ir.netflix.net), July 16, 2020, 1; https://ir.netflix.net/investor-news-and-events/financial-releases/pres-release-details/2020/Netflix-Releases-Second-Quarter-2020-Financial-Results/default.aspx. By April 21, 2020, in the middle of the COVID-19 pandemic, industry analyst Edmund Lee of the *New York Times* observed, "Everyone you know just signed up for Netflix," and reported the media tech streamer had 182.8 million subscribers worldwide and 69.9 million subscribers in the United States and Canada—growing to 203 million global subscribers by the end of 2020. Edmund Lee, "Everyone You Know Just Signed Up for Netflix," *New York Times*, April 21, 2020; Variety Staff, "Netflix Top 10," *Variety*, March 28, 2023.

(Eastman specifically created Double-X black-and-white film in 65mm for IMAX and Panavision System 65mm film cameras for *Oppenheimer*.)

19. Industry trade journals recognized the media industry's shift toward streaming: "The sands have shifted in video." Influential media streamers (like Netflix) churned out noir-styled films and long-form neo-noir. In November 2020, *Variety* named Netflix the Most Important U.S. Streaming Video Brand across all age groups—in every sought-after demographic from age 18 to 64. Gavin Bridge, "Most Important U.S. Video Brands Dominated by Streaming," *Variety*, November 2, 2020; Ben Smith, "The Week Old Hollywood Finally, Actually Died," *New York Times*, August 16, 2020; *Hollywood Reporter*, August 13, 2020; November 12, 2020. Yet a few years later, in the wake of COVID-19, other challenges also arose in the media industry. Digital streaming companies emerged from the pandemic, and companies struggled to compete and outpace corporate losses, regime change turnovers, and plunging cable subscriptions as cord cutting accelerated. The television industry lost 5.8 million pay-TV and cable subscribers in 2022 and 4.7 million in 2021. Media conglomerates were hoping that streaming could eventually make up for losses, but such an offset was slow to be realized. Caitlin Huston, "Pay TV and Cable Providers Lost 5.8M Subscribers in 2022," *Hollywood Reporter*, March 3, 2023. See also Sheri Chinen Biesen, "Nostalgia, Remembrance and Crises in an Evolving Streaming Media Industry," *Film Criticism* 47, no. 1, 2023. https://doi.org/10.3998/fc.5174.

INDEX

Ace in the Hole, 4, 6, 37, 60–62, 65, 71, 77, 81
acetate (safety) film stock, 3, 5, 41, 52–53, 70, 71, 105, 112, 127, 204, 212
Academy Awards: for 1944–1946 noir cycle, 11, 38; end of Golden Age, 65
Act of Violence, 4, 38, 41–50, 181, 202–203
advertising: technology companies using postwar noir, 21
After Hours, 128
Ahlgren, Martin, 155
AKA, 194
Aldrich, Robert, 7, 55, 71–73, 143
Altman, Robert, 123–124, 128
Alton, John, 1, 7, 65–68, 130
Amazon Prime Video, 150, 168–169
AMC, 6, 150–151, 233, 234
American Splendor, 169
Americans, The, 169
Andor, 169
Apartment, The, 130
Apocalypse Now, 137
Apple TV+, 169
Asphalt Jungle, 52, 81, 186
Army of Shadows, 114, 138
Aviator, The, 149, 157–158

Babylon Berlin, 6–7, 150, 152, 171, 174–176, 181, 193
Bacall, Lauren, 14, 34–36
Ballhaus, Michael, 133–134
Band of Brothers, 169
Barefoot Contessa, The, 7, 78, 80, 84, 86, 89, 105, 110, 124
Barnes, George, 15
Barton Fink, 5, 8, 134, 135, 138–139, 148, 152
Basinger, Kim, 142–144
Bateman, Jason, 178–182
Batman, 134, 148
Batman, The, 169, 187–188, 193–195
Beatty, Warren, 118, 137, 222
Belfast, 189, 192–195
Benton, Robert, 118, 222
Bergman, Ingrid, 18–21
Berlin Station, 169
Berkeley, Busby, 117, 139, 142
Bernstein, Leonard, 106–109
Big Combo, The, 4, 5, 7, 52, 55, 62, 64–69, 74, 80, 209
Big Heat, The, 4, 71
Big Lebowski, The, 8, 134, 135, 139–142, 145, 147, 148, 150

Big Sleep, The (1946), 3, 10, 14, 17, 35, 125, 129, 131, 135, 140, 165
Big Sleep, The (1978), 125
Billeter, Manuel, 164–167
Billions, 187
binge watching, 150–151, 152
Bird, 8, 128, 132–133, 137
Black Bird, 169
Black Widow, 80
Blade Runner, 128, 129, 146, 148
Blanchard, Terence, 272
Blanchett, Cate, 190
bleach bypass process, 136–137, 154
Blood Simple, 128
Blue Gardenia, The 71
Blues in the Night, 130
Bob le flambeur. 114
Body and Soul, 4, 36, 38–40, 127–128
Body Heat, 128
Bogart, Humphrey: as actor, 11, 14, 25, 28–30, 34–36, 43, 89, 209; comparisons to, 27, 131, 134, 140, 165, 171
Boardwalk Empire, 154, 167, 169–170
Bonnie and Clyde, 5, 8, 110, 114, 116, 117–118
Brackett, Charles, 36, 38, 60, 88–89
Brackett, Leigh, 125
Branagh, Kenneth, 135–136, 192–193
Brando, Marlon, 121–122
Bridge of Spies, 5, 6, 8, 110, 114, 149, 152, 154, 157–160, 169, 193
Bridges, Beau, 133–134
Bridges, Jeff, 133–134, 140–142
Breaking Bad, 6, 151, 163
Breathless, 112
Breen, Joseph, 18, 26, 38, 40, 56, 65, 75
Brooks, Richard, 40, 116
Bullitt, 8, 114, 119–120
Burks, Robert, 97–101, 108
Burr, Raymond, 96, 99, 170
Buscemi, Steve, 140

Cabinet of Dr. Caligari, The 32, 36, 84, 148, 158, 190
Cain, James M., 11, 22, 23, 25, 105, 106, 113, 142
Call Northside 777, 79, 87
Cardiff, Jack, 84, 89
Carlito's Way, 128
Casablanca, 11, 134

Cercle Rouge, Le, 114
Chandler, Raymond, 23, 37, 135, 140, 142, 171; script adaptions of, 9, 12, 14, 125
Chapman, Michael, 126–128
Charman, Matt, 158
Chilling Adventures of Sabrina, 2, 6, 177–178, 180–182
Chinatown, 118
Chernobyl, 186
Choose Me, 128
CinemaScope: *A Star Is Born*, 92–93; color required, 5; introduction of, 79
Citizen Kane, 13, 109, 129, 135, 158, 179
Clockers, 137–138
Cluzet, François, 129
Coen, Ethan, 138–142, 158
Coen, Joel, 138–142, 158
Collateral, 6
Collection, The, 169
color film: abandonment of black and white (1966–1967), 115–116; early development of, 212; early Hitchcock ideas, 97; emergence of, 80; Hitchcock, 95–105; move to less expensive single-strip, 84–85; noir style, 4, 5, 7, 77–95, 78, 90–92; predicted shift to color in 1948, 78–79; 70mm large frame, 107; "subdue the color," 117; use of red 98–100
Come and Find Me, 151
computer graphic imagery (CGI), 147
Connelly, Jennifer, 145–146
Contagion, 186
Cooper, Bradley, 190–191
Coppola, Francis Ford, 5, 118, 120–123, 137
Cotten, Joseph, 87–89
COVID-19 pandemic, 2, 6, 152, 154, 157, 172–173, 182, 183–195
Cox, Charlie, 154–156
criticism: 1940s crime film trend recognized by critics, 11–14; praise for noir style, 181–182 television "too dark" 7, 154–155, 170, 172–173, 180–181; women-centered recognized by critics, 14
Cromwell, John, 28
Cronenweth, Jordan, 129
Crossfire, 4, 36, 38, 40–41, 43
Crowe, Russell, 142
Cukor, George, 90–95, 130
Curtis, Tony, 74–75

Index 245

Da 5 Bloods, 3, 157, 162, 171, 193, 194
Daredevil: as long-form noir, 6–7, 150, 152, 163, 180–181; production 154–157; move to Disney+, 168, 187
Dark City (1998): as color noir, 5, 134; postmodern, 135; production, 144–149
Dark Passage, 4, 22–23, 33–36, 49
Darkest Hour, 162, 174, 185
Dassin, Jules, 51, 112, 161
Davis, Miles, 113, 130
Davis, Sammy, Jr., 115
Dead Again, 8, 134, 135–136
Dead Reckoning, 2, 4, 22–23, 27–30, 41, 165
de-aging digital effect, 161–162
Deakins, Roger, 137, 138–139
Decaë, Henri, 113
Deep Cover, 137
Defenders, The, 163, 169
de Keyzer, Bruno, 130
del Toro, Guillermo, 190–192
Delbonnel, Bruno, 162
Delon, Alain, 114
De Niro, Robert, 126–127, 161
Departed, The, 158
Desert Fury, 80
Detour, 190
deuxième souffle, Le, 114, 161
Devil in a Blue Dress, 137–138
Dial M for Murder, 136
DiCaprio, Leonardo, 158
Dickerson, Ernest, 137
digital cameras: Arricam 162; Arri Alexa, 162, 174, 185, 188, 191; differences from film 157, 169; importance for streaming, 151; low-light performance, 162, 179–180; Panasonic VariCam, 179, 182; Red Dragon, 164–165; Red Helium, 162; Red Ranger 190, 194; Sony Venice, 182; using vintage lenses, 165, 178, 183
digital intermediate, 147
digital streaming, 2; compression 155–157; handling of smoke and shadows 6
direct-to-consumer (DTC) streaming, 151
Dirty Harry, 120
Disney+, 150, 168–169
Dmytryk, Edward, 41, 112
documentary style. *See* newsreel style; semidocumentary style

Double Indemnity: documentary technique, 17; influence in France, 112–113; key film noir, 9–14; style and dialogue, 1, 9–10, 51
Douglas, Kirk, 61
Doulos, Le, 114, 161
Doyle, Peter, 148
Dr. Strangelove, 112
Dragnet, 52, 54, 80
Drive, 152
Dunaway, Faye, 118, 119, 222
Dune, 169, 188, 192, 194–195
Dunn, Linwood, 109
Dupont film stock, 70, 224
dye transfer. *See* Technicolor

Earthquake Bird, 152, 177
Eastmancolor: 4, 7, 93, 105, 107, 124; deterioration, 123, 124; development, 79; later improvements, 5, 8, 129, 224
Eastwood, Clint 128, 132–133
El Camino, 163
Elevator to the Gallows, 112–113, 130
Ellroy, James, 142
Enforcer, The, 4, 54, 71
ENR process. *See* bleach bypass process

Fabulous Baker Boys, The, 8, 128, 133–134
Face in the Crowd, A, 55, 74
Fapp, Daniel, 107–110
Farewell, My Lovely (1975), 125
female gothic: films, 14–15; novels, 15; popularity, 21
film gris visual style, fade to gray, 4, 51–55, 70, 72, 204
film noir critical discourse. *See* noir critical discourse
film noir visual style: 1–7; 1940s, 9–50; 1950s, black and white, 51–79; 1950s, influence on color film, 80–110
Finch, 169
Fincher, David, 137
flashing process, 123–125
Force of Evil, 40
400 Blows, 113
4K. *See* UHD
Fraker, William, 119
Fraser, Greig, 187–188
Freeman, Jonathan, 169–170
French Connection, The, 120

246 Index

French New Wave Cinema, 112, 117
French noir films, 112
Fujifilm, 179–180
Fujimoto, Tak, 138
Furie, 151
FX, 169, 233

Gabin, Jean, 161
Game of Thrones, 7, 154, 167, 169, 170, 172, 177, 180–182
Gardner, Ava, 89
Garfield, John, 38–39, 41
Garland, Judy, 90–95
Gaslight (1940), 14
Gaslight (1944), 11, 14–15, 17
Genre Experimentation, 134
Ghost and Mrs. Muir, The, 14, 89
Ghost Who Walks, The, 151
Gilda, 11, 14, 94, 134, 166
Girl with a Dragon Tattoo, The, 169, 176
Glenn Miller Story, The, 86
Godard, Jean-Luc, 112, 118
Godfather, The, 5, 8, 110, 114, 119, 120–123, 152, 169, 173–174, 187
Godfather, Part II, The, 5, 119, 120–123, 152, 169
Godfather, Part III, The, 137, 152
Goodfellas, 128
Goodman, John, 138–141
Gordon, Dexter, 129–132
Grahame, Gloria, 40, 71
Grant, Cary, 18–21, 101–104
Green, Jack N., 132–133
Greyhound, 169
Gun Crazy, 5, 52, 62–64, 68, 117, 118
Guffey, Burnett, 117, 222

Hall, Conrad, 116, 129, 223
Handmaid's Tale, The, 169
Hanson, Curtis, 142–144
Hanks, Tom, 160, 169
hard-boiled fiction adaptations, 12, 14, 22–29, 64–67, 96, 113, 144
Hathaway, Henry, 81, 87
Hayworth, Rita, 31–33, 134
HBO, 154, 167, 169–172; HBO Max, 150, 168
Hellinger, Mark, 41, 51
Helgeland, Brian, 142–144
Herrmann, Bernard, 126, 225

Hickox, Sid, 34
High Dynamic Range (HDR) technology, 155, 172, 184, 190
Hiroshima, Mon Amour, 112
Hitchcock, Alfred: color style, 5, 78, 86, 95–105,130, 218; influence of, 183–184, 190; newsreel style, 17; 1940s noir films, 9, 15, 17–21, 27; sunlight style instead of urban darkness, 104
Hoover, J. Edgar, 19
Hopper, Edward, 35, 92, 148
House of Cards, 6, 150–151, 152, 155, 162
House of Strangers, 89
House Un-American Activities Committee, 41, 43
Howe, James Wong, 16, 39, 74–75, 77, 127
Hulu, 169
Hurt, William, 145
Huston, John, 81, 119, 186

I am a Fugitive from a Chain Gang, 117–118
I am the Night, 169
I-B imbibition process. *See* Technicolor
In a Lonely Place, 52
In Cold Blood, 114, 116, 129
independent film production: Enterprise Studio, 38–40; postwar trend, 64–66, 70, 71, 74–75, 89; postclassical, 111–112, 115, 119; 1980s neo-noir, 128; Netflix distribution, 151–152
Inferno, 80
Irishman, The: as example of noir style, 1, 6, 8, 149, 154, 170; production of, 157, 158–162, 169, 170, 192, 194
Iron Fist, 163–64, 169

Jack Ryan, 169
James, Lily, 184–185
Jane Eyre, 3, 11, 14–16
jazz: notable jazz scores, 66–67, 74, 113, 126, 171; inspiration for *L.A. Confidential*, 143–144; "The Man that Got Away," 90, 93, 94; noir-styled films about jazz musicians, 115, 129–134, 137–138, 226–228
Jessica Jones: as long-form noir, 6–7, 150, 163–169; move to Disney+ 168, 187
Johnston, Eric, 41
jour se lève, Le, 130

Kaminski, Janusz, 6, 110, 158–160, 188
Keitel, Harvey, 161
Kelly, Grace, 97,99
Kloves, Steve, 133–134
Kodak: bleach bypass, 137; development of single-strip color, 79, 85–86; improved film stocks in 1980s-2000s, 5, 129; film use in digital era, 158–159, 161, 170, 189. *See also* Eastmancolor
Khondji, Darius, 137
Killing, The, 112
Kim, Shawn, 182
Kiss Me Deadly, 4,5, 7, 55, 71–74
Kiss of Death, 30, 36, 41, 87, 201

L.A. Confidential, 5, 8, 134, 135, 142–144, 147, 148, 150
Lady from Shanghai, The, 4, 22, 30–33, 41, 80
Lady in the Lake, 34
Lancaster, Burt, 74–75
Lang, Fritz, 71, 112, 129, 134, 148
Lansky, 169
Laszlo, Ernest, 72
latensification process, 59, 124
Laura, 3, 11, 14, 152
Laurents, Arthur, 106
Laustsen, Dan, 190
Lawton, Charles, 30–33
Leave Her to Heaven, 80, 81
Le Carré, John, 112, 159, 176
LED lighting and noir style, 167
Lee, Spike, 3, 137–138, 157
Lehman, Ernest, 74–75, 101
Leonetti, Matt, 136
Levinson, Sam, 189
Lewis, Joseph, 62–69
Lewton, Val, 26
lightweight equipment. *See* portable cameras and lights
Lilyhammer, 176
location shooting; *Ace in the Hole* and desert, 61–62; *Act of Violence*, 42–50; 52; *Body and Soul*, 38; *Dark Passage*, 35; difficulty during pandemic, 187, 191; Europe, 84; increase in 1960s and realism, 114–115; Los Angeles, 72; New York, 40, 70–71, 74–75, 165–166; Niagara Falls, 87–89; opening of *West Side Story*, 108; postwar trend toward, 36;

San Francisco, 119; stagecraft as digital alternative, 173; Venice, California, 76
long form serials: as extended movie, 150–151, 164
Long Goodbye, The, 114, 120, 123–125
look up tables (LUTs) and digital color grading, 147, 179–180
Lost Weekend, The, 4, 11, 36–38, 56, 58
Love Me or Leave Me, 86, 105; sunlit location, 112
Luke Cage, 6–7, 154, 163–164, 169

M, 148
Mad Men, 6, 150, 177, 233, 234
Magic City, 169
Malcolm & Marie, 189, 193, 194
Malle, Louis, 112–113, 130
Maltese Falcon, The, 81
Man Called Adam, A, 114, 115, 116
Mandalorian, The, 7, 167, 169, 172–173, 180, 188
Manhunt, 177
Man in the High Castle, The, 169
Mank, 189–190
Mankiewicz, Joseph, 89
Mason, James, 90–95, 131
Matrix, The, 147
Max. *See* HBO
McQueen, Steve 119
Mean Streets, 5, 114, 119, 125
Meizler, Steven, 194
Melville, Jean-Pierre, 113–114, 138, 161
Meridian, 6, 152, 170
Messerschmidt, Erik, 190
Metropolis, 53, 129, 134, 148
Milland, Ray, 36–38, 70
Miller's Crossing, 134, 137
Mirish, Harold, 107–108
Mitchell Camera: BNC Camera, 54, 121; noir ads, 21;
Mitchum, Robert: as actor, 11, 23–27, 40, 43; comparisons to, 131, 165
Mo' Better Blues, 134, 137–138, 171
Monopack. *See* Eastmancolor
Monroe, Marilyn, 87–89
Montgomery, Robert, 34
Moon Knight, 169
Moore, Julianne, 140–142
Moreau, Jeanne, 113

Moriarty, Cathy, 128
Motherless Brooklyn, 169
Moulin Rouge (1952), 81, 84, 86, 87
Murder, My Sweet, 3, 10, 14
Musuraca, Nicholas, 25, 27
My Name Is Julia Ross, 62, 64

Naked City, The, 4, 36, 41, 49, 51–52, 53, 79
Narcos, 152
neo-noir: 1960s–1970s, 5, 7, 111–128; 1980s–1990s, 8, 128–148; streaming era, 8, 149–195
Netflix: 2, 6, 8; begins operations, 150; competing streaming services, 150, 168–169; competitors pulling content, 151, 168; joins MPAA, 152; noir house style, 150; noir Marvel shows, 154–157, 163–167; pandemic spike in viewership, 189; technical specifications for digital shooting, 6, 152–153, 170, 179
Newman, David, 118, 222
newsreel style, 14–18, 36
Niagara, 4, 7, 78, 80, 81, 84, 86, 87–89, 105, 110, 124, 127
Nicholson, Jack, 119
Night Agent, The, 6, 193, 194
Night and the City, 112
Nightmare Alley (1947), 190
Nightmare Alley (2021), 6, 8, 149, 169, 182, 188, 190–192, 193–195
Nightmare Alley: Vision in Darkness and Light, 189, 190
Night Moves, 123
Night Of, The, 169
nitrate film stock, 2–4; influence on Scorsese, 127; replaced by acetate, 52–53, 55, 112; role in film noir imagery, 10–11
noir critical discourse: noir as style, 1–2, 52, 77, 90, 91, 211; recognized by French critics, 1, 7, 14, 54, 55, 166; trend recognized in United States contemporaneously, 1, 9, 12–13, 22
noir as visual style: 78; color 77–78, 90
noir musicals, 81, 84, 86–87, 94, 108–109, 169, 182, 188, 192, 213
North by Northwest, 4–5, 75, 78, 80, 86, 96, 101–105, 110, 114, 124, 130
nostalgia, 135, 146, 150, 152, 154, 168

Notorious, 11, 14–15, 18–21, 22, 95, 101, 102, 105, 166
No Way Out, 89

Obi-Wan Kenobi, 169
Odds Against Tomorrow, 55, 74
Offer, The, 169
Official Secrets, 151
Oklahoma!, 81, 105, 107
Old Guard, The, 194
Old Man, The, 169
One Night in Miami, 169
On the Waterfront, 97, 106, 109, 126
Our Kind of Traitor, 176
Outbreak, 186
Outer Banks, 186, 187
Out of the Past, 4, 11, 22–27, 80, 109
overexposing and printing down, 128–129
Oz, 169
Ozark, 6, 7, 150, 162, 177–182, 187, 193, 194, 195

Pacific, The, 169
Pacino, Al, 121–122, 161
Panic in the Streets, 52, 186
Parallax View, The, 123
Paramount: Alfred Hitchcock films, 96–99, 103; Billy Wilder films, 54, 56, 58, 61–62; Paramount decision, 106; digital television productions, 169, 236
Paris Blues, 130
Peacock, 150
Penn, Arthur, 5, 117–118,
Perry Mason (2020–2023), 7, 154, 167, 169–172, 180–182, 194
perspective shift from criminal to crime-fighting, 54
Pesci, Joe, 126, 161
Pete Kelly's Blues, 105
Pfeiffer, Michelle, 133–134
Phantom Lady, 3, 10–11, 166, 190
Pierce, Guy, 142–143
Point Blank, 116
Polanski, Roman, 118–119
Polonsky, Abraham, 38–41
Postman Always Rings Twice, The, 14, 22–23, 112, 128
portable cameras and lights: cramped noir spaces, 165–167; importance for

location shooting and style, 115, 117, 119, 142–144; shooting inside car, 63; wartime development, 17, 204. *See also* Steadicam
Powell, Michael, 81–84, 130
Power of the Dog, The, 192, 194
Pressburger, Emeric, 81–84
Priestly, Jack, 115
Prieto, Rodrigo, 161
Production Code Administration censorship: 11, 40; adapting Spillane, 72–73; *Body and Soul* and interracial fight scenes, 38–39; Breen's retirement, 65; "crime horror trend," 15; *Notorious*, 18–19; *Out of the Past* and criticism of noir, 26–27
Proyas, Alex, 145–148
Punisher, The, 163, 169

Queen's Gambit, 193–194
Queen Sono, 187

Rabbit Hole, 169
Raging Bull, 39–40, 126–128
Rains, Claude, 18
rear projection, 20–21, 63, 170, 173, 199
Rear Window, 4–5, 78, 80, 84, 96–104, 108, 110, 124, 130
Rebecca (1940), 14–16, 95, 136, 183
Rebecca (2020), 6, 8, 149, 182–186, 193–194
Rebel Without a Cause, 5, 86, 105–106
red meat crime cycle, 1, 9, 49, 51, 207
Red Shoes, The, 4, 7, 79–84, 86, 92, 94, 105, 110, 124, 127
Reid, Tara, 140
Rév, Marcell, 189
Resnais, Alain, 112
Rhys, Matthew, 170–182
Rififi, 112, 161
Ritt, Martin, 112
River, 176–177
Robbins, Jerome, 106
Robson, Mark, 11
Roma, 2
Rose, Laurie, 185–186
Rosemary's Baby, 119
Rossen, Robert, 38, 41
'Round Midnight, 5, 8, 114, 128–130, 137, 148–149
Rózsa, Miklós, 36–37

Rudolph, Alan, 128
Ryan, Robert, 40, 43–49

Saint, Eva Marie, 102–104
Salas, Armando, 182
Salón México, 112
samouraï, Le, 113–114, 116
Sayed, Malik Hassan, 138
Scarface (1932), 118
Scarlet Street, 14, 71, 166
Schindler's List, 159
Schrader, Paul: as critic, 117, 188; "Notes on Film Noir," 52, 75, 77, 90–91, 118; as scriptwriter, 118, 126, 128
Scorsese, Martin, 5, 39, 118, 125–128, 157–158, 160–162
Scott, Lizabeth, 28–30
Scott, Ridley, 129, 177
Search, The, 42, 79
Seitz, John, 16–17, 36, 54–60, 77
self-aware noir, 7, 55, 135
Selznick, David O., 17, 90
semidocumentary style, 4, 22–23, 33, 36, 51–52, 63, 71
Serenade, 105, 106
Set-Up, The, 128
Se7en, 137, 187, 241
Sewell, Rufus, 145–146
Shadow (2019), 6
Shadow of a Doubt, 14, 15, 95
Shining Girls, 169
Shurlock, Geoffrey, 72, 75
Shutter Island, 158
Siodmak, Robert, 41–42, 112
Skarsgård, Stellan, 176
Snake Pit, The, 79
social problem films, 40, 201–202
social realist noir, 36–50
So Dark the Night, 62
Song to Remember, A, 80
Sonnenfeld, Barry, 138
Sopranos, The, 169
Spacey, Kevin, 142
Spellbound, 11, 14–18, 37, 95, 105, 166, 190
Spielberg, Steven, 6, 158–160, 188
Spillane, Mickey, 72–73
Spinotti, Dante, 142–144
Spy Who Came in from the Cold, The, 112, 159

stagecraft technology, 173, 188
Star Is Born, A (1954), 4, 7, 78, 80, 84, 86, 89–95, 98, 105, 110, 124, 130
StartUp, 187
Starz, 169
Steadicam, 128, 144, 181, 191
Stevens, George, 17
Stevenson, Robert, 15
Stewart, James, 96–97, 102
Stockhausen, Adam, 158–160
Storaro, Vittorio, 137
Stormy Monday, 138
Story of Three Loves, The, 84
Stranger, The, 22, 152
streaming video: 150–151; noir effects and image compression, 152
Street With No Name, 79
Sun Gun lights, 115, 117
Sunset Boulevard, 4, 7, 37, 52, 54–60, 65, 81, 152, 158, 186
sunlit look: 1950s, 7; postwar, 22–23, 30, 49, 62–63, 78, 112
Surtees, Robert, 41–50
Suspicion, 14, 18, 95, 102, 105
Sweet Smell of Success, 55, 74, 101
Sylvie's Love, 169

Tavernier, Bertrand, 5, 129–130
Taylor-Joy, Anya, 194
Taxi Driver, 5, 114, 125–126, 152
Technicolor: antitrust decree against, 84–85; dye-transfer I-B imbibition process, 85, 122–124; ENR process, 136–137; *Godfather* films, 122–123; lab shutdown, 122–23, 126; look emulated digitally, 157–158; memories, 146; preservation, 123–124, 126; single-strip limitations aiding noir style, 93–94; single-strip processing, 4, 5, 79, 84, 124; three-strip, 7, 81–84, 87–90, 98, 105, 124
television: early visual style of, 4, 52–53, 69–70; Hollywood competition with, 79, 106, 107; influence of low-contrast lighting for, 106, 112, 130; *Kiss Me Deadly* controversy, 73; streaming and convergence, 149, 153–154, 231–232, 194
Tennant, David, 165
They Made Me a Criminal, 117
Thief, The, 54, 70–71

Third Man, The, 41, 112
Thompson, Emma, 134–135
Three Days of the Condor, 123
To Catch a Thief, 102, 105
To Have and Have Not, 11, 35
Tokyo Vice, 154, 167, 169, 187, 194
Toland, Gregg, 18, 21, 201, 222
Top of the Lake, 169
Touch of Evil, 4, 5, 41, 52, 55, 74–76, 163
Tourneur, Jacques, 22, 27, 130
Towne, Robert, 118
transnational productions, 112–114, 174–177
Trauner, Alexandre, 5, 130
Treasure of the Sierra Madre, The, 157
Trouble in Mind, 128
Truffaut, François, 113, 117
Turner, Lana, 28, 127, 142
Turturro, John, 138
Two Men in Manhattan, 113–114

ultra high definition (UHD), 151, 153–157, 165, 170, 179, 184
Undercover Man, The, 36, 49, 62, 65
Unforgiven, 132
United States vs. Billie Holiday, The, 169

Valentine, Joseph, 15
Van Patten, Tim, 170–171
Van Upp, Virginia, 28
Venetian Bird, 112
Vertigo, 86, 101–102, 218–219
Vietnam War, 5, 111, 117–118, 126, 157, 222
violence: calls to curb, 65–70, 72–73, 186; misogynistic, 14, 71, 99, 163, 165–166; wartime, 14, 16–17, 22, 29

Wagner, Fabien, 170
Walbrook, Anton, 82–84
Wald, Jerry: planning for noir film, 43; waning popularity of noir in 1949, 54
Warner, Jack, 11
Warner Bros.: noir cycle productions, 11–12, 14, 35–36; production of *A Star is Born*, 92–95; productions in 2022–2023, 168–169, 187–188; sold *Act of Violence*, 43
Washington, Denzel, 137–138
Washington, John David, 189
Watchmen, 169
Waxman, Franz, 57, 100

Welles, Orson: 135, 158; *Jane Eyre*, 15–16; *The Lady from Shanghai*, 30–33; move to Europe, 41, 112; *The Stranger*, 22; *Touch of Evil*, 75–76, 163
West, Nathaniel, 142
West Side Story (1961), 4–5, 7, 75, 78, 80, 101, 124; production and color noir style, 105–110; studio shooting and noir style, 108
West Side Story (2021), 110, 182, 188, 192, 194–195
Wheatley, Ben, 183
Where the Sidewalk Ends, 52, 186
Whirlpool, 52, 166
Whitaker, Forest, 132–133
widescreen: cropped or masked, 98; introduction of, 71–72, 78–79, 86, 92; Super 35 and spherical lenses, 144. *See also* CinemaScope
Wilder, Billy, 6, 9–13, 16–17, 36–38, 42, 54–60, 77, 88, 112, 152, 158, 186
Willis, Gordon, 120–123, 137, 169, 173–174, 187

Wire, The, 169
Wise, Robert, 107–109, 201
Without Remorse, 169
Wolski, Dariuz, 145–148
World War II: influence of, 2–3, 7, 9–11, 78; labor market and audience, 15, 22, 80, 152; location shooting, 15; rationing and limitations 9–11, 16, 21, 198; violence and popularity of noir, 22
Wright, Joe, 162
Wuthering Heights, 15

Yates, Peter, 119
Young, Loretta, 22
Young, Robert, 40
Young at Heart, 84, 86
You Only Live Once, 118

Zanuck, Darryl: championing color and widescreen with darker style, 86–87; 1950 criticism of noir, 60, 186, 205–206
Zendaya, 189
Zinnemann, Fred, 41–50, 81, 107, 112

GPSR Authorized Representative: Easy Access System Europe, Mustamäe tee
50, 10621 Tallinn, Estonia, gpsr.requests@easproject.com

www.ingramcontent.com/pod-product-compliance
Lightning Source LLC
Chambersburg PA
CBHW031240290426
44109CB00012B/370